Electric and Hybrid Cars

SECOND EDITION

W9-BZA-671

Electric and Hybrid Cars

A History

Second Edition

Curtis D. Anderson *and*
Judy Anderson

 McFarland & Company, Inc., Publishers
Jefferson, North Carolina, and London

LIBRARY OF CONGRESS CATALOGUING-IN-PUBLICATION DATA

Anderson, Curtis D. (Curtis Darrel), 1947–
Electric and hybrid cars : a history / Curtis D. Anderson and Judy
Anderson.— 2nd ed.
p.   cm.
Includes bibliographical references and index.

ISBN 978-0-7864-3301-8
softcover : 50# alkaline paper ∞

1. Electric automobiles.   2. Hybrid electric cars.
I. Anderson, Judy, 1946–   II. Title.
TL220.A53   2010   629.22'93 — dc22   2010004216

British Library cataloguing data are available

On the cover: (clockwise from top left) Cutaway of hybrid vehicle
(©2010 Scott Maxwell/LuMaxArt); 1892 William Morrison Electric Wagon;
2010 Honda Insight; diagram of controller circuits of a recharging motor, 1900

Manufactured in the United States of America

McFarland & Company, Inc., Publishers
Box 611, Jefferson, North Carolina 28640
www.mcfarlandpub.com

To my family,
in gratitude for making car trips
such a happy time. (J.A.A.)

TABLE OF CONTENTS

ACRONYMS AND INITIALISMS

ACEEE — American Council for an Energy Efficient Economy
AFV — Alternative Fuel Vehicle
ALABC — Advanced Lead-Acid Battery Consortium
AMC — American Motors Corporation
APS — Arizona Public Service
AT-PZEV — Advanced Technology Partial Zero Emission Vehicles
BEV — Battery Electric Vehicles
CaFCP — California Fuel Cell Partnership
CAFE — Corporate Average Fuel Economy
CARB — California Air Resources Board
CAUCA — Californians Against Utility Company Abuse
CFA — Central Facilities Area
CMA — California Manufacturers Association
CMAQ — Congestion Mitigation and Air Quality Program
CNG — Compressed Natural Gas
DOE — Department of Energy
EPA — Environmental Protection Agency
EPAct — Energy Policy Act (1992)
ERDA — Energy Research and Development Agency
ETA — Electric Transportation Applications
EV — Electric Vehicle
FCEV — Fuel Cell Electric Vehicles
FCV — Fuel Cell Vehicle
FOP — Field Operations Program
FTA — Federal Transit Act
GM — General Motors
HEV — Hybrid Electric Vehicle
ICE — Internal Combustion Engine
INEEL — Idaho National Engineering and Environmental Laboratory
ISTEA — Intermodal Surface Transportation Efficiency Act
LAW — League of American Wheelmen
LEV — Low Emission Vehicle
LEVP — Low Emission Vehicle Program
LiION — Lithium Ion (battery)
LNG — Liquefied Natural Gas

LPB — Lithium Polymer Battery
NELA — National Electric Lighting Association
NEV — Neighborhood Electric Vehicle
NiMH — Nickel Metal Hydride (battery)
NREL — National Renewable Energy Laboratory
OTEC — Ocean Thermal Energy Conversion
OWC — Oscillating Water Column
PEM — Proton Exchange Membrane
PEPCO — Potomac Electric Power Company
PHEV — Plug-in Hybrid Vehicle
PNGV — Partnership for a New Generation of Vehicles
PZEV — Partial Zero Emission Vehicle
QVT — Qualified Vehicle Tester
RFG — Reformulated Gasoline
SCAT — Southern Coalition for Advanced Transportation
SCE — Southern California Edison
SULEV — Super Ultra Low Emission Vehicle
TEA-21 — Transportation Equity Act for the 21st Century (1998)
ULEV — Ultra Low Emission Vehicle
USABC — United States Advanced Battery Consortium
USCAR — United States Council for Automotive Research
ULSD — Ultra Low-Sulfur Diesel
USPS — United States Postal Service
V2G — Vehicle to Grid Technology
VRDC — Vehicle Recycling Development Center
ZEV — Zero Emission Vehicle

PREFACE

When the first edition of this book came out, the Prius hybrid was king. Electrics had a small following and were being used in test markets. A few cities were experimenting with recharging stations on a very limited scale. Since then, the worldwide movement away from fossil fuels to more sustainable solutions for our autos and energy needs has spurred both government and private investment for research and development of new technologies, alternate fuels, more cost-effective, durable batteries, and expanded infrastructures to support the innovations. New auto manufacturers in India and China have joined the competition; a wide variety of makes and models of electrics and hybrids are appearing in concept cars and production models. This edition brings the reader into the excitement that surrounds this next phase of automotive development and stewardship of our planet. Beginning with a chronicle of more than a century of the politics, technologies, environmental controversies, and marketing strategies that have shaped the auto industry, the book takes the reader from the electric "women's car" and hybrid cars of the late 19th century to today's "green" microbial fuel cells, hydrogen refueling and electric recharging infrastructures, and high-performance hybrids and electrics. It contains illustrations of batteries, fuel cells and chassis for the earlier models and photographs of both early and newer electric and hybrid vehicles, with short descriptions of each. A selected annotated bibliography, list of acronyms and index are included for quick reference.

This work does not include mass transit vehicles, neighborhood electric vehicles (NEVs), solar-powered vehicles or detailed explanations of a car's electrical systems. Nor does it explain the technical workings of the various fuel cells beyond the limits of a general reader's understanding. It is not meant to be a comprehensive history of electric vehicles. We concentrate on their history in the United States, with some references to United Kingdom, Asian, Scandinavian and western European vehicle development. Readers interested in blueprints of the electrical systems in electric cars might find works of Ernest Henry Wakefield[1] helpful.

This is an overview for the inquisitive, a snapshot of the industry for the entrepreneur and a starting point for student researchers.

Introduction: The Birth
of the Automobile Industry

Driving with Parents

Children today have an entirely different experience driving with their parents than children of 100 or even 50 years ago. In the early years, everyone was dressed in the proper attire and motoring was a wonderful excursion, the adventure possibly including a picnic basket for a stop along the way. Sunday drives were still common in the 1950s: driving along listening to a baseball game on the car radio, or everyone singing and playing travel games, or just watching the scenery fly by. Today, look at the inhabitants of the SUV next to you in traffic. The children are strapped in appropriately, according to state and federal laws, and are either looking down while playing a video game or looking up at the video monitor as mom or dad drives them to their soccer practice or music lesson. Cars have become a mainstay, a necessity. Maybe it is time to recapture that magic and adventure that only an auto ride can give. As Nick Emmanouilides says in an *AutoWeek* column, "Take your kids for a ride this weekend, and leave the electronics at home. Take them to a greasy spoon. Let them ask questions. Answer them."[1]

Cars as Identity

Cars provide common ground. They have the ability to cross social, ideological, religious and economic barriers and give people a way to relate to one another through a common interest or conviction. The encounter may be as simple as a parent and child working on a car engine or installing a new piece of technology. An environmental issue may find a staunch conservative Christian joining forces beside a radical liberal idealist through their shared interest in taking care of our planet, being good stewards of our world, using alternate fuels and alternative energy sources to power our cars. At one point in the authors' lives, we owned a Morris Minor Traveler, a small 4-cylinder "woody" station wagon, vintage 1960s, from England. Top speed was about 50 miles per hour and every trip was an adventure. We would use it for trips to the ballpark or short runs for shopping, and whenever we walked through the parking lot to get in our car to return home, we would see a small circle of men, and occasionally a woman or two, standing around it having wonderful conversations about memories from being stationed in England in World War II. We met a new neighbor one sunny afternoon when we had parked the Traveler in the driveway. He came over and began telling us of his experiences with his Morris Minor and his memories of taking out the engine and fixing it on the kitchen table. Cars hold magic for bringing people together.

The computer may soon lead in this category, but for the last one hundred years, the most ubiquitous item in America has been the automobile. It has captured our imagination. As computers invade our environment, they have borrowed terminology from the automobile, like information superhighway, infobahn and i-way. Cars provide a security, freedom and comfort some do not find in mass transit or other public transportation. They are statements about ourselves. Models like the Prius provide an image; they invade our culture. Celebrities left the limos at home and drove up to curbside at the Academy Awards in a Prius to "make a statement." Television shows like *The West Wing* and *The New Adventures of Old Christine* made the Prius part of their storyline.

Today's options even include hybrid SUVs. This fact seems to drive the anti–SUV crowd to distraction. Their anti–SUV crusade has been compared to the "global warming frenzy, a matter of belief in an ideology, close to a religion."[2] Even young people are buying SUVs, apparently unaware of the "Approved Technology List, posted by the Alliance Against Fun."[3] Cars have provided jobs to move our economy, freedom to travel the roads and off roads, sparked interest in alternative fuels, and raised awareness of the need for stewardship of the earth. They affect all parts of our lives, and most importantly, where we live. The car created suburbia by providing the means to commute greater distances from home to work. In over 100 years of inventions, such as the telephone, radio, television and computers, the automobile clearly influences our world.

Birth of an Industry

In 1900, consumers shopping for motorized transportation were offered a choice of steam-powered or gasoline-powered internal combustion engines (ICEs) or electric vehicles (EVs). The marketplace was divided, with no clear indication of which type would dominate. Steam-powered vehicles had speed and were less expensive, but required a long time to fire up and frequent stops for water. The ICEs were dirtier, more difficult to start and moderately more expensive, but could travel longer distances at a reasonable speed without stopping. EVs were clean and quiet, but slow and expensive. Each fought to be competitive in the open market in performance and price.

Electric and hybrid vehicles have a colorful past filled with ingenious inventions, patent wars and idealistic goals. Their designers strove to produce non-polluting, elegant, easy-to-maintain transportation for the motoring public. The advertising has reflected the woman's right to independence, appealed to the environmental cause, and frequently has a stylish flair that can bring a smile to motorists.

As with many products, the most logical solution does not always capture the consumer's imagination. In early years, EVs held a competitive share of the market, holding their own against the popular steam-engined and the faster, rumbling internal combustion engine automobiles. The prominence of electric vehicles at the Electrical Exhibition in Madison Square Garden in 1899 showed that the industry was well established. By 1904 one-third of all powered vehicles in New York, Chicago and Boston were electric. The advent of the electric starter, improved roads and the expansion of the road system in the second decade of the 20th century changed that. Autos with longer range and higher speed, and the emergence of a refueling infrastructure, had the market's attention. Since the 1920s, EVs have balanced on the edge of the market, becoming popular for brief periods during fuel shortages and environmental crises. Their alternate fuel source and non-polluting motor have historically been popular until the crisis passes, then interest wanes.

The underlying reality is that the ICE is still a gasoline-burning engine, with a transmission, wheels and gears, and so on. The most modern is simply a sophisticated version of the Model T.

Innovation resulted in many improvements and variety in the first EVs. The first horseless carriages were just that. The body design was similar to a horse-drawn carriage with a battery, a motor and a means of steering added. Until about 1895 the wheels were the standard wooden spoke variety with solid rubber tires. The ride mimicked the rough jolting of the horse-drawn carriage, subjecting both passengers and batteries to the bumps and ruts in the roads. Creative minds of the day saw a need for improving the ride. Pneumatic tires were introduced, smoothing out the ride and helping reduce the damage vibration caused to the batteries. The run from Paris to Frouville in the fall of 1905 that covered about 130 miles on one battery charge, and the 100-mile trek from Cleveland to Erie over ordinary country roads, some of sand, others with steep hills that taxed the battery charge, showed expanded potential for this auto that usually averaged 35 miles on a single charge. The spirit of winning also gave impetus to improving the speed of the electrics. In the first decade of the 1900s, electric autos were worthy opponents in auto racing. A. L. Riker won a 1908 race at Narragansett Park, Rhode Island, driving five miles in 11 minutes and 28 seconds. The best gasoline car finished over a mile behind. As for touring around the northeastern United States, in 1909 some avid automobilists took electric vehicles on trips up to 1,500 miles. Such innovation put the EVs in a viable market position during their early years.

Competition, safety and a potential revenue source impelled local and state governments to pass laws and regulations for these new vehicles. Registration payments on new vehicles were initiated. Rules for right of way and speed appeared in the statutes. Lawsuits between horse-drawn and motorized vehicle owners hit the courts. All autos were assessed equally in the early decades, but by the 1920s the criterion for fees had changed. A vehicle's weight became a factor. Electrics, because of the extra weight from their onboard batteries, were charged a higher fee to cover wear and tear on the road's surface. Laws and regulations like the additional charge for weight gave electrics a slight disadvantage in the marketplace and a new source of financing for state and local governments.

Concern about the quality of life in the cities was prevalent at the turn of the 20th century. Horses, although hardworking and dependable for pulling wagons and cabs, did come with some drawbacks, such as manure on the city streets (although the need for cleanup gave employment to many men). The electrics did not have the obnoxious smell and noise pollution of the ICE, and were considered a fine solution to the environmental problems caused by horses. Dirt and dust clouds along the roadways were still considered problems common to and created by each type of vehicle, but these would be addressed later through the improvement of road surfaces. EVs garnered a reputation early in their history for being environmentally friendly.

Individual owners may have sparked their neighbors' and friends' interest to purchase their own electric vehicles, but the introduction and growth of the taxicab electric fleets gave the industry a core market. The electric taxicabs made their debut in New York City in 1896 and were being considered by other large cities as the ideal answer to the enormous problem of pollution by the horse-drawn carriages. Henry Morris and Pedro Salom of the

 **Automobiles**

Electric ⊱ Gasoline

**RUNABOUTS,   SURREYS,   TONNEAUS
DELIVERY WAGONS, VICTORIAS, CABRIOLETS,
BROUGHAMS,   TRUCKS,   AMBULANCES,
POLICE PATROL WAGONS.**

*Write for our latest Catalogue illustrating and
describing seventeen different Columbia Models.*

ELECTRIC VEHICLE CO., ⊱ Hartford, Conn.
New York, 100 Broadway. Boston, 43 Columbus Ave. Chicago, 1421 Michigan Ave.

Columbia electric, 1902[4]

Electrical Vehicle Company in New York produced Electrobat electric taxicabs in 1896 and began their New York taxi service as a means for the average citizen to have the benefits of transportation without needing the expertise to maintain the vehicles. They claimed that selling individual vehicles to customers was impractical "because it would be impossible for them to send a skilled engineer out with every carriage they sold, and the average layman knows nothing about the electric business."[5] They believed the electric vehicle was too complicated and unreliable for lay operators and decided to create a transportation service company rather than an automobile sales company.[6] Morris and Salom were in the minority in this opinion. Most people of the day thought that the electric vehicles were so easy to drive and maintain that even a woman or child could operate one. Morris and Salom did prove the electric taxi to be a very effective competitive alternative to the horse-drawn cab.

> The judgment of the people is in the main favorable [and] is proved by the statement of the company that the cabs are in almost constant demand and that more will be put in service soon. For the enterprise they have shown in being the first to introduce [electric] motor cabs in the streets of New York this company is entitled to a great credit and will no doubt reap a commensurate profit.[7]

The *Horseless Age*'s author proved to be an accurate predictor. Electric cabs provided service to city dwellers for over a decade. The cabs proved to be reliable and sturdy.

> The first step away from the time-honored horse-drawn hack was the electric cab, a number of which were placed in service on the streets of New York City as early as 1899 [sic]. These cabs were naturally crude and cumbersome, but the majority of the original vehicles that were placed in service in New York more than ten years ago are still doing duty today [1910]. If a gasoline car of the "vintage" of 1899 were to be seen on the streets now, it would create a furore.[8]

By 1899 there were about sixty Electrobat II cabs in service, then produced by William C. Whitney. He envisioned a nationwide business. The vehicles would run for about four hours, then be taken to a station where the run-down batteries would be replaced by fresh batteries and the cab would be back on the street making money in a very short time.[9] An article in an 1899 *Scientific American* claimed,

> Undoubtedly the most important development in transportation has been the remarkable success of the [electric] automobile carriage in this country. The horseless cab has established itself as a thoroughly practical and popular means of travel with the general public in New York, while its high speed, its ease of control, its comparative noiselessness and its conven-

ience for use in the city in place of a two-horse carriage is rendering it increasingly popular with the wealthier classes. The electric cabs of New York are standing the test of winter work, and, during the recent snowstorms, they ran under conditions which discouraged even horse [drawn] time.[10]

The Electrobats had become a mainstay for the emerging electric taxicab services. In 1902 New York Edison began a fleet with the delivery of one electric truck made by the Electric Vehicle Company. By 1906, they had purchased six more and eventually expanded to fifty-three.[11]

The Association of Electrical Vehicle Manufacturers was formed in 1906 to promote electrics and provide a concerted effort to obtain better exhibition space for the machines in upcoming auto shows. Pope, Studebaker and Baker were on the board of directors. They felt at the time that "the electric vehicle is destined to occupy a wider field of usefulness in the near future than in the past, due to the improvements constantly being made and the ability of electric cars to travel much longer distances than formerly on a single charge."[12]

Colonel Pope, of the Pope Manufacturing Company, makers of the Columbia Motor Coaches,

is of the opinion that in the present state of the art electricity — while not without its limitations, fulfills more of the necessary conditions of a successful motive power than the steam or gas engine.... The storage electric motor is clean, silent, free from vibrations, thoroughly reliable, easy of control, and produces no dirt or odor. While it is not so cheap in such mileage capacity as some other forms of motors, it is certainly not extravagant in proportion to the service rendered, and its capacity has been proved to be more than equal to the demand of the average city or country vehicle.[13]

Scientists researching electric current and its possible uses for the general population saw great promise for using electricity to power automobiles and commercial vehicles. Thomas Edison devoted efforts to a battery that ran direct current. From his laboratory in West Orange, New Jersey, he said the invention could be the key to cheaper, more efficient transportation: "In 15 years, more electricity will be sold for electric vehicles than for light." Edison's wife Mina was the proud owner of an electric, while Thomas preferred the gas-powered Model T. Nearly fifty companies produced electric cars between 1900 and 1910, when they were at their height of popularity. By 1912, more than 34,000 were registered.[14]

Dr. Charles P. Steinmetz, a contemporary electrical researcher with Thomas Edison, believed that for short hauls the electric truck would prove superior to the gasoline truck.

Reductions in the cost of delivering merchandise would be distinctly a service to the public, for the merchant who effects such savings is usually able and eager to pass them on to his customers. One of the greatest evils in our economic system today is the high cost of distribution, and I am convinced that a greater use of the electric truck will mean a considerable decrease in the cost of distribution especially of food commodities. It has always seemed a surprising thing to me that electricity — the greatest driving power known — has not yet been given its full position in the transportation world. I do not think I exaggerate when I say that the use of electric motor trucks for short hauls will mean a savings of millions of dollars to the people of the country.[15]

In 1910 the *Cyclopedia of Automobile Engineering* introduced its Volume 3 with a note of the specialized use for the electric automobile.

With the successful development of the gasoline car and its production on a large scale, it is more or less generally thought that the day of the electric vehicle had passed, and there are still many who are of this belief. It must be borne in mind, however, that the electric is a specialized type particularly well adapted for certain classes of service, and without an equal in its own field. The misconception regarding its status usually arises from the erroneous idea that the manufacturer of electric vehicles is attempting to compete with the make of gasoline cars. Despite the great and constantly increasing number of the latter, as well as the fact that the improvements on the score of reliability and silence have made them strong competitors in the electric's chosen field — town service — there will always be a constant demand for electric vehicles. Where pleasure driving is concerned, the electric is without a peer as a ladies' car, while its extreme simplicity and great economy in service give it a strong hold on the commercial field, in which the question of obtaining competent drivers militates against the gasoline type.[16]

Even with the efforts of the Association of Electric Vehicle Manufacturers and the optimism shown by Edison and his fellow researchers and developers, marketing the efficient city car proved difficult, but did meet with some success and created businesses to support the EVs. Although the industry anticipated batteries being developed for greater distance between charges, their current product came with some drawbacks— short range and very few suitable recharging facilities. To stay competitive, sellers had to develop a better market strategy. Some chose to deal with the mileage problem head on. Their strategy depicted the electric as safe, silent and free from offensive odors, smoke and grease, with roominess, comfort and luxurious equipment. They were also rugged, and the right vehicle —*their* product —could cover greater distances. One innovative Columbus agent gave a test drive for a customer, taking him about fifteen miles out of the city to farms where they ran over stubble fields and tall grass up to the axle. Then they returned to the city to climb a steep hill that had never before been ascended by an electric car. They made the climb and had traveled a total of seventy miles on the same charge in one day. The demonstration worked, and the car was purchased. Others touted the car's easy operation and maintenance. While the ability to operate the electric without the services of a chauffeur was definitely a strong advantage for the product, the advertising tactic seemed questionable since the upper levels of society, who were least likely to want to drive and maintain the vehicle themselves, were their primary market. In spite of its seeming contradiction, the marketing campaign was surprisingly successful. Members of society purchased the electrics for their city driving, and because they preferred to have others maintain the vehicles, convenient and numerous charging stations sprang up that could also provide minor overhauling tasks. An expanded EV auto service industry began in a few of the larger cities.

Convenient, cost-effective charging stations beyond the major population centers had been an issue from the beginning for electrics. In 1895 a firm in London displayed a sign indicating it was prepared to charge "accumulators" of all sizes at any hour of the day or night. At the same time, L'Energie Électrique in France painted a glowing picture of the future of electric vehicles, with charging stations being available at any of the 10,000 establishments that had electrical plants. By 1906 a battery exchange system had been developed in Hartford, Connecticut. A customer could purchase a vehicle without a battery and would then pay a flat fee for service and battery exchanging. The Philadelphia/Baltimore area, for example, had twenty-seven charging stations in 1910. In 1911, *Electrical World* wrote, "If a suitable automatic equipment can be installed in each private garage much will have been accomplished toward success. At present the high cost of most charging outfits stands in the way of their general use."[17]

Electrical World also examined a boom in the number of electric vehicles, recognizing them as a "vehicle of convenience, not ordinarily adapted to covering very long distances or running at very high speed, but immensely handy and workable within its limitations."[18] The cost for electricity to charge an electric vehicle was about five cents per kilowatt-hour in 1911. Electric car enthusiasts assumed that if a person thought this was too high a price, he could not afford to use electric energy. At the time, it was a competitive price with the horse or gasoline. With this in mind, proponents suggested emphasizing the electric's "cheapness, simplicity, economy and longevity."[19] They felt this had to be done to make a serious encroachment in the pleasure vehicle market, a market being taken over by the gasoline vehicles. By this time roads were improving, and distance became a swaying factor for many. "If charging stations could readily be found in every town where there is electric service, the use of electric pleasure cars on fairly long runs would become much more common than it is now."[20]

At the 1914 Electric Vehicle Convention, Day Baker, treasurer and enthusiast, promoted his belief that electrics could be used for touring. He said he regularly made a trip from Boston to Providence, a distance of forty-six miles, in three hours. For this distance he did not need to recharge the batteries. For longer touring trips, infrastructure was a problem for an electric car. By 1914 the Lincoln Highway stretched from New York to San Francisco, but there were only fifty charging stations along the way, with only fourteen west of the Mississippi River. Even between New York and Chicago, there was one space of 123 miles between stations. There were no stations between Salt Lake City and Sacramento.[21] To make it through these areas, the driver had to arrange to have his vehicle either put on a railroad car or towed to the next city with a charging facility. This made it very difficult, if not impossible, for the average man to consider touring in his electric car. The adventure became more of a vocation than an avocation or vacation.

By 1915 supporters were proclaiming that the increased use of electric vehicles would naturally be followed by an increase in the number of charging stations. EV enthusiasts' confidence was high, but the reality of finding a market balance between the number of EVs purchased and the availability of charging stations did not materialize. Potential EV buyers needed to see a convenient way of recharging the battery. To stimulate interest in providing charging stations, manufacturers needed to see a market. Fuel was not an issue with the ICE. Their owners continued to have an abundance of almost "free" fuel from the discovery of vast amounts of oil in Texas and exploration in other areas of the northeastern United States and an abundance of liveries, farms and stations that willingly stocked the product. Electric grids were not in place to provide such convenience to the EV drivers to energize their autos. They were convenient for short trips but remained hampered by limited recharging services.

The invention of the electric starter in 1912 dealt another hard blow to the competitiveness of the electric automobile. ICEs had been difficult and dangerous to crank-start, making EVs the preferred model for the more timid and genteel. The invention made starting the ICEs easy and fast, taking away another of the electric's strong selling points. Even with this discovery, the marketplace might have absorbed the new competition for the electric city autos if the roads between cities had remained rutted and difficult to traverse, but this was not to be the case. Roads improved. Electricity, however, was limited to urban areas. With ICEs being easy to start and EVs limited distance per battery charge, the EV was fast becoming a niche market.

By 1913, the general perception of electric vehicles was that they were not in competition with gasoline cars. They were meant for comfort, cleanliness, reliability and economy. Their owners used the vehicles in making professional, business or social rounds, or for a daily commute to and from the office. Designer fashions clothed the driver and passengers as they ventured out for dinner and the theater or an afternoon of shopping. Suffragists praised the independence the electrics gave women, the freedom to drive on their own. Great improvements in both the storage battery and in the body styles in the previous five years increased the range to about eighty miles on one charge. It was assumed that most people did not need to travel eighty miles a day, making that range sufficient. Careful, conservative driving at low speeds increased mileage and were expected to satisfy any reasonable craving by the driver. Driving instruction suggested that one should drive at a steady rate and climb hills at ten miles per hour to conserve the battery. The electrics were not advocated for cross-country touring, primarily because of the lack of charging stations, and, according to a contemporary writer, "[e]lectrics are useless to speed maniacs; they are comfort vehicles giving legitimate speed for a reasonable running distance."[22] At the same time, gasoline vehicles were being written up in stories as "'racing' between towns, 'speeding' past cars leaving a cloud of dust, passing others so fast that the occupants could not recognize the faces in the other vehicles, buzzing, roaring and screaming through the air. Cars approaching at speed seemed to go by 'like meteors.'"[23] The EV and the ICE branched off to serve different market needs. The American love affair with gasoline-powered vehicles had begun. The EV as a personal vehicle of choice moved to an aficionado market. Yet, by 1915 supporters again proclaimed, as their counterparts had done ten and twenty years earlier, that the increased use of electric vehicles would naturally be followed by an increase in the number of charging stations. EV enthusiasts' confidence was high: "The progress in the electric passenger vehicle field during 1915 ... has been greater standardization and factory economies in production, all of these making possible considerable price reduction in nearly every case."[24] The niche supporters continued to tout the benefits of EVs and lament the continued lack of infrastructure for providing power conveniently throughout the countryside, but the majority of the buyers moved to ICEs and did not return to purchase the clean, quiet electrics.

The years from the late 1920s to the 1970s were a very lean time for the electric automobile. The depression of the 1930s, followed by World War II, did not lend itself to daydreaming about or experimenting with alternative fuel vehicles. Very few articles concerning electric vehicles or alternative fuel vehicles even made it to the scientific publications. Emphasis was on patriotic involvement in the war effort. Countries on both sides of the war encouraged their citizens to do their part to support their troops. In Europe during World War II, a scattering of electric car companies supplied small electrics for personal and commercial use to conserve gasoline for the war effort and as an alternative to gas rationing. In the economic prosperity after the war, very few people thought about saving energy. Oil and gasoline supplies were abundant and cheap; ICE cars got bigger and faster. Businessmen and "Sunday drivers" saw the potential for extended travel by automobile and looked to the ICE for range and speed. In 1956 President Eisenhower established the Interstate Highway System throughout the United States, linking roadways from state to state and simplifying driving for those enthralled with the wanderlust of touring. EV technology did not keep pace with the needs of the distance traveler in either speed or convenient charging station infrastructure. The electric vehicle did not make it back into the general public's eye again until public concern about air quality grew after mid-century and concerns about air pollution's role in global warming emerged around the millennium.

Politics and legislation involving use, registration and licensing of automobiles have been a part of the world of electrics since their inception, but a political climate actually favoring the electric automobile may be argued to have started with the Clean Air Act of 1963. This act has been amended and updated over the years. In 1975 Corporate Average Fuel Economy (CAFE) gasoline mileage standards were established for the ICE. The regulations passed by the California Air Resources Board (CARB) in 1990 depict the struggles involved in promoting electric vehicles. The rules forced manufacturers to sell a certain number of zero emission vehicles (powered by battery only) in the state by 1998 or incur severe monetary penalties. Over the intervening years, CARB has been compelled to amend its strict regulations to include hybrid and alternative fuel vehicles, lower standards, and allow "trading" and "banking" EV credits to make it possible for manufacturers to comply. The modifications demonstrated that consumer demand and new technologies could not just be created by political mandates. CARB has changed its strategy over the years from "command and control" to a "partnership" strategy.[25] Much of the money for projects comes from tax incentives and subsidies for industry and government funding given to government research labs. The public looked to technology for answers, and industry and government partnered to find a better battery.

Commenting on the research and development of new battery technologies in 1989, DeLuchi, Wang and Sperling added:

> The availability of an economical means of quickly recharging EVs, or the successful development of mechanically rechargeable batteries, may be the most critical factor in the future of EVs and could mean the difference between a minor and major role for EVs in transportation. Therefore, as research and design on powertrains and batteries continues, and the commercialization of advanced EVs draws near, research and design work on charging systems, and the cost and performance of batteries designed to accept very fast (20-minute) recharges, should commence. The development of a suitable infrastructure and the successful completion of advanced EV development programs will bring the electric vehicle dream much closer to reality.[26]

Battery development has moved the EVs forward with the lithium-ion, lithium polymer and NiHM by increasing storage capacity with less weight, but EVs gained an even higher profile with the promotion of clean energy sources for stopping global warming.

By 2005 approximately 20 percent of the oil used in the United States was used in transporting ourselves and our goods. Carbon dioxide, a main ICE pollutant, was officially declared a "greenhouse gas" by the Supreme Court in 2007 and will, according to some in the science community, lead to climate change. This has led to a growing entrepreneurial market that focuses on emissions for reducing "greenhouse gases." One of the most widely known markets comes in trading carbon credits. This practice was brought to the consumer's attention when Al Gore used the process to offset the carbon pollution from his private jet. Countries within the European Union, after the Kyoto Protocol, also introduced carbon credit trade. There are hundreds of Web sites and organizations committed to the monies found in carbon credits. Each is similar, offering the user a chance to calculate his own carbon footprint by entering the type of car they drive, how many miles they fly, or simply keeping their lights on, etc. Then a calculation is made to determine how many pounds of carbon they add to the environment. The next step is to calculate the amount of money to send in to the Web site to buy carbon credits so they can become "carbon neutral." The Web sites state the money supports clean, green energy projects like wind farms and solar farms, and helps farmers capture and destroy methane (another global warming gas) which forms when animal (cow & hog) waste is not properly managed. Monies may be used in research, or to provide the equipment needed to turn wind, solar, or various gasses into usable energy. Companies specializing in backup power supplies, for example, Katolight in Mankato, Minnesota, have offered a methane powered generator option for agricultural use. It is predicted this "carbon credit" industry will expand to become a five trillion dollar industry by 2015. Clean alternate energy sources give greater possibilities for bringing cars with reduced emissions and convenient refueling capabilities to the consumer.

In a straight comparison of today's EVs and ICEs, the EV shows a number of practical advantages, but that advantage is narrowing as technological advances occur with ICEs and hybrids. The EVs do not have tailpipe emissions. They have about 70 percent fewer moving parts than an ICE. This means less maintenance — no oil changes or replacement of items such as filters, fuel pumps, alternators, and the like. EVs also pollute less, conserve energy and are cheaper to run, averaging about twice the distance on each dollar spent. The main disadvantages of electric cars continue to be their short range and high initial price. As EVs approach the ICE performance levels for the speed and acceleration, more efficient, cleaner ICEs are getting closer to EVs in tailpipe emissions. Overall, the environmental advantage provided by EVs has been negated by the greater improvements in gasoline and hybrid engines. Internal combustion engines are currently running very clean due to reformulated gasoline and computer-assisted combustion systems.

The popularity of the hybrid concept may have had a slight negative impact on the research and development of even more fuel-efficient, clean-burning ICEs by diverting resources to develop the more marketable image of the hybrid. Hybrids became the research and design hotbed in the first decade of the 21st century with a variety of potentials in fuel and propulsion types ranging from corn-produced ethanol to lithium-ion batteries to hydrogen fuel cells. Their higher price tag is not keeping buyers from owning one. Hybrid mechanics are dotting the landscape and avid amateurs are retrofitting their cars with advanced technologies. Although the convenience of not having to plug in the car was a definite selling point for hybrids, the plug-in hybrid returned to the fray with the interest generated by the Hybrid Electric Vehicle Working Group's Report. The report saw EVs as a contender if battery storage units improved. By 2006 advancement in battery technology moved plug-ins to the testing and niche market stage. CalCars Initiative provided conversion kits and promoted the concept, and soon kits came on the market costing from $10,000 to $38,000. Small companies like AFS Trinity began their marketing campaigns to raise capital and markets for their Extreme hybrid, a car which could run farther on electrics only. Governments began incentive programs to be in effect "when cars are available." Cities joined forces with environmentalists through a grassroots effort, Plug-in-Partners, to promote plug-in cars as part of their climate protection plans. Competition continues to be influenced by regulation and competing technologies.

CARB rules and restrictions that regulate the allowable level of ICE pollution are being relaxed, prolonging the advantage of the ICE. The environmental value gap between the ICE and the EVs is lessening. During the first decade of the 21st century, even though electric vehicles come in many types— generating electricity from batteries, solar energy, fuel cells, and biomass, among others— and hybrids combine the power of fossil fuels with electric energy created by on-board chargers, the technology for the electrics is still limited. The optimistic feeling about electric cars during the 20th century has always been "This time it will catch on." If the optimists meant the hybrids, there was definitely a market swell for many varieties of the gas-electrics, backed by President Clinton's research and development funding. Here were cars that used electricity to boost power, to save gas and to lower pollution ... and they didn't have to be plugged in.

As the decade progressed, more options became available. "Green" car options expanded as manufacturers saw potential market opportunities demonstrated by the success of the Toyota Prius and the Honda Civic Hybrid. Another oil crisis, and more federal monies available as subsidies sponsoring research and development, resulted in a variety of hybrids, flex-fuel (usually ethanol or ethanol-gasoline blend) and alternate fuel cars and trucks. Models began appearing at concept car shows; some models even moved to production. Even the plug-ins showed promise again because larger-capacity battery packs were developed and more external refueling sources were being installed. Biodiesel hybrids, hybrid SUVs that shut down unneeded cylinders during highway driving to save on fuel, and ultra low-sulfur diesel (ULSD) are also in the mix. ULSD is creating interest in using diesel more widely again. It has the advantages of high mileage, high performance and less pollution. Unfortunately, there is limited fuel availability, the age-old problem for alternative fuel vehicles. Europe leads in marketing and refueling stations for this option. Fuel cell vehicles continue to suffer this same fate. The technology dates back to 1839 when Sir William Grove demonstrated the first fuel cell; its practical applications appeared with the Apollo space travels. In 2003, President G. W. Bush provided $1.3 billion in funds for the Hydrogen Fuel Institution to speed development for domestic use. Cost and infrastructure continue to be its major obstacles.[27] The Standards Council of Canada contributes to fuel cell development by providing fuel cell standards and conformity assessment, giving consumers confidence in product safety. In the early part of the 21st century, gasoline costs and environmental green marketing combined with government subsidies again made exploring electrics, alternative fuels and fuel cell vehicles worth the industry's time.

The solution is always just around the corner, down the road, and all the other automotive metaphors, but the reality is that most consumers want internal combustion engines and are not willing to change this conviction as long as they have the money to pay for the car and the oil and gasoline to run them. The early 20th century brought inventions in motor and battery design that increased the range possible for an electric vehicle before it needed recharging. The electric automobile was a serious competitor to steam and internal combustion engines during the early 1900s. The new millennium offers a great opportunity for developing technology to advance the acceptance of alternative vehicles. Moore's Law — a prediction of technological progress — may soon apply to battery and fuel cell technology. Hybrid vehicles are providing excellent mileage, and have gained popularity through yet another gasoline crisis when U.S. gas prices almost tripled between 2006 and 2008. Fuel cell and hybrid vehicles, for the near term, seem to be the best choice to answer the question of tailpipe emissions and pollution, but competition with biofuels and more efficient ICEs is narrowing the gap and providing alternate environmentally friendly high-performance vehicles. This is an exciting time for developing new, cleaner technologies for the future. Improvements in utility power generators and advances in nonpolluting fuels show a positive approach to transportation and energy. These solutions appear to be the realistic, sensible and necessary methodology needed today as they rely primarily on the marketplace (consumer demand) over the political (social awareness demand) as an approach to the problem. Time will tell.

The Competitors in the Early Years

The steam-powered vehicle was a viable competitor to electrics and ICEs in price and performance during the first quarter of the 20th century. Its main drawback was the time required to warm up and produce steam to begin locomotion. In 1906 a steam-powered vehicle set a land speed record of 127 mph. The steam cars were competitive in the early automobile market for a little longer than the electrics and were still in production in the 1930s, in small quantities.

Grout Steam Carriage, 1902[28]

In 1899 the Stanley Steamer's success attracted the interest of John B. Walker, publisher of *Cosmopolitan* magazine, who wanted to buy the business. To dissuade him, the Stanleys named what they thought was a ridiculously high price — a quarter of a million dollars in cash. To their surprise Walker promptly paid it, and the Stanleys were temporarily out of the car business. The new owner changed the company's name to the Locomobile Company of America. The Stanleys went back to producing steamers in 1901.[30] Like the electrics, the steamers were environmentally friendly, running approximately 100 miles on one fill of water and fuel for the boiler. The advertising also touted its cleanness: "lady need have no fear of even soiling a glove in running the car."[31] The year 1905 saw the White steamer bus beginning its 6½ mile run from Osaka

White Steam Car, 1906[29]

and Sakai, Japan; it ran the route for 20 years.[32]

Why did the steamer drop out? Quality versus quantity. Steam-powered cars were manufactured by a number of small manufacturers who were content to build a few hundred cars, while Henry Ford was thinking in the numbers of millions for his machines. Most of those small manufacturers (approximately 200 of them) only lasted a few years before they went out of business.[33] Even the leading steam car manufacturer, the Stanley Motor Carriage Company, was primarily interested in providing cars to local markets and was more concerned with quality craftsmanship than volume and lower prices.

The environment, the infrastructure and market timing also played roles in the demise of the market for the steamers. Hoof-and-mouth disease broke out in 1914. To prevent the spread of the disease, most public water troughs were removed. Stanley Steamers were not designed with condensers to recycle the water; owners were obliged to stop frequently to refill the boilers. Without the water troughs, water was not readily available. The epidemic forced the Stanley Company to rethink its design and develop a condensing system. It took two years, at great expense and with a drop in production, for the condenser to be integrated into the design. When the United States joined World War I in 1917, the government limited consumer goods production to one-half the average output over the previous three years. Since Stanley had been in a development phase and had built very few vehicles for market during that time, the limitation put Stanley at a major disadvantage. They needed volume to increase sales and visibility for their new product, but were limited by the government in how many vehicles they could produce and make available for the marketplace. When the war was over and Stanley was about to recover, it was hit by a third bit of bad luck, the 1920s recession. Stanley did not recover.[34] Steam-powered vehicles disappeared around the time of the stock market crash of 1929 and the Great Depression and never found a way back to the marketplace to compete with the ICEs and EVs. In 1962, James L. Dooley and Allan F. Bell brought a modern steam car to a Los Angeles auto show. It used a Paxton steam generator mounted in a 1953 Ford coupe. Although steam cars give high performance, are fuel efficient and relatively service free, the concept did not catch the market's attention.[35] Today, steam vehicles occupy a hobbyist niche. Steam engine clubs build and drive their machines, display them on festive occasions and keep the technology alive, providing a glimpse of the past for avid admirers.

Companies such as Ford, Studebaker, and Porsche produced internal combustion engine autos for the marketplace from its early years. Gasoline-powered automobiles became the market-shaping force over both electric and steam cars early in the 1900s for four reasons:

(1) Better road systems connected many cities by the 1920s, promoting a need for longer-range vehicles.

(2) In 1901 vast oil reserves were discovered in Texas. Gasoline was a waste by-product of the oil industry, which was in the business of producing kerosene for lamps. When the Spindletop oil gusher was brought in at Beaumont, Texas, the country's oil production doubled almost overnight. Fuel was cheap and readily available by 1905. An infrastructure of gasoline fuel stops began to appear. Cars could fuel up at many convenient locations. General stores, shops and even liveries had a supply of gasoline cans on hand to fuel the new vehicles. The first gasoline station was built in 1913 by Chevron. They were widely present by 1920, and most service stations were not hooked up to an electrical grid at that time.

(3) In 1912 a reliable, easy-to-use electric starter for gasoline engines was introduced. ICEs in the early 1900s were difficult and dangerous to start —cranking the motor was a chore for even an able-bodied man. If the engine backfired during the crank start, the crank could spin backwards. Broken arms and other injuries were not uncommon. The technical advancement of the electric starter invented by Charles Kettering in 1912 made the option of starting not only electric cars but also ICEs open to less-athletic men and women.

(4) Henry Ford decided to pro-

Winton Phaeton gasoline automobile, 1899[36]

duce affordable gasoline-powered cars[37] using mass production and interchangeable parts to streamline automobile maintenance. His method worked. He supplied large quantities of product at low prices. By 1912 electric roadsters were selling in the $1,750 to $3,000 range, while a gasoline car built by the new production processes sold for $650. By World War I, low-priced fuel and advanced technology gave a distinct advantage to the ICE, an advantage it has enjoyed through the turn of the 21st century.

The Battery

The battery, its reaction to heat and cold, its recharging capabilities and its weight are key to the success or failure of electric vehicles. The impact of its slow technological development when compared to improvements in the internal combustion engine cannot be minimized. It has been the main roadblock in the EV's fight for consumer market share. From the earliest days of Thomas Davenport's experiments with electro-magnetism and his invention and patents for an electric motor in 1837, and the development and refinement of the storage battery by Gaston Planté (1860) and Camille Faure (1881), the battery has been key to market potential and consumer acceptance of the electric car. Surprisingly, some of the early inventors of the electrics were actually interested in building a better battery, not in creating a mode of transportation. In late 1880, N. D. Possums used an electric tricycle to demonstrate the qualities of the pasted-ribbed lead acid battery for Brush Electric Company. Charles F. Brush of Euclid, Ohio, is best known for inventing the electric lightbulbs used during that era in streetlamps. His bulb was also mounted on the tricycle and may be the first appearance of an electric headlight. William Morrison made his fortune through royalties from storage battery patents. It took an association with Harold Sturgis of Chicago to put Morrison's six-passenger electric into the public eye as part of the American Storage Battery exhibit at the 1893 World's Columbian Exposition in Chicago. The battery held fascination and profits for these early entrepreneurs. Automobiles were a convenient way to show what their batteries could do. High-performance, low-maintenance batteries are key to the electrics' appeal and success.

For the past 100 years, competition between the electric and the internal combustion vehicles has see-sawed. Just when confidence in EVs is rising and the electric seems poised to make a breakthrough, circumstances change and the ICE moves ahead. Whether it is in fuel infrastructure, technological advances or road infrastructure (mud, hills, and cold weather), the electric finds itself at a disadvantage.

An editorial in *Scientific American* in 1917 proclaimed that a new battery would be invented any day, which would change the look of cars and the infrastructure of the automobile. As in the past, the EV would continue to improve on the quality of the battery so that it could be a major viable competitor to the ICE. The following year brought the promise of a breakthrough in battery technology that would benefit EVs. A 1918 article in the *Scientific American Supplement* proclaimed, "Through many adverse conditions and numerous objections that have to some extent been overcome, the electric vehicle for both pleasure and commercial applications has come to stay." At the time a battery exchange system and a growing infrastructure of central recharging stations were developing, but battery performance continued to plague the EVs.

Cold weather and bad roads seriously tax the battery, affecting the mileage, amperage generated and battery life. Throughout the 20th century an answer to the problem of dealing with climate and cold-weather performance eluded the inventors. In the 1990s fleet owners were reporting less range during the colder months. At the turn of the 21st century, federal regulations required climate control in all automobiles, both heating and cooling. Designing a battery that can generate the additional energy needed while withstanding the cold temperature without increasing weight or price continues to be a research dilemma. Manufacturers have tried to find solutions since the early years of EVs when the performance problem first surfaced. In 1918, the traveling distance (range) of the battery was noted as being less in winter than in summer — the colder the day, the greater the difference. During cold weather, the roads were also in poor condition, adding to the increased ampere-hours required from the battery per mile. Battery technology at the time was unable to meet the problem. Instead, inventors concentrated efforts on two approaches to making the battery immune from the cold. One approach was to install the battery in a box that had the insulating characteristics of a Thermos bottle. The second was to use a small amount of energy from the battery itself (about 100 watts) to provide an electric heater to control the temperature around the battery. Neither proved effective for the marketplace. There was a general call at the time from conservationists asking for cooperation between the manufacturers and central-station companies to advance these improvements to make the electric vehicle a success. Such cooperation did not happen until almost a century later with the advent of partnerships, such as the U.S. Advanced Battery Consortium (USABC), and an increased emphasis on battery research and development.

In the 1950s, it was estimated that if as little as five million dollars per year were invested in research and development of a battery of high specific energy, light weight and low cost, the United States would have electric vehicles in 1990 that would be able to travel at fifty miles per hour for 150 miles on a single charge. Even if the money had been allocated, it is unlikely, based on the technological challenges still being examined, that the desired results would have been produced.

Since the 1960s, any electric car viable in the competitive marketplace has required subsidies from the government or the energy industry. This may change as the technology develops incrementally over the next few years, but battery technology has seen very little improvement over the last one hundred years and is still in need of a great breakthrough to move EVs into the industry mainstream at a competitive price. Nickel-metal-hydride (NiMH), lithium-poly, and lithium-ion batteries are the first major breakthrough in batteries in close to one hundred years. They have put hybrids and plug-ins into the marketplace and continue to evolve into smaller size with greater storage capacity. The possibility of using cars as places to store and transmit power to the grid (grid-to-vehicle) is emerging and may provide incentive for buyers through utility bill adjustments or income to car owners who provide electricity back to the utility companies.

For over one hundred and ten years proponents of the electric vehicle have been predicting that it would take command of the marketplace soon. A technological breakthrough favoring EVs has been long expected in "just a few years." The present technological buzz is the fuel cell, but fuel cells have been around longer than batteries. Will someone invent a new, cost-effective battery? This also has been predicted for over one hundred years, yet based on past development patterns, it should not be expected any time soon. Consumer demand for a vehicle powered by battery only is still low. People just do not want to put up with the inconvenience of plugging in their cars. Hybrid vehicles and fuel-cell-powered vehicles hold promise as a bridge to achieve the California Air Resources Board's (CARB) requirements of a zero emission vehicle (ZEV). It is more likely that a hybrid vehicle will capture the market's interest as the next stage of development in saving fuel with hydrogen fuel cells providing advancement to clean energy. The problem again is the cost. How long will automakers be willing to sell a car for $20,000 when it costs $41,000 to build and diverting the profits from sales of their ICE models to subsidize their ZEV requirements? Historically, EVs have appeal during times of energy crises, such as World War I, World War II, the 1970s oil shortage and when environmental and industry leaders create peaks of interest by calling attention to EVs as a solution to dependence on foreign oil, energy shortages and pollution problems. But overall, the electric vehicle industry is still struggling to become financially independent and a viable option in the consumer market. There is no conspiracy in the auto industry to prevent the electric vehicle from being built and sold. Automakers will sell any product that consumers want, and the first one to create such a car that captures the consumer's interest at a reasonable price can expect to enjoy striking profits.

Fuel shortages, the Iraq War and the global warming issue caused a concerned public to look to electrics and hybrids as a way of reducing dependence on foreign oil imports. American transportation needs a large supply of fuel daily. In 2007, the United States used about 20 million barrels of oil each day. A barrel of oil contains 42 gallons and will yield about 20 gallons of gasoline. This converts to about 400 million gallons of gasoline per day. Assuming there are about 100 million households in the United States, this would mean each one consumes about four gallons per household per day. The United States consumes about 146 billion gallons of gasoline each year.[38] Oil supplies to the U.S. were being affected by the war in Iraq and the growing automotive markets in Asia. Repeating the past, as gas prices increase and availability is threatened, the market turns to alternate fuels and various types of vehicles. In the first five years of the 21st century, hybrids caught the attention of consumers. The Toyota Prius led the field with competition from hybrid versions of the Honda Civic and Accord, Ford Escape and Lexus 600hL. Their customer base is between one and three percent of total vehicle sales.

Success for hybrid technology is evolving as automakers are seeing other possibilities with SUVs and crossovers. It is a core, adaptable technology. In each commonality, computers are used to balance the amount of power the vehicle delivers and reduce the amount of gas used. Even with higher gas prices, buyers were not giving up their SUVs. As hybrid technology development expanded, advances came in many forms to put the marketing draw of "hybrid" onto SUVs.

Efforts to move consumers from petroleum to other forms of energy are also coming from entrepreneurs. They see a market building among consumers who want to plug in their vehicles, consumers attracted by the idea of solar panels on the roof and technology that allows the transfer of energy back to the grid when it is not needed for driving. In the period 2005 to 2007 there was a small surge of interest in plug-ins, both electric and hybrid.

States and cities moved from relying on federal mandates and began taking charge of their own projects and programs to improve air quality and energy efficiency, working locally through initiatives and projects like Clean Cities and taking steps like converting fleets to hybrid and alternate fuel vehicles to meet the challenge. Governor Schwarzenegger of California was quoted as saying, "We don't care if Arizona is going to do the right thing; we take action ourselves."[39]

In the private sector, all-electric promotions are emerging. Project Better Place is working with governments and selected auto manufacturers. Their initial partners are Israel, Denmark, and Australia. The project is focusing on infrastructure, building electric refueling stations in those countries with the intent that they will expand the size of the coverage to neighboring countries or (in Australia) other parts of the country as more people in those countries start driving electric cars and trucks. Partnerships along the United States' West Coast are also testing the water by adding recharging and battery-swapping stations in parking lots and along commercial streets, and experimenting with various methods for drivers to pay for the recharging. The Tesla Motors company thinks more in terms of convenient recharging for their more affluent clientele. Tesla made a deal with the Hyatt hotel chain to provide recharging for its customers along the route from San Francisco to Lake Tahoe. The cars have a range of 140 miles, and it is estimated that three stops should cover the trip.

Motor vehicles have been a fascination since the first motor was attached to a bicycle in 1881. They are used for work, for leisure, for prestige and for entertainment. Whether the power source is steam, gasoline internal combustion or electric current, cars are interwoven in the fabric of our society. They both support and are shaped by the energy industry. Their styles reflect individual personalities and their versatility echoes our functional needs in work and play. The automotive industry is at the heart of the way American business works— mergers, acquisitions, patent fights, partnerships with government and the "bottom line."

Triggered by environmental issues, interrupted oil supplies, tighter emission controls in some states, and the accuracy of Moore's Law in technology, among other factors, manufacturers have again begun to revisit electric and hybrid vehicles as possible solutions.

At the beginning of the 21st century, the field looks similar to the rivalry of the early 20th century. Consumers and the auto industry are exploring options with electrics and plug-in electrics, hybrids and plug-in hybrids, flex-fuel, diesels and many alternative fuel vehicles. Consumers are trying to find the cars will match their lifestyle, their ideology and their pocketbook. Infrastructure, batteries, fuel cells, the price of gasoline, environmental awareness and cost effectiveness are all a part of the mix as the auto companies struggle to provide consumers with their passport to the freedom of the road: their car.

1

THE EVOLUTION
OF THE ELECTRIC VEHICLE

"The growth of industrialization ... saw the escalation of one of the most basic needs of humans—transportation."[1] No one person can be credited for the invention of the automobile that you are driving today. It developed bit by bit from the ideas, imagination, fantasy, and tinkering of hundreds of individuals through hundreds of years.[2]

The early years of automobile development showed a keen rivalry among gasoline-powered, steam-powered and electric vehicles. Innovation spawned more innovation as a wide variety of manufacturers and entrepreneurs sprang up, supplying an infatuated public with a broad range of cars to pique their interest and match their needs. A few enterprising manufacturers even had gasoline-electric hybrids on the road. It was an exciting time.

Today's market mirrors early development with its bustle of evolving technologies, designs, and innovations to fit current lifestyles. A recent concept car, the Chevrolet Volt, is the company's first plug-in hybrid vehicle. The car features an "E-flex system," an innovative drivetrain that runs on electric power only until the battery runs down. Then a small ICE (internal combustion engine) kicks in, not to propel the car, but to feed the onboard generator that produces electricity to store in the battery. A fascination with the electric car flowed through the past century, and it has its followers, but it has been difficult to sell to consumers since the ICEs won the marketplace around 1912. Today's buyers believe their all-purpose, powerful SUVs work best with their active lifestyle, so the market has responded by providing diesels, hybrids and flex-fuel engines as options for beating the high price of gasoline. Thanks to improved technologies that produce better gas mileage, the SUV, or sport/ute, meets many personal transportation needs, hauling both people and cargo, while maintaining a perceived quality of life.

The market is expanding; consumers are being offered more choices for their driving pleasure. In 2008 alone, there were over 7 million flex-fuel vehicles on the roads of America. Approximately 3 million of those vehicles were made by General Motors Corporation. GM was the leading producer of E85 flex-fuel vehicles, offering 11 different models using E85 or biodiesel, and 8 hybrid models. The 2008 Saturn VUE Green Line Hybrid offered the best highway mileage for an SUV at 32 mpg. Hydrogen-powered electric vehicles may be in our future as fuel cell development finds more cost-effective designs, battery storage improves and solar-powered hydrogen refueling stations begin appearing on the landscape. The increased interest in hybrid cars and in moving to alternative fuels has improved the climate for research for both battery and fuel cell innovations, making the early 21st century a mirror of the innovations that occurred at the beginning of the automotive era in the early 20th century.

The history of electric vehicles can be generally divided into three parts: the early years (1890–1929), including their golden age of dominance in the market from about 1895 to 1905; the middle years (1930–1989); and the current years (1990–present). In the early years, England and France were the first nations to experiment with electric vehicles, with the United States showing some interest in about 1895. The first electric vehicle may have been a converted Hillman Sociable tricycle created by M. Raffard in France in 1881. The first commercial application of EVs was a fleet of New York taxicabs in 1897. The general perception of the electric vehicle in 1899 was that it had many advantages over gasoline-powered cars. It was clean, silent, free of vibrations, thoroughly reliable, easy to start and control (no shifting required) and produced no dirt or odor. The disadvantages were short range and high initial cost. It was not as cheap to run as other forms of automation and could average only about 18 miles per day, but this met the needs of much of the population in the larger cities. Electric vehicles outsold all other types of cars in America in the years 1899 and 1900. A wide variety of automobiles were built during the "brass era," from 1895 through 1914, when designers experimented with different body styles and engine configurations. But, as the 1920s approached, "It was the end of an era of experimentation. It was pretty much the end of steam and electricity as viable sources.... The writing was on the wall.... Things became patented, standardized. In a sense they became better that way, but the experimentation was over. Everyone was following the same route, so to speak."[3]

The middle years saw a brief peak of interest in EVs brought on by the gasoline shortages during World War II, the environmental concerns of the 1960s and oil shortages of the 1970s. The current years brought renewed interest in air quality and the impact on the environment of pollution from the internal combustion engine, resulting in legislation such as the Clean Air Act of 1990, regulations put in effect by the California Air Resources Board (CARB) in 1990, and the Energy Act of 1992. The terrorist attacks of September 11, 2001, and the Iraq War made becoming energy-independent a high priority for many nations. Since 2002, statutes have encouraged research in EVs and re-energized the development of environmentally friendly vehicles through tax incentives, grants and government-industry collaborative projects. In each era, the EV was touted for its quiet, reliable, environmentally friendly advantages over its competitors.

Automobiles had a market in Europe earlier than in the United States. The first automobile put into production is thought to be the German one-cylinder, gasoline-powered three-wheeled Benz in 1885. Gottlieb Daimler put a four-wheel, gasoline-powered automobile into production in Stuttgart, Germany, in 1886. In 1890 the first American to build an electric vehicle was Andrew L. Riker. It was a tricycle imported from England with a motor attached that could deliver $\frac{1}{6}$ horsepower and speed along at eight miles per hour with a range of about thirty miles. The United States did not have a production industry until 1896 when the Duryea brothers of Springfield, Massachusetts, produced thirteen matching "motor wagons."

In 1900 France led the world in car production, innovation and ownership. There were 5,600 automobiles in France; the support infrastructure shows a total of 3,939 stores for oil, gas, and other necessities, and only 265 electric charging stations.[4] New York State had about 4,000 registered vehicles in 1903. Of these, 53 percent were steam powered (made primarily by the Locomobile Company), 27 percent were gasoline powered and 20 percent were electric powered. Automobile production was about to explode in the United States and the ratio of support stations associated with gasoline and electric vehicles remained about the same as that of France in 1900.

The electric car was the most conservative form of the automobile in that it bore the closest resemblance to the horse-drawn vehicle in both appearance and performance. Manufacturers of electric vehicles closely copied fashionable carriage forms. The Woods Motor Vehicle Company, a prominent early maker of electric cars, for example, hoped to supply hundreds of thousands of gentlemen's private stables with fine carriages in all variety of styles rather than a creation of a machine which will transport a man from town to town, or on long country tours.[5]

The Automobile, an extensive two-volume treatise on steam, gasoline and electric cars and their parts, stated in 1905:

It [the electric vehicle] is managed easily, is docile, has a noiseless motion, and the motor itself is mounted in a very simple manner. Over petrol cars it has the advantages of easier starting, greater cleanliness, and perhaps lower cost of upkeep. There is but little vibration with the electric automobile, no bad odour, and no consumption of energy whilst the car is stopped. The inconveniencies of electricity as automobile motive power are increase in dead weight carried, maintenance and renewal of accumulators ... and the loss of time in charging. These inconveniences are lessened greatly in cars for town work.[6]

Considering hybrid cars of the day, it states, "It certainly seems that there is a big future before the petrol-electric car."[7]

The Automobile Club of America was incorporated in 1899 with the objective "to maintain a social club devoted to the spread of automobilism and to its development throughout the country; to arrange for through runs and encourage road contests of all kinds among owners of automobiles."[8]

The 1893 World's Columbian Exposition in Chicago (Chicago World's Fair), in addition to housing the world's first Ferris wheel, featured six electric automobiles. The only American entry was the Morrison electric surrey, built by William Morrison in Des Moines, Iowa, in 1892. It was a twelve-passenger open surrey wagon with twenty-four battery cells and a 4 hp motor. It could attain a speed of 14 mph. Charging time was estimated at ten hours. Steering was accomplished by rotating the wheel on a vertical steering apparatus, and it was claimed to have been perfected "to such an extent that a light touch on the wheel will alter the course of the vehicle."[9] Morrison sold the electric automobile to the American Battery Company of Chicago. This is thought to be the first sale of an American automobile.[10]

Harold Sturges began building an electric surrey in 1895 fashioned on the model of Morrison's carriage. He removed the third seat to allow more room for batteries and claimed a range of seventy miles on a flat and even surface. Morrison and Sturges entered the vehicle in the *Chicago Times-Herald*'s

William Morrison Electric Wagon, 1892[11]

Chicago-to-Evanston race in 1895. It ran thirteen of the fifty-three miles in six inches of snow before running out of power. Duryea's gasoline-powered vehicle won the race.

Charles Jeantaud, a famous French carriage builder and inventor of complex gearing and differential systems, proclaimed in 1895, "The electric carriage has a future, and already in London there is a firm which displays a sign saying they are prepared to charge accumulators [batteries] of all sizes at any hour of the day or night."[12] In that same year in France, he decided to develop his own vehicle to compete with the petroleum and steam carriages. He was looking for a smaller and lighter source of electricity and found it in the Fulmen accumulator. The accumulator consisted of lead plates and acid, as did other batteries of the day, but the weight was lessened by covering the plates with a perforated celluloid envelope. It was a nonconductor and was not attacked by acids. The box was sealed and watertight, and was resistant to shocks and bumps. Jeantaud used twenty-one of these elements in his carriage, enclosed in seven small boxes, each containing three accumulators. The accumulators were stowed away under the seat. On a level road, he managed a speed of thirteen miles per hour, while in hilly country the speed was reduced to about seven miles per hour.[13]

By 1899 Jeantaud was the head of a fairly large carriage establishment that produced some of the finest and best-known electric vehicles in Paris. He was one of the founders of the Automobile Club de France and was a leading member of the civil engineers' society. He established a taxicab service for use in the city with vehicles that carried two or three passengers. Jeantaud also experimented with a chain-drive system to drive the rear wheels, and different types of transmissions. One type had each rear wheel driven by a separate motor, with a large gear wheel affixed to the main axle. This eliminated the use of differential gearing and made the system less complicated. It was similar to the system developed by Krieger for his Electrolette machine. Jeantaud's motors primarily drove the front wheels and not the rear, which allowed for the vehicle to be steered in any direction without interfering with the working of the driving mechanism.[14] Differing speeds of 4, 8, 12 and 16 kilometers per hour were obtained, with a reverse speed of 4 kilometers per hour. The electric brakes were very efficient and were tested by a run down a steep grade at full speed. When the driver got a signal to stop, the brakes were applied and the vehicle came to a full stop within a distance of eight meters. These brake tests were conducted by the Automobile Club de France. The club also tested distance and speed. Jeantaud entered a number of his electric cabs in these tests and showed they could cover a distance of sixty kilometers in less than four hours, averaging fifteen kilometers per hour. The tests covered a ten-day period and a distance of over 6,000 kilometers. In a presentation to the Society of Civil Engineers of France, Jeantaud gave his opinion that the problem of city service could be solved by electric cabs and the competitive tests conducted by the club proved it feasible.

In 1898 Jeantaud convinced the Automobile Club de France to organize races. The race trials lasted nine days and the winners were Jeantaud and Krieger. The lone ICE Peugeot fared so badly one journalist declared, "The petroleum-spirit cab will never be a practicable proposition in large towns."[15] Jeantaud held the land speed record at the time of 39 mph, until rival Camille Jenatzy beat it with 41 mph. This rivalry led to a competition resulting in streamlined cars with bullet-shaped coachwork. Jeantaud's driver Chasseloup-Laubat set a record of 58 mph, which was again beaten by Jenatzy on April 29, 1899, when he reached a speed of 65.8 mph.[16] Deciding to take another tactic to find greater speed to win races, Jeantaud switched to a hybrid gasoline-electric vehicle, as did Austrians Ludwig Lohner and Ferdinand Porsche.

The first Lohner-Porsche debuted at the Paris Exposition in 1900. An automobile historian wrote, "Dr. Ferdinand Porsche (1875–1952), although not the first with hybrid electric vehicles, probably carried the concept furthest of early pioneers at the turn of the century and later."[17] Porsche was an employee at the Lohner's Electric Vehicle Company in 1898, when his employer boasted to the press: "He is very young, but he is a man with a big career before him. You will hear of him again."[18] Porsche helped develop a hub-mounted drive system that eliminated a transmission by mounting the electric motors on the front wheels. This hybrid automobile was not cost effective for production and Porsche turned to gasoline-powered vehicles.

In America in the 1880s carriage-building was considered an art. The invention of the horseless carriage as a new form of self-propelling machine was less impressive than the production of the fine artistic carriages that would surround the mere electrics and mechanics of the vehicle. The Woods Motor Vehicle Company, founded in 1898 by Clinton E. Woods and also known as the American Electric Vehicle Company, was an excellent example of that art. It produced eight different models. Many had electric side lanterns, electric lights in the interior and even electric foot warmers. The company devoted its efforts to fine coachbuilding in a variety of styles and claimed it could work easily with electricians and mechanics—with one exception. They could not accommodate rubber tires. For the 1915 season, the company completely remodeled its line of electric vehicles. They used a new type of spring suspension, improved brakes and replaced the bevel gears with a worm-drive system. The new body style also included headlamps that were set into the body. The motor was suspended by a ball-joint mechanism to prevent jarring. The Anheuser-Busch Brewing Company owned a fleet of fifty Woods electric delivery wagons for trans-

Lohner-Porsche Electric Coupe, 1899[19]

Woods' Victoria Hansom Cab, 1899[20]

porting beer. By 1916 interest in electric vehicles began to fade. In response, Woods began development of a hybrid (gasoline-electric) car.

Another electric vehicle whose manufacturer concentrated on the tradition of coach-building was the 1895 Holtzer-Cabot. It was promoted for its comfort, simplicity and ease of operation. Powered by forty-four chloride cell batteries, it had a three-speed transmission operated by a lever near the steering shaft and boasted a top speed of fifteen miles per hour. Part of adapting to the coachbuilding process involved applying many layers of acid-proof paint to prevent damage in the event of a battery cell's breaking.

From their inception electrics have had difficulty with distance and battery recharging. Racing and popular journals of the time brought the problem to the public's attention, and solutions appeared on a limited scale. One of the first organized automobile races in the United States took place in Chicago in 1895. Very few electrics competed; the batteries did not have enough storage capacity and the race course did not have charging stations. In 1900 *Scientific American* noted that an important aid in popularizing the electric car would be to have central station owners provide their plants with the necessary apparatus to charge the carriage, for the convenience of drivers traveling in unknown territory. A new feature at the time in New York was the charging "hydrant." It was being perfected by a prominent electric company and consisted of a coin-operated mechanism with a wattmeter, voltmeter, rheostat, switch and terminals. After the driver deposited the necessary coins he could draw upon it for a certain number of watt-hours. It was assumed that general adoption of this type of device would greatly simplify the use of electric automobiles. Prices for charging storage batteries varied considerably, depending on the locality and the differing conditions contributing to varying daily loads of electric use. The novelty of the service also added cost to the product. The average price was about two and one-half cents per kilowatt-hour. The greatest financial problem facing the central station operators was the relation between the cost of installation and the possible return on that investment. The start-up cost at the time was high. It was a chicken-and-egg situation, with the prediction of more electric cars demanding more charging stations and more charging stations causing a higher demand for electric cars. EV supporters like H. M. Maxim were confident that the industry could meet the challenge. In one article he said, "It does not seem to me to be an exaggeration to say that the [electric] horseless carriage builder now offers the solution of this vexed problem."[21] Researchers and entrepreneurs continued work on battery design and charging possibilities to improve the EV powerplant.

Electrics were especially useful in commerce; they were efficient and practical work vehicles for the cities. Fleets were less affected by the need for charging stations. The company garages maintained the units and the distance most cabbies traveled was well within the electric's range. Electric taxicabs became a thriving business in the larger cities on both sides of the Atlantic. On August 19, 1897, W. H. Preece inaugurated an electric taxicab service in London to compete with the hackney carriages. Thirteen cabs were ready for use and the company expected to have twenty-five more cabs available in the near future. The cabbies were very enthusiastic about the new vehicles and underwent instruction in managing switches and steering. The motor was a three-horsepower Johnson-Lundell with a variety of speeds and a range of about thirty-five miles. The storage batteries were hung on springs beneath the vehicle and could be recharged in place or taken to a supply station and exchanged for fresh batteries by using hydraulic lifts.

On the west side of the Atlantic, Henry Morris and Pedro Salom built one of the first American electric cars and called it the Electrobat. They took the suffix "bat" from a Greek word meaning "to go." Morris was a mechanical engineer and Salom was an electrical engineer when they formed a partnership in 1894 and called it the Electric Carriage and Wagon Company. They were ahead of their time with the concept of offering several different models of their product simultaneously, giving the consumer a choice within the same company. They were also one of the first to make electric vehicles for commercial use. Morris and Salom thought electric taxis would be cheaper to operate than horse-drawn cabs. They produced Electrobat taxis for New York City from 1896 to 1898. In August 1897 they wrote a letter to the editor of *The Horseless Age* indicating the success of their taxi business. It showed a total mileage for the previous six months of 14,459 miles with 4,765 passengers being carried. They wrote, "While we do not care to publish the actual receipts and expenditures for contracting the service, we would say that the results have been so satisfactory as to warrant the organization of a new company with a large capital stock for the purpose of manufacturing and operating electric motor vehicles of all styles, and that the construction of 100 additional electric hansoms will be begun within the next thirty days."[22] Their brougham featured a new concept known as the "Tracteur" principle that consisted of mounting the motors, gears and batteries on the front part of the body. This allowed for standard carriage construction of the body built on the same line as those intended to be drawn by horses. The motors were mounted on the axle and would swing radially about it. The average speed was six miles per hour with a range of about thirty-six miles. In 1898 Morris and Salom sold their company to Isaac L. Rice, who expanded the service to 200 taxis by the end of the year and renamed it the Electric Vehicle Company.

Like many entrepreneurs of the era, Rice took advantage of trusts and mergers. He went on to create the Electric Boat Company in Groton, Connecticut. The company then became part of the Lead Trust, a very powerful monopoly directed by William Whitney. Whitney initially ordered 200 taxis from Colonel Albert A. Pope, and then increased the order to 1,600. In 1899 Colonel Pope's Columbia Automobile Company acquired the factory, and by 1900 both Pope and Riker Electric Motor Company's automobile division had become part of the Electric Vehicle Company. In 1900 the Storage Battery Company gave Electric the right to use storage batteries on vehicles around the country and agreed to sell batteries and machinery to them at all times at a rate of 15 percent below the market price. The Electric Vehicle Company was sued in 1901 for illegal dividends payment. The directors of the company were held responsible and were directed to repay $800,000. This did not stop the business from thriving.

In 1895, before doing business with Whitney, the Pope Manufacturing Company of Hartford, Connecticut, a well-known bicycle manufacturer, decided to enter the horseless carriage field. Pope was one of the first companies to take another approach to producing EVs—it produced electric vehicles, not merely coaches with electrics. The company began experimenting with this new approach without regard to expense and by 1897 produced the Columbia Motor Carriage. The electric motor was powered by four sets of batteries consisting of forty-four cells, and produced about two horsepower. Unlike its competitor Woods, Pope saw great advantage to pneumatic tires. It was this vehicle's most exceptional feature. The Columbia's wheels were fitted with heavy rubber pneumatic tires that could travel 3,500 miles before needing to be replaced and were considered practically unpuncturable. The carriage had a range of thirty miles at a maximum speed of 15 mph. The company claimed this range could be increased if "the roads are good and free from mud." It promoted the electric vehicle as being very economical since charging the batteries cost about fifty cents, which corresponded to a cost of about a cent a mile to operate. In a testing session on May 13, 1897, the scientific press found that the carriage was as easy to handle as "guiding the gentlest horse," even by those totally unfamiliar with a horseless carriage.[23] The company did not ignore fine coachbuilding. Its top-of-the-line 1899 brougham offered a fine oak frame with a mirror-like lacquer finish, a satin roof and goatskin upholstery. Standard equipment included a hand mirror, electric reading lamps and a small clock. It also had a meter on the dashboard that allowed the "coachman" to read the condition of the batteries. The first brougham was made for a prominent physician in New York City and was shown there in the Electrical Exhibition in 1899. This model sold for $5,000; only the wealthy could afford it.[24] The Electric Vehicle Company absorbed Pope's company in 1898.

By 1902 the company was producing a hybrid (electric-gasoline) vehicle.

Another gasoline/electric hybrid appeared in the Third Annual Automobile and Cycle Show in Paris in 1901. It was designed by Camille Jenatzy and carried an electric motor and a gasoline engine, which could work independently or in combination. The gasoline engine could be coupled to a small dynamo and used to charge several accumulators. This would also charge the batteries when going down grades. The 1902 Jenatzy cab and delivery car had two motors, each geared to drive a rear wheel. The single controller was replaced by a rheostat with a handle that allowed ten different speeds. The forty-four battery cells were split between front and rear boxes to balance the body.

The City and Suburban electric car company produced electric and hybrid cars from about 1901 to 1905. It made many styles, from a light and cheap runabout to the graceful Victoria. The larger hybrid (gasoline-electric) car was experimental, but was thought of as a good performer for its day. It was a four-seat double phaeton with a chassis consisting of two frames. The upper frame (the chassis itself) was mounted on double elliptical springs on the lower tubular framework, consisting of front and rear axles connected by a tubular span. The electric motors were mounted on the tubular rear axle and

Left: Columbia Motor Carriage, 1897.[25] *Right:* Columbia hybrid vehicle, 1902.[26]

Left: Jenatzy cab, 1902.[27] *Right:* City and Suburban Electric Victoria, 1902.[28]

drove the rear wheels with a pinion gearing system. This gearing system worked in combination with the brakes. When the control pedal under the driver's seat was depressed, the first movement cut off the current; if it was depressed further, the brakes would engage. The gasoline engine was a twin-cylinder five-horsepower Daimler set in front. It charged the batteries on flat roads. The battery supplied power to the vehicle when climbing hills, or it could provide a range of up to twenty miles on a flat surface without using the gasoline engine.

The Milde electric car company produced a variety of body styles from about 1901 to 1906. The electric motor was enclosed in a case to protect it from dirt, but was said to be readily disassembled for access to the parts. The forty-two battery cells weighed in at 1,014 pounds and transmitted the power via pinion gears to the rear wheels. The controller, operated by a handle, provided nine forward speeds ranging from one to eighteen miles per hour and three reverse speeds. Milde made a gasoline-electric hybrid four-seat car in 1904 that weighed about the same as its electric car and was capable of a range of 400 miles. It incorporated a de Dion-Bouton nine-horsepower gasoline engine that was housed under the driver's seat. This charged the batteries, and would come into use when climbing hills or when the gasoline engine was stopped for short distances in traffic.[29]

Another early hybrid gasoline-electric vehicle was built by the Munson Electric Motor Company of LaPorte, Indiana. It used a two-cylinder gasoline engine in conjunction with a dynamo and flywheel. The controller could be used to connect the batteries in series or parallel. The car had a total of four speeds, but two of these speeds involved running the gasoline engine at half power, making the car unacceptably slow.[30]

W. C. Bersey manufactured open motorized horseless carriages and electric buses and cabs in England from 1895 to 1900. The Bersey carriage was the focal point of the 1896 auto show in South Kensington, London. A highlight of the company's history came in 1917 when the prince of Wales rode in a Bersey cab. The carriages were powered by two motors and contained an unusual feature for an electric car — a clutch. According to one account, "Three of these carriages ran in the London-Brighton Emancipation Run in November 1896, though it was widely rumoured that they completed the journey by train. This was finally confirmed by Walter Bersey in a speech to the Veteran Car Club in 1935."[31] Bersey is best remembered for building taxis between 1897 and 1900. Bersey's "Hummingbirds" began operating on the London streets in late 1897. These cabs, owned by the London

Electrical Cab Company, had removable battery packs to make recharging easier, Mulliner bodies supplied by the Great Horseless Carriage Company, and three and a half hp Lundell motors. Reliability was a problem for this design. A larger package was also supplied by the Gloucester Railway Carriage & Waggon Company. Breakdowns were frequent with this model as well, and cost of batteries was high. The company closed in 1899. Bersey switched to selling gasoline-powered cars.

Ransom E. Olds of Lansing, Michigan, built his first steam-powered automobile in 1892 and a gasoline-powered vehicle in 1897. He began producing electric automobiles in 1898. Olds was the only manufacturer to offer all three types of powered vehicles until he finally decided to pursue the gasoline Oldsmobile in about 1900. In 1904 Olds was approached by his head of engineering, Henry Leland, with a lighter, more powerful engine that could improve the runabout. To the dismay of his backer, Samuel Smith, Olds refused to use the new engine. Smith forced Ransom Olds out of the company. Olds went on to found the Reo Motor Car Company, and Oldsmobile went on without him. Henry Leland took his motor elsewhere to power the world's first Cadillac.

In 1897, the identical twins F. E. and F. O. Stanley produced a steam-powered car as a hobby. It was designed to be a racer that would set a new land speed record. The following year the Stanleys introduced the Model K, a hybrid with a 26-inch boiler and a two-cylinder gasoline engine. It carried 26 gallons of water and 13 gallons of fuel and featured left-hand drive. It took about 30 minutes to produce enough steam to reach the required 85 pounds per square inch (psi) once the burner was lighted. F. E. Stanley, always an optimist, thought this length of time before start-up was a good opportunity for the owner to polish his ride.[32] In 1906, Fred Marriot, the Stanleys' chief mechanic, decided to modify the auto body in hopes of improving speed; he set an inverted canoe on the chassis. It worked. He set a speed record of 127 mph against a Mercedes, a White and other contenders at the Ormond/Daytona Beach trials. In 1907, with a few alterations to his machine, he attained 197 mph on that same track — a land speed record that lasted for 25 years.[33]

In 1897 M. A. Darracq displayed his electric coupe in the Salon du Cycle show in Paris. It was possibly the first vehicle to use a regenerative braking system. When the brakes were applied, the kinetic energy was converted to electrical energy to charge the battery. It had a steel tube chassis, hard rubber tires on wooden wheels and forty Fulmen batteries weighing a total of 800 pounds. It could reach a speed of six miles per hour and had a range of about thirty miles.

The Riker Electric Motor Company of Brooklyn, New York, built a four-wheel one-person vehicle in 1895. It was as sparse in design as a bicycle and it may have been the first vehicle to be equipped with wire spoked wheels. In 1897 Andrew Riker drove a Victoria model six hundred miles around New York City at a cost of $10.35, averaging 1.7 cents per mile. Riker also saw economic possibilities in the hansom taxi market. By 1899 he designed and produced the Demi-Coach cab, which positioned the driver at the rear of the passenger compartment, giving the occupants an unobstructed view of the road. Half of the batteries were stored in the boxlike front compartment and the other half under the driver's seat. This gave the taxi a well-balanced and symmetrical appearance. It was elegantly upholstered and had a full glass front with an electric light on the roof and exterior lamps. Instruments attached to the back of the vehicle and in front of the driver included a voltmeter and ammeter. It could carry four passengers and travel twenty-five miles on one charge at about ten miles per hour.[34]

The newly named Riker Electric Vehicle Company expanded by opening a new plant at Elizabethport, New Jersey. The facility was equipped to make every part of the vehicle. In 1899 Riker produced a surrey, a delivery wagon and a brougham with a system of electric motors and a controller stored under the front and rear seats. "The Riker System" was considered to be one of the new ideas of the time. The design fitted a large number of storage batteries into a small space. It was seen as a portent of things to come and projected a confidence that expected improvements would continue to produce greater efficiency for the electric car. The system used forty-four Willard storage cells (batteries) approximately 3 × 5 × 9 inches

Riker Electric Demi-Coach, 1899[35]

in configuration. The system could be modified to produce different energy exchanges. Each battery was compactly placed so that either only a few cells would operate at one time, or the batteries would operate in parallel, or in series, or with the direction of the current reversed. The car approached 15 mph on a level road. Instead of a steering wheel, the driver guided it by a vertical steering shaft. In 1896 a Riker electric car decisively defeated a Duryea (ICE) at the first auto race in the United States on a racetrack at Narragansett Park, Rhode Island.[36] In December 1900, Riker merged with the Electric Vehicle Company, maker of the Pope-Columbia, and thereafter only electric trucks were made under the Riker name.[37] That did not stop Riker from racing his electric automobiles. The Long Island Automobile Club ran one-mile straightaway races in 1901 featuring one electric vehicle (Riker), eight gasoline-powered and six steam-powered vehicles. The vehicles were stripped of all unnecessary equipment, leaving only the motor, wheels, a frame and a seat. Mr. Riker had a man riding behind him clinging to the frame. Henri Fournier set the new one-mile land speed record with a time of 51.5 seconds. A. L. Riker's electric finished with a respectable 1 minute, 3 second run for third place.

Fifty thousand people watched and occasionally some fans wandered onto the course as there was very little supervision by the club, but miraculously no one was hurt. After the race, A. L. Riker switched to producing gasoline-powered cars. He became vice president of the Locomobile Company of America in 1902 and was influential in replacing its steam-powered cars with gasoline cars.

The 1900 Waverley used a braking system based on a

The Electric Surrey constructed on the "Riker System," showing details of working parts.[38]

bidirectional controller concept that charged the batteries as the driver was applying the brakes. It incorporated a recharging motor. By continuing to run the motor downhill instead of immediately applying the brakes, the motor continued to increase in speed "until the counter electromotive force of the armature equals that of the battery, which would be 80 volts with the controller on the third position or notch. At this point the motor will take no current and ... if the speed increases ... will generate a current in the opposite direction."[39] The inventor claimed this process would provide from 20 to 40 percent greater distance than the conventional wound motor. The Waverley had two unique features: a rear-facing front seat and a steering lever in the center of the backseat, allowing the driver to converse face-to-face with the passengers. In 1904 Waverley merged with Pope's American Electric Vehicle Company. The company became Pope-Waverley in 1908. Pope sold the company in 1908 to a group of executives who renamed the car simply the Waverley and introduced a front end resembling a gasoline-powered car as a new design feature.

The 1914 Waverley electric brougham incorporated many new design principles, including rounded corners on the body. It also featured larger windows for a wider range of vision and a spacious "four chair" seating arrangement with maximum "knee, shoulder and elbow room."[41] The construction of the body included the use of new lightweight aluminum in the roof and panels. A standard forty-two-cell battery gave a range of about seventy-five miles. At a slightly higher cost the purchaser could have the optional new Edison or Iron-clad Exide battery installed. The battery boxes were located at the front and rear and were covered with sloping decks that rounded off to present graceful lines. The battery compartments were lined with acid-proof material to prevent any damage to the paint should the liquid be spilled. Other unique features of this brougham included a trussed hardwood beam frame, five quarter-elliptic springs front and rear and a double set of expanding brakes. The standard color was black with blue panels, but the company offered to paint the vehicle to suit the demands of the customer. With luxurious bodywork and leather upholstery, the Model 109 sold for $3,150.[42]

The Electromobile, made in Britain from 1902 to 1920, was one of the best-known electric vehicles in England. The British & Foreign Electric Vehicle Company was founded in 1900 and sold a Krieger under the name Powerful. They changed their name to the British Electromobile Company in 1902 and began to assemble vehicles with parts from different sources. The chassis was from Greenwood & Batley in Leeds, bodies were obtained from the Gloucester Railway Carriage & Waggon Company, which also supplied Bersey, and motors from France. In about 1905 they offered a "for-hire" leasing service in which a brougham could be hired, including maintenance and free charging, for £325 per year. Chauffeur services were extra. Reportedly, "In 1908, a fleet of 20 taxicabs went into service in London, some still being on the streets in the 1920s."[43]

Pope-Waverley Surrey, 1908[40]

The first horseless carriage for

Studebaker was a light runabout built along buggy lines. It had leather fenders, bar-lever steering, chain drive and a leather dashboard. The advertisement claimed "Reliable Brake Control ... with All Machines equipped with Two Brakes." The Studebaker brothers of Fort Wayne, Indiana, were the largest wagon makers in the United States by 1895 and became interested in supplying the federal government with wagons for the Spanish-American War (1898–1902). They also wanted to supply the army with electric vehicles, but were slow in developing the complete product. Their first electric appeared in 1902. By 1904, electric production ceased and the company moved to producing gasoline vehicles.

In 1903 Thomas A. Russell produced an electric two-passenger Ivanhoe runabout, called the "Thoroughly Canadian Car," in a Yonge Street plant in Toronto. Production of the electric car only lasted two years. Then Russell turned his attention to gasoline-powered vehicles and began making a two-cylinder Model A.

Studebaker Electric ad, 1902[44]

De Dion-Bouton produced an electric car in France in 1904 that featured a large, slow-speed four-pole motor, mounted in the position occupied by the gearshift in a gasoline car. This was a simple arrangement to provide for speed changes, but it added to the overall weight of the vehicle. The motor was completely enclosed in an aluminum casing with inspection openings near the brushes and incorporated a direct drive to the rear axle by means of a bevel gear. The steering mechanism and thick treaded tires copied the design and construction of contemporary gasoline vehicles.

The Babcock Electric Carriage Company (1903 to 1912) of Buffalo, New York, promoted safety and comfort in its vehicles. They were advertised as having "sufficient speed, besides greater mileage than is required in city or suburban riding." Founder Frank A. Babcock claimed a world record for range when he drove a runabout 100 miles from New York to Philadelphia in 1906 on a single charge. The actual distance to Philadelphia was 105 miles. The car consumed the last kilowatt of electricity a half-mile from the Camden, New Jersey, city limits and was towed the remaining five miles to the Philadelphia ferry, but the record had been set. It had a top speed of 30 mph and was claimed to be able to climb any hill at better than 20 mph. In 1911 Babcock maintained an electric garage at 66th Street and Euclid Avenue in Cleveland, Ohio, for the convenience of electric car owners "who wish to leave their cars downtown while attending business or the theater."[45] A special inspection

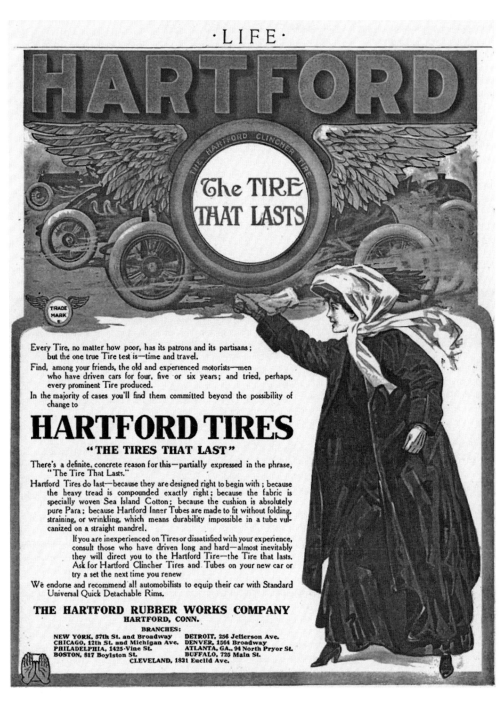

Hartford Tires ad, 1909[47]

service, provided as part of the manufacturer's guarantee, was furnished free for the first
year and included batteries being charged, inspection and adjustment of chains and minor
repairs being made "at the great convenience to electric owners."[46] The service could be
extended after the first year by a payment of $2 monthly. Frank Babcock merged his com-
pany with the Clark Motor Company, changed the name to the Buffalo Electric Vehicle
Company and continued production until 1915. Attempts were made to increase sales by

designing the body to look similar to a gasoline-powered car, but the company went out of business in 1915. Their Model 6 Victoria sold for $1,700.

In 1908 Henry Ford introduced the first Model T at a price of $850. The gasoline-powered "Tin Lizzie" was his idea of a universal car. Ford kept reducing the price of the car until it reached $265 in 1923. In 1914, Clara Ford, Henry's wife, bought a Detroit Electric car for herself, claiming Henry's cars were too noisy.

By 1911 electric auto manufacturers were experiencing increased competition from the Fords and other ICEs. They

Babcock Electric Coupe, 1912[48]

decided to combine forces to enhance market share. A 1911 article in *Electrical World* reported:

> Each Wednesday noon, all representatives of electric vehicle manufacturers located in the Boston district gather at the Edison Building for a pleasant social hour, after which, under the oversight of the chairman elected each week, a large number of imparted topics in connection with development of electric vehicles in the district are discussed. It is inspiring to see these competitive interests putting their shoulders to the wheel with the single object of advancing the industry. Reference was also made to recent decision of the Boston Electric Company to replace all its gasoline and horse-drawn vehicles by electrically driven machines. On Memorial Day, an electric vehicle parade occurred in Boston in contrast to the annual work-horse procession, sixty two electric vehicles being in line.[49]

Thomas Edison made moving pictures of the parade. The movies were used by W. C. Baker in his lectures to promote electric vehicle transportation in the New England territory.

Another well-known and successful company in business from 1905 to 1923 was the Rauch & Lang Carriage Company of Cleveland, Ohio. The firm produced in quantity compared to most and offered a variety of open and closed vehicle models. As was common during this time, companies merged and diverged when they needed capital investment. In 1915, Rauch & Lang merged with the Baker Electric Company to settle a dispute over Emil Gruenfeldt's rear suspension patent (held by Baker) and became Baker, Rauch & Lang; some of Lang's interests spun off to form the Lang Body Company. Raymond Owen became vice president of sales, bringing Owen Magnetic with him. Raymond Deering bought the company in 1919; he was also owner of Stevens-Duryea Co. in Chicopee Falls, Massachusetts. That company went bankrupt in 1924 and its assets were purchased by the Owen brothers for $450,000.[50]

The Columbus Buggy Company of Columbus, Ohio, had been a prominent maker of horse-drawn vehicles since the 1860s. It entered the electric automobile market in 1903 with a folding-top runabout and added a station wagon, surrey and coupe in 1906. Columbus began making gasoline vehicles in 1907. The company was sold in 1915.

The Hupp-Yeats electric vehicle was promoted as a "town car designed and built for the twentieth century" with a low-slung construction that was easy to enter or exit. It was claimed to be safe and graceful without the dangerous tendency to skid or swerve that the high-ride electrics had. The Hupp-Yeats used Westinghouse motors and attained a range of 75 to 90 miles on one charge. The auto was first manufactured by the R.C.H. Corporation, from 1911 to 1912. The Hupp-Yeats Electric Car Company took it to a level of high fashion from 1912 to 1919. In 1915 the company introduced three models, replaced a bevel drive axle with a worm drive and reduced the price to $1,500. Hupp-Yeats offered a unique feature for the buyer. The purchase price included, as part of the standard equipment, a Lincoln

Rauch & Lang, 1923[51]

(motor generator type) electric battery charger. This was a good selling point, aimed at reducing the customer's anxiety about the additional investment in maintenance and charging. In 1919, when interest in the electric car was waning, the Hupp-Yeats was discontinued.

Although the concept of the gasoline-electric hybrid auto had been used with some success in the late 1800s by Jeantaud, Porsche and others, it was only marginally used. The Hybrid Electric Vehicle (HEV) concept came to wider public view in November 1905. H. Piper filed a patent to produce a vehicle with an electric motor augmented by a gasoline motor for greater performance. The patent was not issued for three and one-half years and by that time the internal combustion engine achieved better performance. The HEV concept

Columbus Electric Coupe, 1912[52]

all but disappeared except in a few companies, like Galt, soon after 1910 and was not looked at again seriously until the oil shortages in the early 1970s and the first decade of the 21st century.

There are two types of hybrid vehicles, series and parallel. In the series, a gasoline engine generates power to drive an electric motor. In parallel, the two systems are distinct and separate, able to propel the vehicle independently or together.

The Galt Motor Company was founded in 1909 and produced a series hybrid vehicle in 1914 called the Galt Gas Electric. It was one of the early Canadian entries into the efficient hybrid market. The auto was powered by a small gasoline engine, which turned a Westinghouse generator to produce electricity. The electricity powered the motor and charged the batteries. It had five speeds forward and three in reverse, was reported to get seventy miles per gallon and have a top speed of 30 mph. Traveling on battery power only, the Galt could tour 15–20 miles, reducing the risk of being stranded without gasoline. As an added feature the Galt's front headlight was coupled to the steering gear and turned with the front wheels. This car did not sell well, possibly because the 30 mph speed was no match for the gasoline-powered competition.

The Flanders Electric Company of Pontiac, Michigan, produced a three-horsepower electric vehicle in 1914 with a worm drive to the rear wheels and a horizontal steering controller lever on the left side. Walter Flanders, the company's director, had set up the Ford Model T production line. He later went on to build the Maxwell made famous on *The Jack Benny Show.*

By 1913 the Electric Vehicle Association of America was working overtime to promote its product. The association was formed with twenty-nine charter members in 1911 and had grown to 885 members by 1913. The members included seventeen electric vehicle makers, fifty-six central charging stations and ten manufacturers of accessories. Its promotion campaign targeted every aspect of the industry. It vigorously encouraged central station managers to open more stations for more electric cars. It persuaded the managers to lower their rates. It also approached insurance companies to lower rates so that the rates for electrics were about one-half that of gasoline vehicles. It promoted standardization of parts for electrics and had practically succeeded in standardizing the charging plug. It called for a standard speed limit and recommended a standard sign for battery charging stations. The association also called for the establishment of electric garages to more rapidly advance the introduction of electric cars. The association worked to bring about cooperation among the manufacturers, the central station owners, the battery trade and others in a nationwide advertising campaign for the benefit of the electric vehicle.

The National Electric Lighting Association (NELA) conducted a survey of seventy-five central station representatives and discovered that the electric vehicle as an off-peak revenue producer was not yet fully appreciated by many central stations. By 1914 there were approximately 1,500 electric vehicles in New England. The NELA committee recommended the purchase of at least one electric vehicle by each central station of any size, membership in the national organization and the introduction of charging equipment into their facilities. *Electrical World* wrote, "The day is at hand when the companies will be forced by the public to give the electric vehicle its proper service and when the companies themselves will have to use this class of equipment or become hopelessly out of date."[53]

The "dual-powered" car was a 1916 attempt at making a commercially viable hybrid vehicle. It was capable of running on either electricity or gasoline or both simultaneously. On electric power alone, the vehicle could speed up to 20 mph. Adding the gasoline power increased the speed to 30 mph. Running the gasoline engine now and then was sufficient to recharge the batteries. The power plant consisted of a small gasoline motor and an electric motor generator combined into one unit. The movement of a lever on the steering wheel connected the gasoline motor to the electric motor generator, which transmitted power through the armature shaft of the electric motor and the propeller shaft directly to the rear axle. As the lever was moved forward it caused the car to be operated more and more on gas. With a variation of another lever on the steering wheel, the battery could be charged or used for the electric motor. It was promoted as having 40 percent greater speed than electric vehicles of the time, and was simple, efficient and had more power. It was not competitive with its gasoline powered counterpart.

The Baker Motor Vehicle Co. of Cleveland, Ohio, was an industry leader from 1899 to 1916. The company offered fifteen different models of EVs. The earliest Bakers sold for $850 and one of the first customers was Thomas Edison. Other famous owners of Bakers were Mrs. William Howard Taft, the king of Siam and "Diamond Jim" Brady. In 1905 annual production reached 400 vehicles. Production doubled to 800 the following year, making Baker the largest producer of electric vehicles in the world.[55] In 1910 company advertising claimed, "It outsells all other Electrics because it outclasses them. More than three times as many Baker Electrics are sold each year than any other make." In 1911 Baker maintained a charging garage at 71st Street in Cleveland, Ohio. The garage had facilities for charging 66 vehicles simultaneously and providing care for 100 automobiles. "The front of the building is given over to sales offices for the Baker ... while above these are high-class bachelor apartments."[56] Baker supplied fleets of Baker Electric trucks to over 200 companies in 1912. Baker introduced a two-passenger roadster model in 1914 featuring a very sleek body style, high speed, and a steering wheel instead of a lever. By 1915 Baker acquired the R. M. Owen Company, maker of the Owen Magnetic car. After this acquisition, production was divided: the chassis was built in the Baker factory and the body was made by Rauch & Lang. Also in 1915, Baker and its competitor Woods each switched from a straight bevel drive train to worm drive, providing quieter operation and fewer gear reductions between the motor and the rear axle. The 1915 Baker models sported two head lamps, colonial side lamps and rear quarter interior lamps that lit automatically when the right-hand door was opened. Simplicity and reliability were the watchwords used to promote the Baker as the "standard" of the industry. Walter C. Baker referred to his vehicles as "The Aristocrat of Motordom." The company claimed to produce the most efficient, simplest-to-operate vehicle, with the fewest parts and fewer adjustments than others. An advertisement went so far as to call it an "automobile without a repair bill." The company maintained that its vehicles were the safest and simplest to operate and the cheapest to maintain, but it did admit they were

The Dual-Power Car, 1916[54]

Baker ad, 1908, showing 5 of its 15 models[57]

not the cheapest to buy. The initial cost factor again was a deterrent in a time when few
people had the extra money to spend on such an extravagance. Baker tinkered with a gasoline-electric hybrid for a short time, but decided it was too cumbersome. The Baker electrics
were discontinued in 1916. Walter Baker moved on to form a successful electric forklift
truck business.

The Owen Magnetic Company, founded by brothers Raymond and Ralph Owen, began producing a gasoline-electric hybrid car in 1914. It featured an electric transmission that replaced the clutch, gears, starter motor and magneto. It was known as the "Car of a Thousand Speeds." The Baker, Rauch & Lang Company acquired the Owen Magnetic in 1915 and moved production from New York City to Cleveland, Ohio. Baker produced the chassis, while Rauch & Lang produced the body. Famous owners included operatic tenors John McCormack and Enrico Caruso.[58] The price kept rising ($6,500 in 1918) while sales were falling, and in 1919 Baker discontinued production of the Owen. The company was acquired by J. L. Crown, who continued production on a small scale until 1921 under the name of Crown Magnetic.[59]

The Beardsley Electric Car Company of Los Angeles, California, marketed three models in 1915, a victoria, a brougham and a roadster. The brougham sold for $3,000 and the roadster for $2,600. They all had the same chassis and used wire wheels exclusively.

The Columbian Electric Car Company of Detroit, Michigan, began in 1915 and offered three models. The first was a very low-priced two-passenger roadster listing at $950, the second a three-passenger coupelet selling for $1,250, and the third a four-passenger brougham listing at $1,450. All employed the same chassis, and the standard body color was dark blue with silver-gray trim.[60]

The Storms Electric Car Company, founded by William E. Storms, formerly of the Anderson Electric Car Company, was another 1915 start-up. He produced two low-priced models, a coupe for $950 and a roadster for $750. They were shorter than most, with a wheelbase of only 90 inches, and had large, 44-inch tires. The motor was located in the center of the chassis to create a direct drive by a shaft to bevel gears in a tubular full-floating rear axle. Two sets of brakes were operated by a pedal.

The Century Electric Car Company of Detroit, Michigan, manufactured electric vehicles from 1911 to 1915 in cooperation with Westinghouse. The motor was geared directly to the rear axle. The company offered only one model in 1915. It was the first to incorporate an underslung frame and came with a choice of solid or pneumatic tires.[61] The company went bankrupt in 1915.

The Grinnell Electric Company, founded by Ira and C. A. Grinnell, produced electric cars and enjoyed moderately successful sales from 1912 to 1915. In 1915, it offered a dual-drive model with a set of control levers operated from either the front or rear seats; it sold for $3,400. As interest in electric vehicles faded, the Grinnell brothers changed their entire business strategy to move from a loss in automobile sales to a profit by establishing a chain of piano and music stores in Detroit.

In 1916 the Walker Vehicle Company produced a product line termed the "Edison models" designed spe-

Century Electric, 1915[62]

cifically for use with the new G-Type Edison battery. The new battery provided increased power with reduced weight. The models included a five-passenger car, a four-passenger car and a sleek cabriolet roadster. The rear seat of the roadster was wide enough to carry three passengers, and an auxiliary folding seat would carry a fourth person. The car body design avoided sharp angles and a new crowned fender design gave it a sleek look. Aluminum was used exclusively for all parts exposed to the weather. Luxury items in the interior included

Grinnell Electric Coupe, 1912[63]

dome lights, reading lamps, arm rests, arm slings, a concealed vanity case and smoking set, a clock, and dash instruments. The chassis was a one-unit rigid frame thought to be well-adapted to the solid tires. The construction included better lubrication of the steering gear and a worm-bevel gear axle drive similar to that used in the Chicago electrics. Cooler winter weather took its toll on the battery performance in the electrics, but the new batteries included in the package were claimed to be less affected by temperature changes than other batteries. To promote sales, Walker offered a battery exchange system and lowered prices from an average of $2,600 to $1,985. If a buyer wanted the battery exchange system, the new list price would go up another $270. The purchaser could "rent a complete battery service at a minimum charge per month."[64] This service covered all maintenance and repair expenses whether the car was driven fifty or one thousand miles a month, and if the battery wore out, it was replaced with a fresh one.

The most successful company in the electric vehicle field was the Detroit Electric Car Company, operating under various names from 1907 to 1939. It produced one of the most popular electric cars in the United States. The popularity was due in part to a false front end resembling the radiator of a car with a gasoline engine. The company started as the Anderson Carriage Co. in 1907. It became the Anderson Electric Car Co. in 1911 and finally the Detroit Electric Car Co. from 1919 to 1939. The Detroit Electric in 1915 featured a new beveled worm-gear drive and large expanding brakes. Window glass was fitted into the bodies mounted on thick rubber, with a dovetailed channel to prevent rainwater from entering the interior. Six models were offered. To encourage sales, the company dramatically lowered the prices of various models from $600 to $725, bringing the average selling price down to about $2,000. The Anderson Electric Car Company produced a four-passenger model Detroit in 1917 that featured windows operated by a patented window lifter. In the warm summer, the car could be converted to an open-air vehicle with a permanent roof. Detroit Electric sales dropped from 4,669 cars in 1914 to less than 200 cars in 1920. There was a bankruptcy in 1929, and a man named Alfred Dunk bought up all the assets. People were still ordering cars, so he went out and bought up all the old Detroit electrics he could find, and with a few renovations to the bumpers, fenders, and so on, sold them as new 1932, 1933 and 1934 models. While the basic body design changed little over the years, in 1930 Detroit offered an option of a body supplied by either Dodge or Willys. Production gradually declined from its high in 1914 to "by-order-only" in the later stage of the company. The company continued to produce cars (mostly electric conversions of the Dodge or Willys) until it faded in 1939 and finally closed in 1942.[65] During its thirty-five years in business, it produced over 35,000 vehicles, far more than any other electric car company.

The Milburn Wagon Company, founded in 1848 in Toledo, Ohio, was another of the more successful electric car makers of the time, producing thousands of vehicles from 1914 to 1922. In 1909 it leased part of its wagon plant to the Ohio Electric Car Company. When Ohio moved to its own factory in 1911, Milburn's directors became interested in electric vehicles and began their own production in September 1914. Milburn produced a variety of coupes and roadsters and a delivery van. They used aluminum, hammered by hand, to produce arched fenders and sweeping curves in the body style. The craftsmanship of the bodywork was excellent, reflecting the Milburn Company's concern for the artistry of the coachbuilding business. In 1915 they introduced a battery swap-out system with the batteries on rollers that allowed the owner to roll out the discharged batteries and roll in the charged ones. President Wilson's Secret Service staff used Milburns. General Motors (GM) bought the Milburn factory in February 1923 and proceeded to make Buicks. Milburns may have been produced on a "custom-order" basis as late as 1927.

Detroit Electric two-seater, 1912[66]

In 1917 electric vehicles in general were thriving in the commercial vehicle industry. The electric truck was being used in over one hundred types of industries, some having been in use for about ten years. Express companies, department stores, breweries, bakeries, central stations, laundries and warehouses were the major users of electric car fleets. The fleet managers began gathering data on their performance and were pleased with the results. Fire departments in particular held great appreciation for

Detroit Electric Roadster Model 46, 1915[67]

the electrics and converted from horse-drawn vehicles to EVs. Horses sometimes balked near fires and the gasoline engine was considered too flammable. The Camden, New Jersey, Fire Department modernized its entire fleet in 1917 and made a thorough investigation using a rigid set of tests. The results showed the new fleet had a quick getaway and the ability to negotiate crowded streets easily and climb hills readily. They were easy for anyone to operate, economical and generally had good reliability. The city council was so impressed that it ordered a charging apparatus for each fire station. Many other cities followed suit, including Philadelphia, Pennsylvania; Brooklyn, New York; Grand Rapids, Michigan; and Akron, Ohio. Police departments and most hospitals in large cities with ambulance service relied increasingly on electric vehicles.

In Europe, World War I materially added to the development of the electric vehicle. In the United States, as well as Germany, France and England, electric vehicle fleets began to be used for street cleaning and sweeping and garbage collection. In England, when gasoline cars were commandeered for the war effort, many merchants began experimenting with electric vehicles. England had a nearly inexhaustible supply of coal to produce electricity, one of the few items it did not have to import. In the three years following the beginning of the war, England increased its electric truck sector from 150 to over 1,000. Electric vehicle use expanded in England by 400 percent during the war. By 1917, Birmingham had

Left: Detroit Electric Coupe, 1917.[68] *Right:* Milburn Coupe, 1915.[69]

Milburn ad, 1916[70]

twenty-two charging stations in the area and seven stations in the city. Growth was expected to continue after the war. Germany was mining an abundance of coal in occupied France to provide cheap electricity. It used the electricity to power railroads and trucks to support the war effort. Italy was generating cheap electricity using waterfalls to supply the energy needed for large numbers of electric vehicles. The market for EVs was plentiful, and United States auto manufacturers came forward to meet the demand. In 1917 the United States became a major exporter, delivering electric vehicles to South America, Norway, China and England. During this era, a solution for recharging also seemed within reach. A battery exchange system had been developed four years earlier for taxicabs and was being used in most large American cities and in Berlin. Under the new system the charging station owned the battery, leased it to the customer at a fixed rate, and charged the customer per mile instead of selling electric current for charging a battery by the kilowatt-hour. The batteries could be exchanged in a few minutes and showed a possibility of unlimited mileage.[71] It was expected that studies conducted by qualified engineers, in the analysis of transportation after the war, would show that electric vehicles were the most efficient mode of transport. The future of electrics looked bright.

James H. McGraw, president of the McGraw-Hill Company, presented a paper to the Electric Vehicle Section meeting in June 1918. In it he stated, "The supply of electricity for the big developments to come in cheapening the cost of handling goods in terminals and warehouses, and in cutting the cost of deliveries on our city streets, is worth the attention of every central station."[72]

Cheap electricity, gasoline shortages, improved battery recharging after World War I had all the elements for marketing electric vehicles, and the United States auto industry was poised to deliver. European and Scandinavian factories needed time to refurbish and rebuild. The U.S. auto factories had expanded production to meet demand during the war. In the United States alone there were an estimated 50,000 electric vehicles, 10,000 of them in Chicago. Now the U.S. auto industry was the only source for supplying large quantities of autos quickly to the war-torn recovering nations. The Central Palace Auto Show in New York in 1918 had four electric companies as exhibitors— Rauch & Lang, Ohio, Milburn, and Detroit Electrics. The show drew several representatives from Scandinavia, Europe, South America and Japan who were prepared to place contracts for large orders of passenger motor vehicles. Demand for electric vehicles was exceptionally high. Rauch & Lang sold ten new taxicabs to Japan. A Norwegian representative ordered one hundred Rauch & Lang broughams for $3,000 each, with arrangement to buy forty more within two weeks. Norway and Sweden were producing abundant and cheap electricity using their water power systems. With electricity plentiful in Norway, the representative expected to sell the cars as soon as they had been shipped. Milburn featured a model with a long hood holding the batteries and a radiator to mimic the appearance of the high-powered gasoline vehicles. Studebaker had an exhibit, but did not feature any electric models at the time. The volume purchased gave indications that the interest in electrics would continue after the war, but even with the postwar interest, they did not regain the popularity they had seen ten years earlier.

In an attempt to revive the electric automobile, Harry E. Dey of Jersey City created a revolutionary vehicle in 1919. It was a hybrid billed as having its own portable charging plant — a three-horsepower air-cooled gasoline engine to charge the two-horsepower electric motor. The gasoline engine could be removed and used as a stationary charging unit for charging a separate battery or powering house lighting. Of its many new features, the motor combined a rotating armature with field magnets connecting to a driving wheel by way of reduction gears. This eliminated the expense and weight of a differential gear. The construction of the vehicle included a number of tapered slip rings and was called the "nutless" car as so few were used. The chassis was made of wood and the commonly used elliptical spring suspension was replaced by air springs. The construction consisted of a helical spring inside a cylinder providing for the static load, while the air would take up all the shocks. If an air leak occurred, the spring would bring the load back to normal position and the air would return. Many other points of the construction reduced the overall weight of the car. The battery was carried underneath the floor of the chassis housed in truss rods. This permitted more room for passengers and luggage. The battery could be lowered to the floor of the garage, or, by lifting a trap door in the floor of the car, water could be added to the battery. The "nutless" lightweight revolutionary new vehicle never made it to mass production.

By the 1920s roads were crisscrossing throughout the cities and towns, making driving both difficult and dangerous. There were bicyclists, horse-drawn carriages, pedestrians and a variety of cars, all competing for the same space. Accidents were inevitable. After seeing a serious crash between a carriage and an auto, Garrett Augustus Morgan, an African American inventor and businessman, invented America's first traffic signal system. The device had a pole with a bell on top and three "STOP" signs. Two of them were controlled by a hand crank at the base of the pole; one remained stationary. He received a patent for the device in November 1923 and later sold it to the General Electric Company for $40,000. It was used for a time in Cleveland, Ohio, until the more familiar three-light system replaced it.[73]

The stock market crash of 1929 and the beginning of a ten-year global depression virtually ended the production of the electric automobile in the United States and crippled companies in England and Europe. Dozens of major companies went bankrupt, though the Detroit Electric Car Company survived until 1939 and Studebaker and Willys lasted in the United States beyond that. Electric car production was not seen again in the United States until World War II, when fuel shortages caused consumers to find an alternative to gasoline vehicles.

The renaissance of electric vehicles had begun in Great Britain about five years before the war. They were used primarily for delivery service, carrying items such as coal, bread and milk. There were about 1,400 electric vehicles in Great Britain in 1933, and by 1940 the number had grown to 6,500. By 1939, due to the war, milk delivery had been reduced from two rounds a day to one. This created an opportunity for marketing larger electric vehicles to meet the delivery need. Attempts at producing EVs with a larger capacity resulted in the same problems earlier manufacturers had had. The battery was not robust enough to handle the added weight of the battery and the larger vehicle. The battery, used under these conditions, had a guaranteed lifespan of only two years. It was hoped that a newer, lighter battery would soon be invented and produced, but the prospects looked bleak.

By 1940, England and Germany were in the midst of war. Every gallon of gasoline saved was important to the war effort on both sides. Germany had already taken advantage of the use of electric vehicles and had promoted their use by making them tax-exempt. They had over 27,000 EVs in service. Their postal service alone had more electrics in operation than the total number of electrics operated in England. Some in England realized that if electric vehicles could replace even more gasoline-powered cars in the transport of everyday items such as milk and bread, it might free up an estimated 70 million gallons of gasoline each year that could be redirected to military needs. To promote the move from gas to electrics, a strong marketing campaign that used many of the advertising points of thirty-five years earlier was put into place. Several advantages of the electric car were pointed out. The long life of the electric vehicle would conserve natural resources. The cheaper operation of the electric vehicle would keep transport costs down and reduce the cost-of-living increases and the risk of inflation. The sales pitch to English customers was that they must be made to realize that the electric car was not intended to be a direct competitor to the gasoline car. It would provide reliable transportation and reach a cruising speed of twenty miles per hour with a range of about fifty miles per day. The buyer should think of the electric as the perfect purchase for transport and delivery vehicles. Hills were not a problem. Even the hilly districts of Sheffield and Bristol already had over three hundred Morrison vehicles operated by the Co-operative Society. Advocates pointed out that slight hills gave somewhat increased mileage to the electrics compared to traveling on flat roads as the batteries could be recharged when going down hills. Supporters of the electric vehicles campaigned that they were not more expensive to purchase when one took into account the expense of gasoline being four times the price of electricity. Another selling point was the lack of maintenance. Simplicity and efficiency were a keynote point that had made the electrics a favorite vehicle for unskilled or even careless drivers since the beginning of the century. Fewer components to get out of order made them less likely to break down. Forgetting to top off the battery was the most common maintenance problem. With fewer components to maintain, the electric cars could expect a longer lifespan. Gasoline-driven vehicles were expected to have a lifespan of about five years, while electric cars were averaging ten years and sometimes up to thirty years. It was anticipated that increased demand would bring about an increase in mass production. A few manufacturers were involved in what they called semi-mass production of electric vehicles in Great Britain in 1940 to meet the limited demand.

Other countries also looked for alternative fuel possibilities to serve the civilians' needs for transportation. European and Japanese civilians began exploring alternate energy possibilities; many turned to the electric vehicle. Some of the manufacturers who made efforts to meet the demand include:

- The Bleichert Transportanlagen Company of Leipzig, Germany, manufactured two-seat electric vehicles from 1936 to 1939.
- The Electrolette was a two-seat light electric vehicle manufactured in France from 1941 to 1943. It was powered by a single 1.5-hp motor and attained a speed of 20 mph. Only a few hundred vehicles were produced.
- The French Faure was produced from 1941 to 1947.
- The Netherlands produced the Story (1940–1941), a three-wheeled electric that attained a top speed of 18 mph with a range of 60 km.
- The French Stela (1941–1948) was a four-door vehicle used by private citizens and government officials, and served as taxis.
- The C.G.E. was a two-seat vehicle produced in France from 1941 to 1948 by the Compagnie Générale Électrique of Paris.
- The Dauphin (1941–1942) was another Paris example of a four-door two-seat electric vehicle.
- The Paris-Rhone (1942–1944) was a tiny three-wheeler car with a 2 hp electric motor driving the rear wheels.
- The Partridge-Wilson Company of England produced electric vehicles from 1935 to 1954 in small numbers (perhaps fifty) with a top speed of 27 mph and a range of forty miles.

All of these vehicles were mildly successful during World War II due to the shortage and rationing of gasoline. When the war was over and gasoline became more available the marques vanished, with only a few continuing into the 1950s.

The Tama Electric Motorcar Company of Tokyo produced a popular electric car from 1949 to 1951, a time of severe gasoline shortages in Japan. It had a range of 125 miles and a speed of 35 mph. In 1952 when gasoline became more readily available, the company began making gasoline-powered cars and changed its name to Prince.

The hybrid Symetric (Arbel) was produced in Paris from 1951 to 1953, and again from 1957 to 1958, when it incorporated plastic bodywork. It featured a four-cylinder engine to power four electric motors, one for each wheel, following the early design of cars like the 1901 Krieger. Many options were offered, including Electric-Drive transmission, Thermogum suspension, phosphorescent bumpers and a choice of powerplants that included a Genestatom nuclear reactor. However, according to one source, "The Arbel quickly disappeared in a haze of unpaid debts."[74]

An unusual vehicle at this time was the Electronic, made in 1955 by the Electronic Motor Car Company of Salt Lake City, Utah. It was a hybrid sports car powered by a small gasoline engine with an electric motor attached to the rear axle. The company had an outrageous idea for the time of setting up a system of radio transmitters coast to coast that would relay electronic signals to a receiver in the car. The signal was to be converted into electricity to charge the batteries.[75] The concept became a forerunner of the vehicle to grid (V2G) concept that emerged around 2000.

Environmental concerns again spiked interest in EVs in the 1960s, but the 1960s' electric vehicle production was confined to small experimental types such as the Peel (1962–1966), a small three-wheeler with a fiberglass body, and the Marketour (1965), intended for short shopping trips. In 1960 the American Motor Company (AMC) experimented with a hybrid vehicle in collaboration with a battery maker, Sonotone Corporation. It ran on nickel-cadmium batteries charged by a small gasoline engine. The companies regarded it as the wrong direction to take as it still emitted gasoline exhaust fumes.

Possibly the most successful electric car of the '60s was the Enfield 8000, produced in London, England. It was a two-door, four-seat car that claimed a range of 90 km and a speed of 60 km/hr. It had a steel tube frame chassis and rack and pinion steering. The eight-horsepower motor was powered by eight twelve-volt batteries. Only 106 cars were made, and the price was too high for most private buyers. The Electricity Council of England promoted the practicality of electric cars by purchasing seventy Enfields to be used by electric utility companies.

Next to the Enfield, the Electracation (1976–1980) was the only serious electric

Enfield 8000, 1969[76]

car produced in England in the 1970s. It had a fiberglass body and a 7.5-hp Lansing-Bagnall electric motor. The three models were a town coupe, a van and a rickshaw with a soft top. Reportedly, "There were a number of appearances at international motor shows and the famous sports car maker AC was lined up to make up to 2,400 cars per year, but nothing came of the plan."[77]

During the same time, the Battronic Truck Company of England delivered electric trucks to the Potomac Edison Company in the United States for fleet use. The Battronic had a range of sixty-two miles and a speed of about 25 mph with a payload of 2,500 pounds. General Electric worked with Battronic from 1973 to 1983 developing passenger buses and fleet vans for the utility industry. By 1977 gasoline in the United Kingdom cost twice as much as in the United States, and England had about 70,000 electric vehicles being used to deliver milk, mail and other products or to provide transportation in some type of service capacity.

In 1966 GMC experimented with the Electrovan, a GMC Handivan converted to a fuel-cell-powered vehicle. It contained a very dangerous combination of fuels that included tanks of pure hydrogen and oxygen behind the back seat and hot potassium hydroxide running through pipes beneath the floor. The safety factors included a hydrogen shut-off switch in the glove compartment and a large knife switch to kill the power. It was destined to travel just a few "well-chosen miles."[78]

Ford produced a small number of electric city-cars in 1967 called the Ford Comuta. It had four batteries and two electric traction motors and had a very limited range.

In 1972 AMC produced a concept car called the Electrosport, a conversion of the AMC Hornet to an electric vehicle. Two other examples of independent manufacturers in the mid–1970s electric car arena were the Sebring Vanguard CitiCar and the Elcar 2000. They were both very small two-seater wedge-shaped vehicles, not much larger than a golf cart, with only about 3.5 hp. Sebring Vanguard was the only American firm at the time producing electric passenger cars on an assembly line. The CitiCar had a top speed of thirty-eight miles per hour and a range of about forty miles. It was not allowed on limited-access highways. *Consumer Reports* judged both the Elcar 2000 and the CitiCar as "Not Acceptable" in its 1976 review. During testing, the cars showed a number of safety and operating problems. At one point in testing, the CitiCar's brakes failed. Production was stopped in 1977.

Nissan of Japan experimented with concept and prototype vehicles in the 1970s, producing the EV4P, powered by a lead-acid battery. It also made a variation of a battery-battery hybrid vehicle known as the EV4H, which combined lead-acid batteries with zinc-air batteries. It claimed a range of 250 to 490 kilometers on a charge and a top speed of 85 km/h.

In Australia in the late 1970s, experimenters produced the Investigator Mk II, a battery-powered electric based on a Fiat 127 body. It had a top speed of 75 km/h with a range of 60–80 kilometers.

The Marathon Electric Car Company of St. Leonard, Quebec, Canada, produced more than six hundred battery-powered vehicles by 1978. The Marathon C-360 van was a six-wheeler. The body was lightweight foam-core aluminum. The company closed its doors in 1980. By the 1980s, Canadians, such as the Ballard Company in Vancouver, were concentrating on fuel cells.

The Elcar, built by Zagato of Italy, was a two-door, two-seater light electric car. It had a fiberglass body shaped like the Fiat 124. About 500 were produced in the mid–1970s. It had a range of sixty miles and a top speed of 45 mph. Fiat itself began experimenting with electric vehicles in the 1970s. Some of its products were the two-seat X1/23, the 900 Evan, the Iveco Daily van, and in 1990 a twenty-two-passenger electric minibus.

In 1980 the Bradley Automotive Company produced a line of kit cars based on the Volkswagen Beetle chassis. They sold several thousand units of the Scorpion and GTII models, but fell into bankruptcy in 1981.

The General Engines Company of Sewell, New Jersey, produced the 1980 Electro-Sport, a full-scale replica of a 1929 Mercedes-Benz roadster. It had a range of fifty miles and a top speed of 50 mph. It was powered by twelve 6-volt golf cart batteries that weighed sixty-two pounds.

The CityCom was a popular city commuter German vehicle built from 1987 to date with a range of thirty miles at 30 mph. The current CityEl is a 3-wheeled vehicle powered either by lead acid or lithium-ion batteries. The range continues to be around 30–35 miles and the top speed 35 miles per hour.

Ford developed the Ecostar utility van in the early 1990s. Its top speed was 75 mph. It had a range of 80–100 miles and regenerative braking. If the driver maintains a constant speed of 25 mph, the range could be extended to 200 miles. Gasoline-powered vehicles tend to creep forward when put in drive; EVs do not. To help in the transition from ICE to electrics, Ford built an electronic "creep" into the Ecostar to satisfy the disconcerted traditional ICE drivers.[79] The Ecostar was considered a "research and design" vehicle, and while about one hundred were produced and delivered to Southern California Edison and Detroit Edison to monitor their performance in the controlled fleet environment, they were never sold commercially. Around this time Ford was also in the process of developing a natural gas pickup truck for fleet use.

In the 1990s Ford introduced its Th!nk City car in Norway. The Th!nk is a subcompact battery-powered vehicle designed for urban transportation. It provides acceleration of 0 to 30 in seven seconds and has a range of 53 miles. Although the response in Norway was positive, Ford executives believe there is only a limited customer demand for battery-electric vehicles and plans to focus its resources on hybrid and fuel cell technology. Ford began work on a battery-fuel cell vehicle, the Escape Hybrid, anticipating it would be released in 2004. It came to market in 2007. The Th!nk continues to be manufactured through subsidies in Norway and is now under Norwegian ownership. They are also considering starting a manufacturing facility in Portland, Oregon.

General Motors experimented with EVs throughout the last decades of the 20th century, primarily making prototypes. The Impact (universally acknowledged as badly named) was introduced as a prototype in 1990 and became the predecessor of the EV1. The Impact was capable of 0–60 in eight seconds, could top 100 mph and travel 120 miles on one charge. The bad news, as usual, was the battery pack—it would only last 25,000 miles and cost $1,500 to replace. Many advanced technologies contributed to the introduction of the General Motors EV1 in 1996. In order to help extend the limited range of the all-electric vehicle, GM designed the car to minimize weight, power consumption and drag. They used molded plastic body panels filled with hollow glass beads and supported by cast aluminum. The body shape had a drag coefficient of only 0.19.[80] Part of the development of the EV1 bodywork and efficient ride came from experiments with GM's Ultralite vehicle in 1992. The prototype vehicle was a four-door design that incorporated a high-tech carbon fiber body that weighed only 1,400 pounds. The biggest drawback of carbon fiber is the price— ranging from $40 to $150 per pound, versus about $2 per pound for plastic and forty cents per pound for steel. The Ultralite could go from 0 to 60 in nine seconds. The inductive type Magne-Charge charging system used a plastic paddle at the end of the charger's cord which was inserted into the front fascia of the car. The system could be used in the rain; GM claimed water could run over the paddle without damage. This type of system was selected for safety and was the only charger to be approved by Underwriters Laboratory.[81] The car was offered for lease only. GM wanted select customers who were green minded, had an annual income over $125,000, and wanted to use the EV1 as a second car. By 1997 disappointing sales of the EV1 forced GM to lower the monthly lease payment by 25 percent, from $530 to $399. The 176 people who had already leased the cars were given the same lower rate. The new rate also included the $50 per month cost previously paid for a home charging station.

In the late 1990s Ford developed an electric version of its Ranger pickup that had a range of about 65 miles and a top speed of 75 mph. GM added an electric Chevrolet S-10 pickup to its product line. Honda offered its EV Plus sedan and Chrysler presented its EPIC minivan. Honda's EV Plus was discontinued in 1999. The Chrysler EPIC model became the Chrysler Town & Country. Its main use as of 2009 was with the U.S. Postal Service. Chrysler plans on having an electric for the consumer market sometime in 2010. Options are either their Dodge sports car, Jeep Wrangler or the Town & Country already in fleet service. Recharging sites for the EPIC are still available in parts of California around the Los Angeles area. All of these vehicles were equipped with nickel metal hydride (NiMH) batteries except the Town & Country, which uses lithium ion batteries. Nissan announced in 1998 it would provide its Altra EV station wagons to California fleets, equipped with lithium-ion batteries. Ford's Ranger EV pickup and Toyota's RAV4 EV are very popular fleet vehicles and are also available to the general public.

The Corbin Sparrow, made in Hollister, California, is a one-seat, three-wheel electric zero emissions plug-in vehicle that was introduced in 1999. The company was cofounded by Mike and Tom Corbin, who began researching their vehicle in 1996. As of 2001, Corbin had sold 200 Sparrows and had a waiting list of over 1,000 orders. The Sparrow is rechargeable in three hours at a 220-volt outlet or six hours at a 110-volt outlet and travels at 50 mph for a range of 50 miles on one charge. It does the quarter-mile in fifteen seconds, reaching 95 mph. The company suffered from lawsuits and financial problems and filed for bankruptcy in 2003. Myers Motors of Ohio bought the Corbin in 2004 and continues to sell it under the name MM NmG (no more gas).

The Honda Insight, introduced in the United States in 1999, is an Ultra Low Emission Vehicle (ULEV) hybrid with a compact electric motor. Regenerative braking recharges the NiMH batteries. It boasts a drag coefficient of 0.25. The gasoline engine is the primary

Corbin Sparrow, 2000[82]

source of propulsion with the electric motor assisting when additional power is needed. Honda began producing the natural gas Civic GX in 1998. The engine was similar to the 1.7 liter, four-cylinder gasoline engine of the traditional Civic with small modifications made to run on natural gas. It has a range of 200 miles and was sold primarily for fleet use. The Nissan Sentra CA (Clean Air) was the first vehicle (2000) to receive Partial Zero Emission Vehicle (PZEV) credits from CARB. It has also qualified as a Super Ultra Low Emission Vehicle (SU-LEV). GM's Precept is a hybrid vehicle with an electric motor driving the front wheels and a lean-burning gasoline motor driving the rear wheels. GM's Triax is unique in that it has three propulsion options: all-wheel-drive electric, all-wheel-drive hybrid electric or two-wheel-drive internal combustion.

In July 2000 GM introduced a prototype fuel cell vehicle called the HydroGen 1 that produces about sixty percent more power than its predecessor. Up to two-thirds of the energy generated by the fuel cell is transferred to the wheels, about four times as much as in a gasoline vehicle. GM was predicting at the time that the HydroGen 1 would be competitive in the showrooms by 2004. The HydroGen 3 was tested by FedEx as a delivery van. The GM HydroGen 4, a minivan operating a 440-cell fuel cell stack with a 73 kilowatt electric motor, is being tested as part of *Project Driveway* in Germany.

In November 2000 DaimlerChrysler unveiled its Necar 5 fuel cell vehicle powered by methanol. The fuel cell stack is 50 percent more efficient than the previous model Necar 3, and the Necar 5 can reach speeds up to one hundred miles per hour. DaimlerChrysler spokesmen admit the fuel cell is still in the development stage, but feel they can be competitive with the ICE in a few years.

In November 2000 Volkswagen introduced the Bora HyMotion, known as the Jetta TDI in the United States. It contains a fuel cell engine that runs on liquid hydrogen with the only by-product being water vapor. The hydrogen storage tank has a capacity of fifty liters, equal to twelve liters of gasoline for a range of about 350 kilometers. Volkswagen continues to develop this product.

In 2001 the U.S. Army announced plans to develop a hybrid diesel-electric truck based on the Dodge Ram. The diesel motor will power the vehicle with added acceleration supplied by the electric motor, or it can run for a short range on electric power only. In 2004 a prototype was developed but never made it beyond the test phase; 2007 brought the Aggressor into the prototype realm. The Aggressor is designed to run on battery only for reconnaissance purposes. Eliminating the need for a transmission and conventional drive train to allow room for additional shell protection is a main concept pushing this option. The Association of the U.S. Army show in Ft. Lauderdale, Florida, in February 2008 had prototypes of vehicles with this configuration.

At the Detroit Motor Show in January 2002, General Motors introduced its prototype fuel cell vehicle called Autonomy. The new fuel cell stack is only 15 cm thick. The x-by-wire computer control systems are held in a six-inch "skateboard" structure that attaches to four wheels. The Autonomy's unusual chassis has four attachment points for different body styles. The bodies can be manufactured and sold separately. They include a choice of standard sedan, coupe, pick-up truck or sport-utility styles. High cost keeps the prototype from moving to the current marketplace. GM has continued to develop their fuel cell concept car line with the Sequel, and, in 2007, a hydrogen fuel cell version of the Chevy Volt was demonstrated as a concept car at the Shanghai Auto Show.

In May 2002 Toyota introduced its all-electric RAV4 EV to the public, available in California only. It had been road-tested for four years within Toyota's fleet division. California incentives included a rebate of up to $8,000 over a three-year period, driving in the carpooling lane even if there are no passengers aboard, and parking in desirable spaces designated for electric vehicles only. According to the Board of Equalization's Taxpayers Information section, tax incentives are no longer offered in 2009.

For the 2001 model year, Toyota introduced the Prius sedan to the United States market. A five-seat compact with a 1.5 liter four-cylinder gasoline engine and an electric motor powered by a 275-volt NiMH battery pack, the Prius was a more practical car for the average American than the Honda Insight. It came into its own with the introduction of the second-generation model, featuring a distinctive five-door hatchback body, in the 2004 model year. A sales success, the 2004–2009 Prius became the most recognized hybrid on the market.

Although plug-ins are still very much a niche market, by 2005 a few models were being tested in limited markets. Nissan and Renault partnered to supply cars for the Better Place Project. The Chevy Volt was shown as a star concept car, and most car makers had some type of plug-in vehicle on the drawing board. CalCars, a nonprofit organization formed to promote plug-in vehicles, is a leading force in this effort. The concept vehicles range from commuter cars to trucks and buses.

By 2006, Honda and GM were testing fuel cell cars. Honda's FCX was claimed capable of 350 miles on a single tank of hydrogen; GM's Sequel SIV offered quick acceleration and a 300-mile range, and the Chevy Equinox boasted redundant safety systems to dispel concerns about hydrogen onboard.

Ford Motor Company introduced a new all-electric car model in January 2007, powered by a plug-in lithium ion battery and a hydrogen fuel cell.[83] General Motors also introduced an all-electric car in January as a prototype, but both models needed work to make them affordable and technologically efficient. The 2008 Mercury Mariner Hybrid featured regenerative braking to improve fuel economy and is ranked a competitor to the Toyota Prius and Honda Civic in consumer comparisons for safety and fuel mileage.

The first few years of the 21st century saw a leap in battery development with the lithium-ion concept. Being smaller and more durable than the nickel metal types, this battery showed more promise for bringing the hybrids and all electrics greater range and power.

A small company called AC Propulsion, located in San Dimas, California, is making an all-electric vehicle called the eBox electric vehicle, based on a Scion xB. It seats five and has room for luggage. It has a range of about 120 miles, but is costly, with a starting price around $70,000. The eBox showcases their main product, the Tzero Technology, which is available for customizing vehicles.

Meanwhile, the Toyota Prius hybrid, with its recognizable design, enjoyed record sales. The first six months of 2007 showed an increase in sales to 94,500 cars, up

AC Propulsion eBox

94 percent from the previous year. Part of the success of the Prius is that the model is sold only as a hybrid. Other models perhaps are too subtle for those who want to "send a clear message" about hybrid vehicles. Consumers wanting their neighbors to know they are mindful of foreign oil dependence and global warming see the unique styling as a means to convey their message. Other hybrids such as the Ford Escape, Mercury Mariner or Honda Civic have a subtle insignia on the rear or side panel to indicate that the car is a hybrid. Like the Detroit electrics, the styling of these models conforms to the body style of the counterpart ICE models.

Toyota's third-generation Prius was introduced in the spring of 2009, with more power and a more compact powertrain. Lithium-ion batteries were tested but not adopted, possibly due to the fire hazard risks, but Toyota at the time of this writing expected to offer a plug-in Prius in late 2011.[84]

In June 2007, Honda announced that, due to lack of sales, it was discontinuing production of its Accord Hybrid. Just over 6,000 Accord hybrids were sold in the U.S. in 2006. Honda has concluded that hybrids are more efficient in small cars (the Civic Hybrid) and is looking to diesel engines as a green alternative for larger vehicles. At the same time, the Toyota Camry Hybrid, roughly the same size as the Accord, was selling well, perhaps because it was seen as getting better gas mileage. For 2010 Honda introduced an all-new hybrid Insight, now in a five-door hatchback form similar to the Prius, but at a lower price.

The market success of the Toyota Prius combined with higher fuel prices (above $4.00 per gallon in 2008) across the U.S. prompted a "bandwagon" expansion of hybrid cars throughout the industry. GM had been the world's largest carmaker since 1931. Toyota was expected to beat GM in 2007. When the figures came in, Toyota outsold GM in 2006. Toyota's total sales included one million hybrids.

GM began moving into the hybrid market with small quantities of the Saturn VUE Hybrid and planned to add up to 12 hybrid models to its new environmentally friendly Green Line. Saturn introduced a 2007 vehicle called the Aura Green Line, which mimicked its best-selling sedan and featured an electrically assisted four-cylinder 2.4L Ecotec engine. Saturn claimed it was the lowest priced hybrid vehicle on the market, starting at $22,695 (including a $1,300 federal tax credit). GM introduced a large SUV hybrid in late 2007 called the 2-Mode. It had two electric motors with four fixed gear ratios employing a wide range of speeds. The fuel management system incorporated a shift from eight cylinders to four cylinders and could cruise easily at 80 mph on those four cylinders.[85] Later that year, GM introduced the GMC Yukon and the Chevy Tahoe hybrids. General Motors expanded its popular pickup line for 2009 with hybrid versions of the Chevrolet Silverado and the GMC Sierra. The engine is the standard 6 liter Vortec V-8, equipped with the hybrid late-intake valve closing technology and active fuel management, which allows the engine to shut off half of its cylinders and run in a V4 mode during cruising.[86] In 2009 the Silverado became available with an estimated 21/22 mpg.

Toyota continued with its promotion of the successful SUV Highlander Hybrid in 2007. Safety features included seven airbags (even a driver's knee airbag), electronic on-demand 4-wheel drive, electronic brake and throttle control and active steering.

Ford's Escape Hybrid sales were up about seven percent in 2007, slightly less than the expected total of about 22,000 vehicles. Ford has another small SUV model called the Mercury Mariner, which was rated fourth in the 2007 IntelliChoice Analysis for being cost effective. Mariner sales rose 2.7 percent in 2007.

In 2007 General Motors introduced its Chevrolet Volt concept car. It was the company's first plug-in hybrid vehicle. The concept car featured the "E-flex" system, which could travel 640 miles without a fuel fill-up or a battery charge. The innovative idea is that the Volt runs only on electric power until the battery runs down, then the ICE kicks in to feed the onboard generator that produces electricity to store in the battery. Regenerative braking also sends energy to the battery. Batteries were recharged by plugging into a common 110-volt household electrical outlet.

In 2007 Ford researched a fuel cell car called the Edge. It used the HySeries Drive, which was flexible, centering on an internal combustion engine, a hydrogen fuel cell or an all electric vehicle. It is different from the parallel system used in the Ford Escape. The hydrogen fuel cell will generate electricity to charge the batteries when they drop below 40 percent of their capacity. The Edge has a range of 225 miles and can get at least 40 mpg, and, if driven less than 50 miles per day on the electric motor, possibly as high as 80 mpg. Ford is taking the lead in the hydrogen vehicle domain, but is held back by the initial costs and the lack of a hydrogen infrastructure.

Meanwhile, Ford's Fusion 999 set a new land speed record of 207.297 mph on August 15, 2007, at the Bonneville Salt Flats in Utah, becoming the world's fastest fuel-cell car. It was powered by a Ballard Power Systems 400-kilowatt hydrogen fuel cell and, in 2007, was the world's first and only production-vehicle-based fuel-cell racecar. Using no petroleum-fueled power, it is pollution free. Ford is also exploring using fuel cell technology with a plug-in instead of the gasoline engine. Its Airstream is based on the Edge and can run about 40 km on the electrics and 490 km on the tank of hydrogen. This also remains a concept car because the fuel cell is currently too expensive to put in a production model. Ford does see the possibility of using a gasoline engine in the near future until the fuel cell cost is more competitive. In each case, having a reliable battery developed is key to putting the models into production. Until that battery is available and cost effective, these models will continue to be concept cars.

The Ford Escape Hybrid taxi had been used in San Francisco since 2005, the same year that New York City passed the Clean Air Taxis Act. Taxi drivers in San Francisco claimed a saving of $30 per shift, adding up to a saving of $6,000 per year. Ford promoted a nationwide tour to promote the advantages of Escape Hybrid taxis, and the cities of Chicago and Austin introduced them into their fleets in 2006.[87] On May 22, 2007, New York City mayor Michael Bloomberg announced a change in taxi policy toward increasing fuel economy, highlighting hybrid taxis. That city planned to have an all-hybrid taxi fleet by 2012. The Ford Escape Hybrid and the Mercury Mariner Hybrid meet the standards and were being considered. In March 2008 the Broadway Cab Company in Portland, Oregon, introduced a fleet of six Toyota Prius hybrids with a long-term goal of replacing traditional vehicles with alternative fuel vehicles. Broadway Cab is the oldest and largest taxicab company in Portland, founded in 1930, and has been involved in the "green industry" for some time, even housing its offices in a certified "green" building.

Honda introduced its version of a natural gas car in 2008 with the Civic GX. It had a range of about 200 miles per tank, but finding a natural-gas station could still be a problem. As of this writing, there are fewer than 750 natural-gas stations in the United States. The majority of stations are located in the West, primarily California, and some are restricted to refueling with permit only. A product called Phill is available. It operates off the homeowner's natural gas line. Honda claims this car to be the world's cleanest certified internal combustion engine. The GX was available in New York and California in 2007, but could be obtained by special order in other states. Federal tax credits of $4,000 are in existence for the purchase of the vehicle and an additional $1,000 tax credit for the purchase of a Phill system.

Honda also has a two-seat hybrid gasoline-electric concept car called the CR-Z ("Compact Renaissance Zero"). It has a high torque level with clean performance and is intended to compete in the affordable sports car market, offering the only manual transmission in a mass-produced hybrid. Production was expected to begin in 2010.

Chrysler entered the large-vehicle hybrid fray with its hemi-powered Aspen two-mode hybrid and the Dodge Durango full-sized vehicle, which had a 5.7 liter hemi V-8 engine backed up by electric motors. These vehicles utilized regenerative braking and claimed superior power for driving steep grades, passing, or carrying a load, such as a trailer.

Mercedes was developing a combination of an ICE and diesel engine in early 2007. It is a small displacement engine called the Dies-Otto. The emission is promoted as being as clean as a gas engine and as efficient as a diesel engine. It involves a concept called auto ignition. Auto ignition is compression ignition with gasoline fuel at lower temperatures than those of diesel engines. The fuel management system has a variable compression system that changes the compression ratio while driving. This gives maximum output to the spark ignition and maximum economy with the compression ignition.

In December 2007, the Electric Vehicle Symposium, a 23-year-old event held in Anaheim, California, showcased many types of electric vehicles, including scooters, bicycles, skateboards, mini-cars and even trucks. A new concept vehicle called the BugE was introduced. It has three wheels and seats one person. The big buzz of the meeting was the lithium-iron (not ion) phosphate battery. This battery has slightly lower energy levels than the lithium-ion and requires some care in recharging, but, on the positive side, it has a lower fire risk, lower cost and is longer lasting. As shown at the symposium, it has been incorporated into everything from bicycles to a Shelby Mustang Cobra.

Lexus joined the green fray with its 2008 model LS600hL hybrid luxury car, priced starting at $104,715. *AutoWeek* writer Mark Vaughn poses an interesting question. "Is it possible to hug a tree even if you own the forest and are exploiting the trolls and elves for cheap labor?"[88] The 600hL gets 21 mpg and Lexus claims it is 70 percent cleaner than its competitors. It has received a super-ultra-low-emission rating from CARB. Lexus expected to sell a total of about 30,000 cars a year beginning in mid–2007. They sold about 20,000. Lexus also has a crossover car, which was shown at the Tokyo Concept Show in November 2007. The Lexus LF-Xh has a hybrid powertrain that combines a V6 engine with the electric motor. The model came to market in late 2009.

Roger Penske, entrepreneur, race car owner, and chairman of Smart USA, introduced the Smart "microcar" to the American market in 2008. The Smart ForTwo is five feet tall and less than nine feet long. Top speed is around 90 mph, and fuel economy is rated at 33/41. Smart USA is a division of Daimler AG Mercedes-Benz and its cars have been manufactured in France since 1998. Although an electric version using lithium-ion batteries goes into production in 2010, the gasoline-powered ForTwo is more a novelty than a true competitor in the hybrid alternate fuel marketplace.

Tesla Motors has been producing an all-electric two-seater, high-performance car, the Tesla Roadster, since February 2008. Priced at $109,000, it has a carbon-fiber body with a performance speed of up to 130 mph and a range of 220–250 miles. The company plans to expand to a full line of electric cars, including the Type S sedan unveiled as a concept in March 2009.

Left: Tesla Type S prototype.[89] *Right:* Fisker Karma prototype.[90]

On the plug-in hybrid vehicle (PHEV) front, Fisker Automotive expects to launch its first car, the Karma, in 2010. Aimed at high-end buyers, it is a four-door sports sedan that emphasizes style, performance and luxury.

Chevrolet introduced a fuel-cell electric vehicle in 2008 — a converted Equinox SUV. The big news about this car was its claimed range of about 160 miles on a single fill-up of hydrogen. This is due to three carbon-fiber-wound storage tanks that can hold up 10,000 psi of hydrogen each, or about twice the fuel pressure of previous storage tanks.

General Motors claimed a 50 percent increase in fuel mileage with its 2008 Saturn VUE Green Line 2-Mode Hybrid over the nonhybrid V6 VUE. This small sport utility vehicle was to provide a range of over 500 miles, with part of the efficiency due to GM's mild hybrid system, which consists of a belt-assisted unit that controls an automatic stop/start engine function. Although the termination of Saturn was announced in 2009, the 2-Mode Hybrid powertrain is expected to survive in other vehicles.

Mazda is developing a smarter stop/start system. Most gasoline-electric hybrids shut down the gas engine in periods of stop/start city driving. This requires a need to restart the gas engine. Mazda's new system, called the Smart Idle Stop System (SISS), employs no electric motors for restart. When the engine stops, Mazda uses the alternator to "brake" one cylinder at a point midway through a stroke, then injects fuel into the combustion chamber. When needed, the mixture is ignited and the engine restarts in reverse. But only for one stroke; this sets up an immediate compression and power stroke to restart the engine in the proper running direction. This method saves the weight of a larger starter/alternator and gives about a 10 percent boost in fuel economy. Mazda hoped to have this in production by 2009, though at this writing it has not yet become available.[91] The 2010 Mazda3, fitted with SISS, received a Smartway designation from the Environmental Protection Agency in the light duty vehicle class.

The 2008 Toyota Highlander Hybrid upgraded and refined its Hybrid Synergy Drive system to increase both economy and power. This SUV offered a full EV mode running off the battery power up to twenty-five mph. At higher speeds, there is an ECON mode. By watching the gauge and altering their driving habits, drivers can smooth out the peaks and valleys of acceleration and deceleration and increase their fuel efficiency.

Mercedes-Benz added a hybrid-powered SUV to its line in late 2009. The ML 450 Hybrid luxury SUV is a full hybrid powered by the two-mode system co-developed with GM and BMW. The all-wheel-drive vehicle combines a 3.5-liter V6 gasoline engine, two electric motors and a 288-volt battery pack to produce 321 horsepower, and is rated at 21/24 miles per gallon. A light hybrid sports model similar to the C300 is scheduled to arrive on the market by 2011. A full hybrid integrates the electric motor, battery and ICE and is considered more fuel efficient; the light hybrid uses the electrics to boost power when it is needed.

According to the Hybrid Owners of America, March 2008, the "top ten" list of the greenest hybrid cars begins with (1) the Toyota Prius, (2) the Saturn Vue Green Line, (3) Honda Civic Hybrid, (4) Toyota Camry Hybrid, (5) Lexus RX 400h, (6) Toyota Highlander Hybrid, (7) Ford Escape Hybrid, (8) Chevrolet Tahoe 2 Mode Hybrid, (9) Saturn Aura Green Line, and (10) Lexus GH 450h.

All these new vehicles will soon require maintenance, and the face of the auto shop is moving with the times. A company in San Francisco, started in August 2007, may be starting a trend. Luscious Green is an earth-friendly auto repair shop that services mostly hybrids in an environment of green plants and natural light. The shop keeps a small carbon footprint using various techniques, such as using biodiesel for parts cleaning and electric tools instead of pneumatic. The cordless electric tools are recharged at night, saving daytime energy consumption. Work orders and receipts are e-mailed to customers, saving on paper.[92]

Auto racing has served as a proving ground for new technology in the past, but has not played a major role in recent development of electric vehicles. The year 1996 saw the beginning of several all-electric races, such as the Solar & Electric 500 at the Phoenix Firebird International Raceway and the EV Grand Prix in Virginia. Entries tended to come from educational institutions, and public response was minimal.

Since the late 1990s electric auto racing has moved to college and university campuses with the races being presented as competition among engineering students worldwide. There have been a few exceptions. One of these is Ian Wright. Following in the tradition of Charles Jeantaud, Wright, a former employee of Tesla Motors, has taken his electric Wrightspeed X1 proof-of-concept car (http://www.wrightspeed.com/x1.html) to the races— in this case, the drag races— to raise awareness of what an electric can do. According to its website, the car was clocked at:

- 0–30 mph: 1.35 sec
- 0–60 mph: 3.07 sec in 117 feet
- 0–100 mph: 6.87 sec
- 0–100–0 mph 11.2 sec

It gave an admirable performance. The car uses an AC propulsion system and is intended to be concept only. It is not fitted with additional safety gear required for production autos. Drag racing this auto proves that electrics can go fast. They are not just for commuting cars or local commercial delivery.

In 2004, only one car rental company offered a hybrid in its fleet. Budget rented the Honda Insight in Phoenix and the Toyota RAV4 EV and GM EV1 in Los Angeles. Budget found that its customers liked the option, and, once familiar with the car, frequently asked for a hybrid for their next rental.

By 2008, hybrid rental competition had increased to the point where all the major rental companies were offering a variety of hybrid cars. Hertz, Budget, Alamo, Avis, Dollar, National, Fox, Discount and AutoEurope offered a wide selection. For those who prefer a taxi to a rental, there are hybrid taxis in most of the world's major airports. Taxicab companies throughout the world are incorporating hybrids into their fleets both because customers are requesting them and because they are proving to be cost effective. In New York and San Francisco, Luxor Cabs and Yellow Cabs were the first onboard. In New York, an "eco-luxury" private car service, Ozocar, provides a Prius equipped with Sirius Satellite Radio, Wi-Fi and an iBook computer for Internet access.[93]

Vancouver, British Columbia, is using hybrid cabs, too. The city's oldest taxi company, Yellow Cab, runs some of its newest technology. In 2008, 40 of their 208 cars were Prius hybrids.[94]

"Eco-friendly" does not necessarily mean economic savings. Costs will eventually come down when the competition is stiff among batteries, fuel cells, new models, and so on, but buying patterns remain conventional for most drivers. A poll taken in December 2000 showed 71 percent of Americans would probably not buy an electric or hybrid vehicle if they were only available at a price higher than most new cars. The annual Portland (Oregon) International Auto Show in January 2008 featured the latest in research and design. Many expected that this event, held in a city with the highest per capita Prius owners and known for its green attitudes, would attract many hybrid enthusiasts. In the local paper, an editorialist wrote, "After all, this is Portland, where people worship at the altar of the Prius."[95] But the crowds strolled past the Honda Civic Hybrid and the Volkswagen clean diesel and hovered around the new Corvette and Dodge Viper, many having their pictures taken while sitting behind the wheel of those powerful ICE-powered cars. The editorialist decided, "We respect them, we turn to them in time of need, but we don't love them. Not yet."[96]

Throughout their first century, electric vehicles have proved to be reliable, clean, low-maintenance transportation. Their manufacturers have created coaches for the style-conscious, improved the auto's speed and mileage, and risen to the challenge of developing a more environmentally friendly vehicle. Its second century has brought back the hybrid concept in many creative forms. Electrics and electric hybrids have captured the imagination of countless drivers and car makers. They have gone from a popular choice in the early years to an alternate in times of fuel shortage, and continue to be a best choice for an environmentally friendly mode of transportation.

2

POLITICS

Who Killed the Electric Car? is a 90-minute documentary that premiered at the Sundance Film Festival in 2006 and was narrated by Martin Sheen. It was the third highest grossing documentary in 2006 and was shown widely with Al Gore's film, *An Inconvenient Truth*. It had a definite agenda that conveniently ignored facts, such as: batteries are very expensive, DOT crash tests are very expensive and most people just don't want to change their lifestyles to accommodate a new technology, or "save the planet." According to an *AutoWeek* writer, the movie suggests there is a "dark conspiracy" between the oil companies and automakers to prevent the development of EVs, which in theory, would help the environment and lessen our dependence on foreign oil, but it is "never solidly proven."[1]

"Policy makers do not value market exchange because it maximizes liberty and personal satisfaction of wants," the writer continued. "Instead, policy makers value the market because they can manipulate it to produce a centrally planned outcome. This approach describes so-called market-based environmental policy."[2]

How do governments influence industry and vice versa? Since the first automobile began using public roadways, the automotive industry has been affected by laws and regulations. Today, the transportation sector of the U.S. economy is a major energy consumer. Automotive technology developers tend to look at government as one of many groups they need to deal with, along with utilities, the oil industry and the automotive industry. Of these various factors, only government is a regulator.

In *Future Drive*, Daniel Sperling discusses the need to invoke creative technologies to produce environmentally benign automobiles, and government's role in encouraging development and sale of the technology through tax incentives, fees and credits.

> The answer is founded on technical fixes. Technical fixes preserve the fundamental attractions of vehicle travel — mobility, convenience and privacy — while requiring few behavioral changes. They support rather than subvert travelers' wishes and needs. Given the shortcoming of travel reduction strategies, and the huge promise of new technologies, the focus of any effort to create a more environmentally benign transportation system should be technological innovation.
>
> The public strongly prefers this approach to restrictions on their behavior. In a 1991 survey conducted in the Los Angeles area, over half the respondents (57 percent) expressed willingness to purchase an alternative fuel vehicle as a response to air pollution problems, compared with only 17 percent who were willing to carpool, 16 percent who would use mass transit and 6 percent who would walk or bicycle.[3]

Like many safety features on cars, such as the seat belt and the air bag, legislation for electric vehicles is being driven without consideration for manufacturing costs or demand.

Advocates think that legislation will help advance the electric cars, but is it the most effective way to promote the product? While environmental concerns and legislation can provoke public awareness, new technology is needed to make the autos succeed in the marketplace. New batteries, fuel cells and hybrid vehicles need to be in place, alongside improved internal combustion engines to meet the government regulations, or the regulations will need to be adjusted.

Through laws, regulations, subsidies, tax incentives, research support and purchasing, federal and state governments assist and promote research and provide markets for alternate energy vehicles. Governments have a direct effect on the technological research and development. The Ballard Fuel Cell Company, for example, is succeeding partially due to the market created because manufacturers needed to meet the low emissions standards regulations initiated by the California Air Resources Board (CARB). Australia has offered subsidies to entice partners for its green car innovation program. Partnerships formed between government agencies and private industries allow each to benefit from the discoveries made in the national labs and the testing available through the consumer marketplace. During the last one hundred years, government alliances have sustained the development of electric vehicles that have not succeeded through market forces alone.

The United States imports billions of gallons of oil each year. It is estimated that 10,000 fuel cell vehicles running on hydrogen (the most abundant element in the universe) would save seven million gallons of gasoline each year, and if fuel cell cars occupied ten percent of the market share, the United States could reduce oil imports by 130 million barrels per year.[4] One writer claimed, "European research shows that hydrogen energy could reduce oil consumption in road transport by 40 percent by 2050."[5] This premise is based on hydrogen coming from natural gas, biomass, and water using wind energy. In 2008 numerous hydrogen-powered vehicles were available, including the Honda FCX and BMW Hydrogen 7. Many analysts had predicted this type of fuel cell engine would not be available until well into the second decade of the 21st Century, but innovation and research spurred by rising costs in fuel and environmental concerns for CO_2 beginning in 2002 created a market for alternative fuel autos, causing the timeline to move forward. Government intervention in the form of tax rebates and subsidies for technology innovators helped speed up this development. President George W. Bush announced in mid–2002 that his administration backed the development of fuel cells.

In July 2002 California governor Gray Davis signed bill AB 1493 into law. The law sought to reduce greenhouse gas emissions from automobiles sold in California starting with the model year 2009. This law is unique in that it spells out a direct connection between global warming and exhaust emissions from automobiles. As one commentator pointed out, "whether you believe global warming exists or that man-made CO_2 has a role in it, the perception of its existence is now a reality and businesses need to [start] living with it and planning accordingly. AB 1493 may be the sire of many similar, perhaps even more draconian measures to come, if we fail to act in a prudent and timely fashion."[6]

In March 2004, after public discussion under the Alternative Fuel Transportation Program; Private and Local Government Fleet Determination (10 CFR Part 490), the U.S. Department of Energy (DOE) concluded that creating such regulations "would not appreciably increase the percentage of alternative fuel and replacement fuel used by motor vehicles in the United States and thus would make no more than a negligible contribution to the achievement of the replacement fuel goals set forth in EPAct [Energy Policy Act]," and wasn't required by the EPAct of 1992, which provided financial incentives for developers and owners of clean-fuel vehicles. Its main focus was to encourage expansion of natural gas, and, by implication, a more clean method of increasing electricity production.

The global warming concept, coupled with rising oil costs in the early 2000s, again gave impetus for moving from the traditional ICE to hybrids and electric cars. Although Al Gore's film, *An Inconvenient Truth,* was shown to have less than accurate information (the British Department for Children, Schools and Families, in response to a 2007 High Court ruling, issued an information packet for teachers which was meant to counter Gore's partisan views), it did spark a renewed interest in decreasing auto emissions. This triggered a revitalizing of the hybrid market, and to a lesser extent, the electric car market.

Opponents to car manufacturers taking the test electric vehicles and later the Toyota Rav4 EVs off the test market and recycling them (crushing them) had a very dedicated and colorful activist group in the first few years of the 21st century. DontCrush.com campaigned tirelessly to get electrics out in front of the public and let the testers continue to use the test and to buy the vehicles. In 2005 the group took its cause to the streets, picketing and handing out flyers in front of the Toyota North American headquarters in Torrance, California. In discontinuing the testing, Toyota had allowed private participants to purchase their vehicle, possibly because they were swayed by the DontCrush.com efforts, but the commercial participants returned their cars to Toyota. Again DontCrush intervened, with support from the Sierra Club, and, although they could not get agreements that more cars would be made available to those interested in buying, they were able to convince Toyota that allowing the commercial testers the option to purchase the vehicle was a smart move. Toyota also agreed to not crush the cars that were sent back to its plant. It was a small victory for DontCrush.com, but definitely one that raised their spirits. In 2005 the organization felt a new image was in order and became Plug-In America.[7]

A study conducted in New Zealand in 2006 compared the purchase and running costs of an HEV with that of a gas-powered car to promote the sales of HEVs and thus reduce carbon emissions (in accord with the Kyoto Protocol). The net fuel efficiency of the HEV amounted to about $644 annually, while the net purchase price was about $7000 higher than an ICE. The study concluded that even if a "carbon tax" were applied to ICE purchases there would not be sufficient incentive to buy HEVs.[8]

In January 2008 Israel announced a major initiative to promote electric cars. Part of the proposal included building hundreds of thousands of electric charging stations across the country. The goal was to get 100,000 electric cars on the roads of Israel by year 2010. Taxes on cars in Israel can be as high as 100 percent; a $20,000 Fiat may need financing of $40,000. On January 13, 2008, Israel slashed the tax rate on electric cars to ten percent to encourage consumers to buy the vehicles. However, mass production was not expected until around 2011. The government has a contract with Renault-Nissan for manufacture of the cars. Even though range is limited to about 100 miles on a charge, very few drivers in Israel go more than that distance at any given time. For longer drives, battery-swap stations will be available, with new batteries supplied by a California-based project called Better Place. Better Place, not the individual driver, will own the batteries. People will buy the cars and lease the batteries at low cost. The promoters are looking forward to advancing this concept in China. It remains to be seen how successful this idea will be in a small country like Israel and how it could be adapted to a large country like China.

Increased interest in hybrid cars initially had a negative impact on improving ICE mileage, but as hybrids in various forms became more prevalent, so did impetus to develop other alternate fuel models. Development of biodiesel and fuel cells expanded as manufacturers looked for the next wave of market possibilities.

Early Laws and Litigation

In the United States, patents had an early impact on which automobiles would be successful in the marketplace. At the turn of the 20th century, great industrialists like Rockefeller, Morgan, and Carnegie and financiers like William C. Whitney were using trusts to further their interests by controlling prices and protecting patent rights. They combined business interests by turning over their management to a single board of directors. These trusts followed two designs, each having the capability of creating a monopoly in the marketplace and curbing competition. The horizontal type brought together and controlled companies with a similar product. The vertical type controlled the production from raw materials to finished product. Patent rights held by each company on each model were owned by the trust. Financiers P. A. B. Widener and William C. Whitney saw the potential for profit in automobiles, electric taxis in particular, and put together the State Trust Company, later called the Lead Cab Trust. This trust included trolley franchise holders, lead-acid battery manufacturers and electric vehicle companies.

George B. Selden, a Rochester, New York, lawyer, had foreseen the future success of the internal combustion engine, and on November 5, 1895, he was granted patent no. 549,160 for any automobile concept using a two-stroke internal combustion engine. The Electric Vehicle Company, as part of the Lead Cab Trust, bought the rights to the Selden patent in 1899 for $10,000 (Mr. Selden retained the rights to one-fifth of any royalties gained from the patent). Each ICE manufacturer was obliged to secure a license and pay royalties to the Lead Cab Trust in order to use an internal combustion engine. Under the Selden patent, early autos would display a plaque on the engine indicating that they had legitimate rights to use that engine structure.

The Lead Cab Trust saw this as an opportunity to profit from the rising popularity of the internal combustion engine, as individuals and small businesses making cars started to dot the landscape, and as a hedge to develop electric vehicles by preventing the development of gasoline vehicles should they prove superior.

The first lawsuit concerning the Selden patent was against the Winton Motor Carriage Company in 1900 when the company at-

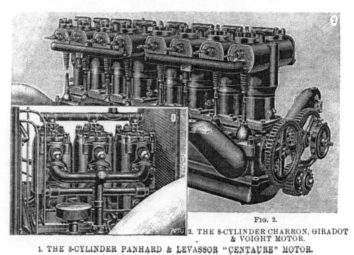

FIG. 2.

2. THE 8-CYLINDER CHARRON, GIRADOT & VOIGHT MOTOR.

1. THE 8-CYLINDER PANHARD & LEVASSOR "CENTAURE" MOTOR.

Competitors of the Otto engine[9]

NOTICE

To Dealers, Importers, Agents, and Users of our Gasoline Automobiles

WE will protect you against any prosecution for alleged infringements of patents. Regarding alleged infringement of the Selden patent, we beg to quote the well-known Patent Attorneys, Messrs. Parker & Burton: "The Selden patent is not a broad one, and if it was, it is anticipated. It does not cover a practicable machine, no practicable machine can be made from it, and never was, so far as we can ascertain. It relates to that form of carriage called a FORE CARRIAGE. None of that type have ever been in use; all have been failures." "No court in the United States has ever decided in favor of the patent on the merits of the case; all it has ever done was to record a prior agreement between the parties."

We are the pioneers of the GASOLINE AUTOMOBILE. Our Mr. Ford made the first Gasoline Automobile in Detroit, and the third in the United States. His machine, built in 1893, two years prior to the issue of the Selden patents Nov. 5, 1895, is still in use. Our Mr. Ford also built the famous "999" Gasoline Automobile, which was driven by Barney Oldfield in New York on July 25th, 1903, a mile in 55 4-5 seconds, on a circular track, which is the world's record.

Mr. Ford, driving his own machine, beat Mr. Winton at Grosse Pointe track in 1901. We have always been winners.

Ford Motor Company
688-692 Mack Ave., Detroit, Mich.
Write for Catalogue

The Ford notice[10]

tempted to sell ICEs without first purchasing a license. Winton settled out of court in 1903.

Henry Ford was offered a Selden patent license in 1902 and refused it. In 1903 the Electric Vehicle Company and the Lead Trust sued Ford, and for eight years the case was in the courts.

Ford eventually won the case because the court ruled the Selden patent was valid only for the two-stroke (Brayton principle) engine and not for the four-stroke (Otto principle) engine. This important decision allowed internal combustion engine auto manufacturers to develop their products unhampered by royalty payments. The Electric Vehicle Company suffered greatly financially and in 1908 Pope abandoned electrics to make internal combustion engines. This court decision lessened the control the trusts had on early auto development.

Other early laws and court cases were concerned with speed, competition with the horse and accidents on public roads. It was generally agreed that the public wanted protection against dangerous driving, but there was great debate over how this should be accomplished. Speed limits were a frequent point of discussion. Automobilists claimed that "speed" and "danger" were not equivalent terms, any more than "slowness" and "safety." Horse breeders and dealers, fearing competition from the new invention, put up a constant effort to limit the speed of the automobile to the same as their own animals. Motorists argued that speed limits were of no use in preventing accidents and that the use of discretion by the driver was a better guarantee of safety to the public than the mere limitation of miles per hour.[11]

British motoring enthusiast the Honorable John Scott-Montagu, a fervent advocate of eliminating speed limits, identified several stages of legislation in 1904. He branded the first stage as contemptuous indifference, wherein legislatures believed it was not likely that the automobile would become popular or numerous. The second stage was fear and jealous dislike due to the inability to understand the great power of the new machines. The third stage was panic legislation, once it was seen that there was a rapid increase in motorcars in every country. Railway companies were a good example of this. They first ignored the automobile, then feared it, then began to use it in conjunction with their own established systems.[12] Scott-Montagu said, "Future generations in all civilized countries will laugh at the cumbrous and illogical efforts their forefathers made to restrict the use of the automobile, and smile at the assumption that it was a dangerous and uncontrollable vehicle."[13] He spent a great deal of time trying to convince legislators that motorists value their own lives, like other people, and they did not have a desire to maim or kill their fellow man. He maintained that the mere ownership of a valuable machine such as a motorcar tended to make the owner more cautious as to what he does with it.

Scott-Montagu also suggested that a reasonable solution to protective legislation be fashioned on the precedent of maritime laws. The underlying principle of marine legislation is that the onus of avoiding collisions lies upon the faster and more easily controlled vessel. Thus the fast liner must give way to a sailing ship or pleasure yacht, providing the liner itself is not forced into a dangerous position. Using this logic, motor vehicles would give way to the less maneuverable horse-drawn carriages.

As clashes between the automobile and the horse-drawn carriage sharing the same roads became more common, so did the number of lawsuits. One case in Bridgeport, Connecticut, in 1901 involved a silent electric vehicle (a Riker surrey) approaching a doctor's horse-drawn carriage from behind. The horse was spooked and the doctor was thrown down and dragged about fifty feet. He sued for $50,000 for the dislocation of one finger and "general nervous shock." Part of the complaint argued that the electric vehicle was too noiseless. The doctor lost the case, but its historical importance lay not in the verdict but in the judge's instructions to the jury. He articulated several important points that were becoming clear at the time: "[T]he mere fact that an accident happens does not make it the fault of someone else.... The highways are for us all; all can use them, with reasonable regard, to be sure, for others who use them. The most common motive power on the highway is a horse; but the horse has no paramount exclusive right to the road; and the mere fact that a horse takes fright at some vehicle run by new and improved methods, and smashes things, does not give to the injured party a cause of action.... You and I, in our experience, have seen a great change in the highways, not only in this town in which we live, but in the highways out of town. The great advantage is that people can exercise their right of locomotion more easily and accomplish more; that we can go to and fro ... much more swiftly.... Within limits, too, the swiftness with which persons are enabled, by modern vehicles, to go from place to place, is of great moment also."[14]

Between 1895 and 1905 many laws, rules and regulations were passed in Europe and North America addressing speed limits, licensing and registration. In general there were parallel ideas put into law, but there were also many variations. If speed limits were posted, some viewed them as an indication of what might be a reasonable speed on that road or curve while states and municipalities enforced the limit as best they could, using stopwatches and astute officials to gauge the speed of the motorist. In every case, the national government did not take control, but left the legislation to the states, counties, cantons and cities.

In the early 1800s, the stagecoach and horse-owning industries set to work to establish laws restricting steam carriages and any other road locomotive. This began in Britain with the Red Flag Act of 1836, which required all self-propelled vehicles to be preceded by a man carrying a red flag by day and a red light by night to warn fellow travelers of its approach and to help keep any frightened horses under control. The act also restricted speed of the vehicle to two mph in town and a maximum of four mph in the country. This regulation stifled innovation by placing limits on speed and discouraged travel in the motorized vehicle by making the adventure a group effort. By 1895 the laws were being reexamined to keep up with the new auto technologies. Great Britain passed the Locomotives on Highways Act of 1896, also called the Light Locomotives on Highways Act, which abolished the red flag rule (along with many other restrictive enactments concerning self-propelled carriages) and increased the speed limit to fourteen miles per hour. It defined light locomotives as those under two tons, not used for hauling other vehicles and emitting no smoke or other vapors. It also held the driver of such a vehicle accountable for a fine not to exceed £10 if he drove negligently or lost control of his vehicle. Motorists celebrated the occasion of the new law by holding an "Emancipation Run" from London to Brighton on November 14, 1896. After several years of public agitation by motorists about this speed limit, Parliament enacted a new law in 1903 establishing a maximum speed of twenty miles per hour. This was seen as a compromise between those who wanted a 12 mph speed limit and motorists who wanted no speed limit at all. This new act also required vehicle identification by numbers, registration of the vehicle under the authority of county governments and a license for the driver.

In the United States, government officials were also facing disputes between horse and motor owners. The popularity of motor carriages was growing, and in many cities rides through the parks were becoming trendy social outings. Controversy arose when horse-drawn and motor carriages appeared in parks side by side. The New York City Parks Commissioner made a serious political faux pas in November 1899 when he declared that no automobiles would be allowed in the city parks. One editorial in the *New York Times* objected thus: "The old ladies of both sexes and of every age who are alarmed at the effect of automobiles on their horses may be commended to imitate the example of the most eminent of living old ladies."[15] The editorial was referring to Queen Victoria, who had her carriage horses put through a course of special training to accustom them to the sights and sounds of the automobile in all its varieties and modes. "People who will not take the trouble to educate their horses should at least have the grace not to make the ignorance of their horse a matter of public complaint."[16] Uproar concerning the ban was so constant that later in the month the parks commissioner reversed his decision and allowed the automobile the right to use all public roadways. He established rules and regulations to ensure safe driving conditions for both horses and automobiles. The conflict was settled for the time being. Baltimore, Maryland, showed another example of a community establishing a means for promoting safe driving through its parks. To drive in Baltimore parks in 1900, drivers had to secure certificates of competence from the general superintendent.[17]

France was viewed as a country naturally receptive to new ideas in 1904 and generally had more liberal legislation than other countries. It had passed some legislation in 1899 requiring that construction of the automobile be safe enough to prevent explosive material or fuel that might cause a fire. Each automobile must be equipped with two lamps, one white and the other green, to increase its visibility to others, and to have secure steering gear and brakes. If the vehicle was to be manufactured for sale, the automobile must bear the name of the maker, the type and number of the machine and the name and address of the owner.[18] It also established a certification of capacity of owners and an examination by an official of the Mining Department. As for the question of speed limits, the law only required a special permit from the Prefects of Departments to hold races through communities at a speed of no more than eighteen miles per hour in the open country and twelve miles per hour in congested districts. Since the races were bringing a good deal of money into the districts, permission was easily obtained and the laws were rarely enforced. There was no general speed limit for the touring car, and the police were seen to be applying common sense in the enforcement of the regulations. They did not set speed traps between cities and would seldom interfere with the driver of a touring car, unless they spotted reckless driving near or through towns. One law that was never enforced was a requirement that the approach of the automobile must be signaled by means of a trumpet. This broad-minded treatment made France a very popular touring place and French hotels benefited greatly from this liberal outlook on regulating vehicle speeds. France became a more popular country for touring than its neighboring countries or Great Britain.

At the same time in Germany, a total prohibition of automobiles was in effect in some provincial towns in order not to frighten children and horses. Other German cities established a number of minute regulations concerning what a driver should or should not do, including a speed limit of four miles per hour. Berlin laws required that each motorcar be equipped with two separate braking systems that could bring a car traveling at a speed of nine miles per hour to a stop within a distance of twenty-five feet. The speed could be increased according to the judgment of the driver on open and straight roads; however, the driver would be liable in case of any accident. Each motorcar was required to carry identification marks, and drivers needed to obtain a driving certificate from a school of instruction recognized by the authorities. Foreigners traveling into Germany were required to have their driving certificates from their own country examined and passed by the German authorities.

Switzerland had a different situation. Its steep roads were not very suitable for the automobile. Many roads had a rock wall on one side and a steep precipice on the other. Each canton had its own very restrictive rules and regulations. Several were as strict as in some German towns, prohibiting automobiles altogether. Hotel owners complained bitterly about the negative economic impact on tourist business due to the restrictions, but had little power at the time to overturn the strict restraints.

A royal decree in Belgium in August 1899 required a license plate bearing the name and address of the owner to be displayed on the left side and front of the car. It also established a speed limit of 18 mph on roads outside towns and villages. The speed limit for Brussels and large towns was set at 6 mph. The town of Antwerp was the exception. It established a speed limit equal to that of a horse-drawn vehicle. Other than these few strict laws, Belgium generally followed the more liberal regulations of the French system. The Belgian gendarme was seen as very fair-minded and would tend to render a liberal interpretation of the laws in favor of the motorist.[19] Austrian laws were very stringent. A 1903 Austrian law required severe official inspections of all vehicles, the use of identification numbers, and a speed limit of only 7 mph. It was also the only country that passed a regulation forbidding women to drive a motorcar. In 1904 the Municipal Council of Vienna proposed that even more restrictive regulations be imposed.

The laws in Italy during this time were very lenient, modeled after those of France. The government alleged that speed limits were of no use in preventing accidents.

In the United States in 1904, each state controlled its own laws and regulations concerning the motorcar. The state laws did not differ as much from one another as they did in European countries. In towns, the speed limit ranged from 8 to 12 mph. The speed limit was generally 20 mph on open roads, and the motorist was to be held responsible for any accident occurring while passing another vehicle or any domestic animal. This became a controversial clause, and the Automobilists of America club named it the "pig and chicken" clause. The sense at the time was that the western states were more lenient in their penalties and more lenient in enforcing their speed limits than states in the East. This could have been due to the fact that many roads in the West were in such poor condition that it was almost impossible to drive a car, much less exceed any imposed speed limits.

By 1906, with the help of automobilists squarely in favor of good roads and uniform laws concerning the use and licensing of automobiles, automobile legislation debates at a national level were beginning in earnest in the United States. The states were intent on setting their own standards for motoring laws. Sidney Gorham of New York said, "I do not think the [federal] Government can ever pass a law to regulate the speed of motor vehicles or make other stipulations. It appears to me that this is more in the line of State legislative action."[20] Gorham proposed federal involvement in the "laws licensing machines, and the regulations governing tourists while passing from one state to another."[21] He was particularly interested in convincing farmers in what were then the western states that improved roads would add value to their property. Many farmers at the time were opposed to automobiles, having seen some wild tourists careening through their property, and would just as soon keep the bad roads to deter the "invasion" by automobilists. Gorham encouraged farmers to see the benefits of both greater opportunities to take their goods to market and more money coming to the district because more people would be traveling through the area. He claimed railroads would also benefit as freight could be more easily handled and larger shipments could be made from longer distances.

As cars toured from one state to another, they ran into state licensing wars. In 1906 New Jersey required motorcars licensed in other states to also be licensed in New Jersey. The license fee was $3 for machines under thirty horsepower and $5 for machines of greater horsepower. New York adopted a similar stance and the fight was on. Massachusetts and Connecticut were a little more tourist- and commerce-friendly. They allowed vehicles from other states to visit for a few days with no additional fees. General discussion suggested that the federal government could be helpful by providing good roads and promoting consistency among state laws.

During the first decade of the 1900s, the eastern United States began campaigns to improve safety and promote revenue. New Jersey, in addition to enacting legislation requiring a speed limit of 8 mph in cities and 20 mph in open locations, also established a Commissioner of State Vehicles office, with the power to inspect vehicles and register them at a rate of seventy-five cents per horsepower. A minimum age of eighteen was set for a license to drive and chauffeurs were required to pass an examination. More than 100 women drivers were licensed in the state and some were "practiced chauffeurs."[22] One prominent woman driver was Mrs. Margaret L. Johnson, daughter of Thomas Edison, who claimed she had traveled 5,000 miles in her automobile in seven years. Licensing violations included a fine of up to $500 and possible imprisonment. The money collected went to the State Road Fund. Monies from the road fund were to be used to improve roads and to provide street signs and possibly lights at dangerous intersections.

New York State believed it could prevent automobile accidents by providing perfect roads from one end of the state to the other. To accomplish this goal, it appropriated $50 million over a ten-year period for road improvement to insure that the state would have the best roads in the country. As much as $11 million had been spent on road improvements by cities and counties from 1898 to 1905.[23] A committee of citizens in Elizabeth, New Jersey, in 1906, charged that automobiles injured the roads. The state engineer called this idea "ridiculous," contesting that the wide tires on the vehicles prevented any damage to the roads. This attitude had changed greatly by 1909, when state engineers recognized that they had a serious problem with automobiles being the most active agent in the breaking down of macadam roads. They believed there were only two solutions to the problem — either restrict automobile traffic or create new and improved methods of road construction. In either case, the states recognized well-kept roads as an element for the successful driving experience.

By 1906 automobile accidents were being reported regularly in the daily newspapers. New York State had twenty-five thousand automobiles, with five hundred persons injured by motorcars annually. Many of these accidents were charged to the stupidity of the street-crossing public; the rest were ascribed to the "road hog."[24] London and Paris combined had fewer automobile accidents than New York. This was attributed to the perception that people in Europe were more accustomed to both driving and seeing cars. It was more likely due to the severe penalties that offending chauffeurs were dealt. One well-known American in Paris was given a jail sentence and a heavy fine payable to the family of the person he killed. The fear of being jailed was used as a deterrent to prevent accidents. America looked to the driver to behave responsibly. An *Outlook* magazine article in 1906 outlined a series of "Don'ts" for motorists to prevent accidents. Some of these included:

Don't allow your chauffeur to drink liquor while in charge of your car and if running your own car, avoid rum yourself.
Don't try to see how close you can run to pedestrians.
Don't put oil on your registration number and throw dust on it. An honest man isn't afraid of identification.
Don't toot your horn at passing horses.
Don't blow your Gabriel horn in a city street.
Don't grab at things that concern the chauffeur.
Don't run away after hitting somebody. You'll stand a better chance if you stay.
Don't ever act like anything but an intelligent gentleman.[25]

There were an estimated 75,000 cars in the United States in 1906. Reckless driving, accidents and lawsuits led many states to enact or consider legislation requiring a driver's license, as well as a speed limit and a variety of other laws. Until about 1905, any man, woman or child could drive an automobile. Manufacturers of electrics advertised that theirs were the easiest to handle and did not require a chauffeur. They created the women's market. That market was to have some challenges. With the rise of the suffragists came a backlash of opinion questioning a woman's ability to handle an automobile. A 1909 editorial in *Outlook* magazine carried on extensively about the ability of women to drive a vehicle because they were unable to "think of two things at once." Men, on the other hand, were seen as being trained from the earliest youth by playing baseball to pay attention to two or three bases at once, along with home plate and "numerous other points. With few exceptions, a woman seldom reaches this particular phase of mental activity, called for time and again in automobiling." It was also asserted that a woman who meets a person with whom she wishes to converse will almost invariably stop and do so while blocking traffic. One slight exception was given if the vehicle was electric. "No license should be granted to one under eighteen, or possibly twenty one years of age, and never to a woman, unless, possibly, for a car driven by electric power."[26]

Laws governing speed had their own set of challengers, but most acknowledged the need for some regulation for safety. The 8 mph speed limit in New York City in 1906 had its share of dissenters and advocates. Some argued the speed limit had two disadvantages: (1) that the speed of an automobile can only be determined by an expert with a stopwatch while the car is passing over a measured course, and (2) the speed limit is already constantly exceeded without protest from the authorities and seems to be impossible to enforce.[27] Charles S. Adams wrote an editorial in *Scientific American* in October 1906 in favor of speed limits. He stated his theory in a very logical, scientific manner, claiming that drivers did not realize that danger increases to the square of the speed. He used an example of three identical vehicles, one traveling at five miles per hour, one at twenty miles per hour and one at forty miles per hour. The second vehicle has sixteen times as much stored energy as the first. It will take sixteen times the distance to stop, and if it leaves the road and strikes an obstacle such as a tree, it will strike with sixteen times as much force. The third vehicle will do the same at sixty-four times the force of the first vehicle. Although enforcement was a problem, the dangers of too much speed were acknowledged.

By 1907 there was great concern about "speed mania" and how to cure it. The perception was that the automobile provided "an exhilaration in flying through the air at forty miles an hour that no other sports could give."[28] Actually, automobiles were beginning to reach speeds of a mile a minute at the time. An article in *Harper's Weekly* identified the type of man given to reckless speeding as the same type "who speculates in more stocks than he is able to carry, eats and drinks more than he can assimilate, covers himself with gaudy jewels [and] makes an objectionable exhibition of himself at every possible occasion." There was a call for more speed limit laws and for their enforcement. The State of New York speed law was general in nature, stating, "No person shall operate a motor vehicle on a public highway at a rate of speed greater than is reasonable and proper, having regard to the traffic and use of the highway, or so as to endanger the life and limb of any person or the safety of any property."[29] An editorial suggested that perhaps policemen should position themselves in wait for motorists on a downgrade, where the motorcar is apt to run faster and thus "make a case" against a greater number of motorists. At the time, some "speed maniacs" would merely laugh at a fine and then boast about it to their friends. It was also suggested that the driver's license of reckless motorists be revoked, with jail time being the penalty for those who were subsequently found driving without a license. The public wanted action against reckless speeding.

General interest and automobile magazines were in agreement as countries struggled with this new technology. In 1908 *Punch* magazine recognized there was an automobile problem in Great Britain and queried, "How shall it be regulated?" Testimony before Parliament declared, "[t]he enjoyment of English country life has been spoiled for all who do not take to motoring." The speed and dust seemed to be the major complaints. Some argued there should be no speed limits and the law should hold anyone responsible for any damage done; they were ignored and a speed limit of 12 mph was set in law. Max Pemberton of the *London Times* listed a code of rules that he said would end the complaints about automobiles. Some points included:

(1) Submission to and observance of a speed limit of 12 mph.
(2) Faithful observance of the following rules of safe driving:
   a. Never take a sharp corner at more than a walking pace.
   b. Never overtake another vehicle uphill or on a corner.
   c. Never drive the engine downhill.
   d. Slow down while passing pedestrians.
   e. Give cyclists plenty of room.
(3) Be unselfish by lessening the evils of dust.

John Burns, a cabinet minister, "officially warned the [motoring] fraternity that their fate is in their own hands, and that drastic results will ensue if they do not put their house — or their motor car — in order."[30]

Many laws concerning vehicles were soon to follow, such as a German law in 1908 that required the automobile owner to be personally accountable for the least misbehavior of his car.

In June 1909 a jury in New York City convicted a chauffeur of manslaughter and sentenced him to confinement in the state prison for not less than seven nor more than twenty years. The man had approached a boy who was playing in the street with other boys at what witnesses agreed was a high rate of speed, hit him in the back and dragged him half a block, slowed for a moment, then sped on at a higher rate of speed. He left the city and was later arrested in Port Arthur, Texas. This was the first case in the United States of a chauffeur's being convicted of reckless driving and manslaughter with a motor vehicle. There was much outrage at the time over "speed maniacs" and this case was seen to serve notice to all chauffeurs that no leniency would be given.[31]

In May 1911 the Touring Club of America and the American Automobile Association combined forces and called for a national movement to improve the highways in all states. The American Association for Highway Improvement was formed and Walter Page, director of the United States Office of Public Roads (part of the Department of Agriculture), was elected its president. The object of the association was to promote public awareness and to establish a uniform system of road building.

Travelers in the early 1900s in Minnesota relied on colored signs to show directions. The Duluth–Twin Cities road to Port Arthur, Ontario was marked with black-and-white signs and became known as the Black & White Trail. Duluth to Fargo, North Dakota, was the Green & White Trail. The system was set up by the local auto clubs and the American Trail Blazing Association. They also benefited from both the federal military roads and the Good Road Movement. The Good Road Movement had businessmen, politicians, farmers and the railroads banding together to build better roads. By 1916 the movement's lobbying efforts to Congress paid off and the federal government made money available to modernize roads. During that time, the number of registered vehicles had gone from a bit over 7,000 in 1909 to over 200,000 by 1917.[32]

By 1912 many states had enacted legislation requiring automobiles to be licensed, but the license was valid only in the state that issued it. The concept was changing. In March 1912 Maryland recognized reciprocal licensing, with a restriction that touring to New Jersey was limited to a fifteen-day period. The statute was not as well received as expected. District of Columbia motorists feared a lack of revenue for D.C. coffers if they were allowed to travel to Maryland on a reciprocal basis. Maryland visitors had been a lucrative revenue source for D.C. Part of the Maryland bill also required the use of one bright light from one hour after sunset to one hour before sunrise. In that same year Massachusetts called for standardization of traffic regulations. New Jersey also enacted a law requiring cars to have mufflers to quiet the internal combustion engines. In April 1912 New Jersey granted reciprocity between it and New York State, allowing travel from one state to the other without fear of interference by the police. States began to see the value of honoring one another's licenses.

In April 1917 France stopped all private motoring because of gasoline shortages. With the advance of World War I, it expected that there would be only enough gasoline available to cover military requirements.

New York State enacted several laws concerning automobiles in 1917, including requiring adequate brakes and sufficient lighting to "reveal any person, vehicle or substantial object on the road straight ahead of the motor vehicle for a distance of at least two hundred and fifty feet."[33] The same law mandated the use of low/high beam headlights because of the high number of accidents caused by uncontrolled headlight glare. That same year New Jersey decided to mail out blank applications for drivers' licenses to save owners a visit to the office and to ease the problems that arose from trying to process all the new applications.

Deaths from automobile accidents in the United States in 1922 were estimated at fourteen thousand, 1,600 more than in 1921. The number of automobiles in use had increased fivefold since 1915. The Boston *Herald* in 1923 said, "There is only one way to eliminate that class of accidents. Keep such drivers off the highways. Never relent in the search for the driver who 'speeds away in the night' ... and the public at large will support such measures." Another writer suggested that the "motor car psychology" contributes to the accident rate by explaining "why a man of intelligence, experience and caution in any other environment will get into an automobile and pull a fool stunt that will probably cause his death or that of others."[34] Others put the blame on pedestrians who left the curb without looking for approaching vehicles. They called for common sense and the general observance of a few plain rules of safety on the part of both drivers and pedestrians to curb the high number of deaths involving motorists.

By 1920 there was a great debate about the uniformity of state laws and whether there should be an all-encompassing federal law for automobiles. Historically, the states began legislation with the introduction of vehicle registration and a driver's license. Collection of the taxes for these fees began with the secretary of state, while the enforcement called of the laws became a police matter. Eventually the automobile license bureau became a separate administrative department generally titled the Commissioner of Motor Vehicles. One argument against federal legislation held that since the states at that time were roughly divided into manufacturing, agricultural or mining, the best interests of each state varied greatly, as did the laws to be applied. The argument for federal legislation was that the federal government could increase revenue by collecting more taxes. Concerns were raised that federal involvement would increase lawsuits through the federal courts, and it seemed that an enormous clerical and judicial machine would have to be built up to accommodate the increased caseload. Officers' jurisdiction would also have to be addressed. Would the traffic officer be a federal appointee or would he remain the municipal policeman who might have to appear in a federal court against offenders he might arrest? Another argument against federal overall legislation said it would be better to have a simple voluntary association among the motor vehicle administrators of several states to meet quarterly and discuss common problems and policies and work together toward common decisions. In 1921 this, in fact, was already happening. Representatives from Massachusetts, Rhode Island, Connecticut, New York, New Jersey, Pennsylvania and Maryland established a working (not constitutional) rule that all formulated policy would be arrived at unanimously. Meeting on September 23, 1921, a conference, through a variety of committees, adopted several agreements, including a uniform headlight law, licensing, registration and the right-hand, right-of-way rule. It was hoped that eventually the entire forty-eight states would be covered by six conferences.[35] This seemed to be the best solution to untangling the automotive laws and put an end to the controversy of a uniform federal automobile and traffic law.

By 1923 the State of New York passed a law taxing vehicles for wear and tear on the state road system. Electric trucks and some electric pleasure vehicles were penalized — that is, taxed at a higher rate — because the assumption was made that the wear and tear on the state highways was proportionate to the additional weight of the vehicle. Heavy batteries accounted for the increased weight. The *Literary Digest* argued that the taxation on the electric trucks was unjust for two reasons: (1) the rapid development of delivery trucks during the previous three years had been for the use of haulage in town and on local roads, and (2) wear and tear on the roads was not proportionate to a car's weight alone, but related also to speed and the mechanical conditions of driving. It went on to argue that tires last longer on an electric truck than on a gasoline truck of the same capacity, thanks to the smooth starting torque and the absence of shock and vibration. *Literary Digest* called upon manufacturers and users of electric vehicles to take the initiative in reversing this type of taxation and developing some simple method of determining a license fee that would be more fair to both electric and gasoline vehicles.[36]

By the 1920s there were many different types of vehicles in use, making the roads difficult and dangerous to navigate. There were bicyclists, horse-drawn carriages, pedestrians and a variety of cars, all competing for the same space. Some of these road warriors met with disaster at intersections. Garrett Augustus Morgan, an African-American inventor and businessman born in 1877, witnessed a serious crash between a carriage and an automobile, and with "characteristic inventor's intuition, recognized an urgent need for more order on the roads."[37] He invented America's first traffic signal system, consisting of a pole with a bell on top and three "STOP" signs, two of which were controlled by a hand crank at the base of the pole. He received a patent for the device in November 1923 and later sold it to the General Electric Company for $40,000. Another device, consisting of the familiar three-light system in use today, would replace Morgan's, but his was the first invention and it was used for a time in Cleveland, Ohio.

In 1928 the American Association of State Highway Officials created national highway concrete thickness standards of six inches, plus ten-foot lanes and eight-foot-wide shoulders. It also recommended octagonal stop signs.

By 1930, in response to public demand, laws were in force everywhere to govern automobile and driver licensing, speed limits and the means for generating revenue to keep roads passable for safe driving.

Rules and Regulations

"Politics deals with public goods—streets, parks, clean air, and so on—that are indivisible and non-excludable, and therefore must be shared. Markets deal with private goods—food, houses, cars and so on—that are consumed by individuals and cannot be shared."[38] Government must take special care in providing assistance in the form of regulations or financial support to any industry. Changes in rules and regulations concerning an industry may have a major impact on the economy, the public's perception of the role government should play in the private sector, and the potential growth of an industry. The EV, HEV and alternate fuels industries are no exception. One example of the process can be seen in federal safety standards that require that all vehicles have adequate heating and defrosting systems. This is a disadvantage for EVs. Heating alone can reduce the vehicle's range by as much as 35 percent depending on ambient temperatures and cabin temperatures. Another example appears in California regulations. The California Air Resources Board (CARB) policies, begun in 1990, have affected civic values and market direction. Citizens, through government, create policies in the hope that the policies will shape other citizens' opinions, which would, in turn, shape the direction taken in nascent technologies. This premise proved true. Environmental groups, for example, began to promote EVs after the government, in the form of CARB, formed its policies. This prompted some in the industry to revisit EVs, HEVs and alternate fuel vehicles as a means to support a potential market of environmentally conscious buyers, and meet regulations for automotive fuel consumption.

The government's impact on the auto industry through legislation and regulation cannot be underestimated. The automobile contributes substantially to the United States gross national product, involving a large segment of the workforce. It is a major component of the production industry. Any government rules, regulations or laws concerning EVs have a profound effect, not only on the general U.S. economy, but specifically on the oil, steel, and chemical and service industries that are associated with the automobile industry. It was estimated in 1967 that for all road transportation to suddenly go electric, the (then) current electric generating capacity would have had to double. Even the most avid proponents of EVs agree that they must crawl in a small way before they can run on a large scale. Government must promote a balance between social and economic responsibility — between the ideal and what can reasonably be accomplished — because changes in one area of the automotive industry affect much of our labor force and economy.

In 1955 Congress passed the Air Pollution Control Act, which identified air pollution as a national problem. Many state and local governments had passed legislation concerning pollution, but this was the first federal legislation on the issue. Many more would follow. The Clean Air Act of 1963 was the first to use that phrase and was passed to promote public health and welfare. Initially, it set standards for power plants and steel mills, but would later be amended to set antipollution standards for automobiles. It granted $95 million over a three-year period to state and local governments to conduct research on power plants' pollution and the automobile exhaust problem.

In the late 1960s, when concern over air pollution was high, at least eight branches of the U.S. government were involved in electric car research, including the Transportation Department (which spent $10.5 million), Health, Education and Welfare ($5 million), the Post Office and the Army. There were also fifteen federal agencies funding a total of eighty-six projects in battery research (21 government laboratories, 14 universities and 51 industrial companies). Part of the government response to concerns about air pollution was the adoption of emission control regulations in California in 1966. That same year, Congress mandated that beginning in 1968, all cars must have emissions control.

The eighty-ninth Congress passed three bills referred to as the Electric Vehicle Development Act of 1966. They provided funding for research and development of EVs. A fourth bill amended the Clean Air Act of 1963 to promote consideration of electric vehicles to reduce air pollution. This act set standards of carbon monoxide emission levels and required each state to submit a State Implementation Plan (SIP) establishing a clean-vehicle fleet program. The federal government set standards that included a certain percentage of "clean alternative fuel vehicles" to be used in state fleets. The percentage varied by areas of pollution classified as extreme, severe or serious. The government realized some of these requirements could not be met on time and continues to remain flexible in its enforcement.

As early as 1973 the Environmental Protection Agency (EPA) issued standards calling for a gradual reduction of lead emissions from gasoline. As part of its responsibility, it examines the complete economic and environmental impact of automobiles from their manufacture to their disposal. The EPA established an oxygenated-fuel program and the reformulated fuel program in an effort to direct compliance. The agency has worked with the Big Three automakers (GM, Ford, and Chrysler) since 1994 to promote electric vehicles as an environmentally preferable alternative to the internal combustion engine.

Nineteen seventy-three illustrated how difficult it is to locate a reasonable balance between government intervention and government manipulation in regulating industry. The 1973–74 oil shortages spurred the federal government to mediate in energy policy formulation, enacting price controls. This led to funding for energy alternative projects and renewed interest in electric and hybrid vehicles. Neither the federal government nor the energy companies established much credibility in controlling the crisis. The public lacked confidence in the government's ability to provide leadership in formulating a rational energy program for the future. The public had many doubts that the oil shortage was real. This crisis shows the volatility of the public's perception when government and private industry align. A survey in Canada at the time revealed most Canadians did not perceive the energy situation as a serious issue and did not believe it to be a "real" crisis. In the United States, the Federal Energy Office was accused of creating the oil shortages. Ralph Nader, a well-known consumer advocate, contended that "the world is literally [sic] drowning in oil ... and the present apparent shortages in the U.S., and related price increases are nothing less than unarmed robbery by oil companies in collusion with governmental support."[39] Many people suspected oil companies of shuffling oil supplies to hide them and delaying delivery of truckloads of oil to take advantage of higher prices. Many also suspected the government to be in collusion with oil companies to perpetrate the hoax of an oil shortage. Public trust of the government was at an all-time low following the Watergate scandal, and seeing home heating oil plentiful in the Northeast while people in Washington, D.C., were being asked to lower their thermostat settings caused many to question the validity of the crisis. The public perceived complicity. One energy administrator said, "People will say 'See, the oil companies contrived the shortage and so did President Nixon to get Watergate off the front pages.'"[40] Wall Street analysts estimated thirty oil companies would realize profits 40 to 50 percent higher in 1974 then in 1973. Oil companies' crude oil reserves were a closely held competitive secret at the time, and the public demanded that Congress get involved in forcing each company to divulge estimates of its reserves. Mobil and Exxon were summoned before the Senate Government Operations Subcommittee to answer questions about the price fluctuations in their stocks and to what extent refined products were brought in from the Caribbean and how much was produced from Arab oil. Other oil companies did report some data to the Bureau of Mines, but the public was aware that the figures could easily be jiggled by reporting the reserves in "custody" without reporting the crude or refined products held at independent terminals. There was also a loophole called "secondary storage" which could include any tank in the distribution system other than the refiners', enabling middlemen to hoard reserves of crude oil. While the hearings proceeded, consumers voiced their distrust of government accounting and demanded an immediate solution for the shortages.

An article in *Public Utilities Fortnightly* in 1974 suggested three possible courses of action: (1) continue the present course, which may lead to higher-priced service; (2) change restrictive regulations to allow prices to fluctuate, and probably increase; and (3) implement government intervention in the form of tax credits.

President Ford signed legislation in 1975 authorizing the Energy Research and Development Administration to provide $6 billion in loan guarantees to promote the synthetic fuels industry. The president also proposed to set up a new agency, to be called the Energy Independence Authority, to finance $100 billion for the development of nuclear energy and synthetic fuels over the next ten years. The intent of this new funding source was to overcome excessive delays in new energy development, and might encourage businesses to take greater risks in trying solar and synthetic fuel research. The purpose was to channel development of domestic energy resources to private industry. This was the first comprehensive national program to reduce reliance on foreign oil. The bill had a "sunset clause" that expired in 1985. At that time, Congress did not extend the bill's authority.

The fuel shortage generated growing interest in electric and hybrid vehicles. It was predicted that "before very long, a lot of people may get their chance to ride in or even own electric vehicles."[41] The U.S. Postal Service began taking bids from several companies for a fleet of electric vehicles. The two drawbacks were seen to be slow speed and limited range. The advantages were the lack of pollution and the availability of electric power. A fleet manager, Bud Tenney in Youngstown, Ohio, said, "I don't like fumes and it's getting harder and harder to get gasoline, and more expensive."[42] Electrics looked like a good alternative to ICEs.

In an attempt to address consumer concerns from the 1974 oil crisis, automakers turned to improving the average fuel mileage from about 14 mpg to about 22 mpg in 1981. The government also responded. Corporate Average Fuel Economy (CAFE) standards of 27.5 mpg were established in 1975 to recommend standard miles-per-gallon norms for the automotive industry. Because the automakers could not produce a station wagon that would meet the standards, they discontinued the model and put their efforts into manufacturing SUVs. The SUV would have to meet only the lower CAFE truck standards. In 1995 General Motors called for the government to increase gasoline prices artificially and do away with CAFE.

One author wrote, "When California had set out in the mid–1960s to regulate emissions from new cars and other states had threatened to do the same, the auto manufacturers sought help in Washington. They consulted Lloyd Cutler, an eminent Washington lawyer who later served as President Jimmy Carter's White House counsel. He suggested that the manufacturers get Congress to authorize a federal agency to regulate emissions from new cars. The companies could use their clout in Washington to keep the bureaucrats from imposing expensive requirements, but the federal agency's being on the job would dissuade states from regulating."[43] In 1965, the Department of Health, Education and Welfare was given the power to regulate emissions from new cars. In 1967, Congress passed legislation that barred every state except California from regulating new-car emissions. The regulation resulted in minimal changes for emission controls on automobiles. With the coming of the EPA in 1970, guidelines for air quality were being set. States were to comply with the air quality regulations but were not to regulate car emissions, just industrial emissions; there was no flexibility in the law. If regulations were not met, facilities were to be shut down. States refused to comply. The politics of implementation went bureaucratically forward, regardless of which party was in the White House. Although, in theory, cost would not be a factor in enforcing the standards, in reality in 1976 when President Jimmy Carter took office, he initiated cost-benefit analysis as part of the process before issuing regulations.

Federal agencies are at a disadvantage in regulating industry. They must bow to pressures from legislators and the president because the holders of those offices govern the extent of their authority and their budget. Legislators and politicians want credit for supporting clean air, but not the responsibility for "the burdens involved in cleaning it."[44]

Federal legislation increased through the first decade of the 21st century. Again, with fuel costs rising, and reliance on foreign markets for oil, interest in alternative fuel vehicles has come to the forefront. In 2007 alone, over 60 pieces of legislation were introduced that referenced one of the trendy "new" possibilities: plug-in vehicles. Literally hundreds of bills were introduced to support all types of alternate fuels, such as fuel cell development and biofuel research. The legislation was intended to promote use and research through tax credits, guaranteeing loans for research projects, and providing loans and grants for research and development of renewable energy. Electric and other alternative fuel vehicles had again become a popular political asset.

In January 2006, environmentalists called on the government to change the classification of SUVs from "light trucks" because the SUVs use the same amounts of gas as cars. The conservationists argued that increasing SUV fuel efficiency from 17 mpg to the 27.5 mpg CAFE standard imposed on ordinary cars would save one million barrels of oil a day by 2015.[45] The argument came during a time when the United States had military in Afghanistan and Iraq following the terrorist attack of September 11, 2001, and faced rising fuel costs and dependence on foreign oil to maintain current production levels. Congress considered options to address energy independence from foreign oil. One of those options was to allow oil companies leasing rights for drilling the oil reserves in Alaska's Arctic National Wildlife Refuge. Environmentalists raised opposition, claiming that the savings in fuel achieved by simply raising the CAFE standards would far outweigh the yield from ANWR drilling, which would cause a huge negative environmental impact in the region.

Executive Director of the Sierra Club Carl Pope says,

> The president pretends the oil industry will use hypodermic needles to extract oil, but surgical precision doesn't exist in oil drilling. Drilling the Artic Refuge would take a huge industrial development sprawling across the fragile tundra in a vast web of oil rigs, pipelines, roads, landing strips, housing for workers and vast incinerators for waste.[46]

ANWR.org, an organization in favor of developing the oil reserves in that region, reminds the public that 19 million acres of the region are already designated as wilderness and that the only coastline available for oil exploration is the stretch between Colville and Canning Rivers. That leaves over 1,000 miles of Alaskan coastline that cannot be leased for gas or oil drilling. In response to it causing environmental damage, the organization asserts that the North Slope's petroleum industry is heavily regulated and uses the most advanced technology to ensure minimal environmental impact. It also notes that the coastal area is not pristine wilderness; it has been used for centuries for hunting, for military radar sites and for commercial recreation. They point out that the negative predictions of impact on the caribou on the North Slope, proved false. The herds along the pipeline are thriving. The environmentalist's fears have not proven true. (The main source for this information is the Alaska Wildlife Fish & Game Department Reports from their caribou census, which is taken every two to three years.)

Proposed modifications to the CAFE standards came to the House and Senate floors in March 2007 under the Fuel Economy Reform Act. The changes would eliminate the 10,000-pound weight minimum needed for automobiles to come under the gasoline mileage restrictions, and would require 27.5 mpg for all automobiles manufactured after 2012, and a 4 percent improvement each year in gas mileages topping at 35 mpg for all automobile models manufactured on or after 2018.

In June 2007, H.R. 2927 was introduced to revise the CAFE standards for autos and promote development of technology for vehicles and vehicle components. It proposed extending the manufacturing incentives for alternative fuel cars for 10 years. The standards would cover model years beginning in 2022 for passenger and non-passenger automobiles. The standards should be no less than a combined 32 mpg and no more than a combined 35 mpg. Part of the bill also requires the secretary of transportation to issue standards for grams of carbon dioxide per mile. As of 2009 the bill was still pending, but much of its content went into effect in the Energy Independence and Security Act of 2007.

The Energy Independence and Security Act of 2007 updated the CAFE standards by requiring a combined city and highway rating of 35 mpg by 2020. It addressed the lack of rules for trucks by requiring that standards be set for commercial medium-duty and heavy-duty trucks by 2010. The bill included provisions for a new rating system to allow easier comparison for consumers in checking fuel economy and greenhouse gas emissions and extended flexible fuel vehicles (FFV) and dual fuel vehicles (AFV) credits through 2019. A grant program supporting projects to encourage plug-in vehicles and loan programs for constructing battery manufacturing facilities was also authorized. Fuel standards regulation has been one of many approaches by citizens using government means to promote development of personal vehicles that have minimal environmental impact. Initiatives to promote specific parts of the industry have also speckled the legislative landscape with varying results, as the size and number of government agencies has expanded.

Congress passed the Electric and Hybrid Vehicle Act of 1976 over President Ford's veto. It established a demonstration project through the Department of Energy and assigned a budget of $160 million. The Energy Research and Development Agency (ERDA) was set up to administer the act and was committed to the view that the United States would have an all-electric economy by the year 2000. The act authorized ERDA's secretary to enter agreements or arrangements with other major government departments such as the Department of Transportation, NASA, the Department of Agriculture and the Environmental Protection Agency. Its purpose was to promote research on batteries, controls and motors, and vehicle design. It was to conduct feasibility demonstration projects to determine possible commercial use of electric and hybrid vehicles, identify potential customer markets and determine impacts on the long-range planning for roads, utilities, urban design, taxation and maintenance facilities. Much of the funding went to U.S. national laboratories. Interest in researching alternative-fuel vehicles began to decline in the late 1970s when it became evident that the EV and HEV were not practical competitors to the ICE. Automakers were improving the efficiency of the ICE and gasoline was flowing freely again. By 1978, ERDA had not received any funding and there was great congressional debate over the fiscal budget to reduce the amount and defer the demonstration project called for in the act.

The Alternative Motor Fuels Act of 1988 provided CAFE incentives for vehicles that run on alcohol or natural gas, either exclusively or in conjunction with gasoline or diesel. The program had mixed results. As in the past, the lack of infrastructure for fuel availability was a major factor. The manufacturers did increase the number of cars produced with the capability of running on E85 (a fuel mixture that is 15 percent gasoline and 85 percent ethanol) as well as gasoline. The Midwest proved the strongest market for this product. It carried the majority of refueling stations needed to service this market. In 2001, a National Energy Policy Group report stated that ethanol vehicles had tremendous potential if ethanol production could be expanded. The National Academy of Sciences' report on CAFE credit incentive programs, released later that year, recommended that credits for dual-fuel vehicles should be discontinued, with lead time given to allow manufacturers to adjust. This was followed by the Securing America's Future Energy Act (SAFE), passed by Congress in August 2001, which extended the dual-fuel provision through 2008.[47]

The international community was also responding to environmental concerns. People wanted research into the health aspects of automobile pollution. Some international events during the mid–1990s included:

- England — "No new road-building" protestors wanted to save money and protect the trees that would be taken down to build new roads.
- France — A clean air policy was enacted that allowed city governors to close cities to car traffic in times of heavy pollution.
- Italy — The city center of Milan was closed to gasoline-powered cars.
- Japan — Protestors demanded new road designs to accommodate noise and pollution.

In 1990 the U.S. Congress approved a contract with the Department of Energy (DOE), Ford and General Electric to design commercially viable modular propulsion. Known as the Modular Electric Vehicle Program, it was part of the larger Electric and Hybrid Vehicle Program.[48] Also in 1990, the Clean Air Act required the EPA to set air quality standards. The law concentrated on producing cleaner fuel mixtures. Gasoline sold in the most populated, and thus presumably more polluted, urban areas was to contain at least 2 percent of certain additives, increasing the oxygen level to make it burn more cleanly. These additives were usually either ethanol or MTBE (methyl tertiary-butyl-ether). The law recognized that the states must be in charge of their own pollution control problems and the means they would use to meet those standards.

The Energy Policy Act of 1992 was designed to reduce dependency on foreign oil and to improve air quality. The EPAct established the State and Alternative Fuel Provider Program, a Department of Energy regulatory program that required state and alternative fuel provider fleets to purchase AFVs as a portion of their annual light-duty vehicle acquisitions. Fleets earned credits for each vehicle purchased, and credits earned in excess of their requirements could be banked or traded with other fleets. This gave fleets flexibility in meeting their requirements. Part of the act required federal, state and fuel provider groups to purchase increasing numbers of alternative fuel vehicles (AFVs) each year to meet a 10 percent reduction in petroleum use by 2000 and 30 percent by 2010. In 1999 only 1.6 percent of alternative fuel vehicles on the road were electric; by 2006 that number had dropped to 1.12 percent. The majority of the fleets had moved to E85 to meet their credits earned.

In an effort to curb air pollution, New York City enacted the Clean Air Taxis Act (2005). This requires the Taxi and Limousine Commission to approve at least one gas-electric hybrid model for use in the city. This allows the taxi services to bid on the clean-fuel taxi medallions and installs hybrids as standard taxi transports. The change to hybrids allows cab drivers to go an entire shift (approximately 500 miles) on one tank of gas.

In March 2007 Las Vegas received a 63 percent rating, the highest mark for alternative fuel use in its city fleet vehicles. This was reported by SustainLane Government, which tracks data and offers resources for sustainability programs. Dallas was ranked 5th among the 50 largest U.S. cities. At the time, Dallas had over 1,200 compressed natural gas and hybrid electric vehicles, including cars, light trucks and vans in its fleet program.

To promote compliance with the Energy Policy Act of 1992 and the Clean Air Act of 1990, the Department of Energy established the Clean Cities Program. The voluntary program was designed to encourage local communities to find economically sustainable markets for AFVs. The program was founded on the principle that individuals working toward a common goal can best achieve the nation's objectives through local action. By 1993, Clean Cities International had over eighty cities in the United States, and five countries (Brazil, Mexico, Chile, Peru and India), involved in the program. By 2007, the composition of those participating internationally had changed slightly, with Bangladesh, Canada, the European Union, and the Philippines joining the international group, and Brazil leaving it. A number of major alternative fuel projects were funded through the World Bank, the Asian Development Bank, and the U.S. Agency for International Development (USAID).[49] Clean Cities' purpose is to bring private industry, utilities, government agencies and the public together to create a viable alternative fuels market. Some groups work on policies and government initiatives to encourage public support and market interest in electric vehicles and other AFVs, others have begun using AFVs in fleets, buses and shuttle services, and still others institute public awareness campaigns to promote usage. Statistics from 2006 reports show that approximately 375 million gallons of gasoline were displaced that year by the alternative fuels, and 302 million of those gallons resulted from Clean Cities projects. This was a 50 percent increase from 2005.[50] Each Clean Cities Program contributes to the goal of private industry working with community governments to promote the use of alternatives to gasoline and diesel vehicles.

Plug-in Partners was established in 2006 in Austin, Texas, as part of its climate protection plan. It has grown to include over 600 partners—local and state governments, businesses, environmental groups, unions, utility companies and associations—across the United States. It also has a few Canadian members. The organization has encouraged the major automakers to build plug-ins (the Chevy Volt may be a by-product of that support), and promoted federal policies encouraging support for alternate energy sources for the nation's energy grid, including the vehicle-to-grid concept. Some participants of the program offer rebates or tax credits for those purchasing plug-in cars.

Most western European countries have passed legislation to reduce air pollution by reducing auto emissions. In 2001 the United Kingdom passed regulations allowing buses to have remote controls to change traffic lights to green, minimizing the time spent idling. The U.K. is also widening bus lanes and requiring cars to stop and wait behind the buses when the buses are picking up passengers. Beginning in 2003 and extending in 2007, London initiated a congestion charge in parts of Central and West London. This scheme is one of the largest in the world. It requires payment (equivalent to approximately $12 per day) each time a chargeable vehicle comes into the designated zone, and imposes fines for non-payment. Fleet vehicles are charged £7 per visit and other non-exempt vehicles pay £8. Payment may be made via website, text message, at shops using PayPoint or by phone. Emergency vehicles, buses, taxis and hybrids are among those exempt. Honda saw this as a marketing opportunity and increased shipment of the hybrid Civic by over 3,000 autos in 2007. Singapore took a slightly different approach. Instead of considering the emissions as the source for taxation, owners were taxed from 20 percent to 30 percent based on the engine power. This approach did not provide the needed incentive to offset the additional cost of a hybrid. The market for them has not expanded in Singapore at the rate it has in other major metropolitan cities. Some areas have legislation to restrict driving motor vehicles in city centers. Switzerland provides direct subsidies for buying cars to individuals who take part in demonstration programs involving electric vehicles.[51] France is experimenting with electric vehicle fleets for utility companies and is offering recharging services and reduced parking fees for electric vehicles. In 2005, the French postal service tested eight electric vehicles, developed by Société de Véhicules Electriques, in its postal delivery van fleet. The cars used lithium-ion batteries specifically designed for the cars through a joint venture of Johnson Controls, Inc., of Milwaukee, Wisconsin, and Saft Groupe, a French battery company. Although there is still some question about the durability of the battery, La Poste plans on replacing most of its 48,000 vehicle fleet with the electrics over the next five years.

The hybrid market continues to rely on subsidies and tax incentives to encourage buyers to its marketplace. One of these assists takes the form of a United Kingdom grant to Professor Li Ran of Durham University and Professor Phil Mawby of the University of Warwick. Their work, funded by a three-year £500,000 government grant, will address the power fatigue of insulated gate bipolar transistors (IGBTs) such as those used in wind turbines and hybrid motor controls. Toyota Prius uses a 50-kilowatt IGBT inverter to control two AC motor/generators connected to its DC battery pack. Thermal fatigue degrades their delicate structure over time and research will be addressing ways to predict the failure before it occurs. The results of their work should also be applicable to improving servicing parts in renewable energy systems. The researchers hope to demonstrate practical benefits that will lead to more cost-effective designs for equipment such as those used in alternate energy sources and hybrid car motor controls.

California has introduced many incentives and laws concerning free meter parking for alternative fuel and hybrid electric vehicles. The vehicles must display a California Clean Air decal and then may park free for the maximum time limit indicated on the meter. Some of the cities involved in this program are Los Angeles, San Jose, Santa Monica, Hermosa Beach and Sacramento.

In 2008 wind farms were enjoying federal clean-energy tax credit benefits, but Congress has allowed those to lapse several times over the years. Advocates have called for extending these credits and eventually establishing a national renewable power standard that would also require states to be involved in tax credits.[52]

A 1992 study by Southern California Edison (SCE) showed that nearly two-thirds of Californians would buy an electric vehicle if, and again this is a big "if," it was comparable in price to the internal combustion engine (ICE). Nearly half in the study said they would accept a $1,000 annual battery replacement cost as a necessary expense. Michael R. Peavey, president of SCE, said, "If you build them, they will buy."[53] He claimed that electric vehicles could reduce air pollution in California (attributed to the ICE) by two-thirds and would reduce dependence on foreign oil. An air quality official at the New York Department of Environmental Conservation said, "There's a wealth of Yuppie environmental guilt out there to be exploited."[54] Allan D. Gilmore, then a vice president of Ford Motor Company, commented on some focus group studies conducted in California. "Basically, what the people told us was this: 'I think these alternative types of vehicles are marvelous. I'm in favor of protecting the environment, and I think my neighbor should get one.'"[55] Automakers insist that incentives from utility companies and federal and local governments are necessary to get EVs on the road.

In 1993 Michigan senator Carl Levin proposed a consortium of the utilities and the Big Three automakers in Michigan to build electric cars. The Big Three balked, responding that they all knew how to build cars; what was needed was new battery technology and infrastructure. They also noted that having customers was an important detail that would increase their efforts to produce electric vehicles and suggested that the government should put in an order for fifty thousand vans by 1998.

In 1994 a thirty-member advisory panel was charged by President Clinton to achieve a long-term Global Climate Action Plan in a three-stage strategy for the years 2005, 2015, and 2025 to reduce carbon dioxide emissions. The CAFE standard was still 27.5 mpg. The panel was portrayed as an attempt to bring together the automotive, environmental and utility industries. The thirty-member panel contained only five seats for automakers. The Sierra Club considered the effort a shield for the administration to get credit for a clean-air program and an attack on global warming and as a way to appease the auto industry by keeping regulation at bay.

In 1995, oil companies and auto manufacturers were accused of trying to kill the electric car. A spokesman for Mobil stated that they did not fear the competition of electric cars, but at the same time were opposed to the government's mandating "unproven technology" and subsidizing the competition with public tax monies. A Carnegie Mellon University study concluded that recycling lead-acid batteries on a large scale would discharge large quantities of lead into the environment, an amount that would outweigh the benefits of the removal of lead from gasoline. The more efficient ICEs of 1995 were already emitting 95 percent less tailpipe emissions than the cars of the 1960s.[56]

A study conducted in 2001 by the American Council for an Energy Efficient Economy (ACEEE), a nonprofit research group in Washington State, found that new technology improved standard ICE engines to the point of getting about forty miles per gallon. The better engines added about $1,000 to the cost of the vehicle. The same study found that a hybrid Taurus could get fifty-three miles per gallon, but the added cost to the vehicle was about $3,500.

In an effort to find viable alternative fuels, the National Renewable Energy Laboratory (NREL), part of the U.S. Department of Energy, partnered with DuPont and Genencor in 2000, providing over $49 million in grant monies for research and design on improving ethanol processing. In 2008 Iowa State University and ConocoPhillips joined the partnership to research biomass alternatives for fuel — leaves, stems, grass and trees.

The Canadian government is taking a key role in the development of hydrogen and fuel cell technology. It allocated $30 million in 1999 for a five-year partnership whose key component was the National Research Council (NRC) Fuel Cell Program. This program's main objective was to support small and medium-sized businesses in the research and development of fuel cells and the creation of a hydrogen infrastructure. The move was meant to promote high-tech industries, job creation and environmental awareness. By 2005, the program had funded 12 research projects involving six NRC institutes, 10 Canadian universities and over 20 Canadian companies. Ford Canada introduced its Th!nk City car at the Montreal 2000 Electric Vehicle Project symposium in September 2000. In June 2001, the Canadian government's Canadian Transportation Fuel Cell Alliance (CTFCA) was begun. This $23 million venture focused on developing a fuel cell refueling infrastructure. By 2002, Canada had also developed partnerships in hydrogen projects with organizations in Brazil, China, Thailand and the United Kingdom. In 2005, the NRC Institute for Fuel Cell Innovation (NRC-IFCI) was established at the NRC institute in Vancouver, British Columbia. This was made possible through the government's additional $20 million funding. Canada is among the leading nations in fuel cell technology, along with Germany, Japan and the United States.[57] By 2007, the fuel sector profile for Canada had stabilized, with product sales of approximately $89 million and jobs numbering approximately 2,000. Research, development and demonstration expenditures dropped from $237 million in 2004 to $193 million in 2006. This trend indicated a movement toward commercial product sales.[58]

In 2005 the Ford Focus FCV came onto the Canadian scene. This vehicle is a third-generation hybrid-electric that uses a Ballard Mark 902 series fuel cell and Dynetek 5,000-

psi compressed-hydrogen storage tank. Through a partnership among the Canadian government, Ford Motor Company/Ford of Canada, Fuel Cells Canada, and the government of British Columbia, five of the Ford Focus FCVs were monitored through 2008 to collect critical data for improving the development of fuel cell technology. BC Hydro, B.C. Transit, Ballard Power Systems, the City of Vancouver, Fuel Cells Canada, the NRC, Natural Resources of Canada and the government of British Columbia used the vehicles in normal daily driving.[59] July 2007 found Ford expanding its testing program to include a partnership with Southern California Edison to test rechargeable, plug-in hybrids, using its Ford Escape SUV as the model. In December 2009, Ford sent 10 Ford Focus FCVs to Reykjavik, Iceland, to test the vehicles in everyday driving conditions. Iceland has commercial hydrogen fueling stations available for public use. With this new venture, Ford's testing program has logged over 1 million miles as they continue research and development with fuel cell technology.

The freedom that comes from operating one's own car is nearly considered a right in Western society. When the price of gas at the pumps doubles, cries go out for government involvement. The government's roles to date have been to attempt to socially engineer and spur industry through mandates (rules and regulations) and tax incentives (rebates and subsidies).

State Incentive Programs

Almost every state has offered and continues to offer tax credits or deductions for developing and implementing alternative fuel vehicles. As a greater percentage of these vehicles begin displacing conventional ICEs and as programs have tested their effectiveness, the incentive programs have been adjusted over the years. Emphasis before 2005 was on purchase of alternate fuel vehicles; since 2005 incentives have focused on adding infrastructure for refueling stations and promoting the use of hydrogen and biofuels. A few examples are:

- Alabama — Low-interest loans for alternative fuel vehicle (AFV) projects.
- Arizona — State income tax deduction of 25 percent on the purchase cost of AFVs; a lower license tax than that applied to conventional vehicles — $4 for every $100 assessed value; Honda Civic Hybrid, Honda Insight and Toyota Prius may use the HOV lane; up to $75 tax credit for home recharging unit installations; EV recharging-station parking is reserved for EVs; all others are fined a minimum of $350.
- Arkansas — A 50 percent tax credit for any Arkansas taxpayer who constructs a facility in the state that will manufacture EVs, fuel cells or photovoltaic cells.
- California — Up to $5,000 in rebates on the purchase or lease cost of EVs, ZEVs (battery electric and hydrogen fuel cell), plug-ins, and AFVs until March 31, 2009, and a $1,000 tax incentive for NGVs. Free meter parking for alternative fuel and hybrid electric vehicles. The vehicles must display a California Clean Air decal and then may park free for the maximum time limit indicated on the meter.
- Colorado — A credit is available to both new and converted vehicles based on computation of credit. Amounts vary according to the model and year of the auto, and the type of fuel used. It averages between $2,500 and $4,000. Percentages decreased beginning in June 2009. The credit applies to nonprofit and government agencies, the private sector, and individuals. Up to 50 percent rebate on the cost of AFVs. Credit for alternative fuel

refueling stations was added in 2006 and extends through 2010. This credit may extend to 70 percent if the fuel being dispensed is from a renewable energy source.

- Florida — Between 2006 and 2010, sales and use tax exemptions for hydrogen and bio-fuel vehicles.
- Georgia — Tax incentive for the construction of alternate fuel production facilities. Facilities must use biomass such as agricultural products or animal fats.
- Kansas— Up to 50 percent tax credit on the cost of converting a vehicle to AFV that uses biomass. Up to $750 or five percent of cost for purchasing a new vehicle (original owner only).
- Kentucky — Beginning in 2008, up to $1 per gallon tax credit (total allowed, $5 million) for qualified ethanol producers. Must be corn- or cellulosic-based ethanol that meets ASTM (American Society for Testing and Materials) standard D 4806. Unused credits may not be carried forward and applied to a future tax return. However, unused ethanol credits from one ethanol-based cap, such as corn, may be applied to another ethanol-based cap, such as cellulosic, in the same taxable year.
- Louisiana — Zero-interest loans for fleet conversions to CNG or LNG vehicles. Up to 20 percent for the purchase or conversion of an AFV or the building of a refueling station for AFVs.
- Maryland — A tax credit of up to $2,000 for EVs, $500 to $1,000 for hybrid electrics based on their energy efficiency, and $125 to $500 for their ability to regenerate through braking. Hybrids are exempt from emissions testing for the first three years if they meet 50 mpg EPA rating.
- Minnesota — Excludes the sale of propane or natural gas for vehicles from the motor fuel tax. Offers tax incentive (up to $0.20 per gal.) for producing ethanol; payments are limited to $3 million per producer and end in 2010.
- Montana — A 50 percent tax deduction for the purchase cost of an AFV. Up to $500 tax credit to defray costs for converting vehicles to alternative fuels. Ethanol producers and distributors have a credit of $0.20 per gallon if at least 20 percent of the ethanol is made from Montana products.
- Nebraska — Low cost loans (5 percent) toward the purchase or conversion of fleets to AFVs. Investors in Nebraska biodiesel production facilities (must be at least 51 percent owned by Nebraskans) producing B100 biodiesel may receive a tax credit for 30 percent (not to exceed $250,000) for the first three years.
- North Carolina — State and local government credit unions offer green vehicle loans for new AFVs and HEVs. The loans are offered at a one percent interest rate discount.
- New York — Rebates up to 80 percent of the cost of converting vehicles to CNG. Tax credits equal to 50 percent of the cost for installation of a refueling structure for alternative fuels (natural gas, liquefied petroleum gas, hydrogen, electricity, and any other fuel that is a least 85 percent ethanol or other alcohol.) This credit does not apply after December 31, 2010.
- Ohio— A ten percent tax credit for vehicles using ethanol. Retailers who sold E85 or biodiesel are eligible for a tax credit of $0.15 per gallon of E85 or biodiesel fuel sold using a metered pump at a fueling station in 2007, and $0.13 per gallon of E85 or biodiesel fuel sold in 2008.
- Oklahoma — A ten percent tax credit for the cost of AFV conversions and for electric vehicles or hybrids. Until 2010, tax credit of 50 percent for the cost of installing alternative fuel refueling infrastructure (CNG, LPG, LNG, methanol, electricity).
- Oregon — A 35 percent tax credit for AFV projects. Up to a total of $1,500 may be claimed

if the homeowner has both an alternate fuel vehicle and a home refueling station. Up to $10,000 to install or convert fueling equipment at retail gasoline stations and fleet fueling sites to B20 or higher biodiesel blends and E85 ethanol blends.
- Rhode Island — A 50 percent tax credit was offered to businesses for constructing EV recharging stations effective January 1, 1998 through January 1, 2003. A tax credit of 25 percent of the federal credit for electric vehicles.
- Texas — A $2,000 rebate for CNG conversions. Blended diesel/biodiesel is exempt from diesel fuel tax. Austin set aside $1 million for plug-in hybrid rebates.
- Utah — A tax credit for up to 50 percent of the cost of a new EV to a maximum of $2,000 per vehicle. As of 2008, hybrids were no longer exempt. In 2009, alternative fuel credit changed to 35 percent.
- Virginia — No local motor vehicle license fees for AFVs. Beginning in 2008, a tax credit of $0.01 for biodiesel producers up to $5,000 and available the first three years.
- Wisconsin — Taxis may be reimbursed for the amount of Wisconsin fuel tax paid. A minimum 100 gallons of alternative fuel must have been used in that year.[60]

The tax credits did convince some businesses to give their employees incentives for buying alternative fuel vehicles. Google and Hyperion Solutions, for example, offered their employees $5,000 toward the purchase of a high mileage hybrid; a shoe manufacturer in New Hampshire offered $3,000. Some employees who took advantage of the incentives got a bonus from their employer and a credit on their taxes for buying one of the hybrid cars on the market.

In December 1996 the city of Portland, Oregon, opened two electric charging stations downtown that were capable of charging two electric vehicles at once at any time of the day. The city also announced it was considering adding electric vehicles to its fleet.[61] By 2001 Portland had experimented with a few alternative vehicles, such as electric, propane and compressed natural gas (CNG), and had plans to buy three dozen Toyota Prius hybrids in the near future. Portland's Department of Sustainable Resources (formerly the Energy Department) discovered a "Catch-22" during this experimentation period, one that has plagued AFVs throughout the history of the automobile. The department found it easy to buy CNG vehicles, but the infrastructure was not in place to support them. On the other hand, the infrastructure is in place for electrics, but they are too expensive to buy. By 2008, the city advertised electric recharging sites in five facilities, including parking for the main public library. The city's fleet, according to manager Don Taylor, had sixty hybrids, the majority of them Toyota Priuses, and one hundred eighty-five E85 vehicles.

In 1997 Massachusetts and New York enacted low-emission-vehicle programs (LEVP) with tighter standards than the 1990 California LEVP. The LEVP set sales mandates for LEVs, ULEVs and ZEVs. In 2000 federal courts overturned the stricter northeastern state laws in favor of the lower California standards.

In 1999 Arizona enacted a program to promote alternative fuel vehicles. It allowed buyers to recoup up to half the cost of a vehicle if it was outfitted with a natural gas fuel system. The program did not require owners to actually use the system. Many people took advantage of this law (more than 22,000) without following through with the conversion, and estimated costs to the state went from $5 million to over $500 million before the state took action to reverse the program in 2000.

State-supported programs in California also fell under scrutiny. In early 2001 California experienced rolling blackouts. Due to power shortages, the electric grid was shut down

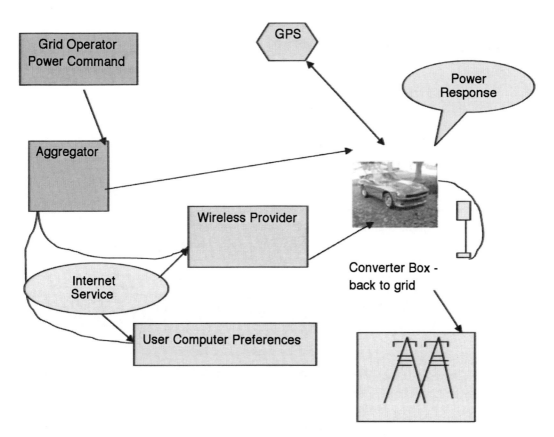

Figure 1. Vehicle-to-Grid Diagram

at various times during the day in many populated areas. California had to buy electricity from Washington, Oregon and Texas. How does this affect EVs? CARB commissioned the University of California at Davis and the AC Propulsion Company to study the potential role of EVs (battery, hybrid and fuel cell) as energy storage devices, which could conceivably feed electricity back into the power grid. They might be used as storage units during the hours of inactivity when the driver is away from the vehicle and the vehicle is plugged into an energy source generated from solar or wind power.[62] Electric vehicles have power within them capable of producing AC electricity, the same type that powers our homes and offices. Connections can be added to allow the electricity to flow from cars to power lines. This is called "vehicle to grid" power, or V2G. The key to this concept is the precise timing of grid power production to fit within driving requirements while meeting the time-critical power of the distribution system.[63]

Results showed the process is possible, but implementation will involve additional work. Rules must be modified to allow mobile vehicles to participate in the power exchange, and accommodations will be needed for various vehicle models.[64]

The public concentrated on reasons for the electricity shortage and the wisdom of state-supported EV projects. Opinions on causes of the shortage varied. Some people blamed environmentalists for not wanting power facilities in "their backyard" and some blamed deregulation of the industry. Whatever the reason, those supporting electric vehicle development began to question the government's interest in promoting electric vehicles when the state's existing electric power system could not produce enough power to keep the lights on all day. Others suggested that California not allow any imported cars, but only electric cars manufactured in the U.S., and then only sell the number that could be supported by electricity produced in California.

Pennsylvania announced in February 2001 that it would provide funding in the amount of $7 million for projects promoting the use of alternative fuels in vehicles. The ultimate goal is to reduce air pollution and dependence on foreign oil. This money supplemented $17 million funded during the previous six years to develop alternative fuel vehicles, build refueling and recharging stations and fund research and development of the various technologies. The alternative fuels being considered included natural gas, biofuels, methanol, ethanol and hydrogen. The Pennsylvania Department of Environmental Protection estimated that this program by 2007 had reduced hydrocarbon and carbon monoxide emissions to a degree that would equal the removal of 200 ICE vehicles from the roads every year.

By 2001, various programs throughout the states had been in effect long enough to begin collecting data. They hoped to report an impact that would move governments, corporations, utilities and private citizens from the ICE to alternate fuel vehicles. A survey[65] conducted by the National Conference of State Legislatures, a bipartisan organization whose focus is to "improve the quality and effectiveness of state legislatures," looked at the type of incentive used (grant, loan, and tax credit) and the reason (public image or mandate) AFVs were being added to fleets. The survey results showed that use of incentives varied from state to state, and that government grant money, not loans, was the incentive most often used by fleets and municipalities. State grants were used most often (64 percent), with federal (31 percent) being the next choice. Small businesses, because they pay personal income tax and so try to have as little net profit as possible, had a clear preference for grant and rebate programs. Loans were used only if grant money was not available. Only Oklahoma had minimal success with a loan program that was marketed by the state to fleets. Its was based on the differential among gasoline, natural gas and diesel prices. New Mexico decided against offering loans, using the rationale that loans are useful only if there is a large differential between gasoline and natural gas prices.[66] Both federal and state tax credits were also widely used. When asked whether public image or mandates was the driving force behind leasing or buying AFVs, federal, state, and utilities were complying with mandates with federal at 100 percent and state at 80 percent and the utilities at 76 percent. Public image scored high in municipalities (58 percent image and 49 percent mandate) and private companies (69 percent image and 15 percent mandate).

The survey and data were collected through interviews with Clean City, fleet managers, grant managers, and other reports from the various government departments and private enterprises. Many viewpoints and tools were used to collect the data. One limitation found was in the way the data had been kept by the various programs. Detailed information about the persons/organizations using tax incentives, for example, was not available as the data were all grouped as "tax incentives." The survey had a 20 percent response rate, which was considered by the NCSL to be quite a high percent-

	Mandate	Public Image
Federal	100 %	
State	80 %	
Municipality	49%	58%
Utility Company	76%	
Private Company	15%	69%

Figure 2. Table for Mandates and Public Image

age. The report gave the states information on the effectiveness of the programs both locally and in comparison to other states' programs.

The California Air Resources Board (CARB) has shown itself to be the most influential political association affecting vehicle emissions in current history. It has passed many regulations affecting the auto industry and its suppliers, beginning with a requirement of an 80 percent reduction in new car emissions between 1992 and 2003, and a minimum of ten percent of vehicles sold to be zero emission vehicles (ZEV) by 2003. California is not the only state to have made this type of legislation, but it has had the greatest influence in regulating the behavior of automobile manufacturers. CARB's adjustments to these regulations also depict the fluidity needed when government and the marketplace combine forces.

California initiated the low-emission vehicle (LEV) mandate on September 28, 1990. This initiative also contained the zero-emission vehicle (ZEV) mandate, which included special rules to allow manufacturers to "bank" credits as well as trade them. In 1994 CARB introduced the ideas of emission averaging, trading and banking credits, as a departure from uniform standards. The board realized it might have to change its standards because the industry could not comply in such a limited time frame given the current technology and consumer market. This led to the decision in 1996 in which CARB changed the relative importance of some technical criteria evaluations and changed the factors it was using to assess consumers' willingness to purchase EVs. The free market's lack of enthusiasm for the products had become evident. CARB's research on consumer acceptance had proved to be flawed. A survey submitted to CARB in 1994 showed that the consumers' lack of enthusiasm was primarily due to their lack of information. From this CARB falsely concluded that once consumers were properly informed, they would begin to want and buy EVs. This did not prove to be the case. Buyers were not willing to purchase the more expensive environmentally friendly vehicles if the cost was substantially higher and the owner was inconvenienced by the fuel supply. The primary objections to these vehicles, as throughout the century, were still lack of range and high price. People were not influenced by civic benefits or citizenship for the public good if the product offered less performance than their current choices. By 1996 CARB realized that its survey tool was unreliable and that it could not create or convert consumer behavior by trying to sway them through data and environmental impact information. CARB returned to adjusting incentives for the manufacturers to encourage compliance to their mandates. CARB provided an incentive for smaller manufacturers with its ZEV credits program. In 1995 a coalition called Californians Against Utility Company Abuse (CAUCA) was formed by 2,700 companies and groups, including some oil companies, to actively attack attempts by utilities to increase rates to finance EV promotion and develop infrastructure. The coalition stated that Southern California Edison should finance its EV involvement by company profits and not by customers. The California Manufacturers Association (CMA) was also working in 1995 to prevent the CARB mandates from going into effect in 1998. CMA claimed the EV mandate was a "well intentioned, but misguided attempt by government to force technology into the marketplace prematurely."[67] "We absolutely oppose any government mandate that forces manufacturers to make a product that isn't ready for the marketplace," stated CMA president William Campbell, citing a U.S. Government Accounting Office warning "that automotive batteries are not well developed, fueling and repair infrastructure is lacking, safety and environmental effects are not known, production costs are high and the market potential is uncertain."[68] He further added that the government should be mandating clean air and not the technology to achieve it. It was also felt at the time by persons actively involved in the research and development efforts in both private and public partnerships, that technological improvements in the ICE would bring emissions down close to zero. These factors led in part to CARB backing away from and revising some of the mandates in 1996.

Since sales were not meeting expectations, banking and trading emission credits provided flexibility among the manufacturers to balance their inventories and still meet the letter of the regulations. For each vehicle sold, CARB gives the company a ZEV credit, which can be sold to any of the Big Seven manufacturers (Ford, General Motors, Nissan, Chrysler, Honda, Toyota, Mazda) for $5,000. In 1996 CARB voted unanimously to do away with the requirement that 2 percent of automotive sales for 1998 be ZEV and 5 percent for 2001. In 1998 automakers convinced CARB to relax the standards by postponing the 10 percent quota until 2003 and allowing 6 percent of the 10 percent quota to be made up of partial zero emission vehicles (PZEVs). In 1998 CARB allowed partial credits for vehicles that achieved near-zero emissions, such as hybrids, and those meeting a new standard for super ultra low emission vehicles (SU-LEVs). In 2000 CARB announced it would allow carmakers to substitute up to 2 percent of the 4 percent ZEV quota with Advanced Technology Partial Zero Emission Vehicles (AT-PZEV). This would allow the acceptance of cleaner engines due to reformulated gasoline, and hybrid and fuel cell vehicles could be counted as part of the solution. To qualify for PZEV status, the vehicles must meet three criteria: (1) meet the SU-LEV standards, (2) have zero evaporative emissions, and (3) ensure 150,000-mile warranty on emission control equipment. These decisions slightly favored the manufacturing industry, while recognizing that then-current "state of the art" battery technology was not yet marketable. CARB offset the possible reluctance by the manufacturers to produce more ZEVs by offering to provide funds to consumers who purchased or leased ZEVs prior to 2003. The initial cost of the vehicles' manufacture required subsidies from California as high as $10,000 to $20,000 per vehicle sold.

In 1999 the Environmental Protection Agency proposed new regulations—effectively a de facto adoption of CARB's requirements—as a national standard.[69] Little progress was made, and in 2000 the House and Senate cut the $1.25 billion subsidy for alternative fuels in half. *Business Week* reported, "Representative John Sununu (R–N.H.), who led the charge to slash the project, says the success of the Insight and Prius demonstrates why subsidies won't work. 'It may well be precisely because the federal government has been subsidizing certain areas of innovation that we're behind the Japanese.'"[70]

In late 2000 CARB advanced the target date of ZEVs to 2007 with the hope of seeing 14,000 annual sales by year 2012. All its efforts went toward a battery solution. It did not promote the sales of alternative hybrid vehicles to help accomplish the goal. New battery technology, such as NiMH and lithium ion batteries, costs more and will not be purchased by manufacturers until the cost comes down. The cost won't decrease until suppliers launch volume production. The technology has not yet been able to produce an efficient low-cost battery to use for EV mass production. CARB's shortsightedness in supporting one energy alternative to achieve their ZEV goals resulted initially in less research being devoted to other power sources that could do more to reduce pollution in the long run. CARB temporarily lost its objectivity and global view for finding viable solutions. This resulted in its having to adjust target dates to give the industry more time to comply. Its view reversed by 2003 when it began backing fuel cell research. This adjustment makes it more probable that CARB may come close to the goal in 2012.

GM filed a lawsuit in 2000 claiming that CARB, as a state regulatory agency, has no authority to require a zero emission vehicle. A General Motors spokesman noted that the mandate would require the government to provide subsidies amounting to between $500 million and $1 billion annually. Dealers noted that consumer demand was not present because of the high price and short range and felt they would suffer, as the mandate only states the cars must "be available." Dealers have no way of knowing how many will actually be sold and eventually wind up on the road. In 2002 GM contracted another manufacturer to build NEVs that might help to meet California's ZEV mandate when the decision is made on what the mandate will specify. By dictating the process instead of ultimate environmental goals, California forces industry to follow specific types of technology solutions, instead of allowing the market to lead innovation and create products that move with the market economics, products that do not require tax subsidies to encourage industry to build them and consumers to buy them. Concerns about the economics of ZEVs illustrate the repercussions that government regulations can have on industry.

In January 2001 CARB revised its requirements from its original idea of 10 percent ZEVs to 2 percent ZEV, 2 percent hybrids and 6 percent natural gas or other clean-burning cars. The January 15, 2001, meeting of CARB readdressed the issue of selling EVs, not just making them available. The chairman of the board emphasized the word "sell" and not just "offer" vehicles to earn the ZEV credits. By 2002 many automakers had accumulated enough banked credits, many from the four credits earned by NEVs (neighborhood electric vehicles, like golf carts), to prolong any serious production of EVs through 2005 and beyond.

A short news article in *AutoWeek* (February 15, 2001) noted that CARB reduced the number of required ZEV sales in 2003 from 22,000 per year to 4,670. This was due to automakers' claims that no one was buying electric cars and the battery technology was not yet capable of satisfying consumers' needs. CARB claims it does not want to eliminate gasoline-powered cars, but to replace two of every one hundred. CARB maintains that mandates and subsidies should be used to correct consumers' and automobile makers' bias against the more expensive EV.

Support for state standards for that effort grew on the East Coast as well. By January 2002 thirteen northeastern states adopted the California standards, with only New York sticking to the 2 percent goal and imposing stricter limits than California.

A number of CARB staff "straw man" proposals were submitted in December 2002 to a workshop open to the public for discussion. The public had until the February 2003 board meeting to respond. The proposals included:

- Move the start of the mandate from 2003 to 2005. This could also allow manufacturers to extend the banking of credits to 2005.
- Lower the 2 percent ZEV requirement to 1 percent until 2012. During the interim, 2005 to 2011, automakers could split the 2 percent ZEV requirement into a 1 percent pure ZEV and 1 percent transitional EV section. This would allow hybrids to earn credit in the transitional portion.
- Split the "gold" section from 4 percent to 2 percent. This would allow advanced technology partial zero emission vehicles (AT-PZEVs), like the Honda Insight and the Toyota Prius hybrids, to get credits under the 2 percent status. The "gold" section is the top section for automaker credits. The change allows vehicles that are "transitioning" to zero emissions (for example, fuel cell vehicles) to be considered in the top tier, giving less

incentives for battery development for manufacturing plug-in and all other electric vehicles.

- Change the requirements for ZEVs to get credits. This would create a four-tier system of categorizing vehicles into NEV, City EV, Full Function EV and fuel cell vehicles. Each would be required to meet a specific mileage range. The NEV would remain the same, the City EV would need to get a 50-mile range, the Full Function EV would have a minimum of 120-mile range and the fuel cell vehicles would need a 100 mile range.[71]

March 2008's forum brought additional revisions to the 1990s mandate. They added the Enhanced Advanced Technology Partial Zero Emissions Vehicle (Enhanced AT-PZEV) to cover plug-in hybrids and hydrogen ICEs. The revision also carried a mandate for 66,000 plug-in hybrids to be available on the market "at a reasonable price." Because the cost for producing the plug-ins is more than the market would consider a "reasonable price," manufacturers will need to subsidize through sales from their other models. Bloggers had mixed reviews of the changes, most stating the need to have reasonably priced cars that can be refueled at convenient locations. The need to subsidize the ZEV and PZEV with profits from the more popular models was criticized.

As of April 2008, CARB reduced the number of ZEVs required to be sold between 2012 and 2014 to 7,500, far below the 25,000 established in 2003.

CARB continues to revisit its mandates, trying to find a balance between the goal of zero emissions and the ability of industry to meet the regulations. This flexibility on the part of CARB shows its willingness to cooperate with manufacturers during a period of new technology development, and demonstrates that it realizes merely instituting a mandate does not change the market. The move to putting more EVs on the road will be a slow and incremental process involving government standards, manufacturers, and consumers.

Government and Private Partnerships

In a 1980 study, the U.S. Department of Energy identified eighty-one attempts in which one or two hybrid electric vehicles were made to yield extra range.[72] The problem of increasing range is being approached today using hybrid engines, fuel cells and improving batteries. The Partnership for a New Generation of Vehicles (PNGV) was formed in 1993. It was intended to be a high-profile $250 million effort, funded by the Department of Energy, NASA, the EPA and the Departments of Defense, Transportation and Commerce, to promote hybrid electric vehicle (HEV) technology. The goal was to produce an 80 mpg family sedan. PNGV also included the Big Three automakers, who contributed about $500 million per year. The preferred HEV design is an electric car with a small internal combustion engine and an electric generator on board to charge the batteries. In addition to hybrid development, PNGV put efforts toward developing new batteries, focusing on replacing the lead-acid battery with NiMH batteries and encouraging manufacturers to develop technologies to make the HEVs more efficient. These include lighter-weight bodywork, more efficient gasoline and electric motors and better batteries and generators.[73] PNGV proposed to have test vehicles in 2004. The Freedom Car and Vehicle Technologies Program, begun in 2002, was the successor to the PNGV. President Clinton's project focused on hybrid car development, and President George W. Bush's on hydrogen fuel cell development. Each focuses on emission free, alternate-fuel cars and light trucks. The Freedom-

Car partnered the U.S. Department of Energy with U.S. Council for Automotive Research (USCAR), representing Ford Motor Company, DaimlerChrysler Corporation and General Motors Corporation. The initiative is putting its efforts into developing fuel cells. It considers this direction a better long-term solution to reducing oil dependence and eliminating harmful emissions. It puts 2010 as a target date to evaluate progress. The automotive industry supports voluntary programs such as the Partnership for a New Generation of Vehicles and Freedom Car that promote collaboration between industry and government. The Sierra Club claims this collaboration on battery and fuel cell development between industry and government is merely a "scam to keep regulation at bay."[74] Automakers like this type of program for its flexibility. It is not binding and they do not have to commit to mass production. They feel the arrangement allows them greater freedom to concentrate on improving product lines.

The U.S. Advanced Battery Consortium (USABC) was established in 1991 to improve the performance and range of electric vehicle batteries. It included three U.S. automobile manufacturers (DaimlerChrysler, Ford and General Motors), the Electric Power Research Institute, battery manufacturers and the U.S. Department of Energy (DOE). The consortium is investigating NiMH, lithium polymer and lithium-ion battery systems. Its goal is to accelerate EV acceptance and sales by supporting research and design in advanced battery systems and to help develop electric energy systems to be competitive with the ICE. USABC is now under the umbrella of USCAR (United States Council for Automotive Research), formed in 1992 by DaimlerChrysler, Ford and General Motors. Among its goals are cooperative efforts to share results of research projects, coordinate with PNGV and seek out funding for joint research and design from public and private resources. In May 2008, USABC and the U.S. Department of Energy contracted with A123 Systems to improve the lithium-ion battery used in hybrid cars by expanding the energy density for longer charges, reducing cost, and increasing abuse tolerance and durability. Emphasis continues on finding ways to improve batteries for use in cars and trucks. In her congressional testimony on October 3, 2007, GM's director for hybrid storage systems, Denise Gray, indicated that a 2009–2014 timeline for demonstration programs would be feasible, with early purchase programs for government to procure early plug-in models of the vehicles being part of the package, realizing that these vehicles would have greater cost than the current models.[75]

In 1992 California began CALSTART, a state-funded nonprofit consortium that called itself a "business incubator" for the alternative fuel automobile. Some members include the City of Camarillo; HaveBlue, LLC; and the California Electric Transportation Coalition. They concentrated on hybrid vehicles at the beginning, with an eye on developing the emission-free fuel cell in the not-too-distant future. CALSTART did run into opposition initially from some in the automotive industry who emphatically stated that battery technology for electric vehicles was not in place and it was impossible to comply with the California zero emissions mandates. Lobbying turned public opinion in the industry's direction, resulting in 1996 in modification of the requirements for 1998. Melanie Savage of CALSTART expressed concern about the amount of money being spent by automobile manufacturers on this anti–EV campaign, stating, "For every dime we [CALSTART] spent, they spent a dollar."[76] By 2008, CALSTART's emphasis had incorporated hybrid truck technology and offered expertise in using that technology in the military as well as the commercial and transportation sectors. Companies such as Peterbilt, International Truck and Engine Corporation, Ford, Kenworth, Volvo and Mack all had versions of hydraulic and electric hybrids in the works. Odyne Corporation of Waukesha, Wisconsin, concentrated on a plug-in hybrid utility truck, while Oshkosh Corporation offered an electric refuse collection truck and Oshkosh and Northrop Grumman supplied diesel-electric joint light tactical vehicles (JLTV) to replace U.S. Army and Marine Corps Humvees. Many companies worked as industry partners with CALSTART to make efficient hybrid options for both local and long-distance hauling and military transports.

The Southern Coalition for Advanced Transportation (SCAT) is a nonprofit technology consortium of more than sixty-five public and private institutions. SCAT provides mechanisms for business and government to bring together resources in electric and hybrid electric transportation technology research and to demonstrate direct market viability. It was formed to promote development and public acceptance of AFVs. Its members include such diverse companies as GM, Delta Air Lines, Advanced Vehicle Systems and various battery companies.

The Surface Transportation Efficiency Act of 1991 authorized $12 million for the Advanced Transportation and Electric Vehicles Program. Four consortia were selected to receive funds to promote the development of electric vehicles. These consortia were to be an example of public/private partnerships. They would receive 50 percent of their funds from non-federal sources.

- Chesapeake Consortium — Consisting of Westinghouse, DaimlerChrysler, Baltimore Gas & Electric and the State of Maryland, it received an initial $4 million from the Federal Transit Administration (FTA), $2 million from the state of Maryland and $4 million from other sources. It has concentrated on developing electric transit buses and school buses.
- New York State Consortium — Members include the New York Metropolitan Transportation Authority, GE and various utility companies. It received an initial $2.3 million from the FTA and a matching $2.3 million from non-federal sources. FTA supplied an additional $750,000 in 1995 with matching non-federal funds of $750,000. The New York State Consortium has developed a hybrid transit bus.
- CALSTART — Formed in 1992, it consists of forty public and private companies representing utilities and state, local and federal agencies. CALSTART initially received $4 million from the Federal Transit Administration and $2 million from the State of California. By 2001 it had received $11 million in federal funds and $22 million in state and local funds. It has completed over 140 public recharging stations in California, developed several electric buses and been instrumental in establishing EV components such as energy management systems, batteries and safety systems.
- Advanced Lead Acid Battery Consortium (ALABC) — Consisting of battery manufacturers and suppliers, it received an initial $2 million from the FTA with matching $2 million from local funds. ALABC is evaluating rapid recharge systems for electric buses.

The Advanced Vehicle Partnership (1998) was part of President Clinton's support for the development of hybrid engines. It teamed the U.S. Department of Energy, the U.S. Department of Transportation and the Advanced Transportation Technology Consortium. Its initial purpose was the development of electric propulsion systems and refueling/recharging stations. Its goal was to demonstrate 50 percent more fuel efficiency through hybrid engines for commercially viable buses, delivery trucks and municipal fleets. A second goal aimed at 30 percent fewer emissions below the 1998 standard. The federal government supplied $20 million to assist the research and development efforts.

One of the major partnerships among government agencies and private industry occurred just before the turn of the 21st century with the forming of the California Fuel Cell Partnership (CaFCP). Its purpose is to explore the viability of infrastructure technology and to increase public awareness by making fuel cell technology more visible. In April 1999, twenty-eight members, including auto manufacturers, fuel distributors, fuel cell manufacturers, and government and transit agencies, came together to work on fuel cell solutions in a real-world test to explore the viability of this technology for commercial use. GM and Toyota joined the CaFCP in October 2000, stating their belief that the activities of the partnership would ensure that consumers and the environment would benefit from advanced technologies. In early 2001 GM and Ford announced they would produce cleaner-burning hybrid gasoline engines for SUVs by 2004, improving fuel economy by 25 percent. This did not happen. CaFCP partners are actively looking for ways to make alternate fuel vehicles a market alternative.

Some agencies that provide funding for alternative vehicle research and development include:

- DOT's Advanced Vehicle Program
- CALSTART
- Alternative Fuels Infrastructure Development
- International Energy Technology Assistance Program
- Renewables Subject Area
- Energy Innovations Small Grant Program
- Public Interest Energy Research (PIER) Program
- Alternative Fuel Infrastructure Program
- Pennsylvania Department of Environmental Protection
- Clean Cities Organizations

Federal Incentive Programs

In 1995, one author wrote, "Government should be creating mechanisms such as taxes, tax credits, fees and marketable credits that marry technology and regulatory initiatives. This would lead to a more flexible, incentive-based public policy."[77] The Federal Transportation Efficiency Act of 1998, managed through the Department of Transportation, set aside $9.1 billion for addressing environmental problems and created the Advanced Vehicle Technology Program (AVP) to encourage the development of AFVs. The AVP is designed to work in conjunction with PNGV to advance technologies that will reduce vehicle emissions beyond the 2004 standards, provide a 50 percent improvement in fuel efficiency, promote a globally competitive U.S. industry in AFVs and increase public awareness and acceptance.

Federal transportation programs have been in effect for many years. The most recent are the Transportation Equity Act for the 21st Century (TEA-21) and the Federal Transit Act (FTA). TEA-21 was initiated in June 1998 as the successor to the Intermodal Surface Transportation Efficiency Act (ISTEA) to provide federal money for AFV projects. Three parts of the act, under the Federal Highway Administration's purview, are:

- The Congestion Mitigation and Air Quality Program (CMAQ), which funds projects that reduce carbon monoxide and small particle emissions. CMAQ will pay up to 80 percent of a project's cost, with the other 20 percent coming from non-federal sources.

- The Clean Fuel Formula Grant Program, which provides funding of $100 million per year to assist fleet operators in purchasing low-emission buses.
- The Access Jobs and Reverse Commute Program which provides grants to local governments to offer transportation services for welfare recipients for employment and support services. The idea is to provide a public transportation link for people transitioning from welfare to work. Funding for this program began in 1999 at $50 million with increases to $150 million by 2003. In 2008 $158 million was requested.

The Securing America Energy Act of 2001 was passed in August 2001. Its goal is to reduce dependence on foreign energy sources from 56 percent to 45 percent by 2012. Some of the highlights of the tax incentives include:

Battery Electric Vehicles (BEV)
- A 10 percent tax credit for low-speed BEVs (up to $4,000).
- A $4,000 tax credit for passenger vehicles and light-duty trucks with a driving range of at least seventy miles on one charge.

Fuel Cell Electric Vehicles (FCEV)
- A $4,000 tax credit for light-duty FCEVs.
- An additional tax credit of $1,000–$4,000 for vehicles that show a 150–300 percent increase in fuel mileage over that of fiscal year 2000.

Hybrid Electric Vehicles (HEVs)
- A $250–$1,000 tax credit for HEVs less than 8,500 pounds gross vehicle weight.
- An additional tax credit of $1,000–$3,500 for HEVs that show a 125–250 percent increase in fuel economy over that of fiscal year 2000.

Hydrogen research and design — Authorizes $250 million for hydrogen research for fiscal years 2002–2006.

Fuel cell research — Authorizes $84 million for a three-year research program.

Fleets — Requires the federal fleet program to increase acquisitions of alternative fuel vehicles by five percent by fiscal year 2005.

After four and one-half years of debate, the Energy Policy Act of 2005 was signed into law by President Bush on August 8, 2005. It specified tax credits through 2007 for HEVs, and possible state tax incentives and rebates. Credits ($250–$3,400) were based on the weight and fuel economy of the vehicle. Companies that purchased hybrid trucks also qualified. The bill brought in renewable fuel standards with its credits system to encourage new technologies by giving equivalencies to various alternative fuel sources. For example, one gallon of biodiesel would equate to 1.5 gallons of corn-based ethanol. Tax credits of up to 10 cents per gallon were available for agri-biodiesel producers. Fuel suppliers also benefited under this act. Refueling stations could claim a 30 percent credit for the cost of installing clean-fuel refueling equipment. This provision runs through December 31, 2010. To assist the over 600,000 owners of alternative fuel vehicles and prospective buyers in locating alternative fueling stations, the Department of Energy put up a web site, mapping locations for electric, natural gas (CNG and LNG), propane, biodiesel, ethanol and hydrogen. As of April 2008, there were more than 5,600 alternative fuel stations in the United States. Of those, 437 offered electric hookups, 789 CNG, 35 LNG, 2,279 propane, 644 biodiesel, 1,430 supplied E85, and 34 hydrogen. The top five states were: California with 859 (electric and propane being the main suppliers); Texas with 630 (propane and biodiesel being the main suppliers); Minnesota with 371 (with ethanol and propane being the main suppliers); Illinois with 240 (with ethanol and propane being the main suppliers); Wisconsin with 161 (with ethanol and propane being the main suppliers).[78]

In his State of the Union Address in January 2006, President George W. Bush introduced his Advanced Energy Initiative. Its goal is to provide support for new technologies to reduce dependence on foreign oil imports. Funding increases are provided for both the energy and automotive sectors. Other points are:

- $2 billion over the next 10 years for clean coal research ($281 million in the 2007 budget; $54 million devoted to the FutureGen Initiative, a public/private partnership to develop initiatives for emission-free coal plants)
- $148 million in the 2007 budget (an increase of $65 million from 2006) for the Solar America Initiative to advance the development of photovoltaic cells that convert sunlight directly to energy
- $44 million in the 2007 budget (an increase of $5 million from 2006) for development of low-speed wind energy research
- $150 million in the 2007 budget (a $59 million increase over 2006) for the Biorefinery Initiative to accelerate research of cellulosic ethanol to make it cost effective by 2012
- $30 million in 2007 (a $6.7 increase over 2006) to aid battery research for hybrid and plug-in hybrid autos
- $1.2 billion Hydrogen Fuel Initiative with $289 million included in the 2007 budget ($53 million increase over 2006) to accelerate the development of hydrogen fuel cells and affordable hydrogen powered cars through private sector partnerships and the Freedom-Car programs.[79]

By 2006, the interest in buying hybrids was established and the incentive tax breaks moved from tax deductions (a straight $2,000 deduction) to tax credits (IRS Form 8910) and the process became more complex. It relied on the make, model and year of a vehicle to assess the amount of credit that could be claimed. For example, a taxpayer who purchased:

- a two-wheel-drive Chevrolet Silverado Hybrid pickup could claim $250
- a Ford Escape Hybrid could claim $2,600
- a Mercury Mariner Hybrid 4WD could claim $1950
- a Honda Insight CVT could claim $1,450
- a Toyota Prius could claim $3,150.[80]

The credit could be applied only to a new hybrid purchase that was purchased no later than one calendar quarter after the hybrid manufacturer sold its 60,000th car. The credit looked at fuel economy and the lifetime fuel savings projections. The calculation was based on a comparison of the hybrid's fuel efficiency and the efficiency of a 2002 ICE vehicle based on city driving. The lifetime fuel savings ranged from 1,000 to 3,000 gallons of gasoline. Credits for fuel economy went to a maximum of $2,400 and for lifetime fuel savings up to $1,000. Taxpayers subject to the Alternative Minimum Tax (AMT) were not allowed to use the credit.[81] The amount of credit depended on the model and year of vehicle, and how many of that model and year were sold.

Even with the Energy Policy Act of 2005, which included tax credits for hybrid car buyers, the money recovered through greater fuel economy does not match the amount spent to purchase a hybrid.

The Energy Independence and Security Act of 2007 was also intended to reduce our dependence on foreign oil through consumer awareness, fuel economy credits, guarantee loans, prize monies, grants for infrastructure development of biofuels, and countless reports and feasibility studies on alternate fuel endeavors. Some of the provisions are:

- Increase in CAFE standard (combined city and highway) to 35 mpg by 2020.
- A new rating standard to be developed by the Department of Transportation to make comparison of fuel economy, greenhouse gas emissions benefits and alternative fuel use among various makes and models of cars and trucks easier for the consumer. This requires an agreement between the DOT and the National Academy of Science for developing an initial and subsequent report every five years through 2025.
- Extends fuel economy credits for flexible fuel vehicles through 2019. B20-capable (20 percent biodiesel and 80 percent diesel) vehicles are included.
- Authorizes a grant program for projects to encourage the use of plug-in EVs and other emerging EV technologies.
- Authorizes awards and loans for manufacturers (original equipment manufacturers) and component suppliers in the U.S. to assist them in producing standard-compliant vehicles and parts.
- Requires studies and reports on the impact of the renewable fuel standard, the challenges in increasing the amount of biodiesel and biogas and how the car's fuel system will be affected by these products,
- Amends Title I of the Petroleum Marketing Practices Act to prohibit future franchise agreements from containing provisions to restrict availability of biofuels at their stations.
- Authorizes a pilot program to establish refueling infrastructure corridors. Authorization is $200 million annually ($1.4 billion total) for the period 2008–2014.
- Requires each federal agency to install at least one renewable fuel pump at each federal fleet station by 2010.
- Authorizes cash prizes for research, development and demonstration for commercial applications of hydrogen energy technologies.

The Emerging Economic Stabilization Act, signed by President Bush, enacted the Energy Improvement and Extension Act of 2008. The act supports biodiesel production, extends the alternate fuel and alternate fuel infrastructure tax credits and provides tax incentives for purchasing plug-in hybrid electric vehicles.

- Extended the timeline for the Fuel Cell Motor Vehicle Tax Credit, which gives an $8,000 credit for the purchase of qualified light-duty fuel cell vehicles until December 2009. Beginning in 2010, the credit is reduced to $4,000, and it expires on December 31, 2010. Vehicle manufacturers must show compliance to the IRS before their vehicles can qualify for the tax credit. A similar credit is also available for vehicles burning compressed or liquid natural gas, hydrogen or fuel containing a minimum of 85 percent methanol. These Qualified Alternative Fuel Motor Vehicles (QAFMV) must have gone into service after January 1, 2006. Compliance to IRS Notice 2006–54 is required as it is with the fuel cell cars, and it also expires in December 2010.
- The Qualified Plug-in Electric Drive Motor Vehicle Tax Credit grants from $2,500 to $15,000 based on the vehicle traction battery capacity and gross weight of the vehicle. The credit phases out when 250,000 plug-in hybrid cars have been sold in the United States, and it will expire on December 31, 2014.

Utility Incentive Programs

A variety of utility companies in many states provide incentive programs. As with so many of the other incentives, the utility company incentives come and go. By 2008, many programs had run their course. Consumers looking for ways to maximize a conversion to an alternate fuel needed to look to state and federal programs for monetary assistance; consultations for business to explore their options became the way in which the utility companies met their obligation to contribute to alternative energy possibilities.

Some examples are:

- Colorado— Financial assistance for CNG fueling stations.
- Connecticut— Financial assistance for NGV purchases.
- Florida—$300 free CNG for private fleets. None in 2008.
- Illinois— Tax rebate of $1,500 on the purchase cost of a NGV. Private consulting firm offers feasibility studies for CNG refueling stations on a case-by-case basis.
- Maryland—$1,500 tax credit for hybrids. None in 2008.
- Mississippi— special rates for natural gas purchased as vehicle fuel.
- Montana— Ten percent tax credit on the purchase of an EV. None in 2008.
- North Carolina— Discounted charging rates for EVs. None in 2008.
- Oregon— A 35 percent tax buy-back credit on the purchase of an EV. None in 2008.
- Washington— A partner in the Seattle Clean Cities program offers assistance and refueling for natural gas vehicles.
- Wyoming— Ten percent tax credit on the purchase cost of an NGV. Assistance in converting vehicles to NGV and consulting services for alternate fuel comparisons.

Southern California Edison (SCE) operates one of the nation's largest electric car fleets. In 2000 SCE started an eighteen-month-long project to test a hybrid utility line truck. SCE, with additional funding from the Department of Transportation's Advanced Vehicle Program, began conversions of existing line trucks to hybrid vehicles using a battery pack and an internal combustion engine. In 2005, SCE introduced the hydrogen powered fuel cell electric DaimlerChrysler F-Cell to its work schedule, and began work with Chevron to build a hydrogen refueling station at SCE's Rosemead, California, headquarters.

Fleet owners benefited under the Energy Improvement and Extension Act of 2008 as well. They qualify for Alternate Fuel Excise Tax Credit, the Fuel Cell Motor Vehicle Tax Credit and the Qualified Alternative Fuel Motor Vehicle Credit (AQFMV). The Alternate Fuel Excise Tax Credit allows $0.50 per gallon of gasoline equivalent (GGE) for CNG and $0.50 per liquid gallon of LNG, LPG, and liquefied hydrogen. The credit expires on December 31, 2009, for all but the liquid hydrogen, which expires on September 30, 2014. Conditions and expiration dates for the Fuel Cell Motor Vehicle Tax Credit and the Qualified Plug-in Electric Drive Motor Vehicle Tax Credit parallel those for individual buyers.

Manufacturer Fleet Incentive Programs

- Ford has offered a $1,500 rebate on its Ranger EV pickup and $2,000 on all of its natural gas vehicles.
- GM has a variety of incentives for its EV1 and S-10 pickup. The 2007 "Fleet Retail Alter-

native" offered fleet customers cash incentives of $500 to $7,500 depending on model for both cars and trucks.
- Honda offers comprehensive collision and roadside assistance. In 2008, its Civic GX, Honda references the $4,000 federal tax credit.
- Toyota offered a home connecting device for its RAV4-EV.

City and State Fleet Funding

Fleets reflect the trends in the market as well as providing excellent testing grounds for durability and practicality of alternate fuel vehicles. States and cities struggle to find the most cost-effective vehicles to run in their fleets, and move toward those vehicles that offer the best reliability and value for the task at hand.

Idaho operates a central facilities area (CFA) as a home base for its fleet of EVs. It includes more than 1,100 buses and other vehicles ranging from carts to large trucks. Research is also being conducted on other vehicles, including passenger buses, using liquefied natural gas (LNG).

Idaho's INEEL (Idaho National Engineering and Environmental Laboratory) has been testing hybrid electric vehicles (HEVs) since 1984, and results show a constant gain in the trend toward improved energy consumption per kilogram of vehicle weight. It also participates in the Field Operations Program designed to test vehicles over several years of traditional real-world fleet-use operations. Infrastructure continues to be a key factor in the success of AFVs. INEEL established a compressed natural gas (CNG) fueling station in Idaho Falls in July 2001. The station is used to fuel the state's fleet of CNG light-duty vehicles and was planned to be available to regional businesses and the public.

Arizona Public Service (APS) in Phoenix, Arizona, began using electric vehicles in 1979, and in 2002 had over forty-one vehicles in its fleet. The vehicles have logged over 750,000 miles. Its fleet consists of GM's EV1, Solectria E-10, Chevrolet Electric S-10s and Ford Electric Rangers and is used on a daily basis by executive staff, meter readers and research and design departments. The object of the program is to test and evaluate electric vehicles in fleet use by collecting battery data and operation and maintenance data. In 1996 APS started a charger test project to explore the use of fast charging to extend battery life. The year 2004 saw INEEL and APS participating in a pilot project for creating and dispensing alternative fuel refueling services for hydrogen, compressed natural gas and a hydrogen–CNG blend. The plan dispenses fuels every day to provide energy for ICEs. The pilot uses Ford, Chevrolet, Dodge and Mercedes trucks.

The Salt River Project (SRP) in Tempe, Arizona, started an electric vehicle fleet in 1991 with four G-Vans and currently runs Ford Rangers and EV1s. By 1998 it had established eight recharging stations in convenient locations such as the Biltmore Fashion Square, Arizona Mills, Scottsdale Fashion Square and Fiesta Mall.

Electric Transportation Applications (ETA) is a private corporation in Phoenix, Arizona. It has offered fleet services to private and government fleet managers since 1996 to support electric vehicle fleets. It has coordinated the development of electric fire and rescue emergency vehicles, promoted infrastructure, and is supported by the Advanced Lead Acid Battery Consortium.

The State of Arizona 2008 Report showed that 3,554 (64.8 percent) of the fleet's vehicles were capable of running on alternative fuels, a five and a half percent increase over the previous year. In 2008, 90.3 percent of the vehicles purchased were AFV. The state has banked 950 credits toward the new vehicle purchase option. Ethanol (70 percent) and compressed natural gas (17.3 percent) are the most common fuels in the AFV fleet, with electrics (4.4 percent) and LPGs (6.3) making up the remainder.[83]

Southern California Edison (SCE) created its Electric Transportation (ET) division in 1991. In 2001 it operated about seventy EVs, and it planned an aggressive expansion of its fleet in the near future. The fleet includes the EV1, Chevrolet S-10, Chrysler EPIC, Honda EV-Plus and Toyota RAV4-EV. Meter readers, field representatives, service managers, mail handlers and security patrols use the vehicles on a daily basis. Primary testing and serving areas include battery and charger technology testing and SCE's "Pomona Loop," which is a twenty-mile urban driving test run. By 2009, SCE had incorporated hybrids, diesel electric hybrids and plug-in hybrids in its testing garage.

Potomac Electric Power Company (PEPCO), an investor-owned electric utility of Washington, D.C., and the state of Maryland, began its electric vehicle leasing program in 1997. It leased ten Chevrolet S-10 electrics to the federal Government Services Agency (GSA) and later supplied thirty electric S-10s to the Naval Public Works Center in Washington. PEPCO also purchased five S-10s in 1997, two of which are being tested by the DOE in Arizona. PEPCO has committed to encouraging the development of the necessary infrastructure for EVs. It is working closely with the DOE, EV America and the electric utility industry to promote fleet applications.

The Electricity Council of England promoted the practicality of electric cars by purchasing seventy Enfield 8000 vehicles in the 1960s to be used by the electric utility companies. During the same time, the Batronic Truck Company of England delivered electric trucks to the Potomac Edison Company in Maryland for fleet use. General Electric worked with Batronic from 1973 to 1983 developing passenger buses and fleet vans for the utility industry.

Federal Fleet Funding

Alternative fuels are as much a political as a technical issue. Those in favor of government involvement in industry see intervention with money and regulations as helping shape a future as they envision it. Those preferring less government involvement find the regulations and subsidies a drain on taxpayers' money and a hindrance to using research and development to create products consumers want and are willing to buy. Most agree that having economical, convenient, environmentally friendly personal transportation is the goal. The practicality of using a variety of fuels began with the first autos. In the early 1900s, Henry Ford, using private resources, experimented with soybean ethanol fuel in some of his early models.* Today, using government resources is common practice to further the use of alternative fuels, and governments, like the car industry, have short memories and tend to "reinvent" when forced to find solutions to problems or issues.

The Energy Policy Act of 1992 provided federal funds for alternative fuel vehicles for fleets. Some incentives for fleet operators included:

---

*He had a great fascination with soybeans, which he personally grew, and to his family's dismay, sometimes created soybean meals. He led the field in the use of soybean products to produce gasoline and plastics to be used in his vehicles.

- A 10 percent tax credit on the cost of an EV until 2004.
- A $100,000 tax deduction for alternative fuel refueling stations.
- A $2,000 tax deduction for converting vehicles to alternative fuels.
- Low-interest loans by the DOE whereby a state could provide 20 percent of the cost to implement alternative fuel vehicles for fleet use.

As of 1995, electric car buyers qualified for a 10 percent federal tax credit, up to a maximum of $4,000. Also in 1995, Vice President Al Gore, with the Big Three auto executives, announced a program to develop clean-fuel-burning cars that would get eighty mpg. This was in conjunction with an update of the Energy Policy Act of 1992. Part of the act required a 10 percent reduction in fuel use in the U.S. by year 2000 and a 30 percent reduction by 2010. The DOE failed to promulgate regulations by mid–1995 and manufacturers were given extra time to comply with the requirements for the model year 1996. The act also required the government to involve itself in providing a nationwide alternative fuels infrastructure. Title IV of the act provides for a financial incentives program for the states. Title V allows for credits for alternative fuel vehicles acquired beyond what is legally required. These credits could be sold or traded by fleet owners.

In 1996, Executive Order 13423, Strengthening Federal Environmental, Energy, and Transportation Management, addressed using alternative fuel vehicles for federal fleets in an effort to decrease U.S. dependence on foreign oil. The agencies were to show a two percent annual reduction each year in their consumption of petroleum, and a ten percent increase annually in use of the alternate fuels annually through fiscal year 2015; waivers were possible if the fuel was not available within a five-mile or 15-minute radius, or was cost prohibitive.

In 1998, Executive Order 13031 mandated that the DOE provide incremental funding to federal fleets of EVs under the Federal Alternative Fueled Leadership group. Under the Incremental Funding Program, the United States Postal Service (USPS) ordered sixty-one Chrysler EPICs, used in three fleets; the DOE ordered fifty-nine vehicles, used in eight fleets; and the Department of Defense (DOD) ordered forty-one vehicles for six fleets. Out of a total of 209 EPICS and Rangers, 59 percent experienced a variety of mechanical problems, primarily with battery packs, coolant pumps and wiring harnesses. Most of these problems were considered minor and were easily remedied. A survey of thirty-seven fleet managers taken in 2000 showed a positive response of 2 to 1. General positive comments included "very happy with vehicle," "ideal vehicle for mission," "very nice ride," "responsive," "perfect for our site" and "no complaints." General negative comments were "winter drains batteries quicker," "mileage not as good in mountainous areas," "distance a limitation," "looking at hybrids" and "lack of range."[84] DOE estimates there are more than 1,350 commercial and government fleets in the Washington, D.C., area using about 150,000 AFV vehicles.

Executive Order 13031 was replaced on April 21, 2000, by Executive Order 13149, Greening the Government through Federal Fleet and Transportation Efficiency. This new order removed the incremental funding, and:

- Required each agency to reduce its fleet's annual petroleum consumption by 20 percent by the end of FY 2005, compared with FY 1999 levels.
- Required agencies to increase the average EPA fuel economy rating of passenger cars and light trucks by 1 mpg by the end of FY 2002 and 3 mpg by the end of FY 2005 compared to FY 1999.

- Stressed the alternative fuel vehicle (AFV) acquisition requirements of the Energy Policy Act of 1992 (EPAct section 303), which states that 75 percent of the vehicles acquired by each agency should be AFVs.
- Required agencies to use alternative fuels to meet a majority of the fuel requirements of AFVs, rather than using alternative fuels only "to the extent practicable," as stated in Executive Order 13031.
- Encouraged agencies to team with state, local, and private entities to expand use of fueling at commercial facilities that offer alternative fuels for sale to the public.
- Increased the credit values for dedicated AFVs and zero emission vehicles towards fulfilling the AFV acquisition requirements of EPAct.[85]

In 2005, the U.S. Congress passed a law requiring the use of 7.5 billion gallons of ethanol as a gasoline additive annually, beginning in 2012. It was reported that "critics denounced the legislation as simply the latest in a long line of federal government subsidies for the ethanol industry, which they said amounted to billions of dollars a year."[86]

In January 2006, President Bush in his State of the Union address called for the development of new technologies, including ethanol production using "wood chips, stalks or switch grass." The president said, "Our goal is to make this new kind of ethanol practical and competitive within six years."[87] As yet, the general public is undecided about the president's endorsement of ethanol. E85 is not readily available in most states and is usually more expensive than gasoline. As of March 2007, about 600 of the 180,000 gas stations in the United States offered E85.

In June 2006 Japan announced it would be requiring all new cars to run on a mixture of 90 percent gasoline and 10 percent ethanol. The goal is to have all cars running on this mixture by 2030. The government claimed it undertook this policy to "fight global warming" and "make itself less dependent on foreign oil."[88]

Supporters of ethanol point to its production as a domestic product that creates new jobs from farming the corn to research and development of new products. Supporters of the ethanol production accuse oil companies of undermining the efforts to establish ethanol as a viable alternative to gasoline. They also claim that ethanol will have environmental benefits, as it will reduce greenhouse gas emissions by 12 percent. This has yet to be proved. Detractors also claim that it is too expensive to produce ethanol for a profit unless the government subsidizes it. The fight seems to have become more political than scientific. Time will tell.

Also in 2006, the military joined the green effort. The U.S. Air Force used 3.2 billion gallons of fuel in 2005, more than the rest of the federal government combined. The Air Force is testing a jet fuel made from natural gas and another derived from coal. The Army is researching hybrid and hydrogen fuel cell cars, possibly for a hybrid Humvee, and the Marine Corps is working on a hybrid combat vehicle, known as the Shadow Reconnaissance.

The power wielded by California in environmental concerns cannot be minimized. In March 2006, the U.S. District Court of Northern California ruled that the Department of Energy must mandate AFV purchases for both private and government fleets. The decision resulted in a new replacement fuel goal in March 2007 and extended the goal of the 1992 EPAct to 2030. A March 2007 modification also allows agencies to choose a fuel reduction option instead of purchasing AFVs. Using the option requires a waiver from the Department of Energy. The waiver states that the applicant must achieve an equivalent of having the mandated miles of AFVs running on alternate fuel 100 percent of the time. In January 2008, hybrids, fuel cell and advanced lean burning vehicles were added to the approved list.

In November 2006, concern for extending federal tax credits for hybrid vehicles prompted Toyota North America president Jim Press to call for an extension of tax incentives. There was a legal production limit of 60,000 vehicles that would be eligible for the tax credits. Toyota reached that limit by the summer of 2005. Hybrid sales of Toyota dropped by the fall of 2005 and the company claimed it was because of the reduced tax credit policies.

On April 2, 2007, the U.S. Supreme Court ruled that carbon dioxide (CO_2) could be defined as a pollutant. The ruling was in response to a lawsuit against the U.S. Environmental Agency brought by the State of Massachusetts regarding its refusal to regulate CO_2 as a pollutant under the federal Clean Air Act. This ruling is remarkable in that CO_2 is what humans exhale with every breath. Car companies are trying to balance the environmental impact of vehicles with price and performance. All alternative combinations of electric, biofuel, hydrogen, natural gas, and the like are being researched.

Meanwhile, in March 2007, the European Union (EU) established regulations to mandate the CO_2 emissions from cars. The numbers are determined by measuring the weight of CO_2 emitted from the tailpipe per kilometer driven. The EU established a prescribed fleet average of 130 grams per kilometer traveled (by 2012), with heavy fines for those who did not meet this standard. The limit allows heavier cars to have higher emissions balanced by lighter cars having lower emissions. By the time of the Frankfurt International Motor Show in September 2007, carmakers were responding to the EU's mandate with new hybrids and also improvements in "new starter-generator technology, regenerative braking systems, efficient new engine concepts and low-rolling-resistant tires."[89] Manufacturers presented a number of eco-friendly, low-emission, and high-mileage green vehicles.

The Toyota Prius comes in at 104 grams per kilometer and the Volkswagen Polo and GM's Opel Corsa Hybrid EcoFlex were the lowest, at 99 grams per kilometer, with the Ford Focus ECOnetic at 115 grams per kilometer. In the U.K., cars emitting more than 225 grams per kilometer will be fined an annual tax equivalent to about $420. Politicians in Germany were looking to increase this tax in the next few years to possibly $4,000.

To put a little perspective on this mandate, some other CO_2 emitters include;

- A Boeing 747 releases 125,000–135,000 g/km
- The Queen Elizabeth II cruise ship: 900,000 g/km
- The London-to-Paris Eurostar electric train: 1521 g/km
- The world's livestock industry: 4.5 billion–6.5 billion tons of CO annually[90]

With regulation and policy emphasizing energy use and alternative energy development, one factor has slipped through the cracks—the quiet. One of the marketing benefits and one of the safety considerations for electric vehicles is their lack of noise. For persons who enjoy a quiet ride and those living near busy streets, the quiet is an added benefit beyond the energy efficiency; for those without sight, the quiet is a menace. For them, there is no warning that a vehicle is coming. Like the adjustment to make curbs at street corners into ramps for those in wheelchairs without taking into consideration that the curb was a safety guard for the visually impaired that indicated the sidewalk ended, the quiet of the electrics may have to have some adjustment in the cause of safety to make sure pedestrians are aware of oncoming quiet cars.

Cooperation, coercion and partnerships between government and industry provide incentives for change. Their impact is seen in technological development of fuel cells, batteries and alternate fuel sources and in government, utility and manufacturer fleet projects. There is interest in promoting marketable alternatives to the traditional ICE that will be kinder to the environment.

3

ENVIRONMENT

In 1977, a proponent wrote, "Civilized is the word for the electric car, not only because it is environmentally clean, but also because it conveys the impression of friendliness and serenity. They offer efficient transportation, yet still they proceed with civility and show compassion for lovers, joggers, bicyclists and walkers."[1]

Families love their vehicles. Whether the vehicles are powered by gasoline, natural gas, hydrogen or electricity, they have become part of our culture and our public environmental concern. They symbolize our independence and freedom to move where we want, when we want. Discussions about the use and type of automobiles reflect our society's wants and fears as we try to protect our independence and freedom while still sustaining a healthy environment. Ride sharing and carpooling programs over the years have failed because people want independence and individual automobility.

Why would people want to buy a hybrid car? "Go back a few years, and hybrids were a political statement," says Kate McLeod, author of the newspaper column GirlDriverUSA. "Owners were more emotionally involved in the idea of these cars, seeing them as a solution to the problem of pollution, oil lust and global warming."[2] But today, given a choice between fuel economy and horsepower, many people will choose more horsepower. Given the choice of whether to use hybrid technology to maximize fuel economy or acceleration, acceleration wins. Cars and SUVs like the GMC Yukon found best sales when they wedded larger engines to boost horsepower with hybrid technology. The hybrid came with an added benefit of approximately 25 percent greater fuel economy. Persons like Scott Nathanson, member of the Union of Concerned Scientists, considers this a "meager improvement in fuel economy"[3]; people who bought those models obviously disagreed. People choose cars that feel right for them. Jim Crockett, editor-in-chief of *Consulting-Specifying Engineer*, made the decision to buy a small, fuel-efficient car. He thought he had his heart set on a Honda Civic, but after driving one, he felt there "was no chemistry." He opted for a Mazda 3 instead, "because frankly it was much sportier — and also had 'zoom-zoom.'"[4]

So the "chemistry," or "love," or satisfaction one gets from one's car is clearly important. Statistics from the U.S. Department of Transportation show that "Americans drive an average of 29 miles and spend some 55 minutes a day in their vehicles."[5] Unlike producers of refrigerators or toothpaste, car manufacturers have to cater to the "chemistry" (love) element. It may be as simple as knowing the car has a reliable heating system and a comfortable ride, or the aesthetic appeal of the car's styling. How many are successful? Maybe very few. As expressed by Denise McCluggage, race car driver and author, "most drivers never experience that emotional connection because they are wheel holders, not drivers."[6] Nonetheless, it is there.

The number of persons owning cars has grown exponentially with growing economies. In 1911 there were 578,000 automobiles in use in the United States, with 70,000 in New York and 40,000 each in Pennsylvania and California. In 1930, Minnesota had 744,000 registered vehicles. Today, there are between 150 and 200 million vehicles in the United States, 18 million vehicles in Canada and about 100 million vehicles in Europe. In China in 2007, 60 percent of the population owned cars. In 2006 China topped 200 million in sales, an increase of 1.5 million over 2005. During that same time period, people in India bought 1.2 million cars, and the figure was predicted to increase by ten percent annually by 2010. In 1950 the world's population was 2.6 billion people and 50 million cars. Fifty years later, there were six billion people and 800 million cars. The population doubled while car ownership rose over tenfold. By 2007 there were 120 cars for every 1,000 people worldwide. The world's car manufacturers produced over 50 million vehicles per year, and, as economies in developing countries grow, more people want more cars. Economists estimate that when the average annual family income in a country reaches $6,000, car sales rise dramatically.[7] As countries' economies prosper, their car owners move from economy models to the larger and more luxurious models. India has been a leader in the purchase of small economy cars like the Altos and the Santios. As India's economy builds, Indian car buyers are looking for SUVs and the more elegant BMWs, top-of-the-line Hyundais and other autos in that class. This growth is also affecting the hybrid market. Even with the higher cost of a hybrid, markets are beginning to appear in Latin America and Asia. Mexico, for example, has dealerships offering the Honda line; Toyota is moving its Prius into China. For the entry-level buyer, there are incentives for starting with electrics. Chile's largest power company, Chilectra, offered its customers a deal in 2007. Customers who purchased Zap electric scooters could finance the bikes on their utility bill. Offering the same option to customers who purchase Zap's e-cars is expected to be the next step. Governments in these developing countries want to attract manufacturers, and it is likely that the automobile industry will expand rapidly as these local economies grow around the world.

How will this automobile expansion affect the global environment? Cars are big producers of carbon emissions, which some environmentalists point to as affecting climate change. Today's urban areas are growing at a 66 percent property use rate and an 89 percent population rate, but suburbs are still a popular place to live and people in America are not giving up their cars, nor are our world neighbors. Other options need to be examined. Using technology is one viable alternative; developing cleaner-burning gasoline and alternate fuel ICE engines and introducing hybrids and EVs should help reduce the amount of harmful emissions. The SmartWay Fuel Economy Guide emerged from the United States Environmental Protection Agency in 2007, giving consumers another set of purchasing standards. This guide gives ratings based on CO_2 emissions per mile, along with the more traditional tailpipe emissions and fuel economy. Carbon dioxide emissions and tailpipe/fuel efficiency are rated on a scale of 1 to 10 each (10 being the best). A score of 13 or higher (e.g., 6 in CO_2 and a 7 in tailpipe/fuel economy) earns the car a SmartWay seal.

Brazil decided that alternative fuel would be the best option. The country chose to build an ethanol infrastructure using its vast sugar cane crop. Since 1977, the Brazilian government required a mandatory 20–25 percent blend of gas and ethanol. By 2006, over 5 million cars in that country were flex-fuel. That same year, Volkswagen Brazil became the first auto manufacturer to move to an all-flex-fuel line, halting production of the gasoline-only cars. Brent Dewar from GM took his experiences with ethanol in Brazil back to the U.S. to promote the concept in GM's line. Other American companies such as Brenco (AOL founder Steve Case is one of their initial investors), GE, BP, Du Pont, and Archer Daniels Midland became investors in the alternative energy boom. China Agri, China's largest processor of agricultural products, expanded its product line to include biofuels in 2007. Investors from Scandinavia, Germany and the Middle East joined in the belief that this market strategy will pay off. In India, a car was invented that runs on compressed air. The Asian market expansion has the benefit of already having leaders in the Japanese and Korean hybrid auto industry. The developing markets are moving in many directions—more efficient ICEs, hybrids, alternate fuels and electric. As with any developing technologies, the market will find which solutions best fit the needs of the various economies.[8]

But just expanding the options available for auto buyers is not the only change needed. If electrics are to be an option, where is that power going to originate? There are still questions about how to produce the electricity needed to power the electric vehicles without adding more pollution, and how to dispose of batteries, tires, and other waste in an environmentally friendly way. Partnerships among manufacturers and government agencies are forming to find solutions to lessen the environmental impact caused by increased demand and auto ownership. Those who favor electric remind those promoting ethanol to reduce CO_2 emissions that they must also take into account the carbon dioxide emissions which occur during cultivating, producing and transporting ethanol. With utility companies finding more efficient and less polluting ways to make electric power, the carbon trade-off gap lessens among the alternate fuels. The energy industry continues to find different paths that will allow car buyers to have choices that minimize impact on the environment.

Persuading both new and return buyers to consider nonpolluting vehicles is a key factor for those wanting to protect the environment. In the early years, electric automobiles were seen as the solution to horse pollution and the noise and fumes of their ICE counterparts. The environmental problems that accompany our favorite form of transportation have changed only in degree. It is obvious that cars have had and will continue to have an adverse affect on air quality. John Barber of the Toronto *Globe and Mail*, wrote in a 1999 article:

> But, we would never dream of giving them up, let alone using them less. The current fascination with new gizmos actually disguises the incredible advances in conventional technology that have occurred over the past 20-odd years. Unfortunately, the explosion in car use over that same period of time has virtually cancelled out all environmental benefits we might otherwise have gained.[9]

Emission patterns in the United States provide a guidepost for air quality concerns for emerging markets, but an economic plateau must be reached before concern about environmental impact becomes a public issue in those countries. It has been clear that at some point, if we want to protect the environment, we must change attitudes about car use, including increasing fuel efficiency, improving the design of the ICE automobile, and expanding options for our energy sources. As with the international market, the U.S. is incorporating biomass into its energy production. This fuel source has the advantage of being domestic and renewable. It is also versatile. Biofuel provides a technology transition to hydrogen as an avenue of energy for autos directly, by using gasification, or indirectly, by using it to produce liquid alternatives to gasoline (methanol, ethanol, bio-oil, and so on). A number of these emerging markets are jumping ahead, seeing the benefits of incorporating environmental positives with the expanding market for vehicles in both their public and private sectors. Attitudes in the United States and markets worldwide are adjusting to the many alternative energy possibilities.

The U.S. transportation industry is about twenty years ahead of other industrialized countries in emissions volume. Carbon emissions from U.S. motor vehicles contribute to about 5 percent of the world's total carbon emissions, more than any other industry sector, including the airline industry.[10] As nations grow into economic viability, the people in them tend to use public transportation less and buy individual vehicles more. Environmental concerns evolve after a level of economic prosperity has been reached. It is predicted that by 2015, 90 percent of the oil in the Middle East will go to the Far East. Most Asian nations will be growing economically and, as they become more affluent, will use more oil and gas for energy for personal transportation. Europe, with over a century of automotive experience, is a leader in recognizing the damage done to our environment by engine emissions and is promoting a number of environmentally friendly transportation policies to discourage the use of private automobiles.

The international environmental community targeted carbon dioxide as a major pollutant and began working on a clean air initiative. One approach requested that countries work together to cut back on carbon dioxide emissions. The Kyoto agreement (1997) was one result of their efforts. It bound the signers to reduce their CO_2 emissions back to the levels of 1990. There is much disagreement among nations about the effectiveness of this agreement as there were no provisions for enforcement and it did not bind emerging nations to the same standards as those who have long-standing use of fossil fuels for energy production. Many nations, particularly in Europe, chose to sign the agreement with a goal of cutting greenhouse gases eight percent between 2008 and 2012; the United States did not sign.

Those who signed the agreement attempted to find reasonable ways to comply with their commitment. To assist companies in the European Union, the EU emissions trading scheme (ETS) was introduced. This created a pricing structure for carbon through the establishment of a liquid market for emission reductions. Prices were based on supply and demand in the marketplace. This liquidity allows companies to bid on allowances per ton for CO_2 emissions. The logic behind the process is that companies that have low emissions are able to sell their allowances, so even if the buyer has not decreased emissions, the emissions are still offset by the seller.

Shortly after the treaty was signed in 1997, questions of its true effectiveness or value emerged. One area that raised some suspicion was this emissions trading provision. Heidi Bachram, in her article "Climate Fraud and Carbon Colonialism; the New Trade in Greenhouse Gases," calls the process a "permit to pollute."[11] Her view is simple and straightforward — turn away from using fossil fuels. She considers carbon trading to be part of the problem, creating escape routes for countries and corporations that are already the heaviest polluters and not providing incentives for emerging nations to adopt cleaner energy avenues or protections against fraud in credit trading. The credit process involves assigning the greatest polluters a number of credits based on units of greenhouse gases (one ton of CO_2 emission equals 1 credit) emitted in 1990. This establishes the amount of emissions that country may continue to emit. If they don't use that amount, they can bank or trade the excess or purchase credits from others to offset their polluting. One loophole involves companies investing in new enterprises in other countries and applying those new facilities emissions to their total, making it unnecessary for them to update the old plants. Other strategies allow planting trees or using wind energy to offset the pollution coming from outdated fossil fuel facilities. Pollutants are interchangeable and there is little oversight on the process internationally, making fraud quite tempting.

By 2006, the phrase "carbon neutral" had been added to our cultural vocabulary. This concept allows a trade for environmental impact. For example, one might buy an SUV and then contribute money to an organization that reforests somewhere on the planet. One company of many, TerraPass.com, provides visitors to its website with a means to calculate the amount of a donation. They just type in the make and model and the number of miles they drive per year and the calculator comes back with a dollar amount for the person to donate to their favorite green organization. By 2008, a number of similar sites had emerged. The term "carbon neutral" became so popular and was used with such regularity that it was added to the New Oxford American Dictionary, defined as "a lifestyle sensitive to climate damage."[12]

The European Union is cooperating with automakers to reduce carbon emissions in new cars.[13] Germany, in particular, has committed to supplying 10–30 percent of its energy from renewable energy resources, such as wind farms.[14] It made good its commitment and, by 2006, became the world's largest producer of energy through wind power. In 1999, Denmark established CO_2 quotas and emission trading and banking allowances for its electricity generating industries. Its goal was to reduce carbon dioxide emissions by 20 percent by 2005 through energy savings and increased use of combined heat and power and renewable energy. The difficulty with managing these projects is reflected in the impact of consumers' need for power. Denmark's program experienced a setback in the period 1994–97 when increased energy was needed for export to Sweden and Norway. Low rainfall during those years in Sweden and Norway, which rely on hydroelectric power as their main energy source, meant that they needed power exported from Denmark to meet their energy demands. This unexpected claim on Denmark's electricity output caused Denmark to have to use less-efficient outdated coal-fired power plants for that period of time to meet its contracts. During this time, Denmark also adopted the European Union CO_2 Quota Act, which allowed power companies to balance emissions between electric and heat generating facilities, or bank credits if the quota had not been reached for that year. The trading is done among electricity producers without government intervention. As of 2002, no trading had taken place.[15]

These efforts are counterbalanced worldwide by the growing use of more traditional energy sources in the emerging economies. As nations improve economically, more power is required to meet new demands and people move to individual automobiles instead of relying on public transportation. Despite efforts among more-established industrial nations to promote the need for adherence to strict environmental quality standards for the burgeoning markets and the increased development of alternate fuels, we can assume, based on existing buying patterns for ICEs over alternate fuel vehicles, that the buying trend will duplicate the U.S. pattern initially. This trend will lead to more carbon emissions globally and the need to address its impact on the world's air quality.

Advocates for the global warming theory are renewing interest in alternative fuel vehicles. In 1998 supporters stated that, given the current patterns of fossil fuel use worldwide, by 2050 we will see dramatic climatic changes causing drought in the Amazon, Mediterranean and eastern U.S. The weather changes experienced in 1998 due to Hurricane Mitch and excessive flooding in China and India were just the beginning, according to this environmental faction. These extreme weather patterns reflected the effects of the excess in carbon dioxide (CO_2) emissions from ICEs and utility plants from thirty years earlier. The global warming theorists see a pattern of increased CO_2 from ICEs and the corresponding cycle of rising temperatures caused by the greenhouse effect, leading to decreased rainfall and a shortage after 2050 in plants to absorb the extra CO_2. They predict this will magnify the greenhouse effect for the second half of the 21st century, resulting in droughts, killer storms and widespread disease.[16] Many adhering to this theory see the agreements made by the scientists of the Intergovernmental Panel on Climate Change in 1990, the Rio conference in 1992 and the Kyoto Agreement in 1997 to be very slow-moving, and consider them effective only in their efforts to create a groundwork for much-needed worldwide regulation on the use of fossil fuels. By 2008, the early believers' contention that auto emissions were the sole cause of global warming was tempered as other scientists and climatologists who saw the climate changes as part of a natural cycle began being heard. Rhetoric changed from *global warming* to *climate change*. The shift did little to alter the growing concerns for the need for more alternative fuel vehicles because, by 2008, oil prices had jumped worldwide, causing increases in the price of gasoline at the pump. In the U.S. prices had climbed to over $4.00 a gallon. Public outcry pressed utility companies, auto manufacturers and the government to identify and put monies toward developing alternative energy sources, both to curb rising costs and to ensure national security against dependence on foreign oil.

Both private enterprise and government responded. Many businesses saw the advantage of "going green." Some hotels and spas allowed free parking for hybrid cars and offered carbon credits by which their guests could offset travel emissions by contributing to Carbonfund.org. These businesses opted for environmentally friendly landscaping, water conservation, solar power, and biodiesel fleets. Residential planners also moved green with porous surfaces on their roadways, floors made from recycled tires, and roof solar panels to generate energy for electric cars.[17] Legislation to improve fuel economy also flourished. The Markey-Platts Bill (H.R. 1506), for example, updated the CAFE standards and was signed into law in December 2007. It stressed both an energetic timeline for improving fuel economy and the need for our military to be independent of reliance on foreign nations for energy supplies. The environmental tax was introduced in the European Union as a new revenue stream, with energy taxes representing 77 percent of environmental taxes (five percent of the total taxes and social contributions) and transportation taxes representing 20 percent of the total environmental tax revenues (1.3 percent of total taxes and social contributions) with pollution and resource taxes making up less than three percent of the rest.[18] The global warming theory (probably helped by the rising cost of gasoline) renewed interest in alternative fuels for the automotive and transportation industries.

Pollution Problems

Environmental issues have been a part of the story of the automobile from its inception. In New York and Chicago in 1890, horse-drawn carriages were as major a traffic problem as cars are today. They were "bumper to bumper," or nose to carriage. Crossing the street in front of mammoth draft horses and avoiding the pollution of manure was a daunting effort. There were ordinances concerning where horses could be stabled to protect the citizenry against possible disease. Although these restrictions were necessary, they were inconvenient. Persons wanting to use public carriages had to wait for livery to arrive from these set-apart areas. Street cleaning in the 1890s was a major industry in New York City, employing 1,600 men engaged in removing 1,035 cubic yards of sweepings per day and carting them to the dump. The average cost for this service was eighteen cents per cubic yard.

The advent of the horseless carriage was expected to reduce this expense considerably. The horseless carriage was looked upon as an environmental godsend. Not only could it be conveniently housed, but there was no need for street cleanup after it passed, and it decreased the need to find places to dispose of the stables' by-product — manure from thousands of draft and carriage horses. A *New York Times* editorial in 1899 suggested "automobilitors" have the right to freedom of the road, and moreover not they, but users of horses, should be paying fees to use the roads: "Horses' [owners should] be charged a license to travel upon the parks and boulevards, inasmuch as they are a source of considerable expense to the public in wearing out the surface of the streets, and causing a considerable additional expense in maintaining forces of men to keep the roadways clean over which they pass."[19] An analysis by *Scientific American* in 1899 discovered that two-thirds of the dust and mud in city streets was caused by horses. The writer concluded that if automobiles could replace the horses, two-thirds of the dirt in cities would disappear. It was also estimated at the time that a horse would eat 12,000 pounds of food a year, or about five acres. The article stated that the ten million horses in the United States provided employment for thousands of stable and street cleaners, and that the iron hammered out for horseshoes by blacksmiths in one year could be turned into 40,000 farm tractors or 60,000 motor vehicles.

Converting from horse to automobile would clear mud and dust pollution in the local environments, but other pollutants also brought distress to the public. Probably the first recorded complaint about automobile air pollution came in 1900 from Burton Peck. Peck had made two gasoline-powered vehicles, then stopped, saying, "There is one great obstacle that must be overcome and that is the offensive odor from gasoline that has been burned and that is discharged into the air. It is a sickening odor and I can readily see that should there be any number of them running on the street, there would be an ordinance passed forbidding them."[20]

Noise pollution was also becoming a problem. In 1899, the "noise and clatter" of horse-drawn carriages "which makes conversation difficult on many streets of New York at the present time will be done away with" by the nearly noiseless electric vehicle.[21] In a lawsuit in 1901 involving an electric vehicle, the judge advised the jury, "Much has been said about the swiftness of the vehicle and its relative freedom from noise. Within limits, freedom from noise is of very great moment to the whole community, not merely to the persons who use the vehicles, but persons living by the roadside and the persons who use the road."[22] Electric vehicles seemed to solve some of these problems. Ladies especially liked the quiet-running electrics. The New York Fifth Avenue trolley line service added electric vehicles to its fleet in 1904. "It is not probable that tracks can ever be laid in any part of Fifth Avenue, as public opinion as well as property holders are extremely opposed to it. There are no objections, however, to the noiseless and clean horseless [electric] omnibus, which will leave the street in good sanitary condition."[23]

"Electricity continues to assert itself as the most suitable power for city and suburban traffic. In the former, it is supreme and for suburban travel, it is growing in favor,"[24] an author asserted in 1904. A century later, Kevin A. Wilson, in an editorial in *AutoWeek* in 2002, illustrated that noise pollution is as much a part of the current environment as it was in the early 1900s. On a vacation in the Maine woods, Wilson discovered he could find no silence. ATVs, powerboats, Jet Skis, and so on all contribute to noise pollution near and within campgrounds to the point where silent campers can be disturbed even at night. He suggests this is a wonderful marketing opportunity for silent-running fuel cell electric-drive machines to provide "quiet transport through the wilderness."[25]

Roads in a constant state of disrepair were another early environmental issue. If roads were dirt, motoring autos created clouds of dust; if graveled, the small rocks would be kicked by tires to the neighboring fields, yards and walkways. Road repair became a public priority. Citizens banded together to improve the roads. Groups like the Good Roads Movement sprang up across the country. In the West in the early 1900s, the Iowa State Highway Commission opened a course in road building at the state college in Ames, Iowa. All across the country, motor vehicles were penalized through taxation for wearing out the roads faster than horse-drawn carriages. Electric vehicles were taxed at a higher rate because they generally weighed more due to the batteries, and it was assumed that the extra weight caused more wear and tear to the road surface. New York State appropriated $50,000,000 to be spent on roads in 1906.[26] There were 74,000 miles of roads and highways in the state; 38,000 miles were repaired and maintained under the "day work program," under which a person could work out taxes owed at $1.50 a day instead of paying the taxes in cash. From 1898 to 1906 the amount of money spent by towns, counties and the state amounted to about $11,508,000. These monies accounted for an estimated 16,000 miles of "good" roads in New York State. It was predicted that the appropriated $50,000,000 to be spent over a ten-year period would result in "perfect" roads from one end of the state to the other. Much time and expense went into keeping the roads maintained to promote a safer, cleaner environment.

By 1909 road resurfacing was a serious problem throughout the country. Many of the highways were being surfaced using John L. MacAdam's process of layering small stones on the roadbed and binding them with tar or asphalt. The auto caused the greatest damage to the macadamized road surfaces. The initial breakdown of the surface, when it was first noticed, was called "suction." This occurred when rubber tires picked up the finely crushed binding material of the surface and threw it to the rear, exposing the broken edges of the top layer of macadam. These loosened "marbles" would in turn be broken down and again picked up by passing vehicles and thrown by the wind into adjacent fields, lawns or other property. Chains and other nonskid devices on tires intensified this effect. The damage was accelerated by the road's popularity. So many automobilists were attracted to the new macadamized roads that, when a new stretch of highway opened up to the public, they would make a considerable detour just to drive on it instead of using inferior roads. This caused greater traffic volume and faster breakdown of the surface. With a high level of traffic, the underlying foundation of macadam was exposed much sooner than road builders projected and the roadways had to be rebuilt on an accelerated schedule. Legislation was considered that would limit the traffic or impose fines for speeding and using chains. Regulation was not pursued because it was recognized that this solution might slow the problem, but would not stop it completely. The only workable solution was to build more-durable highways that could stand up to the increased traffic demands. Engineers looked for a material that would shed water in the winter and prevent the surface from being ground up into dust in the summer. They began experimenting with tar, but found it almost more objectionable than the original material. Eventually, it was decided to use tar with a surface layer of sand, providing a crown to the surface that was sufficient to drain water. Even with this new approach, the roads needed day-by-day attention from repair gangs who continuously patched the surface and prevented the polluting of the adjacent roadsides.[27]

Hard-surfacing all roadways was not economically feasible, so auto enthusiasts looked for other possible solutions to reduce the dust churned up by the automobiles. It was noted that some cars running at high speeds were not accompanied by as much dust as others at lower speeds. *Motor World* magazine in 1909 suggested manufacturers should make designs tending toward the abatement of the public nuisance of dust. This would include devices on the front and rear of cars to accommodate the direction of air currents, and building highways with cohesive surfaces.

By 1917 the dangers of carbon monoxide from the internal combustion engine surfaced as a topic of discussion. Deaths in garages were being reported as men worked on their cars' engines without properly ventilating the space where they were working. The running engines would consume oxygen and expel more and more of the harmful gas. The *New York Times* wrote, "Many persons have succumbed to its poisonous fumes, and scientists have given the cause of death from the gas the name of petromortis."[28] Media of the day encouraged their audience that auto maintenance be done in a well-ventilated area to prevent such carbon monoxide tragedies from happening.

During the world wars and the postwar era, concerns for sustaining a viable economy outweighed concerns about pollution-producing vehicles, but in the early 1950s industrial areas of the country were beginning to see haze in the air. Air quality became recognized as an important aspect for community health. Rachel Carson's *Silent Spring* (1962) reawakened awareness of the damaging effects our culture was having on the earth. In the late 1960s air pollution was the topic of the day. Advocates of electric vehicles at the time admitted that if it were not for air pollution, the interest in EVs would be nil. They also realized that some of the reduction in air pollution gained by driving EVs might be offset by the increased exhaust pollution from the generating plants needed to supply the energy for those vehicles. The federal government responded to the public's increased concern for air quality by passing first the Air Pollution Control Act of 1955, which identified air pollution as a national problem, and then the Clean Air Act of 1963, which set standards for power plants and later for automobile emissions. Having identified the issue, Congress did little to answer the post–World War II dilemma of how electricity to support battery-operated EVs on a large scale could be safely generated by power plants without having detrimental effects on the air, water or earth. In 1970, in an effort to address environmental quality, Congress and the executive branch of the government formed the Environmental Protection Agency. Its primary purpose was to develop standards for air, water and land quality. Environmental interests were surfacing to temper the needs of the economy.

Providing a lasting alternative, renewable energy source for vehicles continues to impede acceptance of environmentally friendly personal transport. Fossil fuels have brought their own share of problems for consumers, but not enough to dissuade the masses from the ICEs. At the time of the 1973–74 energy crisis, 6 percent of the world's population (the United States) consumed 40 percent of the world's oil. After the Watergate scandal, the public's trust in the federal government was waning. Environmentalists noted that the United States began decreasing oil imports in April 1973, and they demanded that Congress enact legislation requiring full disclosure of all oil industry data. The environmentalists suspected that the crisis was being artificially induced to raise consumer prices. They also lobbied to require auto manufacturers to produce cars with 20 percent more efficient fuel usage. The Federal Energy Administration did not ask Congress for gasoline efficiency standards or a horsepower tax, but suggested the auto industry should aim to increase gasoline efficiency by 1985.

During the same time period, the Environmental Protection Agency issued standards for automobile emissions to comply with its mandate to improve air quality. The standards, along with another oil crisis, demonstrated the government's interest in the potential for alternate fuels. Tax dollars were spent on researching the feasibility of electric and hybrid vehicles for commercial and consumer use. Research showed little support for the alternate fuel vehicles, and by the late 1970s, attention turned from EVs to encouraging more efficient ICEs. The efficient ICE continues to be a preferred economic choice for consumers. Air quality auto emission standards require engines to be more fuel efficient. The distinction between the environmental impact of the ICE or HEV versus electrics continues to narrow. For electrics to be the better option, clean-power generators must be available. Environmentalists are in strong disagreement about how that alternate power source might be established and maintained. A constant reliable energy source is key to the electric's feasibility and survival as the preferred "green machine."

In order to have power available to energize EVs as an environmentally friendly alternative to ICEs, a balance must be reached in generating the power needed to operate them. Sometimes laws and court rulings intended to improve the environment become far more influential than originally intended, and they may have a negative impact on the EV industry. Environmentalists, while being advocates for EVs, have thwarted the efforts to promote electrics by decreasing the expansion of the power stations needed to support the high volume of energy needed to keep electrics in service. Although using off hours for recharging vehicles at low-use hours, vehicle-to-grid (V2G) technology, and solar panels on personal and commercial buildings are altering the discussions, they are still not the mainstream energy pattern. Additional power must be available to support a wide-scale move to electrics.

There is much disagreement among environmental factions on how power might be generated, and whether private automobile ownership is in the public's best interest. The objections are varied. Hydroelectric power plants cover Indian ruins in Arizona, deplete salmon runs in the Pacific Northwest and generally disrupt the flow of wild rivers. The whirling blades of windmills can kill birds and bats, including protected species. Solar energy takes up too much land space. Geothermal sites are mostly in protected areas like Yellowstone and have a limited nonrenewable capacity. Coal-fired and natural gas plants are air polluters. Nuclear plants have the problem of waste product storage[29] and must overcome consumers' fear of reactor malfunctions, as occurred at Chernobyl and Three Mile Island, to be considered a viable choice.

Successful environmentalist lobbying was considered a major contributor to blocking the construction of new energy facilities during the 1990s while energy needs continued to increase. The 2001 brownouts in California are one example of negative impact. Clean air initiatives were again a topic of controversy in 2002 with the Bush administration bringing the "Clear Skies" initiative to the table. Its intent was to bolster and simplify the Clean Air Act. President Bush's proposal gave utility companies until 2018 to complete their major production upgrades to accomplish a 63 percent to 75 percent reduction, considered doable under their current technologies. Those opposing the plan supported the Clean Power Act sponsored by Senator Jeffords of Vermont. Jeffords' proposal contained a tighter timetable, proposing completion of from 75 percent to 90 percent reduction of harmful elements such as nitrogen oxide and mercury by 2007. Neither initiative was implemented. By 2008, estimates for power grids being able to support EVs had become more positive. If EVs could be recharged during off hours, the current energy flow could support the demand, due in part to an increase in alternate energy production and increased efficiency in fossil fuel utility companies. These new facilities were not without controversy.

In the summer of 2003, controversy arose on Cape Cod. Residents of the popular, scenic vacation area voiced opposition to Cape Wind Associates' being allowed to build 130 wind turbines approximately six miles offshore. Cables from the generating source would be routed to shore to the regional power facility. According to Cape Wind, the facility would offset one million tons of carbon dioxide and supply 74 percent of the energy needed for the area. Residents' concerns covered a wide spectrum, from politicians who objected to local jurisdictions' authority over regulating offshore wind turbines, to wind turbines on the horizon of a popular tourist spot, to environmental and commercial concerns about possible disruption of local oyster beds, estuaries and fishing areas. Mark Rogers of Cape Wind Associates believed this protesting to be a NIMBY (Not in My Back Yard) objection.[30] This observation has merit. In a 2007 survey of 600 Massachusetts residents, 81 percent favored the Cape Wind project; of those living on the island itself, 58 percent of the residents in the survey favored it. Although opinions differ on the amount and source of energy needed by our communities and the reluctance of some to agree to support new energy sources, it is a generally accepted belief that it is easier to control emissions from a utility plant that supports EVs than try to control people's use of their cars. Compromises must be reached if consumers are going to support nonpolluting alternatives to the ICE. Federal legislation is still pending, but according to a 2009 follow-up of the 2005 survey, the public's acceptance rate is increasing. To assist in raising financial backing for the Nantucket Sound project, the Massachusetts governor, Deval Patrick, is bringing Cape Wind and National Grid together in hopes of providing a buyer for the power generated by the Cape Wind's 130 turbine wind farm project. Getting the project completed before federal incentives disappear could save the project as much as $1 billion.

Other areas of the United States found more acceptance of wind farms. On the Texas plains, a wind farm went into production in 2008, helping to replace tapped-out oil fields. More than three percent of Texas's electricity, enough to supply one million homes, derived from wind turbines that year. Financier T. Boone Pickens announced in 2008 that he would build the largest wind farm in the world, a $10 billion venture that could power a small city.[31] (In July 2009, however, he postponed the project indefinitely.) Wind turbines on Louis Brooks's ranch in Texas are twice as high as the Statue of Liberty, with turbine blades as wide as the wingspan of a jumbo jet. As of 2008, he owns 78 wind turbines with plans to expand by another 76, and gets paid $500 a month for each one.

The number of wind farms was small in 2007, but it grew 45 percent by 2008. With a comparable growth rate over several years, it could make a vigorous contribution to the nation's energy supply. Wind power supplied about one percent of American electricity in 2007, the equivalent of powering 4.5 million homes. According to estimates by the American Wind Energy Association, wind farms power about 5 to 8 percent of the needs for Oregon, Colorado, Iowa and Minnesota. This has even garnered attention by some environmental advocates who predict wind power could supply up to 20 percent of America's electrical demands, as it does in Denmark. Opposition to wind farms is usually based in complaints about the windmills killing birds and bats, or that they are eyesores, or, as in the Cape Cod area, harmful to wetlands.[32]

Wind power does have challenges beyond those raised by some environmentalist groups. One potential problem is the transmission of the electricity generated. The windiest part of the United States is the central plains, from Texas north to Montana and the Dakotas. Most power is needed in the densely populated cities on the East and West Coasts. Is it worth exploring wind power for transport to those coastal locations, or should efforts be put toward other options?

For those who venture forward and are considering personal wind turbines to locally power homes, institutions or businesses, the actual mechanics of the structure need to be taken into account. Carleton College, in Northfield, Minnesota, found out through experience that there is more to operating the turbine than just erecting the structure. The college decided that wind energy might help the campus to go green and lessen carbon emissions. The college began with one unit costing $1.5 million. This cost was to be offset by the revenue-generating possibility of selling an average of $20,000 per month back to the local power company. A warranty was included in the turbine's initial cost, but when a mechanical failure caused a shutdown just three years into its 25-year life expectancy, the college found that it did not cover all expenses. Fixing the turbine required a 300-ton crane (rental cost $28,000 a day) and necessitated waiting for parts to be shipped and waiting for nonwindy days for the repairs to be made. It took three weeks for the structure to be repaired. Vestas-American Wind Technology of Portland, Oregon, honored the warranty and paid for repairs, but the costs of lost revenue and needing to purchase power from the outside for three weeks was not part of that agreement. In order to have a constant production of power for reliable service to the users, there must be a backup unit, and regularly scheduled maintenance is a necessity.[33]

Developing a stable, cost-effective energy source has been and continues to be a roadblock to electric vehicles joining the mainstream market. Current research has branched in many directions, using theories and concepts formulated in the early years. Each has its positives and negatives. Some continue to be cost-prohibitive; others are plagued by the historic problem of lack of infrastructure to provide wide area service. Batteries, fuel cells, alternate fuels—each struggles to find environmentally friendly solutions that the market will accept.

Energy Sources

Batteries

The environmental impact of the battery, with its limited range and high cost, continues to be an obstacle to the EV's development. There are many unanswered questions about pollution generated from old batteries and traditional power plants, the possible toxicity and recycling of current lead acid batteries and the advanced (NiMH, LiION) forms being developed, and the cost of generating electricity to recharge these batteries at home and at commercial recharging stations. By 1990, 12 states (California, Florida, Hawaii, Illinois, Maine, Minnesota, New York, Oregon, Pennsylvania, Rhode Island, Washington and Wyoming) had laws requiring mandatory lead acid battery recycling. They implemented the Battery Council International's recommendation which made it unlawful to recycle at any location except battery wholesalers, retailers or authorized recycling facilities. The plan also required those businesses to accept all used lead acid batteries from their customers, not just those purchased from that retailer. As incentive to abide by the legislation, Minnesota, Maine, Rhode Island and Washington added a deposit (usually $5 or $10) to the retail price. Rhode Island allowed the businesses to keep 20 percent of the deposit monies, with 80 percent going to the state; in Minnesota, Maine and Washington businesses could keep 100 percent of the monies. New Hampshire, Vermont and New York made agreements with solid waste disposal companies to separate lead acid batteries for easier recycling.

In 1996 discussions heated up over the effectiveness of reducing pollution at the tailpipe level, but creating more pollution at the lead mining/disposal and power plant levels. Researchers estimated that the mining, smelting and recycling of more than 500 kilograms of lead batteries per vehicle would cause a far greater environmental problem than the air quality problem it might solve. They estimated that the battery lead hazard to the environment would increase by 20 percent if emphasis were placed on using battery-powered electric vehicles to combat ICE air pollution.[34] In 1998, an estimated three billion batteries were sold in the U.S., with a projected increase of about 6 percent per year. The disposal of the volume of batteries needed to power EVs does affect our world, but with ingenuity and incentives the problem becomes manageable.

Although the battery disposal problem continues to be an issue, it is being partially addressed through recycling. Most parts of the batteries can be recycled. The electrolyte can be neutralized and the lead can be recovered by a controlled-temperature process and refined for resale. This process looks promising in reducing the environmental impact of pollution from EV batteries as long as the industry finds a market for the battery's recycled by-products. The disposal problem becomes solvable when addressed as an environmental recycling issue. By 2001 environmentalists generally agreed that pollution from tailpipes exposes more people to noxious fumes than does pollution from power plants, as the plants are more likely to be located in remote areas and have tall stacks that allow the pollution to disperse before reaching populated areas.[35] Power plants also must adhere to stricter regulations concerning pollutants. Interest in alternative electricity-producing sources such as fuel cells, solar, hydro, nuclear and wind is increasing as improved technologies and public support are making them financially plausible investments. EVs' batteries and utility plants' emissions as they affect air and ground pollution are obstacles, but accommodations are being found in viable alternative power sources, regulation and recycling.

Fuel Cells

Using fuel cells to generate electricity for the EV has caught environmentalists' attention. The only by-products of fuel cells powered by hydrogen are water and heat. The problem of water emissions becoming ice patches on winter streets is of minor concern, but noted as an area to be examined. Hydrogen fuel cells' benign emissions hold the most interest, but emissions can vary depending on the type of fuel used, and developers face obstacles in packaging, marketing and supplying the product to potential consumers. Hydrogen produced by the electrolysis of water would be the ideal solution, but it is not economically feasible at this time. If hydrogen is produced using gasoline, methanol or natural gas, there are trace amounts of pollutants, such as nitrogen oxide and carbon monoxide. The emissions are still less than those produced by current ICEs, but air quality is still negatively affected no matter which alternate fuel is used. As with the shortage of charging stations that electrics have historically faced, a convenient fuel supply also continues to be a problem with these alternates. An infrastructure is not in place for hydrogen or methane fuel sources, and natural gas carries its own drawbacks in the volume it consumes, even when compressed or liquefied. One possible solution to this problem is to extract hydrogen from natural gas in large reformers located at filling stations and then store it in a solid metal hydride form. This would provide about the same amount of energy as a same-sized tank of gasoline.[36] Iceland, with its vast hydroelectric and geothermal clean energy power plants, and its compact population, chose hydrogen fueling as a pilot program to replace their dependence on oil. Iceland's was the first hydrogen infrastructure project open to the public; its Shell stations were opened in 2005 for fuel cell drivers and hydrogen buses.

Another hydrogen refueling station possibility in its test phase uses solar power to provide energy for extracting hydrogen from water. By 2008, major automakers had versions of fuel cell vehicles available on a limited basis. The benefits for using these alternate fuels appears slowly as the market sorts out which infrastructure to support, but innovations like using solar hydrogen refueling for the low- to zero-polluting fuel cells are raising expectations for people interested in a cleaner environment.

The Pembina Institute of Alberta, Canada, an environmental think tank, estimated the impact of using hydrogen derived from fossil fuels against a benchmark traditional ICE to illustrate that just changing to fuel cells would not provide the greatest opportunity for cleaning the air. The choice of fuels used to generate the hydrogen makes a difference in the percentage of CO_2 pollution reduced by this method.

- The ICE creates 248 kilograms of CO_2 per 1000 kilometers driven.
- A car using electricity from a fossil fuel plant would create 237.
- Hydrogen extracted from an onboard gasoline reformer, 193.
- An onboard methanol reformer from natural gas, 162.
- Hydrogen fuel cell reformer from natural gas at urban outlets, 80.
- Hydrogen supplied from large refineries, 70.

The institute's research found that hydrogen pulled from fossil-fuel generating plants (comparisons of hydrogen gained from hydro, solar, wind power or methane escaping from landfills were not addressed in the study) would have minimal impact on changing levels of greenhouse gases and increase smog and heavy metal pollutants such as arsenic and mercury. Pollution would be reduced by 35 percent using hydrogen refined from methanol; hydrogen from natural gas would reduce it 70 percent.[37] This method produces only half as many pollutants as an ICE.[38]

Again, infrastructure, not ideals, is key to what will and will not survive in the marketplace. Gasoline has the existing infrastructure and is familiar to car owners. It is readily available, but is the least efficient hydrogen source. Natural gas has a small infrastructure, which may be expanded, but is less likely to be the major resource for the fuel cell's hydrogen supply. For some urban areas, natural gas may provide the cleaner alternative, but its limited availability makes it a distant second option for most consumers. Though still in its infant stages, the solar-powered station holds potential for a versatile infrastructure, but one needing backup power from the grid for overcast days. In April 2002 the Bush administration put its support behind the development of hydrogen-powered fuel cell vehicles, acknowledging that the technology for getting the autos on the road could be a decade away. Even with the limitations, fuel cells show promise for decreasing pollution from autos and a high possibility for gaining market share.

Fuel cells powered by hydrogen, even in their current emerging state of development, are already proving to be green conscious. They eliminate the immediate problem of piles of dead lead acid batteries accumulating in landfills and the cost of processing for recycling because they use small auxiliary storage units and onboard generators. They also show future potential to further reduce landfill expansion as new designs in fuel cells are being developed as reusable resources. The components of the Ballard fuel cell, for example, are completely reusable. After thousands of hours of use, the parts can be disassembled, cleaned and reassembled into new fuel cells. The drawback with hydrogen is that, currently, energy generated through it is more expensive than coal, oil or natural gas. However, research at the University of Aberdeen led by Professor Hicham Idriss has found a means for creating the hydrogen needed from renewable biofuel. The process generates hydrogen from ethanol. Following another path, university research centers, among them, Pennsylvania State University in State College, Pennsylvania, Oregon State University in Corvallis, Oregon, and Harvard University in Cambridge, Massachusetts, are successfully finding a more cost-efficient way to produce fuel cells for both commercial power and cars, using microbial fuel cells (MFCs). The cell does not have the membrane used in the PEM, and can produce more hydrogen using less electricity. Using bacteria, it converts organic matter in wastewater to electricity. As an added benefit on the environmental side, the used water is cleaned and can be reused elsewhere. Its use as a means for providing power and clean water in areas off the grid is moving forward. The process for use in vehicles is still in the early prototype stage, and holds possibilities for energy production in the long-term.

Even with new possibilities, hydrogen still carries the added disadvantage of being associated with the *Hindenburg* airship disaster in 1937 in which the hydrogen-filled zeppelin caught fire while attempting to dock in Lakehurst, New Jersey. Hydrogen is nonpolluting and safe, but is still perceived by many to be an unsafe gas that could explode, not a comfortable prospect for use in the family car. Even with this stigma, environmentalists and those in the industry see the fuel cell's potential for success if care is given to the source fuel used.

Major industries are experimenting with ways to supply the automobile industry with fuel cell technology. Automakers are branching out and partnering with fuel cell manufacturers, and governments, seeing potential benefits for their economic partners, are providing support for research and development. Honda's Research and Design Center in Torrance, California, was the first auto manufacturer to open a solar-powered hydrogen production and refueling station, in July 2001. The station uses photovoltaic (PV) cells to extract hydrogen from water using electrolysis. Power from the utility company is used as backup for the less sunny days. At opening, the facility could supply 5,700 liters of hydrogen per year. This is enough to support one vehicle for one year. The station is "neighbor friendly"; its operations are very quiet and its building is architecturally attractive. Concerns about hydrogen safety were a top priority in building the station. The system was built to National Fire Protection standards and equipped to shut down immediately in case of earthquakes. No refueling is allowed during electrical storms. Unlike the hydrogen stations run by city governments in Chicago, Illinois and in Thousand Palms, California, for refueling their buses and neighborhood vehicles, Honda's system was designed to be used by the general public. No special gloves or eye protection is required to refuel the vehicle, and the person can stay by the pump while refueling takes place.[39]

The Honda FCV (fuel cell vehicle) came into operation in 2003, powered by a PEM fuel cell and asynchronous electric motor. Four years later, in 2007, we saw the rollout of GM's Project Driveway. Over one hundred Equinox fuel cell electric vehicles were given to government agencies and consumers around the United States to test drive. The Equinox uses a PEM fuel cell system that is scalable to different GM models.

Each manufacturer wants its market share and is pushing to have its version of the product become the industry standard. Research and development expenses are still a reality, and the competition has not had the needed effect of reducing cost for these products. The website Fuel Cells 2000 says, "Researchers are helping to develop technologies to tap into this natural resource and generate hydrogen in mass quantities and cheaper prices in order to compete with the traditional energy sources. There are three main methods that scientists are researching for inexpensive hydrogen generation. All three separate the hydrogen from a 'feedstock,' such as fossil fuel or water — but by very different means."[40]

- Reformers— Reforming is the name of the process used to extract hydrogen from a variety of materials, including natural gas, methanol, ethanol, propane and even gasoline. One type of reforming is endothermic steam, which combines the fuels with steam and then separates hydrogen using membranes. A problem here is that the process uses energy. Another type of reformer is a partial oxidation process. It has a drawback of having CO_2 as a by-product.
- Enzymes— Cyanobacteria are single-celled organisms that can produce hydrogen when growing in water. The organisms use enzymes to split the molecules, producing hydrogen. This process is especially attractive because the by-product is water, which can be used for the next process cycle.
- Solar, geothermal and wind power—Photovoltaics, solar cells or wind turbines can also generate hydrogen by using power to electrolyze water into hydrogen and oxygen. Hydrogen becomes an energy carrier and can be transported from the generation site to another location for use in a fuel cell.

Each of these methods shows that fuel cell technology is a viable environmentally friendly energy source for powering electric vehicles. Both industry and those looking for clean ways to generate power are following progress in its development.

Catalytic Converters

After the energy crisis of 1973–74, many regulations were enacted to conserve fuels and reduce tailpipe emissions to improve air quality. Tailpipe exhaust emissions consist of carbon monoxide (CO), unburned hydrocarbons (HC) and nitrogen oxides (NOX). One of the solutions to reduce these emissions was the catalytic converter. Evaporative emissions are the fuel vapors that seep out of the fuel tank and carburetor. These vapors are prevented from escaping into the atmosphere by sealing the fuel system and storing the vapors in a canister for later reburning. The catalytic converter captures the pollutants that make it into the exhaust and sends them back to be reburned before they can exit the tailpipe. High sulfur levels in gasoline tend to clog up the catalytic converters. This sulfur content problem was addressed by the Clinton administration in April 1999, when it announced new standards, known as Tier 2, to clean up heavily polluting light trucks. This plan lowered the acceptable levels from 330 parts per million to 30 ppm, with 15 ppm being the goal for 2005. The idea was to lower the amount of soot released in the air. The proposal resulted in an additional $100 cost to the vehicle and had minimal short-term effect due to several loopholes. First, it did not take effect until 2004 for cars and not until 2009 for light trucks. Second, it does not apply to trucks weighing over 8,500 pounds, and third, it does not apply to diesel engines, which produce far more soot than gasoline engines. The Tier 2 program is still being amended, and the EPA is producing reports annually. The rulings involve certain provisions for small refiners to average, bank and trade gasoline sulfur baselines for credit with foreign refiners. In a 2006 amendment (effective January 29, 2007) American Samoa, Guam and the Commonwealth of the Northern Mariana Islands were given exemption from having to comply. The reasons were possible fuel shortage and added cost as most of their supply comes from Singapore, and minimal air quality benefits.

Success in using this catalytic converter technology dramatically decreases ICE pollutants. This may dim electrics' allure as a "green machine" by lessening the gap between tailpipe and non-tailpipe emissions.

CNG and LNG

Demand increased in the late 1990s for clean-burning compressed natural gas (CNG) and liquid natural gas (LNG) engines. By 1998 there were about 50,000 CNG and LNG vehicles in the United States. Most were in fleet use, with about 5 percent being transit buses; a few were consumer vehicles. The transit bus segment expanded; about 22 percent of all new bus orders in that year were for natural gas vehicles. Infrastructure was a factor; there were about 1,300 operational fueling stations from Vermont to California.[41] One-third of the stations were privately owned and the rest were run by utility companies. In August 2008, an article in the *Washington Post* written by Jordan Weissmann found that approximately 120,000 vehicles in the United States ran on natural gas, most of them in government and corporate fleets. The difficulty continues to be fuel availability. Of the 176,000 gas stations in the U.S., only 2,000 also carry natural gas.[42]

This clean-air alternative is in direct competition to the electric fleet and mass transit markets. It also shows promise for providing an infrastructure for hydrogen fuel-cell vehicles.

Biodiesel

Biodiesel fuel is a clear liquid similar to diesel oil, but obtained from plants. Biodiesel oil may be made from any type of oily vegetation, including seeds from peanut, castor, sunflower, etc. A plant called rape is being used extensively in the United Kingdom to produce this fuel. The crop grown will produce about three tons of seed per hectare, and 30 percent of this will produce oil. Its one possible drawback is the potential for having a harmful effect on natural rubber seals in an engine. Rapeseed oil burns cleanly. It does not produce carbon dioxide or sulfur oxide emissions when burned and is growing in popularity, especially for heavy-duty work hybrids.

Biofuels

Biofuels are not a new product. In 1908, Henry Ford intended to have his Model T run on plant-based ethanol, but as steam cars lost the market share, so ethanol was beaten by gasoline. Later in the 20th century, the Energy Act of 1978 called for subsidizing the use of ethanol as an additive to gasoline; the 1990 update to the Clean Air Act required some urban areas in the U.S. to use additives such as ethanol to make fuel burn more cleanly. Flexible-fuel cars came into the world market by 2003 and their appeal increased. Major car makers came out with new models each year in the first decade of the 21st century. The U.S. Congress again gave a boost to ethanol by requiring seven and one-half billion gallons per year to be on the market by 2012. President Bush's State of the Union speech in 2006 endorsed ethanol as a means to reduce dependence on foreign oil. His 2007 State of the Union address promoted increasing the supply of alternative fuels to 35 billion gallons by 2017 (five times the original target) and supported the need to update fuel economy standards for additional conservation. The viability of ethanol has both supporters and naysayers. Those questioning its viability point to the need for government subsidies to manage supply. If it were a best market solution, they argue, the subsidies wouldn't be needed. Energy specialist Jerry Taylor of the Cato Institute was quoted in a chemical industry journal as saying, "'Ethanol is the closest thing we have to a state religion.'"[43] It has reemerged as a panacea for our emission woes.

Biofuels spurred a refinery boom in the Pacific Northwest in 2007. The states of Washington and Oregon proposed nearly 30 refineries incorporating ethanol and biodiesel projects to create 1.3 billion gallons of fuel per year to offset the import of crude oil. This would be roughly equivalent to one fifth of the two states' consumption of gasoline and petroleum diesel. Biofuel is made from plants (mostly corn), used kitchen grease and animal fats. The first ethanol plant opened on October 5, 2007, at the Port of Morrow, near Boardman, Oregon. Portland, Oregon, was the first in the nation to require ethanol and biodiesel to be sold within city limits. Federal and state tax breaks are helping to drive the construction. Federal tax breaks include a fifty cent per gallon discount for ethanol blenders and $1 a gallon for biodiesel. As with each of the alternate fuels, some people oppose creating and marketing the product. Some environmental groups and European governments contest the use of biofuels, claiming it will take up a lot of land that currently grows corn for human consumption and drive up food prices. They contend that biofuel demand will increase corn prices and other food products, eventually hurting the poor.[44] Biofuels are made from such a wide variety of sources that it is questionable whether the food supply will be seriously affected. Instead it is possible that products formerly considered waste (e.g. corn stalks and wood by-products) will be recycled. The awareness and use of biofuels is becoming stronger, especially in the auto markets where power is part of the driving equation.

Automobile racing has also come to the attention of environmentalists. Yes, a Formula 1 car will spit out some 60,000 pounds of carbon dioxide and other so-called greenhouse gases during a racing season, more than five times the average household-owned vehicle. But the entire carbon footprint of auto racing is small compared to normal driving. It is estimated that all the race cars in the world will release less greenhouse gases in a racing season than the state of California emits in one day, but the racing industry has seen the benefits of joining the green side.[45] "Green racing" was introduced in Phoenix, Arizona, in 2007 by Dale Jensen, primary owner of the Arizona Diamondbacks baseball team and co-promoter of the Champ Car Series. He billed an environmental expo as part of the Earth-Shift '07 to "educate urban residents on environmentally advanced technologies."[46] With his partner, Bradley Yonover, he organized a "green auto race" in downtown Phoenix near the Jackson Street Entertainment District that promoted environmental awareness and proposed energy stations that would offer drivers ethanol and natural gas as options.

The Indy Racing League (IRL) switched from methanol to an ethanol fuel in 2007. The IRL's ethanol is mixed with a small amount of gasoline, not for performance, but to make it undrinkable. This avoided alcohol taxes and any potential problems with the Bureau of Alcohol, Tobacco, Firearms and Explosives (ATF). In theory, ethanol can be considered to be "carbon-neutral," as growing the corn or other plants (or even plant matter, such as wood chips) to produce it will consume CO_2 from the atmosphere using photosynthesis, thereby negating the CO_2 released during a race. This also fit in nicely with the government policy of promoting the use of ethanol to reduce dependence on foreign oil.

The American Le Mans Series (ALMS) of racing announced in January 2008 that it would partner with the U.S. Environmental Agency, the U.S. Department of Energy and the Society of Automotive Engineers International to become the first racing series to meet the "green racing" criteria promoted by these groups. Competitors will use alternative fuels such as zero-sulfur clean diesel, E10 ethanol (10 percent ethanol, 90 percent gasoline) and E85 ethanol.

Biofuels, such as ethanol made from corn, may be seen initially as providing clean green energy, but it takes a lot of "old" energy to produce the "new" energy. Only about 20 percent of corn-produced ethanol is "new," as it requires fossil fuel to run the tractors to farm the corn, fuel to power the refineries that convert the corn into ethanol, and natural gas to make fertilizer to grow the corn. According to some estimates, if all of the 70 million acres of land that in 2006 were used to grow corn were converted specifically for ethanol, it would supplant about 12 percent of the U.S. gasoline market. The "new" part of that energy would be only 2.4 percent, providing a small return on investment. Another concern is the amount of carbon dioxide released into the air. If farmers cultivated an extra 10 million acres of land in 2008 to produce corn, it would take up some of the millions of acres of land currently set aside for conservation under a separate subsidized government program. In theory, the uncultivated acres absorb atmospheric carbon, and farming them would release more carbon dioxide than would burning gasoline.[47]

This balance of energy is not dissuading energy producers. As long as government subsidies continue throughout the world to promote the growing and processing of bios for fuel, the trend will continue. Whether the plant is sugar, switch grass, corn, wood chips or any of the many other natural resources that yield a burnable energy source, growers will plant and harvest the product, and investors will bet on the product's viability in the marketplace to fuel our worldwide transportation needs.

Reformulated Gasoline

Reformulated gasoline (RFG) is a specially processed and blended product that uses methanol, ethanol or MTBE. It is intended to reduce the emission of pollutants such as hydrocarbons, carbon monoxide and nitrogen oxides. RFG is estimated to reduce hydrocarbon emissions by 15 percent. There are side effects. The vehicle's gas mileage is reduced by 2 to 3 percent, and it may also shorten the life of rubber hoses and seals in the engine. In June 2000 the Environmental Protection Agency (EPA) proposed to make it easier for refiners to use ethanol in cleaner-burning gasoline. The use of ethanol reduces the amount of carbon monoxide from the tailpipe. The adjustment would allow refiners to slightly increase the evaporative property of gasoline in exchange for reducing the carbon monoxide level from the tailpipe. The EPA called on Congress to decrease or eliminate the use of MTBE in gasoline, citing that it can render ground water supplies undrinkable if leaked into the soil. Although this solution originally looked like a promising competitor to the EVs, its impact on the environment is taking it out of the running.

Foreign Oil

Many countries around the world beyond the Middle East produce oil, some for domestic use and some for export. They have marginal impact on the cost of oil for gasoline. After the collapse of the Soviet Union, Russia emerged with the potential for putting vast quantities of oil on the market. By the turn of the 21st century Russia had become a major producer and oil exporter. Oil production is expected to increase and then peak around 2010.

Russia also has vast quantities of natural gas in the Arctic region, perhaps as much as one-third of the world's supply. The Caspian Sea is one of the oldest oil production areas in the world, and after the breakup of the Soviet Union, capitalism emerged in Azerbaijan, Kazakhstan and Russia and they began exporting large amounts of oil to the West. This prompted hope in the United States that the West could be less reliant on Middle East oil supplies. This has not happened. Hugo Chavez's nationalization of oil companies in Venezuela has brought similar disappointments. This situation may change. January 2009 found Chavez courting the possibility of reopening the state-owned companies to private foreign investors as production and revenues from their oil dropped dramatically after private industry was forced out. The possibility of that market opening in the near future relies on how well his negotiations with the private sector go.

Domestic Oil and Gas

Coal remains the main energy source for the United States. Going into the 21st century, about half of the electricity used was being generated through this fuel. With the demand constantly rising, new coal plants are being built because coal is the most plentiful and cheapest means for meeting energy demands. A few of the new plants are moving to a cleaner gasification process to reduce the carbon dioxide emissions. The process turns coal into gases and filters out the CO_2 before the gases are burned. It costs about 20 percent more to build a plant that uses this process, but building from the ground up with the cleaner process is much less expensive than trying to retrofit the older plants. Unfortunately, the plants currently operating in Tampa, Florida, and Wabash, Indiana, have not been as reliable as anticipated. Shutdowns occur periodically. The companies are weighing the costs and benefits as government regulations move toward requiring fewer emissions. Supporters of electric cars, especially the hybrid plug-ins, see a trade-off on the emissions. The need for additional power gained through these facilities generates more pollution, but centralization of emissions is seen as a more effective means of regulating particulates and gases. It's easier to capture emissions from single plants than from millions of cars.

Exploration and development of oil and gas are not being forgotten in the race for alternate fuels. According to Cambridge Energy Research Associates, headed by Pulitzer Prize winner Daniel Yergin, we have enough oil, including the oil locked in shale, to last at least 25 years, ten years longer than the alarmists claim, and this is the fifth time the world is supposed to run out of oil. Each time, inventive technology has extended the timeline previously predicted.

In addition to funding alternate fuel resource exploration and development, venture capitalists also poured money into oil and gas start-ups. In 2006, investors put in $163 million and financed 18 companies. This was an increase of $56 million over the former year. Companies such as Terralliance are stressing the use of technologies to improve efficiency in finding and drilling for new oil and gas reserves.[48] In Mississippi, Denbury Resources decided to use technology to recover more oil from existing fields. By pumping carbon dioxide into the existing wells, it estimated a 25 percent greater return on those wells. The process behaves much like fizzy water in freeing more oil to be pumped to the surface. Horizontal drilling is also being investigated to reach areas that were not cost effective to drill using older methods.[49] Traditional oil and gas, using current technology, continue to be part of the expanding marketplace for energy.

Alternate Energy Sources

Government incentives, whether in tax credits, partnerships or subsidies, drive research and development of alternate energy sources. In 2002 a Sierra Club press release called for senators to promote the development of solar and wind power, claiming that 20 percent of our energy could come from these sources as early as 2020. Sierra Club began a radio advertising campaign calling for a forward-looking vision in developing an energy plan that would provide for a cleaner environment using diversified technologies. Carl Pope, Sierra Club's executive director, declared, "We don't have to dig, drill and destroy to meet our energy needs. We need leadership from senators to ensure that our energy policy is clean, safe, and secure."[50]

As of 2008, the impact of using electric and electric hybrids, such as the hybrid plug-in, is minimal. It is estimated that less than two percent of the vehicles currently on the road need power from the grid. If electric vehicles become popular, utility companies will be faced with a demand for more electricity to recharge batteries in addition to the growth in the domestic market for more power to fuel our nation's electronic lifestyle. This concerns environmentalists who monitor emissions from generating plants that use fossil fuels. Currently about 50 percent of the electrical energy generated in the United States is from coal. The problems with traditional coal plants are varied, on both an environmental and personal health level. The generation process is only about 30 percent efficient. There are also problems with coal miners dying from black lung disease. Between 1973 and 2002, the federal government paid about $35 billion in benefits to miners and their survivors. Although improvements have been made, a by-product of coal-fired plants, acid rain, is still present in the rains of the northeastern United States and parts of Europe and Asia. Alternatives are being sought to meet increased power demands around the world. A convenient, clean power source for battery recharging is necessary for EVs to succeed as an environmentally friendly alternative.

Wind Power

It is predicted that wind-powered turbines placed in the Midwest could provide up to 30 percent of the energy currently produced by coal, without the disease and pollution problems. In 2001, there were about 12,000 turbines operating in the United States. This was expected to double with a federal investment of $70 billion.[51] During the next seven years, the number of turbines increased to over 25,000.

Using wind power to generate electricity is not a new idea. In 1923 A. J. Root, the dean of the American bee industry, constructed two windmills in his backyard to generate electricity for his electric car. He proposed this as a solution for "free" energy for electric vehicles; however, the initial cost was about $1,500. The windmills kept his car fully charged for its regular duty of five or six miles a day, and powered the lights in his house.[53] The idea did not catch on with the public.

By 2008, the largest numbers of wind turbines in the United States were located in California and Texas. Wind power comprised approximately 35 percent of the new energy sources in the first decade of the 21st century. Wind farmers lease land from ranchers and sell the electricity to power marketers, electric utilities and government agencies. Fifteen states, most in the Midwest, have wind energy potential higher than California. Minnesota, Wisconsin, Colorado and Iowa lead in that development. Largely spurred by another

Wind Fever, Wasco, Oregon[52]

increase in oil prices, momentum grows for developing offshore wind farms. The prime locations being considered initially are off the continental shelf of the Northeast coastline. Australia's Babcock & Brown was the first to sign contracts in Delaware to build 67 turbines. The windmills are to be built 11.5 miles off Delaware's shores. Rhode Island, New Jersey and New York City also look to offshore projects. The projects are more attractive on the East Coast because they are less costly to build. Unlike the West Coast where the shelves drop quickly into extremely deep water, the waters off New England and the Middle Atlantic states are shallow. The winds in this area are also some of the area's strongest. Wind farms are still more expensive to build and operate than conventional fossil fuel plants, but the population density, possible continued tax breaks for the developers that have already increased investments in wind farms by over 90 percent, and demand for alternative energy for the grid are expected to make this option economically feasible. Environmental concerns are being addressed by putting these farms far enough off the coast to be less conspicuous from the land.[54]

In May 2002, the British Parliament approved the building of Britain's largest wind farm in the Cambrian Mountains to generate electricity for 40,000 homes. The project cost £35 million ($51 million) and has a total of thirty-nine wind-powered turbines. The government had previously pledged to produce 10 percent of Britain's electricity supply from renewable resources by the year 2010. Work on the wind turbines began in the summer of 2002. The finished product, the Cfen Croes Wind Power Station, began operation in 2005 and is expected to have a working life of thirty years. Opposition to the wind farm from the local environmental society continues. Supporters of the project intend to add farms in other locations along the Cambrian Range.

The United Kingdom is rapidly moving toward being a leader in using wind power. By 2007, it joined the ranks of only a handful of countries that produce over 2 gigawatts of operational power from wind. This marks quite a climb from its push for commercial application less than a decade before, when British Petroleum (BP) invested millions of dollars in green technology and declared a profit in its wind business operation (2001). BP's Connect service stations, for electric-vehicle recharging, are partially powered by solar power. BP also researches fuel cells for cars. To advance a new image in alternate power technologies, British Petroleum is using the letters BP in advertising to promote itself as "beyond petroleum." In 2008, Royal Dutch Shell, which had designated half a billion dollars over five years for research and development of wind and solar power, sold its interest in London Array wind farms to its Danish partners, E.ON and DONG Energy. Soaring costs in building and maintaining the farm was a major consideration for Shell's selling its interests. It will be looking at geothermal, biofuels and hydrogen fuel cells, with emphasis on diesel and biofuels as alternatives to gasoline for powering our cars and trucks.

One of the drawbacks of wind power is what to do when the wind stops blowing. King Island, off the coast of Australia in the Bass Strait, moved to a more efficient means for using wind power. In 2003, the local utility company installed a huge rechargeable battery. The battery stores energy during periods of high wind and draws from that storage during calmer days. To make this happen, the King Island plant uses flow batteries. The chemicals in these units "soak up" energy, the chemicals with that energy are pumped to a storage tank, and fresh chemicals are pumped into the original tank to be ready to store more energy. The process is reversed to produce energy on calm days. These batteries can deliver up to 400 kilowatts for two hours. They increased the proportion of wind-derived energy for that island from about 12 percent in 2003 to approximately 40 percent by 2007. A flow battery's main advantage is its scalability; the lifespan is estimated to double or possibly triple conventional lead-acid batteries' 2 to 3 years, and energy output is similar to the 80 percent of those conventional lead-acid batteries.[55] This flow battery has been scaled for vehicle use as well. VRB Power Systems has tested this battery in golf carts using conventional electric plug-in. *New Scientist* wrote in 2007, "Enticingly, though, flow batteries might one day allow drivers to refill the tank with energized electrolyte. The spent solution can be recycled."[56] Flow batteries offer one means for making wind power a more standard, reliable alternate energy source by providing a constant flow of electricity, even on calm days. Wind power as an everyday energy supply is increasing its profile in the international marketplace.

Ocean Power

Tidal and wave power are being tested as a positive approach to generating energy without pollution. Tidal and wave power does come with drawbacks. Plants may be damaged by powerful waves and storms. Some tidal power devices that are placed in estuaries may affect the habitat of fish and seabirds. And, generally, due to the tidal currents, many of these devices will produce electricity only about ten hours a day, leaving a fourteen-hour gap in which power must be provided by other means. Even with these drawbacks, it offers many areas the possibility of clean, local energy.

In the 1970s Japan and England began research on generating electricity using the power of ocean waves. More experimental programs began in the 1980s in Australia and Norway. The two basic designs for wave-powered generating devices are fixed and floating. The fixed device is mounted to the seabed or the shore (cliffs). Some consider the best way of capturing wave power to be the oscillating water column (OWC). It consists of a fixed column filled with air that is compressed when the waves come up to it. The compressed air, as well as the air sucked back by the retreating waves, is forced through turbines. This motion produces electricity. Only a few of these devices have been built. The most successful plant, in Tofteshallen, Norway, was unfortunately blown out to sea in a heavy storm in 1998. Another fixed device, called TAPCHAN, consists of a tapered channel. The channel forces the waves to narrow, increasing the amplitude of the wave (kinetic energy) and forcing the water up to a reservoir (potential energy). As the water falls by gravity back

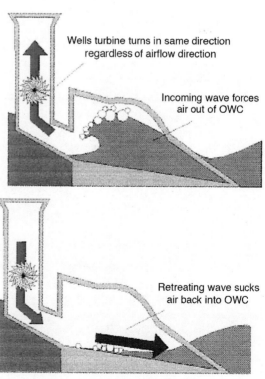

Wells turbine turns in same direction regardless of airflow direction

Incoming wave forces air out of OWC

Retreating wave sucks air back into OWC

Wave power[57]

to the ocean, it is run through a turbine to generate the energy. There are only a limited number of sites for fixed generators.

Floating devices that rise and fall with the motion of the waves and generate electricity through that motion are another type of wave power. Cockerell's Raft, one type of floating device, consists of a line of rafts connected to hydraulic pumps that drive turbines to produce energy. Salter Ducks are floating devices connected in a series that bob up and down in the water. The name comes from its creator Steven Salter and the fact that the devices look similar to floating ducks. The ducks are connected by a stiff shaft. The shaft contains hydraulic fluid that drives a pump to produce electricity. These fixed and floating devices have been part of research and experimentation since the 1970s.

Tidal power operates by building a barrier across a river estuary, an area where the tide meets the current, to allow the tide to drive turbines to produce electricity. One tidal power station, at Rance in northern France, has operated successfully since 1966 without any major breakdowns and supplies approximately four percent of the power needed for the houses of Brittany. The current cost to generate the electricity is slightly below the average cost per kilowatt of other utility plants. As of 2001, North America's only tidal power plant is located on the Bay of Fundy near Annapolis Royal, Nova Scotia. Powered by 20-foot tides, the plant's turbine produces 30 million kilowatt-hours per year, enough to power 4,500 homes. The plant has had such success that Nova Scotia Power is partnering with an Irish company, Open Hydro, to explore use of turbines on the seabed in the Bay of Fundy to see if the units will be rugged enough to withstand the forces of the currents and the debris battering. With their setbacks and successes, tidal and wave power continue to be researched for their clean energy source potential.

Thermal water-based power also holds promise, although it is less cost-effective than the tide and wave models. Ocean Thermal Energy Conversion (OTEC) power plants make use of the difference in water temperature between warm surface waters heated by the sun and colder waters found at ocean depths (about 1,000 meters). A temperature difference of 20°C (68°F) or more between the warm and cold water is required. A great deal of the electricity generated must be reused to pump the cold water from the depths to the surface, making the process less efficient.

Although technology is available to build these power plants, the construction costs are high enough to make the electricity produced from them more expensive than that generated by traditional energy plants. Nevertheless, research continues. Many environmentalists view wave power as a clean acceptable alternative to land-bound sources.

Geothermal Power

Geothermal systems are less used because they must be on site where there is geothermal activity (geysers) that have water or steam of 350 degrees Fahrenheit or more to run turbine generators. Geothermal power plants use the water as the working liquid to generate electricity, but there are problems with corrosion that affect piping and surface equipment in conventional water cycles. One alternative proposed by A. D. Atrens and colleagues at University of Queensland is using liquid CO_2 in place of the water. It doesn't dissolve mineral salts, and the energy generated parallels the amount produced using water. It also has a simpler design.[58] In certain areas, it is a clean, rich, renewable resource. Iceland is a major user of geothermal power for heating, generating electricity, and, most recently, for providing hydrogen fuel for its energy project.

Solar Power

Solar power plants have very little negative impact on the environment, but, as with other clean power producers that rely on nature for the energy source, they need alternate sources for days when nature is not cooperating. Solar plants operate efficiently only when the sun is shining. At night or during overcast days, backup power generators must be in place. Natural gas is used for the power source during these gaps to maintain consistent service. Solar thermal plants use the heat from the sun to boil water to create steam that is passed through a turbine. The collectors are expensive, and the solar industry is working on new technologies to become more efficient. In Gila Bend, Arizona, a solar power plant called Solana is to be built if tax credits make it possible. If the funding is secured, it is slated to be operational by 2011. Energy will be generated from steam turbines with power capacity to supply 70,000 homes. Partners for the project are Abengora Solar and Arizona Public Service Company (APS).

The dream of solar powered autos is a small niche in the market, and development of solar panels that might be adapted to the exterior of a car is a constant in that research. The high cost of this technology keeps it from becoming a viable option for mass production. Flexible solar technology was developed by Texas Instruments, Inc., in the early 1990s; Spheral Solar attempted to make the product financially viable in the market during much of the 1990s, basing its refinement, not on the concept of crystalline silicon wafers, but on tiny mini-spheres (balls) of silicon encased in aluminum sheets and covered in Teflon-protected plastic. The panels have the added advantage of paintability: they can be painted to match the car. In 2007, ATS Automation went into partnership to continue development on Spheral Solar's product as it paralleled development with a product in Photowatt's (ATS's parent company) stable.

Nuclear Power

Nuclear energy has perhaps the lowest initial impact on the environment of any energy source because it does not emit harmful gases and requires less area to produce the same amount of electricity as other sources. Nuclear fuel is used to heat water, creating steam that turns a turbine, creating electricity. The emission-free energy generated by nuclear power plants meets the standards of the 1970 Clean Air Act. The problems with nuclear energy generation are the safety concerns of reactor failure and how to dispose of nuclear waste. The Nuclear Waste Policy Act of 1982 and its 1987 amendments authorize the Department of Energy to build deep, mined geological sites for the storage of high-level nuclear waste. By 2005, opposition to nuclear power plants in the U.S. was waning. Utility companies in the U.S. began identifying existing sites that might offer the possibility for additional reactors if Congress would provide subsidies for those projects. France has decided that the benefits outweigh the problems of nuclear energy. It relies heavily on this form of energy. This possibility was being revisited around the globe in 2008 as a means to offset high oil prices. Although it is a solution, nuclear energy is less favored because it generates extreme potential public safety concerns.

Storing Energy

The way in which energy is stored and moved allows a balance for peak demand times, in the case of wind or ocean wave power, when nature is not providing the means for generating power. The three most common means for storing excess power to ensure a more constant flow of energy are: (1) Pumped hydroelectric storage; (2) Compressed air storage; (3) Batteries.

Pumped hydroelectric storage involves pumping water uphill to a reservoir during off hours and releasing the water through the turbines during peak usage to generate additional electricity to meet the demand. The same equipment is used for directing the flow in one direction or the other. This is the most cost-effective storage and is used by over 300 utility plants worldwide. An estimated 5.5 percent of the power generated in the European Union was stored in this manner in 2006; the figure was 19.5 percent in the United States for that same year. There is also a seawater variation on this process being tested in Japan. Seawater does have the added difficulties of corrosion and barnacles, so it requires more thought for how the system will be implemented.

Compressed air storage uses caverns as a storage medium. During nonpeak times, an electric turbo-compressor is used to put the air in storage. A natural gas heater is used when it is time to expand the air to run the turbines. The process is estimated to be 30 percent to 50 percent more efficient than using the natural gas to generate the power. Plants were built in Huntorf, Germany (1978), and McIntosh, Alabama (1991), with plans for an additional plant in Norton, Ohio (2006). A 30 month extension for the Norton plant was approved on June 2, 2008, and FirstEnergy Generation Corp. purchased the rights to develop the facility from Compressed Air Energy Storage Development Co. on November 23, 2009. Development of this system is ongoing. Finding other means of storing the air and perfecting the heat transfer is the key in this effort. Plastic bags in a large body of water are being tested as one possibility, as this method provides the most stable temperature and pressure.

Batteries have long been the mainstay for electric storage. Development has, over the century, continued to run into difficulty trying to reduce the size and increase the capacity for these units. The lithium-ion battery has been a step forward for electric autos, and the renewed interest in the capacitor has emerged from its discovery in 1740 to be of interest to the researchers at the Massachusetts Institute of Technology at the turn of the 21st century. They are proposing that with the development of the LEES ultra-capacitor comes the plausibility of high capacity storage, no overheating, small size and the competitive cost that batteries have been striving to achieve with the lithium-ion battery. Use of nanotechnology holds promise that this will be one solution; bringing the cost down to the mass-production market is yet to be achieved.[59]

Partnerships

The California Fuel Cell Partnership (CaFCP) is a consortium of automakers, fuel cell makers, energy companies, government agencies and associated partners. The goals for CaFCP in 2002 were extremely aggressive. The organization was committed to promoting fuel cell vehicles by advancing new technology, developing alternative fuel infrastructure and educating the public about Alternative Fuel Vehicles (AFVs). One of its near-term goals was to put 40,000 fuel cell vehicles (FCVs) on the road in California by about 2008, as a mark for a viable market entry. By 2008, CaFCP had tempered its vision a bit to reflect more reachable gains by identifying commercial markets. It continues to promote that form of energy, including the need to provide fueling stations for those preferring the fuel cell model for their cars and trucks. Their efforts have had an impact. Most auto manufacturers targeted 2003–2004 for their FCVs to be tested in fleet use. They conducted studies to determine which type of fuel would dominate the new market. Four current alternatives are hydrogen, methanol, ethanol and gasoline. Infrastructure is still the key problem. When will the cars be ready? When will the fuel be broadly available? Fuel cells powered by gasoline do not require a new infrastructure, but are less friendly to the environment than hydrogen-powered cars. High cost is also a problem that must be offset for FCV marketability. Some of this expense is being absorbed by government agencies to assist the consortium in its program. Although the CaFCP numbers were not reached, major automakers did take notice of the market possibility and by 2008, consumers could choose from a modest range of fuel cell vehicles, among them the Chevy Equinox, the Honda FCV, Daimler FCV, Ford Edge, Hyundai Tucson FCEV, Toyota FCHV, Volkswagen's Touran HyMotion and Nissan X-trail FCE.

The Partnership for New Generation Vehicles (PNGV) has added SUVs to the list of vehicles targeted for improvement. It wants to triple the gas mileage of SUVs and thus diminish the impression that SUVs are gas guzzlers. The PNGV is a longstanding joint research effort between the U.S. government (seven agencies and 19 federal laboratories) and USCAR (United States Council for Automobile Research) formed by Ford, General Motors and DaimlerChrysler (now Chrysler LLC). It is dedicated to collaborative research to strengthen the automotive industry and address environmental concerns surrounding their products' manufacture and use. Its research helps increase automobile efficiency through the development of new materials, fuels and propulsion systems.

Iceland, following up on an idea proposed by Professor Bragi Amason during fuel shortages in the 1970s, took a more energetic approach to moving from a foreign oil based to a more environmentally friendly hydrogen fuel infrastructure. New Energy (comprising Daimler AG, Norsh Hydro, Shell, local utility companies, research institutes and partners in the European Union) was formed in 1999. Iceland's first Shell hydrogen refueling station opened to the public on April 25, 2003. The project has spurred similar business ventures in Denmark and other members of the European Union. Cost for the initial project was $7.7 million, with the European Union supplying $3.1 million of the total. The project's major difficulty is the lack of a supply of fuel cell cars. The infrastructure arrived before the vehicles. Demand was much greater than the supply.[60]

The Vehicle Recycling Development Center (VRDC) is a joint research project to improve recycling of car parts. It was established in 1996 by Ford, Chrysler and General Motors. Of the over ten million vehicles scrapped each year, the VRDC saw about 75 percent of the material by weight being recycled. The VRDC decided to focus on the remaining 25 percent of the vehicle not being recycled. The non-recycled parts consisted primarily of fluids and plastics. Removing fluids can be profitable only if done rapidly. VRDC is promoting an industry standard of design guidelines for fluid caps on all vehicles to aid the fluid removal equipment. Recycling plastics presents a bigger problem, as there may be as many as fourteen different types of plastics used to make just the instrument panel, in addition to a number of different bonding materials. A new method of removing, cleaning and reusing seat foam was developed in 1996. The goal of the project is to take the American automobile, not from cradle to grave, but from cradle to cradle.[61] To this end, the VRDC works with the American Recyclers Association to find new possibilities and recycled product markets to lower that 25 percent of unrecycled material that makes up two percent of landfills. Its success is commendable. By 2008, 95 percent of "end of life" cars were reclaimed through a market-driven recycling infrastructure with no added costs to the consumer. Eighty-four percent of each car is recyclable. The parts are reused in everything from new road surfaces to garden mulch.

Hybrids

Hybrid cars deliver better fuel efficiency and emit fewer pollutants than their ICE counterparts. Vehicles using a hybrid concept generate the power they need from more than one source. How the power is integrated depends on the inventor's and designer's ideas of what makes the most sense. Some use small gasoline motors to generate electricity needed to run the auto and its accessories, while others use a combination of electric and alternate fuel motors or fuel cells to move the vehicle. To provide fast acceleration, for example, both might be used, while in stop-and-go traffic only the electric is needed. Each manufacturer has its concept of what will catch the imagination of consumers and put them in line to buy the product. Regardless of design, this mode of power is a cleaner option both for fuel consumption and air quality.

Two fairly successful hybrid (gasoline-electric) vehicles entered the U.S. market in 2000, the Toyota Prius and the Honda Insight. Toyota has taken an environmental approach, not only to the use of hybrid energy, but also to the product materials themselves. Ninety percent of the Prius is built from recyclable materials, according to Toyota's advertising. The Toyota Prius has been in production and sold in Japan since 1997. Toyota also produces the Estima minivan and Crown luxury sedans that are known as "mild hybrids" in that they use a cheaper and less efficient system. The Estima, introduced in June 2001 in Japan, is a seven-passenger van using a hybrid engine to drive the front wheels. The van's "E-Four" system regulates the drive to the rear wheels and coordinates distribution of electric power to all wheels. Toyota is promoting this vehicle as the world's first electric four-wheel-drive system that represents an achievable environmental solution for a cleaner planet. Both Honda and Toyota products rallied enough consumer interest to have competitors consider expanding their offerings, and Toyota and Honda continue developing hybrids as part of the companies' product lines.

Prototype hybrids of limited production among major auto manufacturers showed willingness for the industry to test the market, but none was expecting to have a competitive mass-produced product until late in the first decade of the 21st century. The marketplace had other ideas. Demand for the Prius showed a burgeoning market as hybrids began dotting the landscape. The automakers listened. Within a few years, various types of gasoline-electric hybrids were available from most of the major manufacturers, each using its own adaptation of the concept to attract customers. Interest in fuel economy spawned additional innovation and products.

In 2006, Ford, through its subsidiary Volvo Cars, established a hybrid systems development center in Gothenburg, Sweden, to serve preferences for its European customers. The center focuses primarily on the development and deployment of cleaner, more efficient diesel engines, hybrids and alternative fuel vehicles, tailored to the European car market. Volvo's participation reflects its continued development of environmentally friendly technology for the auto market. Its early work resulted in the first SUV hybrid, the Ford Escape Hybrid. Volvo also put entries in the Challenge Bibendum race in both 2004 and 2006, introducing its 3CC electric concept car powered by a lithium-ion battery, and its multi-fuel high performance engine, which could run on bio-methane, bio-ethanol, natural gas, gasoline or hythane (a mixture of 10 percent hydrogen and 90 percent methane).[62]

Toyota is producing the FCHV-5, a fuel cell hybrid vehicle that generates electricity from hydrogen derived from CHF (clean hydrogen fuel), using a reformer. Seen as the next-generation liquid fuel, CHF can be produced from crude oil, natural gas or coal, and it has low sulfur content. CHF is also used as a fuel for gasoline engine vehicles and can be supplied by current gasoline pumps. The FCHV-5 could be useful where hydrogen supply infrastructure is not available.[63]

Honda began producing its natural gas Civic GX in 1998. It was certified as a SULEV, and fleet testing proved the engine reduced the CO_2 emissions by 25 percent compared to an ICE. Honda rolled out its Civic Hybrid in 2001.

Volkswagen tested a new concept vehicle, the Lupo 3L TDI, in August 2000 by driving it around the world in eighty days. The Lupo uses the Turbo Direct Injection system to combine a variable blade turbocharger with electronically controlled pump injector units to deliver a precisely measured mist of fuel to its three cylinders. When the car stops, the engine shuts off automatically. It restarts when the accelerator is pressed; the clutch disengages when coasting. These factors contributed to an average of about 80 mpg.

Ford, GM and DaimlerChrysler announced in January 2001 they would expand their offering of hybrid gasoline-electric powertrains. They showed prototypes of cars with claimed mileage of 70–80 mpg at a Detroit auto show that year. As described in Chapter 1, hybrids proliferated rapidly through the decade, but without approaching such economy figures.

In 2007 New York City mayor Michael Bloomberg proposed an aggressive plan to convert all 13,000 yellow taxicabs in the city to hybrid technology by 2012. The proposal was expected to reduce carbon emissions by 215,000 tons annually and perhaps double gasoline mileage. City analysts estimated that the conversion would have the same impact as removing 30,000 vehicles from the streets. New York City has encountered problems using hybrids for its cabs. Hybrids are considered unsafe for taxis. The companies never suggested they should be used for commercial work and don't endorse that use. The Ford Crown Victoria (an ICE) is still considered the safe choice. The Taxi and Limousine Commission's required partitions that provide safety for the driver compromise the safety standards of the hybrids by blocking side air bags; the partitions are easily dislodged in accidents.

In November 2008, in Federal District Court in Manhattan, Paul A. Crotty issued an injunction to keep New York City from enforcing its new fuel efficiency standard. The ruling stated that under the existing EPAct of 1975, only the federal government was allowed to set specific standards. This ruling is still in force.

With an energy crunch beginning in 2006, and the improvements in batteries, the plug-in hybrid reappeared as a concept car and gained attention. The plug-in requires only household current (120 volts) for recharging. In 2007, RechargeIT, a Google initiative, produced a fleet of plug-in hybrids to advance the concept. Their recharging grid included solar-powered stations on the Google campus. This program retrofitted Toyota Prius and Ford Escape Hybrid to be plug-in models. The cars were fitted with data recording devices to track technical and environmental performance. After one year of testing, the data collected showed that overall, the Escape got 49.1 mpg, and the Prius, 93.5 mpg.[64]

The feasibility of solar-powered recharging stations, the production promises for the Chevy Volt's availability, and the Fisker Karma luxury electric are spiking modest interest in the revival of plug-ins in the general marketplace.

The Sierra Club launched a three-year campaign in June 2002 calling for the Big Three automakers to improve the fuel efficiency of their cars. The club maintains that existing technologies could be made more widely available to increase gas mileage in order to cut dependence on foreign oil, save money at the pump and provide a cleaner environment. Sierra Club spokesman Daniel Becker said, "The biggest single step we can take to save oil is to make our cars go farther on a gallon of gas. The technology exists to boost fuel economy in our cars and SUVs, saving 42 million gallons of oil a day."[65] The Sierra Club welcomed Honda's newest fuel-saving car, the Civic Hybrid, in December 2001, stating, "As the nation debates national energy security and the need to reduce dependence on oil, Honda's second hybrid vehicle shows how technology can help cut oil consumption, save consumers at the pump, and curb global warming. Honda's new Civic Hybrid, like the Honda Insight, combines attributes of electric and gasoline motors. The Civic Hybrid's highly efficient gas-powered engine, refillable at any gas station, powers the vehicle and also generates electricity for the electric motor, which helps provide power. The Civic Hybrid additionally captures the energy typically lost in braking, directing it to recharge the batteries. Unlike pure electric vehicles, a hybrid does not need to be plugged in. Because the Civic Hybrid runs on both gasoline and clean electricity, it achieves fuel economy of 50 mpg and therefore emits much less pollution than other vehicles."[66] A study conducted by the National Renewable Energy Laboratory in 2007 estimated that between 1999 and 2006, over 215 million gallons (5.1 million barrels) of fuel had been saved in the U.S. Much of that savings is attributed to more efficient ICEs, and, more prominently, to the consumer's buying power — purchasing hybrids.

Environmentalist clubs and organizations promote hybrid vehicles over the battery-only EVs. There is a web-based car club in Japan, Priusmania, dedicated to the development of the gasoline-electric hybrid car. The members are promoting environmentally conscious vehicles and automakers who support these designs, touting the belief that the gasoline-electric vehicles are "the next big thing" and speculating on whether the next Prius will be a plug-in. Others are taking a more practical approach. Many groups in the United States are concentrating on raising fuel economy and making the CAFE standards higher. They want light trucks and SUVs to conform to the same standards as cars. For the last twenty-five years, CAFE standards for cars have been 27.5 mpg, while for SUVs and light trucks the standard has been 20.7 mpg. The Sierra Club estimated that raising the SUV requirement to that of cars would save consumers over $27 billion at the gas pump and reduce the consumption of oil by over one million barrels a day. The club restates in many of its press releases that the biggest single step to take in saving oil (and gasoline) is to make cars that will go farther on a gallon of gas. It also feels that making a car go farther on a gallon of gasoline will help to prevent global warming. The Sierra Club views the SUV as a monument to environmental destruction because many of the vehicles achieve only about twelve miles per gallon and continue to have higher emission pollutants than regular autos. As part of its fuel efficiency campaign for the Big Three car manufacturers, the Sierra Club also called for more stringent CAFE standards that would require automakers to produce cleaner cars. In 2004, the light truck standard was to meet 22.5 mpg by 2008. In 2006, the Environmental Protection Agency (EPA) proposed adjustments in the mileage rating system. The system then being used was based on test conditions, not real-world driving. The new estimated gas mileage ratings took into account such factors as use of air conditioning and high speed driving. The system took effect in 2008 and showed an estimated downturn adjustment of 10 percent to 20 percent for city driving and 5 percent to 15 percent for highway driving. Gas-electric hybrid vehicles had the sharpest rate drop, with city driving figures falling from 20 percent to 30 percent.[67] The Energy Independence and Security Act of 2007 included 35 mpg standards for all passenger cars and light trucks to be met by 2020.

New Environmentalist magazine promoted hybrid cars in 2002, stating "the gas-electric vehicles offer 1.5 to twice the fuel efficiency of gasoline cars of the same size, cutting carbon dioxide emissions."[68] When the internal combustion engine is running in a hybrid electric vehicle, it emits slightly more pollutants than an electric car, but is far cleaner than a conventional car. A *Scientific American* writer noted, "When pollution from the generating sources that charge its batteries is taken into account, an electric vehicle is about one tenth as 'dirty' as a conventional car with a well-tuned engine. An HEV, in comparison, can be about one eighth as polluting."[69]

In 1990 the transportation industry ranked third in energy usage. By 2006, two-thirds of U.S. oil consumption was earmarked for transportation needs. It is predicted that by 2010 it will be the dominant source of technologically produced CO_2 emissions in the United States. Citizens with an interest in environmental quality have the power to influence manufacturers of our personal transports. Hybrids are capturing the market's attention by their practicality in using existing infrastructure while successfully reducing noxious fumes and pollutants. The possibilities for even cleaner emissions through fuel cell energy is building as its refueling infrastructure expands and less polluting alternatives come to market.

EVs have been viewed at various times in history as solutions to noise and air pollution and as a means to decrease dependence on foreign oil supplies. However, since early days, the electrics have not been able to capture more than a niche in the marketplace. For the environmentalist or conservationist, the electric car is one option that must be viewed in its entirety: Not only "How does the vehicle affect the environment," but also "How does generating the electricity affect the earth?" Acceptance by the consumer must also be weighed. Fuel development and power generation are finding inventive alternatives to the traditional EV, but the market continues to be "just around the corner."

4

TECHNOLOGY

In 1994, an auto company executive said, "We are at the very beginning of a new era of technology [fuel cells], comparable to the days when Gottlieb Daimler and Karl Benz were constructing the first vehicles powered by internal combustion engines."[1] In 1912, *Scientific American* wrote, "The mechanism of an electric car is so simple that there are really only two things upon which there can be any extensive improvement, i.e., the battery and the motor."[2]

Today, technological innovation is needed for the electric vehicle. The public must have a comparable product in price and performance before they will move from their treasured internal combustion engine (ICE) automobiles. The excitement of competition is clear; expanded competition for electrics and hydrogen fuel cell refueling are coming on the scene. Recent developments in battery recharging are aimed at reducing the time needed to recharge the battery from several hours or overnight to 15–20 minutes. This would still take considerably longer time at a recharging station than filling a tank with gasoline, an inconvenience the consumer might not be willing to accept. The choices are battery-powered, fuel cells or hybrids. The most promising long-term solution for a fully electric vehicle is the use of fuel cell technology. The technology itself is not a motor and not a fuel. It is an efficient, environmentally friendly, cost-effective means for creating the electricity needed to run a motor or series of motors for an electric automobile. Its fuel can be as cheap a product as methanol or water. Hydrogen fuel cells fit today's focus on clean green energy since the only by-products are heat and water. The ultimate goal is to have zero-emission vehicles on the road, but until the technology is perfected and costs are competitive, hybrids, using electric motors enhanced by small, clean-burning gasoline engines, continue to be the best interim answer to pollution problems and the most marketable to the auto-buying public.

The deregulation of the energy market in the United States and Europe is another major factor in technology development. As with the expansion of the oil industry in the early 1900s, deregulation of the energy industry has the potential for providing incentives to advance a next generation in the electric automotive industry.

In the mid– and late 1990s, Europe, Britain and the United States each began steps toward deregulating their power industry. This deregulation allowed the industry to segment parts of the process and opened the field for power companies to divide power sources from distribution streams. This change has provided a means for wind, wave and other alternative energy generators to bid for a place in the field. Although they represent a small percentage of the total as suppliers, they are becoming competitors in the marketplace as power producers. Regulation continues in the transmission and distribution sectors to ensure customers have reliable electricity delivery. The deregulation road is not without its potholes. Some restrictions in the legislation, aimed at protecting the consumer against perceived rate hikes once the marketplace dictated price, did have some unexpected consequences. One high-profile example occurred in California. State-imposed price controls forced utility companies to pay more for electricity than they were allowed to charge customers. This led to the bankruptcy of Pacific Gas and Electric (PGE) and the publicly funded bailout of Southern California Edison. Loss of power to the grid formerly supplied by PGE led to a shortage in energy. "Rolling blackouts" in California began in May 2000 and continued until September 2001. On November 13, 2003, Governor Gray Davis declared an end to the state of emergency; deregulation was blamed for the blackouts. Adjustments allowing more flexibility in both the United States and Europe have been introduced. Service agreements now carry, as standard, a consistent power clause. Lessons are being learned. Innovations provide new options. Free market and governments are finding their respective places in providing consistent power to customers. Directive 2003/54/EC in the European Union (EU) is a prime example as it moves to integrate national markets among its members. Many EU members, among them Italy, Norway, Sweden, the UK, Belgium and the Netherlands, introduced Renewable Energy Certificates to promote involvement and generate investment. The system is market based; no government subsidies are involved. This deregulation is substantially increasing the potential for competitive development of new technologies to provide low emission energy at a reasonable cost for both the automotive and residential sectors. Observe the choices now available in the telecommunications industry after deregulation and envision the same happening in the energy industry. The energy industry is only beginning to learn about being competitive, but it is learning rapidly how to survive and thrive in a deregulated environment.

Technology is evolving to provide energy to non-conventional vehicles it is advancing. Inventions in batteries, fuel cells and hybrid vehicles are all options being researched to create the energy needed to run an efficient, convenient automobile. Developments in these technologies will determine whether mass production is feasible and whether a vehicle with comparable performance to an ICE can be produced at a competitive price. If it can, will the public accept it as a replacement? In May 2002 an article in *AutoWeek* stated that "automakers are in agreement in one thing: electric vehicles powered by hydrogen fuel cells represent the best hope for the long-term survival of the automobile."[3] The present argument concerns the source of the hydrogen to use to power the fuel cells. It could come from natural gas, gasoline, water, or a solid state. Once again the problem is that a convenient infrastructure does not exist to get the fuel on board. Building a hydrogen infrastructure, it is estimated, could take ten years or more and cost in excess of $100 billion.

Alternatives are being explored. Solar-powered hydrogen stations developed and operated by Honda in California, Chicago's stations in use by city buses, and Iceland's and Denmark's hydrogen programs are already in service. Other manufacturers are working on a hydrogen supply from on-board reformers that would convert methanol into hydrogen. The reformers are very complex and heavy. John Wallace, executive director of Ford's alternative fuel vehicle Th!nk division, said in 2002, "It's just another layer of difficulty that no one needs."[4] The Ztec Corporation in Woburn, Massachusetts, in 2002 was developing another option: an electric-powered hydrogen generator that could be installed in a filling station's service bay. The generator would vaporize gasoline, mix it with steam, and then pass the mixture over catalyst, stripping hydrogen from the blend. The by-products of carbon dioxide and carbon monoxide would be collected for later disposal.[5] The Big Three manufacturers and researchers in universities and institutes see market potential and environmental benefits and are putting resources into research and development of fuel cells.

The most efficient catalyst in fuel cell electric car technology is platinum, but with start-stop driving in town, the platinum dissolves, reducing its efficiency. In 2007 the Brookhaven National Laboratory in New York discovered that platinum electrocatalysts remain intact when gold clusters are added to them. The gold clusters protect the platinum from being oxidized. It seems a ratio of 10 percent gold to 90 percent platinum is optimal. Yes, it appears expensive, but since gold is about half the price of platinum, the price will not increase too much. Advances in microbial fuel cells, which generate electricity from microbes, are proving interesting because the process can use bio-waste to generate the electricity and return clean water to the environment. The process has come back into the research and design world as an alternate energy resource and a means to provide cost-effective fuel for fuel cell vehicles. This research is moving forward but is still in its infant stages as a marketable product for the auto industry. The University of Aberdeen's research in using biofuels (specifically ethanol) to generate hydrogen needed for fuel cells has more potential for reducing fuel cell costs in the short term and making them attractive alternatives to battery and battery hybrids.

The automotive industry is at the beginning of a generational shift, a sea change that will eliminate the reliance on the standard internal combustion engine. Through this technology-driven change we may soon see an analogy to Moore's law (that computer chips will double in speed every year) in the battery and fuel cell industry. In 2000, a technology analyst remarked, "There is an enormous backlog of innovative ideas in the technology development area."[6] Interest is developing in the energy industry in new possibilities for generating power. The availability of fuel cell kits (prices range from $9,000 to $15,000) for the budding amateur scientist and engineer may provide the next step in much the way that crystal sets of the early 20th century paved the way for advancements in the radio. The technology that is being created today points to solutions that will allow automobile manufacturers to produce an environmentally friendly electric vehicle that is better than the conventional technology currently used in the internal combustion engine, and at a competitive price.

Early Developments

France and England were the first to develop electric vehicles in the late 1800s. The United States followed in 1895, and in 1897 the first commercial fleet of electric vehicles appeared as taxis in New York City. Electric vehicles outsold all other types in 1899 and 1900. This is the peak of their popularity to this point in history. Part of the reason for this popularity was that the only good roads at the time were in towns. Since the range of the electric vehicle was limited, it was a perfect choice for local commuting in cities on both sides of the Atlantic.

From 1894 to about 1900, battery technology made great strides and looked like it had a promising future with the electric cars. Total electricity production increased and battery production flourished. Technology increased battery life and improved durability, needed to withstand the rough roads.[7] Early battery technology blossomed in about 1895 when storage batteries became more efficient and consistent. By that time, the Electric Storage Battery Company had "obtained all battery-related rights, patents, and licenses formerly controlled by Consolidated Electric Storage, General Electric, Brush Electric and Electric Launch and Navigation."[8] Electrics had the promise of a reliable power source.

As steam powered, internal combustion (gasoline-powered), and electric cars vied for dominance, each moved its own technological advances forward, trying to gain market share. In 1895 one-third of all vehicles registered in Michigan were steam-powered, one-third were electric and one-third were gasoline-powered. While the electric and steam-powered vehicles were superior from a maintenance standpoint with fewer parts to repair, they suffered from short range and inconvenient refueling/recharging stations. Although strides had been made in battery technology, development was not sufficient to place the electric automobile in the marketplace lead. Electric automobiles were more expensive to buy and maintain than were steam or gasoline-powered cars. The initial prices for the electric car ranged from $1,250 to $3,500, while gasoline-powered automobiles were $1,000 to $2,000 and steam cars sold for $650 to $1,500. Operating expenses for the electrics averaged $0.02/mile compared with $0.01/mile for the steam or gasoline vehicles. The range of the electrics was only twenty miles and charging stations were not readily available.[9] Increasing the electric car's range meant inventors needed to find a way to improve the battery. That improvement was key to providing electrics with a competitive edge against the ICEs.

The electric utility industry was also expanding at this time. Chicago Edison was busy acquiring every small, local generating station it could afford. By 1898 it had a monopoly. Unfortunately for the EV, most of the Chicago utility company's efforts were spent on advertising the spread of modern electric service (light bulbs and signs) and had little impact on the advancement of sales of the electric vehicle.[10]

The power system of an electric vehicle consists of two components: the motor that provides the power and the controller that provides the application of that power. The motor converts electrical energy into mechanical energy while the controller regulates the energy flow from the battery. The motor may produce alternating current (AC) or direct current (DC). If DC, the controller converts it to AC. If the motor is reversed, the controller converts this action into a generator to recharge the battery. The controller can also be used to regulate regenerative braking to recharge the battery. This discovery came in 1900 when manufacturers began looking at ways to recharge batteries with the automobile in motion. The concept was successful in the 1900 Waverley, for example, which used a braking system based on this bidirectional controller concept. The battery actually charged as the driver was applying the brakes. The motor used was the invention of J. C. Lincoln of Cleveland, Ohio, and was manufactured by the Lincoln Electric Company. It allowed the driver descending a hill to replace the current used in ascending it.

By 1912 the many improvements in electric vehicles prompted people to once again believe the electric would find far greater favor as its advantages became well known and

Automatic Recharging Electric Vehicle, circa 1900[11]

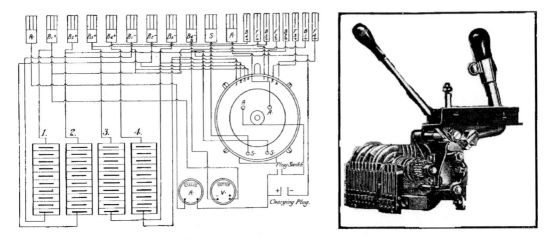

Left: Diagram of controller circuits of recharging motor.[12] *Right:* Knife blade controller, 1911.

appreciated. Technology had made the electric car the easiest to control. It had no gears to shift and no clutch. Starting the car took no more effort than turning a key. There was no noise or vibration, allowing the machinery and tires a longer life. Again it was apparent that the mechanism of the electric car was so simple that there were only two parts that could be improved, the battery and the motor.

Scientific American touted Thomas A. Edison as a genius in bringing out the nickel-iron storage battery. The new battery was just half the weight of the lead battery and was said to increase the electric car's range from sixty-five to one hundred miles.[13] One more improvement of note was the conversion of the transmission of power to the wheels from a chain drive to a shaft drive system. It was silent and could be enclosed, giving a more finished appearance. One failed invention added two more wheels, with motors attached to all six wheels for greater motive power.

By 1913 there were several forms of the lead-acid battery available that could deliver a daily range of about eighty miles, or sufficient charge to travel about the town or suburbs for three days of ordinary travel. A standard thick-plate lead battery was common. A medium or thinner-plate type was also available for lighter body styles, such as the road-

Chassis, 1911[14]

ster. The thinner-plate battery allowed a larger number of batteries to be installed in about the same space and for about the same weight as the standard battery. The thin-plate battery gave longer total mileage per charge, and the total life of the battery was about two to three times that of the thick-plate battery. The improved construction of this battery included a positive plate in the shape of a pencil. Installation of this new battery added about $120 to the overall cost of the vehicle. The additional expense could be justified, since the plates shed very little active material and internal cleaning was seldom required, making it more economical to operate. The nickel-iron battery was another choice. This battery increased the cost of a car by about $600. The added initial price could be offset by reduced maintenance. There was no plate renewal needed and internal cleaning of the battery was unnecessary. The only maintenance required was adding distilled water to keep the electrolyte fluid level above the top of the plate.[16]

Ways for providing interchangeable battery systems for electric cars were being explored again around 1914. The Klingelsmith Electric Truck Company of Chicago, Illinois, devised a system of quickly replacing discharged batteries with charged storage batteries. The batteries were carried to the vehicles on small transfer rail cars. The company proposed that all service stations should own the batteries, relieving the owner of the car of that investment. They estimated that the cost to the driver for fresh batteries and some service offerings would be about half as much as maintaining the batteries themselves. A Chicago agent of the Milburn Electric Car Company developed a battery and rental exchange program in 1917. Harry Salvat, owner of Fashion Automobile Stations, offered to sell a Milburn car for $1,485 minus the battery. The battery would be rented for $15 a month with a one dollar fee for a change. The exchange could be made at any of five stations located in the Chicago area and would take only two minutes, less time than it took to fill a gasoline tank. The company promoted its idea as relieving the car owners of the time and investment in batteries.

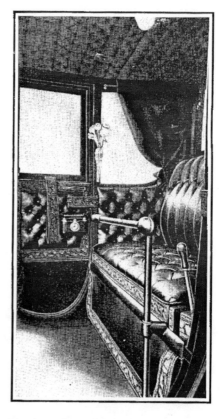

Interior of an electric brougham, 1911[15]

Battery History

Alessandro Volta invented the first battery in 1800 when he generated an electrical current from chemical reactions between dissimilar metals. One writer described it this way: "The original voltaic pile used zinc and silver disks and a separator consisting of a porous non-conducting material saturated with sea water."[17]

Raymond Gaston Plante invented the lead-acid battery in 1860 when he rolled up a combination of thin lead and rubber sheets and immersed it in a dilute sulfuric acid solution. In the 1880s, the efficiency was improved by creating a paste of lead oxides for the positive plate active materials. In the 1960s, German researchers developed a gelled-electrolyte lead-acid battery to help eliminate electrolyte leakage. The two batteries most frequently used in the electric automobiles were a lead pasted battery that contained elements of lead, peroxide of lead, and sulphuric acid, and the Edison battery, containing iron, nickel and an alkaline solution.

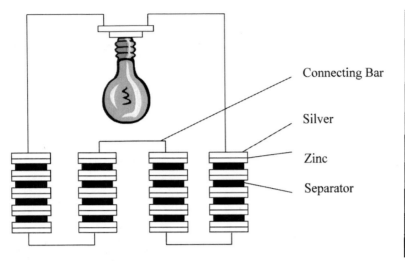

Connecting Bar

Silver

Zinc

Separator

Left: Voltaic pile. *Right:* Edison 4-plate battery cell.[18]

Battery weight challenged the industry. The problem was approached as early as 1899. A *Scientific American* article stated, "The factor of weight is one of the features in an electric vehicle that practical men are working to overcome, and it is said that whenever a storage battery or a system of storing the electric current is invented by which the weight of the battery is greatly reduced, there is certain to be an impetus given to the electric motor vehicle industry such as has never been thought of."[19] The Willard storage cell was one common system of the day, consisting of forty-four batteries measuring 3 × 5 × 9 inches and weighing 950 pounds. Recharging took about two hours. Other designers continued to experiment with new configurations to counteract the battery weight.

A major design obstacle in using batteries is finding the balance between the weight of the battery and the need for a large number of batteries on board to provide performance and range. The problem of large and heavy batteries was partly solved in battery-powered automobiles by redistributing weight. In 1901, to combat the weight of the battery, M. Krieger designed an electric automobile using the two-place "electrolette machine."[20] This system consisted of a gasoline motor, an electric generator and two electric motors. The energy developed by the gasoline motor was delivered to the driving wheels electrically, not mechanically. The front wheels turned at the end of a spur gear, each independently driven by a separate electric motor. The motors represented only 220 pounds of the total weight of 1,700 pounds for the vehicle. The batteries were Fulmen type, having a total weight of only 800 pounds and a range of sixty-five miles on a single charge. The Fulmen battery design was a variation on the original grid type lead-battery plate and used friction to hold the active material in place on the grid. This prevented the lead coating on the plate from "falling off" to the bottom of the battery and causing a short. This design improved battery life, especially against the physical jolts suffered in on-road use. The concept is still in use today.

The speed of the Krieger on an average level grade was about 21 mph. Braking was accomplished by short-circuiting the motors.

The 1900 Waverley incorporated a recharging motor for its electric car. By continuing to run the motor downhill instead of immediately applying the brakes, the motor continues to increase in speed "until the counter electromotive force of the armature equals that of the battery, which would be 80 volts with the controller on the third position or notch. At this point the motor will take no current and ... if the speed increases ... will generate a current in the opposite direction."[22] The inventor claimed this process would provide from 20 to 40 percent greater distance of travel than the conventional wound motor.

Current Battery Technology

Dramatic improvement in battery technology is still needed if the industry is to develop a marketable electric car. Consumers' acceptance of the electric vehicle depends upon the manufacturer's ability to

Krieger automobile, 1901[21]

provide the range, durability, performance and convenient recharging that consumers expect from conventional automobiles. The battery is the single biggest obstacle to the development of an efficient electric car, and thus the most critical component of fulfilling the dream of an electric vehicle revolution. Unless this technology improves, we are stuck with the same roadblocks as in the early 1900s: cost and convenience.

As incentive, the United States Department of Energy (DOE) spent $7 million on advanced battery research in 1976 and increased that to $12.5 million in 1977. The U.S. Postal Service had 350 EVs in operation in 1976 and was slated to purchase 750 more in 1978. In 1978 the Lead Industries Association claimed the lead-acid battery to be the "only viable power source for electric vehicles for the present and near-term future."[23] Partially because of this attitude, almost all research concentrated on boosting the lead-acid battery's performance. The DOE, in a joint project with Argonne National Laboratory, called for the purchase of several hundred electric vehicles with improved batteries by 1979 and for an additional 5,000 electric vehicles with more improved batteries by 1984. The DOE estimated that people would buy an electric car if it had a range of eighty-eight miles. The lead-acid battery of the day was getting a range of only about forty miles. Zinc-nickel batteries were smaller and lighter, but cost-prohibitive.

In 1991 Arizona Public Ser-

	Specific Energy (Wh/kg)	Energy Density (Wh/kg)	Specific Power (W/kg)	Cycle Life	Range (Miles)	Recharge Time (Hours)	Energy Efficiency (%)	Recyclability of Materials (%)
Present Lead-Acid	33	30	130	400	60	8 to 17 hours	65	97
Horizon Lead-Acid	42	93 Wh/L	240	800	100	< 5 hours	na	100
Nickel-Cadmium	57	56	200	2000	120	8 hours	65	99
Nickel-Iron	55	50	100	2000	110	4 to 8 hours	60	99
Nickel-Metal Hydride	70	80	250	600	250	< 6 hours	90	90
Lithium-Ion	100	100	300	1200	195	< 3 hours	na	50

Energy storage devices[24]

vice and Southern California Edison sponsored a new type of battery, a bipolar zinc-air unit. This battery was shown to produce eight times the energy of a lead-acid battery. The system uses oxygen from the atmosphere to combine with a zinc paste and a catalyst to produce electricity. The batteries are renewed by putting in fresh zinc or aluminum rather than plugging them into a charger. The manufacturer, DEMI, claimed a twelve-minute "flash" charge would produce a range of forty miles at thirty miles per hour, while a one-hour charge would give a range of one hundred miles. Honda used the bipolar zinc-air battery in its CRX EV to win the first electric vehicle race in Phoenix with an average speed of sixty-two miles per hour for 108 miles.

In 1996 the United States Advanced Battery Consortium (USABC) awarded seven contracts to research companies to develop mid-term and long-term solutions for the electric vehicle. Because lithium is the lightest metal on the periodic table, research began to explore the possibilities of a lithium polymer battery (LPB) with a five-layer design consisting of an insulator, lithium fuel (anode), solid electrolyte, cathode and a metal-foil current collector. The current focus of the USABC and the Department of Energy (DOE) is on nickel metal hydride (NiMH) and lithium-ion (Li-Ion) batteries, and interest in the lithium polymer (li-poly) is mounting. NiMH batteries have the immediate advantage, offering increased range, but the Li-Ion and the li-poly may take the long-term command in the marketplace. Li-Ion batteries are a solid-state technology that uses carbon as the anode and shuttles lithium back and forth in ion form between the carbon and a metal oxide. The electrolyte in the li-poly battery is held within a solid polymer composite instead of an organic solvent, can take more charge-recharge cycles and is lighter because it needs no metal casing. However, it does not hold a charge as long as the Li-Ion. Lithium is also recyclable. Each design holds promise as an electric car power source.

Sixty percent of the world supply of lithium comes from Australia and Chile. In Australia, it comes from the Greenbushes mine, inland from Bunbury, and in Chile, it is extracted from the large brine lakes in the Andes. With the renewed interest in lithium-ion batteries for electric cars, the price of the concentrate doubled between 2005 and 2008 to about $500 U.S. per ton.

If high-volume production occurs, the price of a lithium ion battery will drop to about $1,200 to $1,500 per vehicle, down from about $4,000 in 2007. One size and type of lithium battery will not fit every type of vehicle. For example, the high performance Lexus RX 400h needs a battery that can be discharged and charged quickly, unlike a Toyota Prius or Saturn Vue Green Line. Either way, the resale value of any lithium ion battery-powered vehicle could be affected by the expensive replacement of battery packs. On the positive side, lithium ion batteries made in Japan were seven times more powerful in 2007 than they were in 1975. There is still a problem of overheating, which GM is approaching in a two-pronged idea of changing the chemical makeup or creating an elaborate system of sensors and computers to shut down the cell. Hyundai brought their retail version, a liquefied petroleum gas with a lithium polymer battery, to market in July 2009 for its Korean market and planning to have a version of their Sonata for their North American market my mid-2010.

NiMH batteries use a metal-hydride electrode that has a theoretical capacity approximately 20–40 percent higher than the equivalent cadmium electrode in a nickel-cadmium battery. From 1991 to 1996, the NiMH battery evolved from small cells used in consumer electronics to larger units capable of powering an EV. It is projected that the next stage of nickel metal hydride batteries will be more cost effective and last as long as the car.

Lithium-Ion (Li-Ion) and lithium polymer batteries became popular for portable electronics like video cameras and laptop computers, and have been scaled for electric vehicles. The cost is high, but they offer longer range and have a long life cycle. The advantage of the Li-Ion battery, and even more for the li-poly, is lightweight and small size. Cells were initially constructed with thin films 100 micrometers thick. The resulting battery was too large for commercial use in an automobile, but its technological evolution mirrors the size reduction seen in the evolution of the computer microprocessor. In 2006 there were reports of lithium ion battery fires in laptop computers. Dell and Apple announced large recalls of the laptop batteries, followed by Toshiba, Lenovo and Sony. This led to an evolution of the battery into a lithium polymer ion battery using a solid polymer composite such as polyethylene oxide or polyacrylonitrile to hold the electrolyte, instead of an organic solvent. Advantages also included lower cost to produce and a battery that, like the Fulmen accumulator of the early 1900s, can withstand more jarring and shaking.

Fuel Cell History

In 1802 an English chemist, Sir Humphry Davy, built a fuel cell that used carbon electrodes and nitric-acid electrolyte.[25] This was the first fuel cell. In 1839, British scientist Sir William Grove discovered that combining hydrogen and oxygen electronically to form water produced by-products of heat and electricity. In 1894 Wilhelm Ostwald, a German chemist, foresaw the dangers of pollution caused by internal combustion engines and stressed the importance of using an electro-chemical process to provide energy. The process was not fully understood at the time and his strategy was not pursued. M. C. Potter began research in microbial fuel cells around 1912. His method for generating electricity used the *E. Coli* bacteria. Fuel cell research surfaced again in the 1930s and '40s, but results produced too little power to be practical for vehicles or utilities. It was not until NASA completed research for the Apollo space missions that fuel cell technology resurfaced as viable for automotive applications. The phosphoric-acid fuel cells showed excellent prospects for better efficiency at lower cost. In the 1960s Karl Kordesch, of Union Carbide, combined a six kilowatt alkaline fuel cell with storage batteries to provide greater power and a longer range for electric vehicles. This hybrid concept was revisited at the Los Alamos laboratory in the late 1970s using a phosphoric-acid electrolyte fuel cell and battery. The hybrid vehicle used the fuel cell to provide a steady speed of 55 mph and the battery provided brisk acceleration.[26] The problem has been that although fuel cell generators are less expensive and more efficient than battery operated units, the fuel cells created to do this are large and expensive.

The current focus by companies such as Ballard, Plug Power, Fuel Cell Energy, Inc., and International Fuel Cells (IFC) and Honda is to make these fuel cells small and inexpensive. Ballard Power Systems is the leader in developing proton exchange membrane (PEM) fuel cell technology, making alliances to develop fuel cell stacks that cost less, are smaller and weigh less. It is developing an oxygen enrichment system and a hydrogen purification system to increase high performance and contribute to cost effectiveness. The Ballard concept consists of a membrane electrode assembly placed between two flow-field plates. The membrane electrode assembly has two electrodes, an anode and a cathode separated by a solid polymer membrane electrolyte. Hydrogen is broken into free electrons and protons. The electrons are used to create electrical current and the protons combine with oxygen to create water and heat. The past decade has shown a great reduction in cost.

The advantage of a fuel cell over a battery is that while batteries eventually lose potency, fuel cells keep producing power as long as the fuel and oxidant supplies are maintained. A pattern can be seen: new technologies are first applied to industrial buildings, then to homes and next to automobiles and computers.

Universities worldwide are rediscovering microbial fuel cells (MFCs) and researching them as sources for electricity for the grid, for commercial use and for vehicles. The environmental benefits of using MFCs go beyond clean fuel cell emissions since biomass, including sewage, can be used as the initial fuel needed to generate the hydrogen or ethanol that in turn generates the electricity needed to power the engine. As with other designs of fuel cells, MFCs have clean water as the by-product at the tailpipe and thus the added benefit of returning clean water back to the environment at the processing plant. This type of fuel cell development is moving from the research lab to prototypes in the academic setting through research efforts like those of Bruce Logan from Pennsylvania State University, whose lab focuses on bioenergy production for the development of an energy-sustainable water infrastructure for both industrial and developing countries.

Fuel Cell Technology

Like the battery, a fuel cell is an electrochemical engine. The fuel is fed in, but not burned, as in an internal combustion engine. Instead, fuel and air react electrochemically in a clean environment. Fuels most commonly used in this process include hydrogen, methanol, ethanol, natural gas and liquefied petroleum gas. Less common sources include energy from biomass, water, solar and wind. Biochemists are developing a method of harvesting hydrogen from algae. The algae are first grown in a standard medium, then sulfur is removed from the mix and hydrogen is produced. Currently this method is operating only on a small scale. Researchers are also working with sewage and other biomass, including wastewater from breweries. Wind and solar power continue to be a niche as well, supplying small amounts of hydrogen to a limited market. The market and developing technology is so diverse that none of these hydrogen-producing methods have emerged as a single winner. Finding sources for separating and packaging the hydrogen is not a problem, but each has its drawbacks. Methanol reformation plants produced a world glut of the product in 2001.[27] Petroleum reformers are not as efficient because the gasoline molecule carbon bonds take a lot more energy to break apart. Petrol reformers therefore need to run at high temperatures, while methanol reformers can operate at about one-third of that temperature range. Fuel cells powered by methanol use a chemical reactor (a reformer) to release the hydrogen. The process has a small amount of carbon dioxide as a by-product. As inventors scale down from large facilities to auto-size fuel cells, they also face another problem — the smaller the reformer, the more carbon dioxide it releases. Probably the best advantage fuel cells have is that they are about twice as efficient as the internal combustion engine, converting about 30 percent of their fuel into useful energy.

In 2003, Iceland opened the world's first commercial hydrogen fueling station. Geothermal power is used to produce the hydrogen. As of this writing, the stations are still without incident. Their major difficulty is the lack of fuel cell cars available on the market. The Shell station's electrolyzer strips the hydrogen from water molecules. From there they can be consumed in specially modified internal combustion engines like the Toyota Prius or turned into electricity in fuel cells like those in the Daimler A-Class cars. The electric option delivers more torque and power.[28]

Hydrogen Link West Denmark started in 2006 in Denmark and had opening ceremonies in September 2008, when hydrogen fueling stations were put in operation in three major cities. The hydrogen is produced by wind power centrally in Holstebro and distributed by trucks to the refueling stations. H2 Logic A/S developed and supplies the hydrogen fuel cell technology. Twenty companies partnered in this project, among them the Danish Energy Agency and Vestas Wind Systems A/S. The stations are making use of the country's wind power to produce the hydrogen and are providing refueling service to fuel cell hybrid vehicles in those cities. The project's budget was about $2.5 million.

In 2008 hydrogen gas vehicles needed storage tanks as large as the trunk of a car. Liquid hydrogen is denser and takes up much less space, but is also very expensive and difficult to produce. Some progress is being made using computers and quantum mechanics to analyze sodium alanate. Computations suggest a reaction mechanism that would extract hydrogen from a diffusion of aluminum ions within the bulk of a hydride. This is very much a computational phase and not in the field of tangible technology engineering.

The industry is concentrating on three types of fuel cell technology today—molten carbonate, PEM and solid oxide.

Molten carbonate is a high-temperature fuel cell technology that became available in the 1990s. It has a market of large buildings and complexes such as hospitals, malls or universities. Known as direct fuel cells (DFC), they use nickel-based electrodes to convert (or reform) fuel into electricity inside the fuel stacks. DFCs are more efficient than external fuel cell systems. The cells produce electricity, with heat as a by-product—enough to provide for large buildings. One example of this application is a 200-kilowatt fuel cell plant in Hamburg, Germany, that was a result of a partnership between the German electric and natural gas industries. Since the by-products are water and carbon dioxide, it is clean enough to be sited next to residential areas and supply additional heat to a nearby apartment building. This shows the potential for fuel cell technology to be cost effective and environmentally sound.

PEM is a proton exchange membrane fuel cell that operates at low temperature and is a good model for uses under one megawatt, such as automobiles and possibly cell phones and small stationary power plants or portable generators. The PEM fuel cell consists of the membrane electrode assembly and two flow-field plates. Hydrogen flows through a flow-field plate, while oxygen from the air flows through the other plate, attracting the hydrogen protons through the proton exchange membrane (PEM). This electrochemical process produces electricity, with water and heat as by-products. Fuel cells are similar to batteries. They produce electricity from an electro-chemical reaction and use the electricity to power an electric motor. Unlike the battery that uses up the chemical reactants during the reaction and must be recharged or discarded, a fuel cell stores the reactants externally, so it will keep producing electricity as long as fuel (hydrogen) is delivered to the fuel cell. This allows a fuel cell vehicle to be refueled instead of recharged. The main drawback of the PEM fuel cell is that it requires an external hydrogen reformer and therefore a new hydrogen infrastructure. One possibility in PEM technology might see the consumer buying a tank of hydrogen (like we now buy propane) instead of gasoline at the pump. While hydrogen or methanol would require a new infrastructure, extracting hydrogen from natural gas could build on an existing service. Natural gas, because of its availability, is the best choice for a hydrogen source, as it is mostly methane and has four hydrogen atoms for every carbon atom. The initial disadvantage of natural gas is that it takes up a lot of space, even when compressed or liquefied, but a product made by the Energy Conversion Devices Co. in Detroit in 2000 provided the innovative technology needed. It is a solid form of natural gas known as metal hydride. It can provide a tank of energy about the same size as an average tank of gasoline. Hydride powder can be produced and sold as a replaceable sealed canister to be inserted at the bottom of the fuel cell stack, requiring only water added at the top of the stack to activate. Though natural gas is currently only available at some gas stations, it is widely used for home heating and thus could be made conveniently available.

In another advance in PEM technology, QuestAir, in a joint venture with Ballard, developed a proprietary pressure swing adsorption technology, a compact PSA gas purification technology that separates and enriches selected hydrogen/oxygen gas streams making the process more effective. This has many uses beyond fuel cells, such as industrial gas applications, diesel emissions reduction, and medical oxygen devices.

In 2000, solid hydrogen storage — whereby hydrogen is kept at low pressure is a safe, solid-compound container — was being considered by some companies as the key to commercializing fuel cell electric vehicles (FCEVs). The technology has increased the limit of two grams of hydrogen per one hundred grams of hydride to seven grams of hydrogen per one hundred grams of hydride. A typical fill-up would require only three to four minutes. Hydrogen gas inserted into the container is absorbed into the interface regions of the metallic powder, and the molecules dissociate into individual hydrogen atoms, forming a metal hydride. Adding heat releases the hydrogen atoms to reform into molecules. The resulting pure hydrogen gas can then be fed into a fuel cell to produce the energy to power the vehicle. In September 2000, GM, in collaboration with ExxonMobil, announced it had developed a unit that would generate hydrogen from gasoline. GM claimed an efficiency of 80 percent and predicted a gasoline processor fuel cell car could be delivered to the consumer

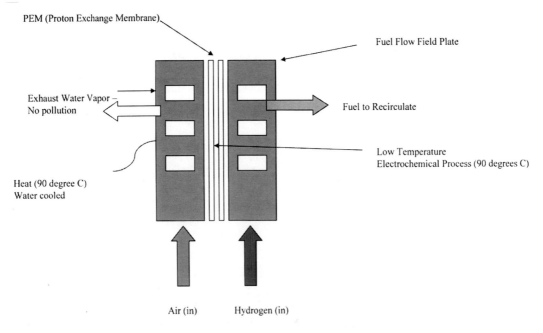

The Ballard Mark 900 Series fuel cell[29]

within ten years. Honda came out with its own fuel cell vehicle in 2003. The Honda FCV uses a PEM fuel cell and asynchronous electric motor. The year 2007 saw the rollout of GMs Project Driveway. The project supplied over 100 Equinox fuel cell electric vehicles, the Sequel FCV model, to government agencies and consumers around the United States to test drive. The PEM fuel cell system in the Equinox is scalable to different GM models. The United States Environmental Protection Agency is one of the testers. The 2008 car has a range of 150–200 miles per tank of hydrogen, accelerates 0 to 60 in 12 seconds, and has a top speed of 100 mph. It has conventional 17-inch aluminum wheels, anti-lock brakes, air bags, and navigation equipment, and is reportedly quiet and smooth to drive.[30]

Solid oxide is the next generation to be developed, within five to ten years, and uses heat to produce hydrogen for the fuel cell. This fuel cell uses a coated zirconia with YTTRIA ceramic electrolyte as an internal reformer. The ceramics used in the fuel stack comprise three of the four layers and become electrically active when heated to between 600° and 1000° C. Oxygen ions diffuse through the solid oxide electrolyte where the chemical reaction oxidizes the fuel. Water and two electrons result. The electrons are siphoned off to become electricity and a new power source. The electrochemical conversion process produces electricity, with a large amount of heat as a by-product. The superheated gas exhaust by-product can be channeled to spin a gas turbine. Mass production of this type of fuel cell is faced with a number of basic manufacturing challenges. BMW is working in this arena to develop a unit that can operate at lower temperatures to run auxiliary motors in cars. The Modine Manufacturing Co. of Racine, Wisconsin, specializes in heat transfer. It has created a fuel cell products group to develop heat exchangers for PEM technology to assist in production of heat cell engines. An advantage to this technology is that it will not require a separate hydrogen infrastructure because it can use a wide variety of fuels. In the early 2000s, a faction of the environmental community was emphatically promoting the development of this type of fuel cell technology.[31] They appreciate that the by-products of fuel cells are water and large amounts of heat.

In an ideal green environment, hydrogen for the PEM fuel cell would be produced directly by the electrolysis of water, using electricity generated from a renewable source. The Scandinavian and California projects are some using this method, but it requires expensive new infrastructure. The alternative is to extract the hydrogen from fossil fuels using the reformer, realizing that some carbon dioxide will reach the environment.

GM began developing a catalytic converter in 2000 that generates hydrogen directly from gasoline. It still creates carbon dioxide as a by-product but is 50 percent cleaner than the conventional ICE. In addition, no new infrastructure is needed as gas stations are already in place. In 2007, GM brought the Chevy Volt concept car, which replaces the generator with a fuel cell, to the Shanghai Auto Show. It uses the fuel cell for primary power with lithium-ion batteries as backup and storage. By 2008, GM had several fuel cell models on the market, including the Chevy Equinox SUV. Honda's FCX hydrogen stack develops about 100 kilowatts of power. The hydrogen is stored in two fuel tanks mounted under the floor in the vehicle's rear end. The cell's electricity propels an 80-kilowatt electric motor and produces no emissions. Ford's HySeries can be charged from either 110 or 220 volt household current and it switches to the onboard hydrogen fuel cell for the road. Fuel cells follow the tradition of a green machine.

People want home energy to be cheap and reliable. The same goes for cars, but powering an automobile by fuel cells is much more complicated than producing a home generator. Fuel analysts' predictions vary with regard to the wide use of PEM fuel cells in automobiles. In 2004, some analysts were claiming it would be ten years before a reliable fuel cell automobile would be available. Other analysts predicted PEM fuel cells would dominate the automotive market by 2010 with an 80 percent share. Skeptics implied GM was not really interested in developing an EV because of its links to "Big Oil." Enron, before its demise, invested in Fuel Cell Energy, Inc., to accelerate the commercialization of fuel cell products. Despite the technology obstacles, the main difficulty with fuel cells being implemented on a large scale is sticker cost. Much like the marketing problems encountered by hybrids in the 1990s, fuel cell vehicles carry a higher price tag because the technology costs for fuel cells run much higher than for conventional battery power.

In March 2000 Purdue University started experimenting with another possible power source. It is a fuel cell that runs on chemical reactions between hydrogen peroxide and aluminum. The hydrogen peroxide works as a "catholyte," having the properties of both an electrolyte (a liquid that conducts electricity) and a cathode (the part of a battery that attracts electrons). A disadvantage is the time it takes to provide a steady current flow.

In 1995, Daniel Sperling wrote:

> Fuel cell vehicles have many advantages, including zero emissions, quiet operation, long range and unparalleled energy efficiency. Perhaps most compelling of all, though, is that they might realize the elusive dream of solar hydrogen. Fuel cells that run on methanol, natural gas or petroleum would dramatically reduce pollution and cut greenhouse gas emissions and energy consumption at least by half. But solar hydrogen would push the fuel cell one giant step further — to a future that would come close to being environmentally benign. No other transportation technology or fuel holds the same promise.[32]

That giant step was met at the turn of the 21st century. Solar hydrogen refueling stations became a reality and are quietly and slowly entering the marketplace. In 2001, Honda opened a station in Torrance, California. The system uses photovoltaic (PV) cells and electrolysis to extract the hydrogen from water. This followed the city government stations located in Chicago, Illinois, and Thousand Palms, California. The Honda station, besides being in the private sector, had the added advantage of allowing refuelers to mimic the familiar refueling pattern used by gasoline stations. No special clothing is needed, and the refueler may stand by the vehicle when the tank is filling. Larger test markets in Iceland in 2003 and Denmark in 2006 show the possibility of having hydrogen fuel cells as a safe automobile option for the buying public. The stations supply a limited number of vehicles, but demonstrate that a solar infrastructure for hydrogen fuel cell vehicles is possible.

The California Fuel Cell Partnership, founded in April 1999, is an alliance of automakers, fuel cell distributors and manufacturers, government and transit agencies and fueling companies dedicated to developing environmentally friendly vehicles. Its automotive partners include Honda, DaimlerChrysler, Volkswagen, Ford, Nissan and Hyundai. DaimlerChrysler introduced its Necar 4 vehicle in March 2000, using liquid hydrogen to power a PEM fuel cell. It can go 90 mph for 280 miles. In December 1999, Ford ordered $4.5 million worth of fuel cells from Ballard Power Systems to integrate into its engines. In May 2002 Nissan confirmed a $2 million order of the Mark 902 series fuel cell from Ballard. DaimlerChrysler directed its efforts toward public transportation.

By 2004, as projected, 30 public buses were operational in 10 major cities worldwide. Among the cities were Amsterdam, Barcelona, Stockholm, Stuttgart, and Perth. The hydrogen buses ranged about 125 miles on the compressed hydrogen fuel cell system. By 2005, cars were added to the equation. Over 100 fuel cell vehicles were on the road through the federal Freedom Car Program. Partnering in this venture was the Sacramento (California)

Municipal Utility District. Its F-Cell is housed in the vehicle's floor, leaving more passenger and cargo space inside the car.

Volkswagen demonstrated its Jetta (called the Bora HyMotion in Europe) ZEM sedan during the California Fuel Cell Partnership meeting in November 2001. The car's fuel cell engine is most efficient when operating at mid-throttle, the range used during most normal driving. It has a range of about 350 kilometers and accelerates from 0 to 100 km/h in 12.6 seconds.[33]

The hydrogen-powered fuel cell is a true zero-emission-vehicle product. There are no air pollutants and the only by-product is water. Electric vehicles with a range and speed comparable to current internal combustion engines, driven by a hydrogen-powered fuel cell, would be a true competitor.

In 2008 Daimler AG, Ford Motor Company and Ballard Power Systems announced a new joint venture, Automotive Fuel Cell Cooperation, to develop fuel cell technology. Ballard transferred its automotive division to the new enterprise; Ford and Daimler AG are supplying the capital and management.

In February 2008 the National Hydrogen Association's Hydrogen Education Foundation launched a campaign to increase understanding about hydrogen. The association's president feels that hydrogen will play a large role in our future energy plans by providing a cleaner environment. Walmart has converted its indoor forklifts to hydrogen-fueled vehicles. Some of America's heavy-duty trucks are partially fueled by hydrogen. Hydrogen fuel cells are currently being used to supply back-up power to cell phone towers in the event of electrical outages. The association feels that people will need to be educated about how hydrogen works as an energy source before more advances can be made.

Mechanics and technicians must be educated and trained in hybrid fuel cell technologies. Columbia-Greene Community College in New York began instructor classes in 2006 focusing on hybrid technology, believing there will soon be a need for technicians who understand and can service high-tech automobiles.

As with the battery, the fuel cell has a long history and is rediscovered periodically when fuel shortages and concerns about a cleaner environment surface. Improvements in fuel cell technology and creating hydrogen refueling stations that use water as the base for producing the hydrogen move the dream of a widespread hydrogen infrastructure from possible to probable.

Hybrid Vehicles

One of the first hybrid vehicles was the 1902 French Lohner-Porsche Electric automobile, which combined electric and gasoline motors. It eliminated the inconvenience of battery recharging. As with the Krieger automobile, the electric motors were mounted on the wheels and the armature was part of the hub. It provided 12 hp and had a range of seventy-five miles.

Two other examples of early hybrid vehicles are the 1904 Krieger and the 1902 Columbia.

Lohner-Porsche Coupe, 1902[34]

Above, left: Krieger Tonneau, 1904.[35] *Right:* Columbia hybrid automobile, 1902.[36]

The Columbia was equipped with a set of twenty Exide batteries installed above the front and rear axles to evenly distribute the weight. (Exide had connections to the Electric Car Company.) Top speed was about fifteen mph and the batteries needed to be recharged every forty miles.

Hybrid vehicles came to the market sooner than the fuel cell vehicle. Most automakers believe the immediate practical answer to the demand for a car that is environmentally sensible is the hybrid gasoline-electric vehicle, with fuel cell vehicles expected to follow. The newest hybrids also include a combination of fuel cells and batteries. Ballard predicted a fuel cell bus line in 2002 and fuel cell cars by 2003 or 2005. This prediction proved accurate. Fuel cell electric buses are being used in test programs in major cities worldwide and fuel cell cars are for sale in limited quantities. Hybrid drive system technology is taking a significant market share sooner than electric vehicles; the technology is on the road in a wide variety of models from most major auto companies. Hybrids have the advantage of using standard fuels and can refuel at conventional gas stations.

The "flagship" hybrid, the one that caught buyers' attention, was Toyota's Prius. It was introduced in Japan in November 1997 and was being marketed in the United States by mid–2000. The Toyota Prius was the world's first mass-produced gasoline-electric hybrid car. The electric motor starts acceleration and the gasoline-run engine kicks in at higher speeds. Its performance is comparable to conventional vehicle's and it gets up to fifty miles per gallon. The key to the Toyota system is a power-split transmission that constantly varies the amount of power supplied by the engine to either the wheels or the generator. Emissions are halved; toxic gases are cut by 90 percent. As with the cars of the early 1900s, when going uphill the battery and electric motor join the gasoline engine to provide more power. When going downhill the wheels are turning the motor, which is charging the battery. The problem is its price. Toyota was said to be losing over $20,000 per vehicle on the first-generation Prius, selling it for $20,000 while it cost $41,000 to build. The Honda Insight, another gasoline-electric hybrid, began selling in the United States in early 2000. The Insight got up to 73 mpg and, like its predecessors, did not require external charging. The electric motor assisted when more power was needed. It used nickel metal hydride

(NiMH) batteries, which are recharged by regenerative braking. When you take your foot off the accelerator, the motor becomes a generator, similar to the 1901 concept used by the Waverley and the Krieger. Some of the energy spent climbing uphill is thus recovered going downhill. Demand was high for the Insight at first but fell off severely as the Prius gained popularity. A new generation of Insight returned to the marketplace in spring 2009 after a three-year hiatus for the model.

Toyota hybrid dash information display panel[37]

Buyers are attracted to hybrids because they solve the problem of extending range and don't require special fuels or a need to plug into an electric source. This makes the transition from the internal combustion engine to the ZEV more comfortable for the buyer. Hybrids create less pollution and use fewer natural resources, right now, today, registering higher mpg without changing their owner's lifestyle or routines.

Hybrids do face a marketing issue. The growing popularity of hybrids has caused some confusions and misinformation. Many Americans still think the battery in hybrid vehicles must be plugged in to be recharged. Another common misconception is that all electric cars are hybrids. All hybrid cars have an electric component, but not all electric cars are hybrids; they can be electric only. The most common misperception is in overestimating the economy of hybrid cars. The U.S. Environmental Protection Agency's "estimated mileage number" is measured on a dynamometer, which does not take into account different and real-world driving styles. When consumers are asked why they want to buy a hybrid car, 47 percent say they want to improve gas mileage, 22 percent want to save the environment and 19 percent want to save money. Hybrids do get improved gas mileage over their ICE model counterparts, but the increased initial cost of hybrids, even with federal and state tax credits, can offset the money saved on gasoline. It is estimated that, unless there is another spike in fuel prices, it will take seven years to recover the purchase price.

In general, hybrid cars are about twice as efficient as gasoline cars, while diesel engines are about 30 percent more fuel efficient than ICEs. However, the new ICE engines in small cars have become very fuel efficient and some models do not have enough space to accommodate larger hybrid systems. Hybrid cars seem to be the immediate answer to the fuel efficiency problem, allowing more time for improvements in fuel-cell technology. The future may well show a wide variety of options among hybrid, diesel, electric and fuel-cell cars with many choices of models and prices.

Diesel is making a comeback. While it has had a poor image historically as a smelly and exhaust polluting fuel, the new, so-called clean diesel utilizes ultra-low-sulfur diesel fuel (ULSD). It can run on pure biodiesel or blended biodiesel. This alternative is popular in Europe where emission control is more stringent and refueling stations are readily available. Its popularity is growing in the United States, with the arrival of the Mercedes E320 Bluetech (range 700 miles), but the "chicken or the egg" problem is hindering the market. Available ULSD refueling must be there for car sales, and drivers must be able to purchase fuel beyond their neighborhood station. Since the current biodiesel gets better mileage than most gasoline hybrids, it seems reasonable to predict that biodiesel, not hybrid biodiesel, will be the gasoline hybrid's competitor. It is clean and is an alternate to high-powered ICEs.

Plug-in hybrids resurfaced during the gasoline price spike around 2004 and gained followers. Most models were conversions from popular commuter hybrids like the Prius, but, like the electric from Tesla, plug-in hybrids have their high-end models as well. Fisker Automotive, Inc., unveiled the Fisker Karma plug-in hybrid four-door sports car in January 2009. The Finland-based Valmet Corporation, whom Fisker turned to to build the Karma, has produced cars such as the Porsche Boxster and Cayman. Annual production of the Karma is expected to reach 15,000 units, with more than half of the sales being overseas. The Karma boasts a fifty-mile electric range and more than 350 miles of total range, with a potential for fuel economy of more than 100 mpg. Top speeds reach 125 mph and it can go from 0 to 60 mph in less than six seconds.

The U.S. Department of Energy established a clean-vehicle competition, Challenge X, in 2006. Andrew Frank, who has been involved in hot-rodding since the 1940s, got involved in fielding a student team to build a 300 mpg plug-in hybrid with an ethanol-powered gasoline engine and a solar-powered electric motor. He says "Last year we had a Ford Explorer that we converted into a plug-in hybrid, and it had so much torque that we couldn't keep the axles from snapping. With six of my students in there, it could still burn rubber."[39]

The disadvantage of the hybrid vehicle is that two systems are more complex, requiring a higher degree of technical expertise to repair if problems arise, but technology in many areas of manufacturing has become more complex. In the early 21st century complex computers and mechanical operations are prevalent in our homes, our appliances and our manufacturing processes. The reappearance of the hybrid fits with this more intricate technological trend.

Toyota's Prius is a good example of a smooth transition from one energy source to another, with drivers reporting that the switch between the electric and gasoline power occurs almost imperceptibly. This is important because acceptance in the marketplace relies on performance as well as cost and convenience.

Toyota also introduced a hydrogen-fuel-cell-powered Highlander midsized SUV called FCHV-4 in mid–2000. The fuel cell stack, developed by Toyota, replaces the batteries and is based on the same drive train as the Prius. The FCHV-4 (2007) uses a polymer electrolyte (PEM) fuel cell stack and four compressed hydrogen tanks at 10,000 PSI. A nickel-metal-hydride battery supplements the fuel cell output during acceleration. A power control unit adjusts the fuel cell output for various driving conditions. Toyota's target is to be competitive in the fleet market.

Fisker Karma prototype, 2009[38]

Left: The 2001–2003 Toyota Prius hybrid.[40] *Right:* The 2000–2006 Honda Insight hybrid.[42]

An issue of *Science* magazine in 2004 compared the energy efficiency of ICEs, hybrids and fuel cell vehicles. The analysis concluded that during urban driving, fuel cell vehicles showed no significant energy efficiency advantage over the hybrid vehicles. The study also showed that hybrid vehicles only offered the potential for improvement in energy efficiency. With the higher cost of hybrids over ICEs, the benefits were seen to be unjustified.[41]

The Honda Insight of 2000–2006 used an ultra low emission vehicle (ULEV) gasoline engine with an ultra-compact electric motor. The gasoline engine was the primary source of propulsion; the electric motor assisted when additional power was needed. Regenerative braking recharged the NiMH batteries. *AutoWeek*'s year-long road test of the Insight found it to be very drivable and practical, with sufficient power. The only complaint was that the heater struggled to maintain a comfortable temperature. Overall, *AutoWeek* found it to be a "dependable, fun little car."[43] The Insight was slightly smaller than the Prius (two and one-half inches difference in length and height and a six-inch shorter wheelbase) and seated only two, but the price came in below $20,000. Equipped with a fuel economy reader and an ECON mode that could be set to optimize fuel consumption by regulating acceleration and deceleration, it carried a 1.3 liter 4-cylinder engine (98 horsepower and 123 lbs of torque) and a continuously variable transmission (CVT). The flat nickel-metal-hydride battery was recharged by the motor and by regenerative breaking. The battery pack size was smaller and lighter than earlier models.[44] Honda introduced its Honda Civic Hybrid in 2002, hoping to rely on crossover sales. The conventional Honda Civic was the best-selling compact car in America. The hybrid version used regenerative braking to charge the batteries, and the battery pack itself was guaranteed for eight years or 80,000 miles. The first Civic Hybrid had four doors, seated five passengers and had an air conditioner. The 2009 model shows it has come a long way with accessories. This model offers a satellite link navigator, Bluetooth link and cruise control among its options. It continues to use NiMH batteries and an aluminum alloy inline 4-cylinder engine.

Many people prefer bigger cars like SUVs, so car manufacturers have addressed this

Left: Toyota Highlander Hybrid SUV, 2008. *Right:* Lexus RX 400h, 2006.

basic need by providing hybrid SUVs, among them the Toyota Highlander Hybrid SUV and the Lexus RX 400h.

These vehicles work like other hybrids, with the important exception of weight and size. It is generally known that the heavier the vehicle is, the less fuel mileage it will achieve. Smaller hybrids aim for 50 mpg and the heavier SUVs get about 28 mpg, which is better than a regular SUV, but far from offsetting the extra cost for the purchase price.[45]

The manager of Pricing and Market Analysis for Edmunds.com, Alex Rosten, says, "Our study revealed that high gas prices and generous tax credits now offset the high sales prices of some hybrids, assuming owners keep their hybrids for a few years."[46]

BMW, Mercedes and Volkswagen in 2007 were all making four-cylinder hybrids using gasoline or diesel engines that incorporate a start-stop technology to cut the engine while it is idling. This is an efficient way of using less fuel.

The Marine Corps jumped into the hybrid fray in 2007 after a report from the Marine Expeditionary Force (MEF) study showed that almost 90 percent of the fuel used by MEF ground forces would be used by tactical wheeled vehicles (TWVs). This category includes HMMWVs, 7-ton trucks and logistic vehicles. The Marine Corps decided to commit to the development of hybrid electrics, with a goal of improving fuel economy by 20 percent. The fastest-growing requirement on the battlefield is electric power. The current solution is towed generators that can supply twice the amount of electric power for a tactical electric vehicle fleet.

In January 2001, GM announced plans to research specific fuels for its fuel cells, say-

Vehicle	Hybrid Cost Premium	Annual Hybrid Gas Savings	Years to break even @ 15,000 miles per year	Years to break even @ 25,000 miles per year
2007 Saturn VUE Hybrid	$1,660	$294	5.7	3.4
2007 Ford Escape Hybrid	$1,218	$425	2.9	1.7
2006 Toyota Prius	$1,393	$671	2.1	1.2
2006 Honda Accord Hybrid	$3,165	$280	11.3	6.8
2006 Toyota Highlander Hybrid	$6,896	$445	12.6	4.5

The best- and worst-performing hybrid vehicles in the Edmunds study.[47]

ing it would concentrate on developing hydrogen in the long term and a clean hydrocarbon fuel in the short to medium term. GM is working with Toyota and collaborating with Exxon Mobil in this venture. Their 2006 report stated that hydrogen fuel cells have potential in the marketplace, but feasibility relies on infrastructure and the ability to bring the cost to a competitive level. One hundred Chevy Equinox SUVs became the key vehicles in Project Driveway 2008. The program tests the potential market for hydrogen fuel cell vehicles in both the private and public sectors.

GM's Precept, a concept car developed as GM's contribution to the Partnership for a New Generation of Vehicles (PNGV), uses a dual-axle setup with a 35-kilowatt three-phase electric motor driving the front wheels and a lean-burn compression-ignition gasoline engine driving the rear wheels. GM's Triax teamed Chevy with Suzuki Motor Corporation to develop a unique concept car. It has three propulsion options: all-wheel-drive electric, all-wheel-drive hybrid electric or two-wheel-drive internal combustion.

Some hybrid enthusiasts tout that tribrids are the next step to energy efficiency and environmentally friendly vehicles. While hybrid vehicles carry two sources of energy (usually gasoline and electric), the tribrid adds a third source, taken from the ambient environment, such as a solar panel, windmill or sail. This represents a source of power that, if left uncaptured, is otherwise simply lost to the atmosphere.[48]

Tata, India's largest automaker, announced in 2007 that production of a compressed-air car was planned. The MiniC.A.T. (Compressed Air Technology system) is made of fiberglass and is glued, not welded, together. The compressed air is stored in fiber tanks and the expansion of the air pushes the pistons to create movement. Range is estimated to be up to 185 miles with a top speed of 68 mph. Refilling the car would require some adaptations by gas stations to provide compressed air. Similar concepts, such as the MDI's MiniCat, are testing the city commuter market for possible profitability. Tata has signed an agreement with MDI for application in India of MDI's engine technology.

Electric-Only Vehicles around the Turn of the 21st Century

The world's major automakers are not the only ones to experiment with new technology. Corbin Motors, located in California, is an example of a small company entering the electric car market.[49] Founded by Mike and Tom Corbin in 1999, the company produced the Corbin Sparrow, an electric three-wheeled zero-emission vehicle.

The Sparrow recharged in two hours at a 220-volt outlet or six hours at a 110 volt outlet, and could travel at 50 mph for a range of 50 miles on one charge. The Sparrow used lead-acid batteries that were rechargeable for 800 cycles, or about 25,000 miles. Replacement cost of the thirteen-pack battery system was about $1,500. An advantage of electric cars is that they have 100 percent torque available at 0 rpm for rapid acceleration. The Sparrow does deliver the quarter-mile in

Sparrow 2000
www.corbinmotors.com
CorbinMotors.com 2360 Technology Parkway Hollister, CA 95023

Corbin Sparrow.

fifteen seconds at 95 mph. Two hundred and eighty-five Corbin Sparrows were manufactured and put on the road. Corbin Motors filed Chapter 7 bankruptcy in 2003. Dana S. Myers of Myers Motors acquired Corbin in August 2004, when Corbin filed for bankruptcy. Myers continues the line as a plug-in under the name MM NmG (no more gas). The MM NmG advertises a 30-mile range with speed up to 75 mph. It runs on 13 sealed lead acid batteries and comes with power windows, AM/FM stereo, and CD player. The optional 220 charger shortens recharging time to 30 to 45minutes.[50]

GM's Saturn division developed the EV1, an all-electric zero-emission vehicle. It was advertised for what it did not have: no engine, valves, pistons, spark plugs, crankshaft, transmission, starter, clutch, muffler, exhaust or oil changes. Called a two-passenger sports car, it could accelerate from 0 to 50 mph in less than seven seconds, had a top speed of 80 mph and a range of 80 miles. The car recharged in about three hours using a 220-volt/6.6 kilowatt charger. It operated with high capacity lead-acid batteries and had a range of 55–95 miles; nickel-metal hydride batteries increased the range to 75–130 miles. Honda's EV+ used nickel-metal hydride batteries and provided a range of 90–100 miles. It took about six to seven hours to charge. The GM and Honda vehicles were available in the test environment for lease only as the manufacturers, like Morris and Salom overseeing their taxicabs in the early 1900s, wanted to maintain control over and monitor the emerging technology. The lease included all maintenance, though there was little to maintain as the cars did not require a tune-up or oil change and there was no transmission, clutch or water pump. However, both models required a special recharging station. GM maintains about sixty-five stations in northern California and far more in southern California, while Honda has about thirty. Both provided free towing, if needed. The Honda was available until 2002. The EV1 was available through 1999 and discontinued in 2003. It was the focus of the film *Who Killed the Electric Car*, released in 2006. The length of time needed for recharging and their limited range (the advertised 60+ miles was more often closer to 40 miles) made the vehicle impractical for most drivers' needs.

Ford's Th!nk City car, developed by the Norwegian company PIVCO, is a subcompact battery-powered vehicle designed for urban transportation. It provides acceleration of 0–30 in seven seconds and has a range of fifty-three miles. It was introduced in Norway with a positive response and became available in the United States in 2002. The car was available

Left: Corbin Sparrow battery compartment. *Right:* GM EV1 (Gen II).[51]

by lease only, in southern California, at rate of $212 per month, including taxes. The body was constructed of biodegradable thermoplastic that can be recycled. Southern California Edison provided the lessee with a special meter to attach to the normal house meter to identify power used for recharging the EV. SC Edison charged a much cheaper kilowatt-hour rate for charging the vehicle.

In September 2002 Ford decided to discontinue promotion and production of its Th!nk City car and Th!nk Neighbor car in the United States. About fifty people then leasing the Th!nk City car organized a

Ford's Th!nk City car, 2002.[52]

protest in San Francisco, probably the first of its kind, in hopes of saving the automobile from becoming extinct. Protesters claimed there were many people on waiting lists for the vehicle and that thousands could be sold if some marketing efforts were applied. One spokesman said that every person who owned one had three or four friends who wanted one. While many of these people may have owned an SUV, they had disposable incomes high enough to afford an environmentally friendly vehicle for trips around town. Ford said it would continue to support the infrastructure and agreements for the cars already on lease. Norwegian companies saw continued potential for the Th!nk in their markets. In 2002, KamKorp bought the rights to produce Th!nk City in Norway. In 2004, Th!nk Global, through an investment agreement with GE (which had put more than $20 million into the company), presented its model at the Geneva Motor Show in 2008. The Th!nk Ox, an SUV crossover, is a 5-door with a choice of three battery packs: a 28-kilowatt-hour Zebra sodium nickel chloride pack, a 26-kilowatt-hour Li-Ion pack from Enerdel and a 19-kilowatt-hour Li-Ion pack from A123Systems. Th!nk Global also has the Th!nk City in its models line. Batteries will be owned and maintained by the company for a monthly fee of approximately €200 (US$305). The company projected that the City 2009 model would sell for approximately €20,000 (US$30,500).[53] By December 2008, Th!nk again faced bankruptcy. It asked the Norwegian government for assistance to keep an all electric car viable in the marketplace. In early 2009, the company was in talks with the city of Portland, Oregon, about opening a production plant for the Th!nk in that city, but in September the company announced its production would be moving to Finland instead.

The India market continues to explore an all-electric city car. The Reva Electric Car Company has a lithium-ion powered car with a range of 120 kilometers that is targeted for the city driver. It was slated for sales in April 2009, with plans to sell approximately 1,000 cars in the first year.

Not all electrics are commuter city cars. The Tesla Motors company in California is producing the Tesla Roadster 100, which can go from 0 to 60 in four seconds in first gear, and has a top speed of 130 miles per hour in second gear. The car uses a regenerative braking system and also comes with a home charging system that operates on a 220V line; recharging takes approximately 3.5 hours. The motor control employs an insulated gate bipolar transistor (IGBT). It is being promoted as a statement against pollution and oil dependence. It incorporates a massive number of lithium-ion batteries, has a range of 250 miles on the highway, and is claimed to be twice as efficient as a Toyota Prius.

In August 2008, Nissan unveiled its new electric car battery lab. It will be used to formulate electrode materials, prototype small cells and evaluate their properties. The lab is preparing two types of cells for batteries, one for HEVs and another for EVs. The EV battery will be larger to increase the energy storage capacity for a longer cruising distance.

As did the battery companies of the early years of automotives, the Chinese company BYD is using cars to promote its batteries. The battery supplier and startup automaker announced plans in January 2009 to build an all-electric hatchback with a 250-mile range. It will be called the e6, and is expected to be in the United States in 2011 at a price of about $20,000. BYD is one of the leading battery supply companies in the world and is now getting backing from billionaire Warren Buffett in the new auto venture.

Reformulated Gasoline for ICEs

The attraction of electric vehicles has been that they are environmentally friendly, clean transportation. Technological changes in fuels for internal combustion engines may affect that advantage.

Gasolines are being reformulated. The U.S. Clean Air Act of 1990 required reformulated gas (RFG) in areas with severe ozone nonattainment status (if an area does not attain the national ambient air quality standards for a criteria pollutant, it is "designated" as a nonattainment area). The program began in 1995, and required that oil companies add oxygenates to gasoline. Oxygenates are additives such as ethanol or ethers such as MTBE. This constitutes an added expense for operating internal combustion engines. A 1999 report from the Wisconsin Department of Natural Resources estimates a loss of about three miles per gallon and an average cost of two cents per gallon more than conventional gasoline. The initial introduction of RFG was met with some negative reports of having a bad smell, giving poor mileage and concern about health problems and possible leaks of MTBE into the groundwater. These problems were addressed during the next five years and the public has generally accepted RFG. Phase two began in the summer of 2000. Compared to conventional gasoline, this phase of RFG is reported to reduce toxic emissions by 22 percent, volatile organic compound emissions by 27 percent and nitrogen oxide emissions by 7 percent. The process added approximately two cents more per gallon over phase one RFG. The product has been extensively tested and shows no changes in performance or mileage when compared to phase one RFG. *Car and Driver* magazine wrote, "The new gasoline cars, for all practical purposes, are zero emitting. It's extraordinary what automakers have done."[54] This simple adaptation for the internal combustion engine may again prove to give the electric vehicles ominous competition.

The Nissan Sentra CA exemplifies the clean-burning ICE competitor. The car qualified and received CARB credits for meeting the standards for a super-ultra-low-emission vehicle (SULEV). ICEs are closing the environmental gap.

Ethanol

Ethanol is an alcohol type of fuel made from corn or sugar. There are two basic methods of making ethanol, dry milling or wet milling. In the dry milling method, dry corn kernels are ground into flour, water is added, and the mash is cooked, cooled and mixed with yeast to produce fermentation. The resulting alcohol product is distilled to 200 proof and then a small amount of denaturant is added, in this case gasoline. This makes it undrinkable and allows the producers to avoid a beverage alcohol tax. The resulting ethanol is called E85, a combination of 85 percent ethanol and 15 percent gasoline. In the wet milling method, the corn kernels are soaked in water and sulfurous acid for 24 to 48 hours. After the bath, the grain is ground down to separate the germ. Then the starch is extracted and the result is fermented.[56]

At the 2007 Detroit auto show, General Motors debuted its Volt concept car. The vehicle is a flexible plug-in featuring new GE plastic technology. Using the new thermoplastic technology trimmed sixty pounds from the car. The Volt carries a small gas/E85 engine to support the lithium-ion batteries, making it a serial hybrid, not the more conventional parallel model like the Prius and Civic Hybrid.

At the 2008 Detroit auto show, General Motors announced a "strategic ownership investment" with a small company called Coskata. This company is converting waste materials, such as grass, wood chips, or old tires into fuel using a patented bioreactor and anaerobic microbes found in nature. The ethanol produced would cost about one dollar a gallon or less. The first phase of making cellulosic ethanol is to gasify the feedstock at up to 4,000 degrees, reducing the product to ash, which can be used in agriculture. The gases resulting from the burn, CO, CO_2 and hydrogen, are fed to anaerobic bacteria that consume them and emit ethanol as a waste product.[57]

Another microbial fuel cell (MFC) produces hydrogen from waste materials. It is a type of microbial electrolysis cell where bacteria consume the acetic acid from fermentation of plants. By placing the material in a tank with an ion exchange membrane and adding a very small electrical input, hydrogen gas will be produced.

Measuring Efficiency

There are a number of ways to measure efficiency of the automobile. The favorite leading holistic approach is called well-to-wheel. It measures everything from fuel extraction (from oil wells) to the turning of the wheels on a car. Oil extraction covers pipeline or truck

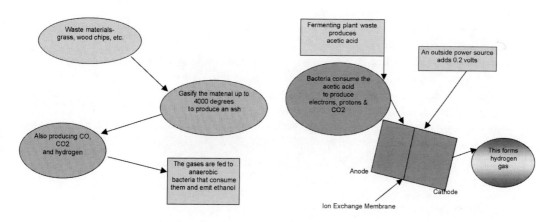

Left: Figure 2. Making cellulosic ethanol. *Right:* Figure 3. Microbial fuel cell.

delivery to a port, tanker delivery to another port, truck transportation to a refinery, delivery to a gas station and finally burning the gasoline in the car. Measuring energy loss that occurs before the gas station is called well-to-pump analysis, while pump-to-wheel analysis measures vehicle efficiency, everything from the pump to the turning of the wheels. The results of these analyses show that diesel is always rated number one in efficiency, followed closely by gasoline, with the electric or hybrid vehicle always in last place. In comparing vehicle combinations, the top four were all hybrids—two diesel hybrids, a natural gas hybrid and a hydrogen hybrid. The Toyota Prius was the only vehicle to come close to the diesel efficiency ratings.[58]

Hydraulic Hybrids

The United Parcel Service, Federal Express, Waste Management and other companies are considering hydraulic hybrid vehicles for their fleets. This different type of hybrid uses hydraulic pump motors and high pressure fluid lines to propel the vehicle. A diesel engine drives a hydraulic pump motor, which charges a high-pressure accumulator, which in turn drives a bent-axis pump motor on the rear wheels to drive the vehicle. The process is completed using a low-pressure reservoir to collect the fluid and send it back to the first pump motor. This results in fuel economy and emissions reductions. This is not meant to be an application for passenger cars; it is specific to delivery vehicles or refuse trucks, as they start and stop repeatedly, often idling, all day long.

New Charging Systems

There are two basic types of electric-vehicle chargers: conductive and inductive. The conductive has a metal-on-metal contact with direct flow of electric current between the two contact points. The inductive has two metal connectors separated by a small gap filled by a magnetic field. The electricity used to recharge the battery flows through a magnetic field.

Fast-charging stations can recharge an EV in fifteen minutes or less, doubling or sometimes tripling the daily mileage for the vehicle. This could become a major factor in establishing a charging station infrastructure in the United States. As early as 1995 some charging stations were offering a "short" charge of one hour, using a paddle system that transferred electricity through a magnetic field rather than a metal plug. In November 1997 the Ford Motor Company purchased a fast-charge system produced by AeroVironment called PosiCharge. This was used to test its fleets of Ford Ranger EVs. The time required for a charge by this device was between six and fifteen minutes.[59] The fast-charge system will recharge a lead-acid battery to 80 percent in less than twenty minutes. The range using this system is about 150 miles. In February 1998 GM announced a new high-speed version of its Magne Charge system. The unit could recharge a lead-acid battery in 7.5 minutes and a nickel-hydride battery in about 10 minutes and provided a range of 60–100 miles. The newer chargers provide faster charging without shortening battery life. The fast charging can allow EV owners to charge their vehicles while having lunch or while on a short shopping trip and increase their range with little inconvenience. Competitors to PosiCharge, such as Edison Minut Charger and EnerSys, generally compete in the industrial markets and for reserve power supplies in homes. As in the past, convenient refueling infrastructure is a key to the success of any automobile.

The search for better ways to power our vehicles continues to evolve. Designs for smaller, more efficient motors and engines spark the industry's imagination. Fuel cell development is improving its potential for use in our vehicles. There have been recent advances in battery technology, but the problems of weight, capacity, recharging and cost seem to be the same as those encountered one hundred years ago. If this does not change, new technology will continue to be directed toward developing cleaner-burning ICEs and a variety of hybrid vehicles. This seems to be the most logical next step away from our heavy dependence on foreign oil supplies and toward a cleaner environment.

5

MARKETING

"[Of] all the electric runabouts I ever saw, while they were very nice cars, [they] didn't seem to go very fast or very far."[1] So wrote Victor Appleton in 1910. Marketing in general is a matter of knowing when to form alliances, when to believe in yourself, when to go your own way and when to follow advice. Automobiles provide more than a means to go from one place to another. They reflect our ingenuity, give a sense of freedom and express our personalities and our politics. The automobile has an emotional aspect tied to our lifestyles that is not associated with other machines, not even our computers. CEO Edouard Michelin calls a driver's license a "passport to freedom."[2] For more than a century the automobile has provided a means for people to go when they want and where they want on their own schedules, not the schedule and route imposed by public transit. Automobile owners can be impulsive and travel where their whimsy takes them. This sense of freedom is blossoming internationally, as the markets of China, India, South America and Africa gain an economic base that provides more of its people with the means to buy their own vehicles. The car has given a stimulus to local economies and shapes and mirrors our social values.

To capture the buyer's attention, automakers need to find the interests of potential buyers. For some, the image of power, speed and rugged individualism appeals; others respond to the environmentally friendly aspects and fuel efficiency in their cars. The extremely successful, high-profile marketing campaign for the Toyota Prius proved once again the importance of finding the personal image that the consumer wants to convey through the vehicle they drive. Similar to the campaigns for the electrics around 1910 that touted the electrics' lack of noise and exhaust and their driving ease, the Prius found its audience in the "think green" buyers. Toyota caught their attention by emphasizing the Prius' greater fuel mileage and less emissions without requiring the driver to change their driving habits. The distinct body style allowed image-conscious drivers to convey to their neighbors that they were helping to clean up the environment. Toyota had found the ideal strategy for its hybrid Prius: Make it fashionable to own; make it an environmental status symbol; and make it reliable transportation. The market opened. The Prius had become the "it" car. Arnold Schwarzenegger, Prince Charles, Brad Pitt and Cameron Diaz were among the early celebrity adopters. Some in the political arena saw its potential too. In 2005, New Haven, Connecticut, mayoral candidate John DeStefano Jr. swapped his SUV for a hybrid.

For a few dollars more than a conventional auto, you too could become one of the special, environmentally aware drivers. The Prius' popularity spurred other automakers to begin supplying their own models of hybrids. The demand created competition, but for a year or so, if buyers wanted a hybrid, they waited in line for a Prius. Toyota boosted production to fill all of its orders, while other manufacturers played "catch up" to get a comparable product on the market. During that period, Toyota touted a fuel economy for the Prius of 28.9 miles per gallon. Ironically, at the same time GM was selling more ICE models than any other car maker and some of its models got more than 30 miles per gallon (Chevy Aveo, Malibu, HHR and Cobalt, Pontiac G Series and Vibe, Saturn Astra, Vue, and Aura). The Saturn Vue Greenline hybrid came quietly into the market a short time later; in addition to mileage and power, its strong selling point was cost. It was priced at $23,495, just $1,995 more than the ICE model. The successful Prius marketing opened the door for other automakers but kept their models out of the limelight. Toyota had become the brand most associated with "hybrid."

When Lexus and other luxury SUV makers began offering a selection of hybrid options in 2006, the hybrid had arrived. Even though hybrids are most efficient in stop-and-start city driving, some commuters like the image of driving a hybrid even though a traditional ICE like a 4-cylinder Ford Escape might be more cost effective. Going into 2006, hybrids had captured 1.2 percent of the market. Of the consumers polled in a J. D. Power study, 35 percent said that they would consider purchasing a hybrid as their next vehicle. The buyers generally are persons over 55 with disposable incomes that allow for more than one vehicle in the household and the capital to afford the higher price tag. The tax credit incentives worked. The industry had found a strong customer base and, although subsidies continue throughout the industry, they are no longer needed as incentive to create a market share.

"It's not that people don't care, I bet if manufacturers made many more of these cars [hybrids], there would be a huge jump in consumption,"[3] said Meredith Williams, a Wall Street executive, in 2006. In a survey conducted in 2007 by the Opinion Research Group, many Americans said they wanted the government to impose a fuel-efficiency standard on American vehicles and, as in the past, 45 percent of them said they would then be more likely to buy a hybrid vehicle. By 2008, with gasoline prices at an all time high in the United States, consumers could choose from a wide variety of makes and models—hybrid, flex, electric, crossover, fuel cell, natural gas and other options—but the buying market remained steady. ICEs are still the most popular models.

According to the American Council for an Energy-Efficient Economy, many four-cylinder ICE compact cars earn better "green scores" than all but three hybrids. Consumer demand for more fuel efficient vehicles and lower emissions influenced the way the auto industry improved the traditional ICE, while accommodating those who found the hybrid appealing. On the one hand, hybrids produce lower emissions; on the other, ICEs in some cases get better fuel mileage. Hybrids typically cost more (at least $5,000) than an ICE, and their costs are sometimes offset by state and federal tax credits of $250 to $3,000,[4] but ICEs still have the appeal and cost effectiveness the consumers want.

An economy is built on supplying goods that meet consumers' wants and needs; automakers are exploring many avenues, trying to find which products we will be willing and eager to buy. Having a convenient, cost effective, nonpolluting fuel supply is a crucial component. In today's world, when the price of gasoline jumps to a new high, people ask, "Why don't we produce and buy more hybrid cars?" "Why don't we get serious about conservation?" "Why don't more people take public transportation or work from home over the Web to save gasoline consumption?" Then the price of oil goes down and we are back to driving our SUVs. The answers lie in more energy production from a variety of sources by (1) producing more alternative energy using all forms of technology, including nuclear, solar, wind, geothermal, and water power and (2) by revisiting fossil fuel production using new technologies and drilling for oil off the coasts of the United States, in ANWR in Alaska, and the many other untapped oil fields around the world.

Innovation in the quest for cleaner, efficient alternate fuels is filling the market with new possibilities. Consumers now have the opportunity to select from many vehicle options in much the same way that the steam, electrics and ICEs vied for dominance in the early 1900s. Flex-fuel vehicles, such as the Chevrolet Suburban, which can burn either gasoline or ethanol, seem to offer a cost advantage for the consumer, but the Suburban gets 12 mpg on ethanol and 16 mpg on gasoline. Ethanol costs more, and even with gasoline at $3.00 per gallon, it is cheaper to use gasoline. Diesel is cheaper, gets better fuel mileage and has a following in Europe, but because of stringent exhaust emissions regulations is not available in many markets in the United States. California, New York and several other northeastern states won't allow the sale of diesel autos. As development of traditional engines advances, electrics and hybrids are again faced with strong competition. The performance and fuel efficiency of clean diesels, efficient ICEs and flex-fuel vehicles brings the vehicles most drivers prefer back into an environmentally favorable arena. Development of both lithium-ion and lithium-poly batteries and fuel cell technology offer much promise, but are the products going to make it to the marketplace in time to be considered strong competitors?

The 2007 documentary *Who Killed the Electric Car?* did put part of the blame on consumers for electrics not being mass produced, but for the most part targeted the federal government, oil companies, hydrogen fuel-cell manufacturers, CARB, and others as the main culprits. The limitations of the EV were downplayed.

Charles J. Murray in his article in *Design News* in 2007 asked, "How much would you pay for a car with a 70-mile range and a six hour refueling time?" He routinely drove from Chicago to Detroit several times a year. He did some calculating: stopping four times to recharge and taking five hours to do so, the EV would make the trip in about 25 hours. An internal combustion engine car could make the trip in five hours. His article was titled "I Killed the Electric Car."[5]

Design News saw flaws in the test program's marketing as well. The electric's limited range kept it from being an all-purpose car; a second vehicle was necessary for the customer to use when the electric could not be used. Having 21 days of access to a minivan, truck or other vehicle might have improved the outcome for the EV,[6] but most families cannot afford to have a $30,000 second car.[7] The electric Toyota RAV-4 and Honda EV Plus were available during this time, and neither one did well in the marketplace.

The all-electric car isn't out of the race yet. Poor acceleration is one reason people don't like the EV. AC Propulsion's 2003 Tzero, a two-seater that can go from 0 to 60 in 3.7 seconds, puts the possibility of "pickup" and speed back in the picture, thanks to a rack of 6,000 lithium-ion batteries. But there is still a question of cost. That little sports car had a price tag of $220,000. The possibility of moving to a more cost-effective model using the smaller batteries continues to inspire those who believe the EV is the best nonpolluting driving solution.

Tesla Motors has focused on those buyers who enjoy an affluent lifestyle. Its EV is priced at $100,000, designed by Lotus and based on the Elise, and is powered by 7,000 lithium-ion batteries. In an effort to provide convenient power for its roadster owners, Tesla reached an agreement in 2007 with the Hyatt hotel chain to supply recharging stations at three of its hotels between San Francisco and Lake Tahoe. This blends well with other EV enthusiasts' strategy to boost EV demand by providing convenient recharging.

In the early 1900s many people thought that the electric, steam and gasoline-powered vehicles would share the market equally, each finding its own market space. The ICE won the market early and has retained its popularity for a variety of reasons, including technology, infrastructure and manufacturers catering to the prospective customer's wants. The EV reflects social changes. It symbolized women's independence during the suffrage movement, patriotism during the world wars, and environmental solutions during periods of concern about pollution. Its market shifts with the social and political climates.

Marketing EVs has posed many challenges. At their inception they fared well in urban areas, but they have had difficulty capturing consumer attention during an expanding economy. When roads between towns were limited and poorly maintained, few people traveled outside their own towns or cities. Electric cars provided convenient, reliable urban transport not requiring a chauffeur. Their performance was adequate. They took less space than a horse and buggy, were quiet and left no tell-tale reminder on the road for the street sweepers, as horse-drawn vehicles did. The short range of the electrics was acceptable for city trips. As roads between cities improved, spurred by a blossoming economy, interest in the electrics declined. The availability of ICE cars grew to meet consumer demand. Electrics could not compete with the greater range and speed of ICEs. As stated, the electrics' usefulness is rediscovered during fuel shortages and increased interest in limiting the environmental impact of ICE emissions. Their potential effectiveness as fleet vehicles for corporate and government operations continues to be examined and tested. Electrics are a possible alternative to what is viewed as a major air pollutant — the carbon monoxide byproduct of the ICE. Electric cars continue to be quiet, clean and easy to operate, but are not convenient or inexpensive enough to capture more than a fraction of the auto market's need for extended mileage and speed. Their reliability, easy maintenance and low environmental impact are major selling points, but their short range and the high cost of batteries are still drawbacks. It seems the pathways to developing an effective electric vehicle are blocked by fundamental limitations of chemistry and physics, and by the limits of our technological capabilities in the development of batteries and fuel cells.[8]

Very few consumers will pay a significant premium just to know they are driving a "clean, green" car that does not pollute the environment. Battery-only electrics must have a competitive price to effectively gain market share. The ICE and hybrids are making great strides in creating an environmentally friendly auto, attacking the EVs' major selling point with more efficient engines. The development of cost-effective fuel cells and smaller, more durable batteries is giving the EVs some traction, but marketing the electric vehicle requires greater incentives if it is to compete with the power and range offered by its major competitor, the internal combustion engine.

How did Henry Ford turn the "inferior" internal combustion engine into a viable force?[9] Not with technology, but by using a better business practice. He understood the nature of the market. He knew that bad roads were a problem to be addressed, and incorporated a design that rode high over mud and ruts. He felt the machine should be easy to buy and repair by the common man. He perfected the moving assembly line to produce large quantities of vehicles with interchangeable parts. Ford was mass-producing 650 cars per day when Stanley was producing 650 steam cars per year. Ford gambled that as people saw more Fords on the road, they would want to buy Fords too. The low cost and availability produced a snowball effect. The discovery of oil in Texas in 1901 made people think they had virtually free energy, and the infrastructure was established. Ford had won the field.

Finding an effective approach for catching the consumer's eye hasn't been easy for EV manufacturers. At the beginning of the 20th century, automobiles fell into two basic categories: "city" cars and "touring" cars. Most automobile owners preferred the romance of the touring car over the practicality of the city car. The city car (electric) became the province of women, doctors and delivery drivers. The speedier, more dangerous, complicated and more "masculine" gasoline-powered car took over the market and never looked back. Is the electric car a "real" car? Hans Fogelberg argues that

> The first two decades of the century were ... characterized by converging technology and converging views on what a car was, what it should be able to do, and where and when it should be driven. Thus the range of interpretations (i.e. the degree of interpretative flexibility) of the technology and the use of that technology decreased drastically during a short time period. Simultaneously, the opinions about the "losers," the failed alternatives of steam and electric propulsion, were also cemented, and have since then been fairly consistent. We "know" that lead-acid battery cars do not fulfil the requirements of a "car." since the notion of the car was integrated and constructed along with gasoline car technology.[10]

He points out that consistency in advertising was key. The electric became established as a woman's car. This tactic did create some interest, but it was for a limited audience.

Electric vehicles, with the exception of some campaigns in the early 1900s, have struggled to identify and sell to their potential market. There is a perceived difference between men and women in their attitude toward what they want from a vehicle. Men are generally felt to want power, racing, travel and luxury, while women are thought to want reliability, comfort, safety and cleanliness.[11] In 1908 Clara Ford — Henry's wife — preferred an electric vehicle to her husband's loud, lumbering, backfiring, gasoline-powered Model T. "Toys for Big Boys — that's what automobiles still are for many men, and that's why electric cars can't cut the mustard,"[12] wrote one critic in 1995. The earliest automobiles weren't sold on functionality; they were sold on the romance of the open road. People took mass transit to go to work. Since the middle class of that day could afford only one car, the male in that culturally patriarchal structure invariably opted for the touring car, not the car that may have made the most economic sense.[13]

In the early 1900s automobiles for family use were looked at romantically for the freedom and elegance they could provide. Sunday drives were a frequent family outing. It was an era of inventions that freed the homeowner and homemaker. Families were emerging from the Victorian model household to a more egalitarian family life. A strengthening middle class was finding income for luxury items already afforded to the wealthy classes. Women's groups were ardently campaigning for more independence for women, and for women to take advantage of that freedom. Mrs. M. R. W. Harper of New York, interviewed in 1971 at age 104, recalled her early advocacy for women drivers. She credited Henry Ford with "emancipating women."[14]

Advertisers were aware of these attitudes, and began to focus on the automobile's image of freedom, romance, refinement and fun rather than its reliability. Advertisers recognized women and physicians as major potential markets for electric vehicles and slanted the ads in their direction. In 1914 *House Beautiful* magazine contained these pitches: "Milady can seek a shady spot with children or friends until the cool of the evening, then glide swiftly back to the city before the dinner hour, rested by the perfect relaxation that an electric makes possible."[15] "There is no question but that an electric automobile is an advantage to a physician. Capable to the last degree of well-rounded usefulness, an electric meets the social, as well as the professional requirements of the professional man, whose wife and daughter are certain to find it most desirable."[16] Advertisers appealed to the fashion conscious by depicting sophisticated owners driving their elegant cars to the theater or the park in style.

Baker ad, March 1909[17]

Not all were convinced of a woman's ability to manage a car. There was a discussion in *Outing* magazine in 1904 as to "Why Women Are, or Are Not Good Chauffeuses."[21] It claimed that motoring was natural for a man, while a woman had to adapt to it. Important factors raised were the judgment needed to control impulse and quick thought, and the ability to concentrate on everyday things. "The weakness that causes a woman to read

Society's Town Car

THE Detroit Electric can be depended upon for all-around service because dependability has been *built into it*. Not only great strength, but great mechanical and electrical principles are *inborn* in this superior motor car.

They are the foundation of your investment and will yield inestimable dividends of pleasure for yourself and friends.

The body designs of the 1912 Detroit Electrics have anticipated the style for years to come. They are dignified and have both character and correct taste. There is nothing "make-believe" or freakish either in the body designs, interior finish or mechanical construction of The Detroit Electric.

Let us tell you about the many *exclusive* features that have contributed to the ascendancy of the Detroit Electric as Society's Town Car.

We offer a selection of nine body designs. Illustrated catalog sent upon request.

Anderson Electric Car Co.
408 Clay Avenue, Detroit, U.S.A.

Branches:

Buffalo
Brooklyn
Cleveland

New York, Broadway at 80th Street Chicago, 2416 Michigan Avenue
Also Branch at Evanston, Ill.
Selling representatives in all leading Cities

Kansas City
Minneapolis
St. Louis

Detroit Electric ad, July 1912[18]

Babcock ad, 1908[19]

the same page of a book twice to get its meaning ... is the same weakness which, in motoring, keeps her looking too long at an attractive bit of scenery ... or for a single instant lifting her hand from the brake.... The only thing about a car which a woman does not have to teach herself with patience and skill is how to dress for it."[22] The writer might have been surprised by statistics gathered two decades later. In 1925 during a six-month period in New York State, one thousand drivers' licenses were revoked. Only twelve of them were owned by women.

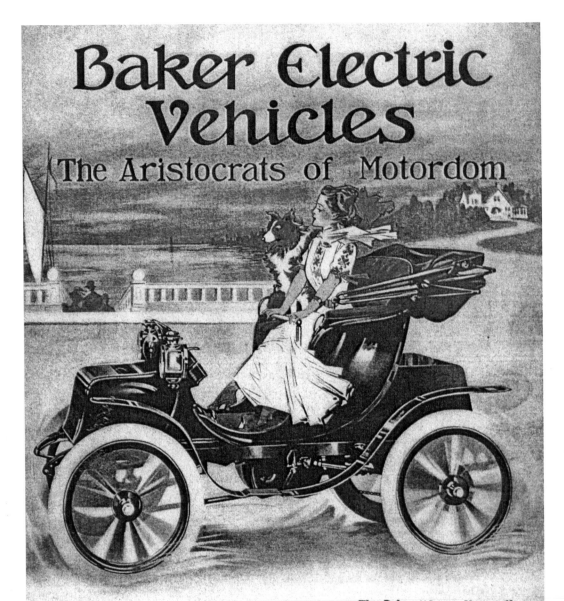

The Baker "Queen Victoria"

Baker Electrics are safest to drive—easiest to control—simplest in construction, and have greater speed and mileage than any other electrics. Where quality and efficiency are desired Baker Electrics are invariably the choice of discriminating men and women who want elegant appointments combined with mechanical perfection.

A request will bring to you our complete catalogue of Baker Electric Runabouts, Coupés, Roadsters, Landaulets, Broughams, etc.

THE BAKER MOTOR VEHICLE COMPANY, 33 W. 80TH STREET, CLEVELAND, OHIO.
Agencies in all Principal Cities.

Baker Electric ad, 1909[20]

There was some controversy in 1906 about automobiles' encouraging the spread of socialism. Automobile ownership, although it began with the upper classes, provided a commonality among the economic classes as more types of automobiles became available and prices became more affordable. Woodrow Wilson, then president of Princeton University, stated, "Nothing has spread Socialistic feeling in this country more than the use of automobiles. To the countryman they are a picture of arrogance of wealth with all its independence and carelessness." The American Automobile Association disagreed and explained that many farmers of the day were buying automobiles for "hard usage."

> Automobiling more than any other sport I know tends to break down class distinctions and brings the poor man with his small runabout into close sympathy and fellowship with the rich man who owns a high-powered and expensive machine.... If a runabout meets with a mishap on the road, the touring car owner does not hesitate to stop and offer such assistance as he can.... In short, a touch of automobiliousness [*sic*] makes the whole world kin, and the sport tends more and more to draw the divergent classes together.[23]

Early magazines explored the adventure of electric auto touring. An article in the 1907 *Scientific American Supplement* described a long-distance touring trip with an electric automobile. The travelers started from Cleveland, Ohio, on September 21, 1906, and covered a total of 314 miles to New York. They averaged 13.2 miles per hour. Charging stations along the way were sometimes only eleven miles apart. They charged up at a street railway plant, a power and heating company, and regular charging stations. The only real troubles they encountered were a flat tire and rain. It began to rain just as they were approaching a hill outside of Erie, Pennsylvania. They waited until the rain was over, but could not climb the hill. The wheels just skidded in the mud. It took them four hours and twenty minutes to cover a forty-four mile stretch. They estimated the car had a range of sixty-two to seventy miles on country roads and were quite satisfied with their experiment.

Touring became very popular by 1907, and many peripheral products were being developed to help the motoring camper. Leather waterproof bags or a steamer trunk could be attached to the deck of the vehicle to carry the necessities of touring, such as a tent, ponchos for rain, and blankets, food and cooking utensils. A speedometer and odometer were recommended equipment, the latter for calculating distances listed in route books, such as "After passing a large red farm house on the left continue straight ahead a mile and a half and keep to right at fork in road."[24] The speedometer was to prevent getting a ticket or being brought before the country justice of the peace at a time when speed limit laws were becoming more common and more severe each year. Many tips about touring could be gained from the publications of the day.

By 1909 electric vehicles were advertised as economical, simple, handsome and free from the complications "which often bewilder the owner of a gasoline car who is not of a mechanical turn of mind,"[25] wrote the *New York Times*, adding, "For park, city and suburban use, the electric is the ideal carriage and will ... remain so, for it is essentially a woman's car."[26] The ads stressed simplicity.

By 1913, manufacturers were expanding their product lines and widening their appeal. EVs came in a wider choice of models. A limousine was the highest-priced model, costing from $3,000 to $5,000. It was claimed to be a direct rival to the gasoline-powered cars. According to a writer in 1913, its "debut proves unmistakably that the maker of electrics is going to demonstrate that the electric is not simply a vehicle for women, but a general utility machine."[27] A brougham model was available in a price range of $2,500 to $3,000 and a roadster model was priced from $2,250 to $2,500. The roadster's design copied the curved hood of the gasoline car. The feeling at the time was that the electric roadster could hold its own in competition with the gasoline vehicle for general utility purposes.

Another new concept also appeared on the scene that year to further the sales of electric cars. One of the largest department stores in New York decided to switch from selling gasoline cars to electrics exclusively. Their sales strategy included selling the vehicles on the installment plan. A customer could buy the car on an easy payment plan that included a year's worth of service on the car. It also offered, for a proper price, arrangements to house and care for the car in the garage nearest the purchaser's residence. The company would pay all the garage bills and see that it is "kept in perfect condition, washed, oiled, charged and so on, and to attend to repair work."[28] The agreement included everything but driving the car, and this could also be arranged if the buyer required the services of a chauffeur. The sales floor consisted of a huge area for the "indoor demonstration of the silent-running machines, with little clumps of foliage here and there, like oases in a desert, sheltering dainty tea tables, where the ladies—and their husbands, if they care to come along—will be taken care of while they are being told about the polished cars flitting about on the floor."[29] They were obviously trying to offer and create a pleasant buying experience for the "fair sex" with a plan that would fit most household budgets.

In 1914 Dr. Charles P. Steinmetz gave a glowing report to the Electric Vehicle Association of America. He stated that the "electric vehicle will surely drive the gasoline car from the limited area of service required in town or suburban life. High speed will not be a requirement of the future small electric car, nor will long mileage per charge be necessary. The distances to be covered are too short for the saving in time effected by high speed to be worthwhile. Even the busy physician rarely exceeds 10 miles to 20 miles per day in his rounds. The electric car is superior to the gasoline car in control and is intrinsically more reliable."[30] He strongly advised the central station owners to perceive and take advantage of the electric vehicles. He concluded with a prediction that "within ten years the electric truck is likely to produce revenue equal to that of the light business and pleasure car."[31] George S. Walker, chief mechanic of the Philadelphia Fire Department, presented a paper to the Electric Vehicle Association titled "Electric Fire Apparatus." He pointed out that numerous tests conducted to compare the horse-driven, gasoline-driven and electric equipment demonstrated the electric to be superior in every fashion. The electric trucks were so reliable they never failed to respond to a call, which was not true of the horse or gasoline equipment. The electric eliminated the offensive odors of horses and gasoline and also reduced the possibility of fire and explosions that characterized gasoline tractors. Flammability, of course, was a major concern for a fire department. The electrics could also be started up and driven off in less time than it would take to crank an engine. This EVA member demonstrated that the electrics had a great deal to offer to the service industries.

In January 1915 there were 25,000 electric passenger cars in use in the United States and over 12,000 commercial vehicles. New York State led the field with 7,455 passenger cars and 2,461 commercial vehicles. Pennsylvania followed with 5,000 passenger cars and 1,000 trucks. When the figures provided by the Electrical Vehicle Association were divided up by cities, they showed that greater New York City had 2,850 passenger cars, Chicago had over 2,000, Cleveland 1,800, and Denver nearly 1,000.[32]

Why did the electric car become popular in some cities and not others? Peoria, Illinois, a hilly city with a population of 100,000, had a fairly high number of electric cars in 1917 for several reasons. The successful electric auto dealerships dealt with electric cars only and did not sell gasoline cars; and the Central Illinois Light Company provided cheaper rates for central stations. The local roads were also a factor. Peoria was not a favorable location for touring. Once a car left the smooth paved streets in town, it would encounter roads nearly impassable, turning the joy of touring into anxiety and distress. The town also made storage and maintenance convenient. Three public electric garages were also available for maintaining and housing the EVs, and individual families were building private garages attached to their homes for their pleasure cars. Many prominent families were also buying electric cars, which helped to make them fashionable. Auto dealers and garages were producing income in the community. The city had 179 private garages that produced an annual income of about $11,000, while the public garages were generating about $3,000 per year. Many families were able to afford two vehicles and bought both an electric and a gasoline car.[33]

World War I created a boom for electric vehicles in Britain and Europe. It was estimated in 1914 that the whole of Europe had approximately 3,200 electric vehicles. About 25 percent of the passenger cars in England and about 10 percent of those in France were manufactured in the United States. Commercial electric vehicles were made primarily in Europe. The commercial electric vehicles were developing along highly specialized lines such as taxicabs, fire trucks and postal vehicles. England had about 150 electric trucks in 1915. Great Britain's Board of Trade removed the embargo tax on American electric vehicles in 1916, allowing for increased sales, especially for commercial vehicles. By 1918 there were about one thousand electric trucks in operation in England, with many more on order. The electric vehicles' dependability, its simple design, and easy operation made them drivable even by inexperienced men. During World War I, England used many electric cars and trucks for delivery of goods. As men of all ages became more and more scarce, women drivers were tried as an experiment and were found to be competent. One of the largest stores in London employed women almost exclusively to drive its seventy-five electric delivery trucks.[34] Harrods department store had a fleet of 60 electric trucks and the Midland Railway Company had a fleet of 73 electric trucks in use.

In the United States, the electric vehicle was drafted to "make the world safe for democracy." Norway and Sweden had a large electric commercial vehicle market and a hydroelectric energy supply, a very promising market for after the war. Italy was also generating electric power using waterfalls, making a continuing market seem probable for the electrics. Australia, Japan, Mexico and France were exporting electric vehicles in large numbers and the future looked very bright. Demand was high.

Motor travel and touring broke all records in the United States in 1917, due partially to the war in Europe. Many motorists who had spent years touring in Europe were forced to do their motoring in the United States. "See America First" became the slogan of the day, and many foreigners were pleasantly surprised by the picturesque beauty of the Northeast and the fine hotel services offered. New England, in particular, spent many advertising dollars to promote the good condition of its roads and its beautiful scenery. The result seemed to be a steadily increasing army of motorists each year. New York State had the most extensive highway system at the time, but travel was somewhat hampered by repair work being completed on many of its important highways. Tourists could also travel at no charge into Canada for a period of three or four days.[35]

Touring gained popularity in the northern states as well. In 1920, Minnesota had 330,000 registered vehicles. One of the most popular tourist routes, the Lake Superior International Highway, linked Duluth to Fort William/Port Arthur, Ontario, Canada.[36] Previously the only connection between Canada and the United States had been ferry service, but, as business saw the potential for increased commerce, they bypassed the bureaucracy that was bogged down in "preparing to negotiate" an official agreement between the Canadian and United States governments, and found lumber donations to quietly build a bridge. In May 1917 the bridge was opened. It immediately became a popular crossing and places like the Pigeon River Resort cropped up to accommodate the travelers caught between the

11 P.M. bridge closing and its 7 A.M. opening. During Prohibition in the United States, the bridge (nicknamed the Outlaw Bridge) became a favorite route for rum runners from Detroit and Chicago.[37]

In the Southwest, painter John French Sloan, in a letter to fellow painter Walter Pach, wrote, "I've been driving a month now and its great fun. I do it much better than I had even thought I would."[38] He included a pen-and-ink sketch of his car driving switchbacks on a lovely winding desert road. Driving had become a major pastime.

In an interview with Thomas A. Edison for *Electrical World* in 1917, the lack of charging facilities was brought to the reader's attention. Mr. Edison said central stations should realize that there is a waiting market for selling current to charge electric cars: "The public is in the curious position of wanting to buy something for which there is no place to go."[39] He proposed that the central station should go into the garage business and should not sell current for charging, but for mileage. The garages should also wash and repair the vehicles at a fixed and reasonable price. "There is an opportunity for big sales of current on a profitable service basis. Business needs imagination. The electrical business is no exception. Sometimes I think the men who ought to see ten years ahead see only next week."[40]

By 1923 car ownership had become common for the ordinary citizen. Some questioned whether there would be a saturation point, and whether people could afford to pay for all these vehicles. One economist predicted a saturation point that would be hit like a brick wall, while another foresaw the doubling of car ownership in the near future. Production was estimated at a half million more cars than the anticipated consumption. One pessimist said, "Fords are likely to sell at cost, and others to retire from the field."[41] Another economist thought people were buying too many cars and not enough washing machines. It was estimated that an income of $2,000 a year was necessary to support car ownership, but statistics from 1922 showed that over a million people with an income of $1,600 a year owned cars. Prices for new cars were coming down and were about 40 percent lower than they had been before World War I. The average price of a new car dropped in November 1922 from $350 to $300, making it statistically possible for millions more people to buy cars. As production and profits went up, the cost of making a car went down. Some in the industry were seriously predicting a $150 car in the near future. According to the census, the theoretical number of purchasers of cars was about twenty million, the same as the number of American families and of white, native-born men above the age of twenty-one. It was also about the same as the number of persons with an adequate income whose occupations indicated they might become car owners. The prosperity of the day and the new developments in the reliability, longevity and performance of the automobile made it a popular household purchase.

Fashions for Motoring

Early automobiles, whether gasoline or electric, exposed their passengers to all types of weather. Books and magazines of the time reflected a plucky attitude. The earliest cars had no tops—and sometimes no windshields—to protect the occupants from rain, wind or snow. To compensate, drivers and fellow passengers adopted greatcoats, ponchos, dusters, goggles, gloves, hats and veils to match the season. Advertisements touted products to protect the skin and hair from the elements. *Life* magazine in 1909 carried an ad for the Scandinavia Fur & Leather Co. of New York, offering "Smart Auto Apparel for Up-to-Date Motorists. The Best Modistes and Tailors of Paris and London are drawn upon for our Selections of Imported Auto-Apparel.... Whatever is 'going' where style prevails can be furnished from our wardrobes at a moment's notice. Man, Woman, Child and Chauffeur can be instantly equipped with everything from a Complete Outfit to a pair of Gloves or Goggles."[42] In 1916 *Life* carried ads for Hansen Gloves featuring "Automobile Gauntlets and Mittens — Exclusive styles covering the widest range in motoring demands."[43]

Women in 1912 were offered "dresses and hats you can launder"[46] and insulated vacuum bottles for picnicking. In 1913 the fashion conscious were presented with a choice of apparel for the cold winter weather and the new spring offerings. Should one invest in a knit coat, skirt and hat, drab in color but very warm, the very thing for a frosty day with the wind whipping around while touring? Or should one anticipate the summer's heat and dust and buy the lightweight, brightly colored silk coats suitable for the opera or a fancy ball? Prices of coats ranged from six dollars to twenty-five dollars. Wet-weather garments, for those in open runabouts, were primarily a poncho style that slipped over the head. A

Left: Clothing ad, April 1916.[44] *Right:* Clothing ad, 1909.[45]

combination warm-weather garment that also had the styling to suggest an evening wrap in cut and richness could cost as much as seventy-five dollars. Straw hats, turbans and bonnets in bright colors, such as cerise, old blues, other blues, and greens of all degrees of brilliance were advertised. The straw hats came with brightly colored veils that tied under the chin. Prices averaged about fifteen dollars. A parasol was considered to be for show only and was not a very real protection against the sun, wind or dust. The invention of the vacuum bottle allowed tourists to carry hot drinks that would remain hot and cold drinks that would remain cold to a picnic. A picnic was just the answer for those weary of roadhouse fare and prices. With a vacuum bottle and a traveling kitchen chest, the tourist could enjoy a "denatured" picnic meal in the "rude state of nature."[47]

Sun, wind and dust took their toll on the faces of early motorists. Cosmetic companies were quick to see the new market and began promoting products to protect and to soothe that chafed skin. The New York Times noted, "Automobiling is very harmful to the complexion and the face should be protected by layers of cold cream and powder, and a veil on top of that."[48] Besides the bad effects of wind and sun, "dust kicked up by your own car [or] from the machine ahead" became another nasty suspect as a cause of bad complexion. Relief of this health nuisance was to be obtained by applying creams and powders.

Advertising also reflected the independence being gained by women of the time. The suffragists were campaigning for a woman's right to vote. More women were looking for their own income. Some worked out of necessity and many found jobs for the independence it gave and the chance to afford more luxury. A popular column in Ladies' Home Journal in 1912 asked "What Can I Do? How Can I Make Money Outside the Home?" and gave suggestions such as working in department stores, typing at home and becoming involved in social service. The column stated that if a woman must teach, she should specialize. Salary ranges for these positions were listed to fall between $600 and $1,800 a year. Home products such as electric washing machines and electric irons were emerging to lighten household chores. Even paper disposable diapers, advertised in 1912, offered more independence for a woman traveling with an infant. Women who had relied on men for transportation and protection were being lured to the EV, with its promises of easy operation, no repairs or need for knowing mechanics, and driving so easy "a child can do it." Women saw the automobile as part of this new independence. It allowed a woman to move about the city without need of a chauffeur or driver, and gave her the convenience of travel whenever the fancy took her. She and her friends or children were free to travel where they pleased.

Men, in the meantime, were reading ads that pictured lovely, stylish women operating electric cars on their own. Even men who felt pressure to be "modern" in their thinking could temper concern for their wife or daughter's safety alone in a vehicle, gathering comfort from ads that stressed the ease of operating these vehicles, even for the delicate woman. Baker, in particular, picked up on this theme in its ads and showed its electrics driven by women in many happy scenes: women and children on a picnic; women chatting off on a drive; women being helped out of the car for an elegant evening out.

In 1909, Alice Ramsey, who had never driven a car before, took up a challenge by the Maxwell Motor Co. to drive across the country. She left San Francisco on June 9, 1909, with three women friends (who also did not drive) headed for New York. The challenge and purpose of the trip was to prove that women could drive just as well as men. She completed the journey in 59 days. There were many trials along the way, as only about 150 miles of paved road existed at the time. She wrote in her diary, "In Utah we hit a prairie dog hole in the road with such force that a tie bolt came out of the tie rod connecting the front

DUST!
A CAUSE OF BAD COMPLEXIONS

The Relief

POMPEIAN MASSAGE CREAM & SKIN FOOD
POMPEIAN MFG CO.

The vogue of the machine has meant the vogue of bad complexions. Not alone are wind and sun enemies to good, clear, soft skins. Dust is an enemy, and often the chief one. Dust gets into the pores and can't be dislodged by ordinary cleansers. A **complete** cleanser like Pompeian Massage Cream is absolute necessary for good skin health of automobilists.

You gather the dust of the machine ahead. Your face is also continually receiving dust kicked up by your own car. This often insensibly gathered over the back by means of the vacuum created by your speed, however slight it may be. This dust g into the pores to an astonishing degree and works havoc with the skin. Hence the necessity of a **complete** cleanser l:

POMPEIAN MASSAGE CREAM
"It Cleans Completely"

Don't compare Pompeian with cold creams. Pompeian is a massage cream. Cold creams get off a little surface dirt, and also *rub in* m dust. This dust stays in the pores. Pompeian Massage Cream is rubbed into the pores—*and then out again*, bringing with it all the po clogging impurities—dust, soot, soap particles, etc. It is this foreign matter in the pores that causes many face disfigurements.

You'll be astonished at the difference between Pompeian and ordinary cold creams. "When I first used Pompeian," wrote a wom "I was as astonished as at my first Turkish bath. The dirt literally rolled out of my face pores." Wrote another: "I had no i so much dirt could get into the pores and stay there, despite soap and water."

Pompeian enjoys the most extensive sale of all face creams, 10,000 jars being made and sold daily. Your druggist should one of the 40,000 that sell it. But don't accept an inferior substitute on which the dealer makes a larger profit—at your expen

Pompeian
Mfg. Co.
25 Prospect St.
Cleveland, Ohio

Gentlemen: Enclosed find 6c., to cover cost of postage and packing. Please send me one copy of your illustrated massage book and a special sample jar of Pompeian Massage Cream.

NAME........................

ADDRESS........................

Sample Jar and Book
☞ **Cut off Coupon NOW Before "Life" Is Lost** ☜

You have been reading and hearing about Pompeian for years. You know it is the most popular face cream made. You have meant to try it, but have not done so. This is your chance to discover what a vast difference there is between an ordinary "cold" cream and a scientifically made Massage Cream like Pompeian. Fill out the coupon to-day and prepare for a delightful surprise when you receive our quarter ounce sample jar. A 16-page booklet on the care of the face sent with each jar. When writing enclose 6 cents in silver or stamps (United States only) to cover cost of postage and packing.

THE POMPEIAN MFG. COMPANY
25 Prospect St., Cleveland, Ohio

542

Pompeian Massage Cream ad, 1909[49]

The Family Car
That Needs No Chauffeur

The utmost in room makes the Silent Waverley Electric Limousine the town car ideal for the family. Ample seating space is afforded for five in this big richly upholstered car. The driver occupies a front seat—and so always has a full view of the thoroughfare ahead. Unusual expanse of plate glass panels, front, sides and rear, gives all the occupants the widest view.

Silent Waverley Electric Limousine-Five

"Full View Ahead"

Needs no chauffeur, because the Waverley No-Arc Controller is so simple and so safe that a child may operate it. It is the Town Car that requires no cranking—presents no mechanical difficulties—yet goes wherever a town car can be used, winter or summer. The coldest weather does not put it out of commission.

Design and Construction Patents Applied For

High Efficiency Shaft Drive, Full Elliptic Springs front and rear. Solid or pneumatic Tires.

Send for the beautiful Waverley Art Book on Town Cars. It shows ten models. Prices $3500 down to $1225.

Also the Waverley Catalog of Commercial Vehicles. Exide Battery.

THE WAVERLEY COMPANY
Factory and Home Office, 194 South East Street, Indianapolis, Indiana

New York, 2010 Broadway
Philadelphia
2043 Market Street

Boston, 25 Irvington Place
Chicago Branch
2005 Michigan Boulevard

Waverly ad, March 1912[50]

Baker ad, March 1916[51]

This theme was even used in a Donald Duck comic in the 1950s. Grandma Duck driving an electric car.[52] Copyright Disney Enterprises, Inc.

wheels. Down went the front end, wheels spread-eagled, breaking the spring seat over the front axle."[53] This is a very impressive knowledge of mechanics for someone who had just taken up the sport. Ramsey was the first woman inducted into the Automotive Hall of Fame, and there is an extensive exhibit covering this journey in the Gilmore Car Museum in Hickory Corners, Michigan.

Being fashionably and properly dressed for social occasions is part of our Western culture, and a woman's ability to face the challenges encountered when she's on her own is a fascination. Young American women of the early 1900s were interested in being properly attired when going motoring. The *Automobile Girls* series of books was advertised with a number of other young adult series as "The Best and Least Expensive Books for Real Boys and Girls. These fascinating volumes will interest boys and girls of every age under sixty."[54] The price was fifty cents per volume. This series followed the adventures of four young women and an aunt as they motored through the countryside beyond New York City. They met gypsies, repelled robbers and kidnappers, and stayed in beautiful country homes as they toured. Although they were motoring in an automobile they had to start by cranking, the clothing and sentiments for driving reflect those of both electric and gasoline motorists of the era.

> They had got into their fresh linen suits and broad-brimmed straw hats, and were waiting on the porch with suitcases and small satchels.... "And don't forget our automobile coats," exclaimed Mollie proudly, as she shook out her long pongee duster, last year's Christmas gift from Ruth. "This is the first time we've had a chance to wear them. I feel so grand in mine!" she continued, as she slipped it on. "With all this veil and hat, I can almost imagine I am a millionaire."[55]

On women driving automobiles:

> "My dear Major," replied Miss Sallie, "you have been away from America for so long that you are old-fashioned. Do you think these athletic young women need a man to protect them? I assure you that the world has been changing while you have been burying yourself in Russia and Japan. Ruth, here, is as good a chauffeur as could be found, and Barbara Thurston can protect herself and us into the bargain."[56]

By 1917 clothing for motoring became high fashion as well as functional, providing warmth in the winter. Raccoon coats were in high demand for men. Women shopped for fur coats made of beaver, wombat, and the fur of a small animal called nutria. The latter provided warmth without extra weight. "The best styled coats of fur are noted at once by the comfortable fullness of their cut. The designers have treated the collars of the coats meant for use in a car. Most of them are cut deep and full, which allows them not only to be warm but permits them to be turned up high in the back to protect the neck and ears."[57] Prices ranged from $55 to $95 with exclusive designs upward to $250. By 1917 motoring fashions stressed comfort, especially in the winter styles. Nearly all coats had pockets trimmed with a contrasting fur. "As for the fabrics that clothe the lady of the car when furs become superfluous, they are many.... Burilla and velour top the list along with 'Anzac Bolivia.'"[58] The well-dressed motorist stayed abreast of the fashion for each season.

Early Advertising

During the early years of the electric vehicle, there were no restrictions for driving, and no training was required. Any child or adult who could manage the vehicle was per-

Left: National Electric Vehicle ad, December 1902.[59] *Right:* National Electric, ad 1902.[60]

mitted to drive without any license or proof of skill. A 1902 advertisement claimed the electric car was so simple to drive that even a child could learn. A 1902 National Electric ad claimed its vehicles were for " those who take no pleasure in mechanical labor. Easily controlled by man, woman or child."

A 1906 Babcock ad targeted women with the slogan: "A contented woman is she who operates a Babcock Electric. She knows there is nothing to fear." Another Babcock slogan was: "When you build it right, IT IS right and works right." EVs were promoted as town cars for shopping and going to the theater and to dinner. A 1908 Baker Company advertisement proclaimed the simplicity and reliability of its car as the standard of the industry. It also promoted luxury and elegance by referring to the vehicles as "The Aristocrats of Motordom." The company claimed to produce the simplest vehicle with the fewest parts and fewer adjustments than others. One advertisement pronounced it to be an "automobile without a repair bill." A 1910 Baker ad claimed, "It outsells all other Electrics because it outclasses them. More than three times as many Baker Electrics are sold each year than any other make."

Early advertising rarely addressed the range of the electric, but a 1900 Riker ad took the problem head on. The ad features a "standard" Riker Phaeton with a map showing the 110-mile route the car took on its run from New York to Philadelphia, on one charge. Another characteristic rarely approached was the electric vehicle's lack of performance in cold weather. This 1902 Studebaker ad claims the car "can be run any day in the year by any member of the family." The same ad claims a range of 40 miles on one charge and the ability to climb hills successfully, even when the grade is "not only steep, but covered with sand and mud."

Automobile shows provided potential customers with glimpses of the new electrics and furnished manufacturers with free advertising in the newspapers. The Cycle and Automobile Show at Madison Square Garden in 1900 featured an electric Foster & Co. runabout weighing about 950 pounds and chargeable in 45 minutes.[63] The same show included entries by the American Electric Company, the Indian Bicycle Company and the Riker Electric Company (eight entries).

Early EV manufacturers formed the Association of Electric Vehicle Manufacturers. Its prime objective was to raise awareness of their product lines. To accomplish this they made efforts to secure better exhibition space at auto shows and to show potential buyers

Riker Phaeton ad, August 1900[61]

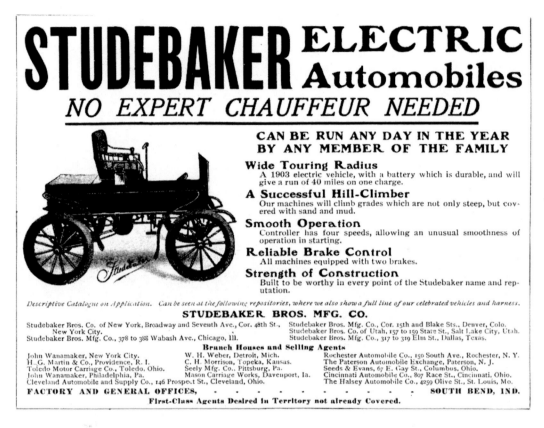

Studebaker ad, August 1902[62]

refinements in their cars and their usefulness for both pleasure and commerce.[64] The electric automobile show held in 1909 at Madison Square Garden was another high profile event. Coverage written by H. A. Harper (who was affiliated with Babcock) for *The New York Times* spoke of the delicate design and mechanism of electric vehicles, and their usefulness for the theater, calls in the afternoon, or a ride in the park. He claimed they were excellent vehicles for ladies and physicians as the cars are economical, simple to operate and require no mechanical aptitude to run. He noted that advances in storage batteries added speed and mileage, and garages "will now charge batteries for a small expense to the owner."[65] These events and articles introduced the public to the EV's style and potential.

Advertisers also turned their attention to accessories needed for the new vehicles. By the midteens, many ads were appearing for batteries, tires, and the like. Some products were successful and others were not. Home battery chargers were one of the unsuccessful products. Companies offered and promoted home battery chargers to combat the inconvenience of relying on charger stations, but the auto recharging plugs were not standardized, so owners purchased these according to the car and model they drove. For people without electric power to their homes in 1900, Baker offered an optional accessory—a Merriman 500-watt electric charger powered by a water-cooled gasoline engine. Women in the ads were shown at their ease in their homes plugging in their automobile for charging. The Lincoln electric battery charger consisted of a motor-generator set and steel cabinet with a knife switch and special connectors. The chargers were notoriously inefficient and did not enjoy widespread success.

Enjoy Your Electric More

Get more speed from your car—Drive it further without recharging—Have it ready the minute you want it—Always start with a full battery.

You can enjoy your electric more and maintain it at lower cost by charging your batteries with the

Lincoln Electric Charger

The batteries are charged with a steadily decreasing current which does not cause gassing or heating. The strength of the batteries is preserved and their service life increased.

The charger can be installed in your garage in twenty minutes. Any member of the family can operate it—just put the charging plug in place and throw on switch. It cannot harm car or batteries no matter how long it is left on charge.

Write for Booklet

The Lincoln Electric Co.
3804 Kelley Avenue
Cleveland, Ohio

Branches in Principal Cities

Lincoln Electric Charger[66]

By 1909 Studebaker's advertising had moved on to recognize the competition from the ICE touring cars. Its answer? Buy both. "Where the one is, there also should the other be — in every garage where there is a high priced gasoline touring car, there ought also to be an electric for city service — Studebaker preferred, of course, since we are considered high class equipment ... YOU MAKE YOURSELF RIDICULOUS, you see, when you compare the gasoline with the electric as if they were rivals—just as ridiculous as if you were to say you preferred a Tuxedo to a traveling suit, without specifying for what occasion."[67]

Columbia and Studebaker, in addition to aiming at the woman's market, appealed to the "rational man" by showing the logic of using the practical electrics in town.

The Columbus Buggy Company advertised heavily in 1909. Its town car was promoted as having the ability to make "99 short trips in one tour," and was meant to "supplant the big gasoline touring and limousine cars *for city service.*" One ad asked, "It is true that no electric will serve the purpose of a touring car but is it *rational* to use a big high-powered machine about town when an electric will carry you quickly and cheaper and you can drive yourself?" Its ads were also directed toward women, emphasizing ease of operation—"Takes

Studebaker ad, January 1909[68]

no strength. The control is easy, simple. A delicate woman can practically live in her car and never tire."—and the modern man who supported a woman's right to greater freedom. "Make the woman of your family independent of a chauffeur and coachman."

The Hupp-Yeats Corporation presented its enclosed vehicle with a sloping front end in 1911. Promoted as having a "French design of the very latest fashion.... With its low-hung

Detroit ad, 1909[69]

body, its curve of roof, and slope of hood — radical changes from accepted design — it presents rare beauty," it was giving the public a "new" design.

The Electric Vehicle Association of America began an extensive national advertising campaign in 1910 to promote the electric vehicle as a "perfected device." By 1912 it was struggling against the popularity of the gasoline car. The association planned an educational campaign to boost the acceptance of electric vehicles. It decided to promote the electric

COLVMBVS ELECTRIC

The town car you will eventually buy

Anyone in the Family can drive it

Cost of upkeep much less than horse and buggy; handsome—graceful in design, roomy and easy-riding; always ready.

You can stop the car *instantly* or jump at once into high speed—both *vitally important in a town car*, both done with one lever, no foot pedals to bother with. It has three positive speeds and a coasting position.

The Columbus Electric is lighter than any other electric—from 100 to 300 pounds lighter. This means greater mileage on a charge, less wear on tires. Extra large tires —3½ inch front and 4 inch rear—also greatly reduces tire expense. The famous Exide batteries are our standard equipment.

Unusually comfortable and easy-riding, due to its luxurious upholstering, long wheel-base and carefully graded springs.

4-passenger. inside operated Brougham, the all-the-year round model.

Just the car for calling, shopping and the theater., You can learn to drive it in 15 minutes; can care for and charge it yourself. No complicated machinery. All moving parts enclosed and run in oil—*dustproof.*

We have agents in almost every city. Our cars are being run by owners in every state. Let us refer you to *users.* Write us for 1909 catalogue showing 4 passenger and 2 passenger styles open and closed and stanhopes with Victoria tops, and name of agent in your locality.

Established 1870.

The Columbus Buggy Co.   382-450 Dublin Ave.   Columbus, O.

Columbus ad, 1909[72]

vehicle's simplicity, economy and serviceability. "The committee felt also that in the preparation of the advertising matter it should be borne in mind that the electric has its own very broad field, and that while the electric in many instances came in direct competition with the gasoline car, the publicity should not include a 'knock,' if you will pardon that expression, aimed at the gas-engine-propelled vehicle,"[73] said *Life* magazine in 1909. The horse, however, was in a different category. "It was further determined that the criticism of the horse and the indication of its being the passing victim of an age of higher efficiency whose elimination was demanded by present-day economy and sanitation would be wise and justifiable." The committee hired the advertising agency of Wm. D. McJunkin. It created the slogans "*Before you buy any car — consider the electric*" for pleasure and passenger vehicles, and "*Public interest and private advantage both favor the electric*" for commercial vehicles. Advertising in six mediums was aimed at different groups: "First, those reached by general publications; second, those reached by publications appealing to the wealthy and fashionable; third, those reached by central-station publications; fourth, those reached by auto trade papers; fifth, those reached by medical publications; sixth, those reached by purely trade publications, subdivided into light and heavy delivery service."[74] Thomas A. Edison commented, "I think the advertising campaign which has been conducted by the Electric Vehicle Association of America will be productive of absolute results in the elec-

Opposite, top: Columbus ad, April 1909.[70] *Opposite, bottom:* Columbus ad, March 1909.[71]

tric vehicle advancement." An observer remarked, "Mr. Edison has expressed himself as being very well pleased with the manner in which the campaign has been handled." The committee decided to place the address of the association under the name in the advertising and welcomed inquiries to the "Information Bureau." Within a few months, it had received 702 inquiries and found it was not in a position to answer the questions about operations and cost, especially the most frequently asked questions—"How far will it run?" And "Will it climb a hill?" It was decided to abandon the term "Information Bureau" and replace it with "Interesting Literature about Electric Vehicles Gladly Sent. Write To-day." The committee also decided that the advertising campaign was worthy of continuing and "that by persistent and proper educational publicity the mind of the purchasing public may be diverted from 'some vehicle' to that of the 'electric vehicle.'"[75]

One of the difficulties faced by the EV manufacturers was improper battery charging, which caused shorter battery life and less-than-expected mileage per charge. An article in 1912 in the New York Times stated that the National Electric Light Association estimated over $10,000,000 was invested in electric trucks and over $30,000,000 in electric pleasure vehicles. The figure was predicted to climb to $80,000,000 by 1913. The association planned to introduce "an ingenious method of determining the real efficiency of an electric vehicle" at its upcoming convention in Seattle. The method promoted for the convention recorded actual hours of use and rates of charging and the expected miles left to be used. The association intended to use the information gathered from this new recording method to teach drivers the proper recharging sequence so they would extend the life of the auto battery. The association wanted to keep the buying public interested in electric vehicles as a solid investment.

A 1912 Detroit Electric ad claimed the vehicle had "dependability built into it ... and electrical principles are inborn." It was also aimed at the higher-income individual—or those aspiring to be wealthy—by proclaiming that the purchase of a Detroit Electric would be a "foundation of your investment and will yield inestimable dividends of pleasure for yourself and friends." By 1919 interest in EVs was dwindling. To prop up sales, designers began emulating the design of the more powerful ICEs. Detroit Electric changed the design of the front end of its enclosed car to resemble the shape of an automobile with a gasoline engine. The advertising proclaimed "A perfect harmony of line—graceful, distinctive, yet dignified" and focused on appealing to the wealthy by promoting "an artistic selection in upholstery and interior fittings which combines beauty, luxury and comfort."

The heyday of the electric vehicle featured advertising directed to women. Women appeared in ads more than men at a ratio of about three to one. An advertising strategy was formulated by L. D. Gibbs of the Boston Edison Company in 1911 as: "In advertising the electric pleasure vehicle the use of illustrations showing a handsomely dressed and attractive lady operating her own car is far more convincing than a bald admonition to use such a vehicle. Such a picture at once conveys a notion of comfort, luxury, cleanliness, elegance and that identifiable element denominated 'class.'"[80] Women were shown in ads taking their children on picnics, attending club meetings and generally enjoying social events and the independence their cars allowed. Electric vehicles were advertised for their reliability, comfort, convenience and luxury, ignoring the technical appeal that interested most men. A 1913 Wood's advertisement proclaimed "The Woods Electric, with all its beauty, its ease, its convenience, typifies the civilization of our times, bearing testimony to man's conquest of the elements and to the constantly advancing status of the American woman, and the desire and intention upon the part of man to supply her with all the luxurious attributes of a real queen."

An Even Finer Detroit Electric

The discriminating public looks naturally to the Detroit Electric for the latest ideas in enclosed car design and construction.

This year's model is a worthy successor to the long line of cars which have maintained Detroit Electric dominance. A perfect harmony of line—graceful, distinctive, yet dignified; an exceptional riding comfort, attained by the use of specially-designed three-quarter elliptic springs, long, wide and flat; an artistic selection in upholstery and interior fittings which combines beauty, luxury and comfort.

Already those who have seen this new model are acclaiming it the finest car of any type yet produced for city and suburban use. You, too, will be delighted with it.

On Exhibition at the Shows

At the automobile shows in New York, Chicago and elsewhere this new Detroit Electric will be shown. At the same time, it will be exhibited in the show-rooms of leading distributors the country over. See it and give yourself the pleasure of a thorough test of its riding qualities.

The electric was the pioneer enclosed car— and it is still the best

DETROIT ELECTRIC CAR COMPANY　　DETROIT, MICHIGAN

Detroit ad, December 1919.[76]

Hupp-Yeats ad, 1911[77]

Utility

Your Rauch & Lang or Baker Electric will carry you in style to the social function or serve as a cheerful conveyance for a day outdoors.

The wonderful ease of control—the silent, efficient, dependable motor—and the genuine Coach Work—all these unite in making your Rauch & Lang or Baker Electric a Car of Utility and Enjoyment.

THE BAKER R & L COMPANY
Cleveland, Ohio

Rauch & Lang Electrics
"The Social Necessity"

Baker Electrics

Baker Electric ad, 1916[78]

As good
as it
is
beautiful

The "Patrician"—100 inch wheelbase ; 30 cell, 13 plate Exide Hycap battery, $2150 F. O. B. Detroit.
The "Regent" — 86 inch wheelbase ; 27 cell, 11 plate Exide Hycap battery, $1750 F. O. B. Detroit.

A car of French design of the very latest fashion.

HUPP-YEATS
ELECTRIC COACH

Design protected by letters patent.

One of the interesting features of the vogue which the Hupp-Yeats is enjoying everywhere is the extraordinary extent to which it is being bought and used as a summer car.

The electric is actually one of the coolest of cars and you will observe scores of the new and larger Hupp-Yeats models — with the luxurious-riding 100 inch wheelbase — being driven daily through the hot months by those who ordinarily confine themselves to the touring car or runabout.

One hundred to one hundred and fifteen miles on one charge in this easy, elegant coach comes as close to perfect comfort in motoring as one could desire.

HUPP CORPORATION, 117 Lycaste Street, DETROIT, MICH.

————————— BRANCHES —————————

BUFFALO, 1225 Main St. ; CHICAGO, 1500 Michigan Ave. ; CLEVELAND, 1992 East 13th St. ; DENVER, 1620 Broadway ;
DETROIT, Woodward and Warren Aves. ; KANSAS CITY, 34th and Broadway ; LOS ANGELES, 816 S. Olive St. ;
MINNEAPOLIS, 1334 Nicollet Ave. ; PHILADELPHIA, 330 N. Broad St.

Hupp-Yeats, 1911[79]

Rauch and Lang marketed their Broughams with the latest conveniences—interior lights that lit when the doors were opened, a cigarette lighter, and windows that could be opened by using a strap pull. Although they did not list it in their catalog, their Roadster could also be purchased with a false radiator hood to imitate gasoline engine autos. Some models came with seats that could swivel. Cost ranged from about $2,600 to $3,200 for most models.[81]

The Owen Magnetic Company, acquired by Baker, Rausch & Lang in 1915, created a vehicle with an electric transmission that eliminated the clutch and gear system. It was advertised as the "Car of a Thousand Speeds."

EV ads reflected trends in language as well as living styles. During the early 1900s "reliability" was the term most often given to the electric vehicle to indicate a stable mechanical performance. "Dependability" is a word that did not appear in very many advertisements until the 1930s. It was first widely promoted by Horace Dodge and used sparingly in early Detroit electric ads. Dodge also included power and rugged construction as attributes of his automobiles.

After World War II, EVs had few supporters. Automobiles were reflecting a different lifestyle. Midcentury advertising brought hot rods and muscle cars and the "Put a Tiger in Your Tank" slogan from Exxon. The roar of the engine and power were emphasized. Popular singing groups like the Beach Boys in 1966 praised ICEs with lyrics such as "She's real fine, my 409," flattering the Chevy V-8. Artists in the early 1950s captured the spirit of that era's image of cars. There was disinterest in painting the car by itself. Instead, artists used it as a symbol for speed and motion.[82] The electric vehicle did not have the power, range or the rumbling noise appeal to compete with this market.

The Green Movement

The surge of the "green movement" in the 1990s and early 21st century made driving an environmentally friendly auto both a political and a fashion statement. A convenient infrastructure, which has been a difficulty throughout the electric's history, began to be addressed. Major cities (London, Seattle, Oslo, Stockholm, Portland [Oregon]) and countries (Israel, Denmark, Australia) launched local and nationwide campaigns focused on promoting nonpolluting vehicles by providing electric charging stations for EV owners. They installed outlets in large parking areas, near businesses, at gas stations and truck stops, and roadside rest areas. They introduced a variety of ways for the car owner to pay for the fuel (subscriptions, credit card, cash). Companies like Elektromotive, Ecofactor, and ventures like Project Better Place saw a possibility and moved into the market. Technology for producing hydrogen fuel from many sources for zero-emission fuel cell vehicles had its promoters too. In their energy independence plans, Iceland and Denmark established hydrogen refueling infrastructures. Iceland has the first fully operational, commercial enterprise.

These projects reflect growing interest in becoming a more environmentally friendly world. During this first decade of the 21st century, interest in stewardship of the earth, called the green movement, attracted a wide variety of followers. Conservation and preservation of the world's natural resources have value; pollution makes a less habitable world for everyone. Environmentally responsible buyers are flooding the marketplace. Venture capitalists see the possibility for making *green* enterprises profitable. The gasoline infrastructure for the internal combustion engine has been the key for that product to remain the preferred transportation model. Building electric infrastructure, increasing the incentives to use the electrics, and pushing the green concept to a receptive public may again catch the attention of the car buyer and bring the electric back to a popularity it hasn't seen in a century.

Infrastructure is important, but fuel availability and initial cost are only part of the total cost of running an auto. Maintenance and insurance must also be factored in. According to the Insurance Australia Group, Toyota Prius and Honda Civic Hybrid are shown to be among the cheaper models to repair. Their tests showed that the cost of repairing a hybrid car was similar to that of a conventional ICE car, despite the hybrid's more complex technology.

The St. Paul Travelers insurance company was the first to begin offering a ten percent discount to owners of hybrid vehicles in January 2006. Its research indicated that hybrid owners fell into a low-risk category overall. One component of the Travelers decision was that hybrid owners are typically married and between the ages of 41 to 60. Soon after that, Farmers Insurance began offering a five percent discount for hybrid owners. State Farm Insurance, however, cited increased repair costs of hybrids and concerns about the risks of electric components as a reason not to jump onto this bandwagon.

Another way to look at the cost of a hybrid versus an ICE is to compare the "dollars per lifetime mile" figures, also referred to as the energy cost per mile driven. Hybrids cost more to build because of the manufacturing, replacement and disposal of batteries, electric motors and the use of lighter-weight materials. For example, the Honda Accord Hybrid has an energy cost per mile of $3.00, while the conventional Honda Accord ICE has an energy cost per mile of $2.18. To look at this over a lifetime of "dust to dust" the hybrid will require about 50 percent more energy than the non-hybrid. The industry average of all vehicles sold in the United States is an energy cost of $2.28 per mile. Surprisingly, the Hummer H3 was only $1.94 per mile. The least expensive was the Scion xB, coming in at $0.48 per mile.[83] Consumers may be saving some fuel in the short term by buying a hybrid, but the broader issue of environmental impact may not be what they expected.

Automobile Racing

From the earliest days of the automobile, racing has been used to demonstrate the superiority of one make or feature over another and to illustrate the potential of a particular machine. Electric vehicles were no exception. They also used racing and setting land speed records as important methods for putting themselves into the public eye. Race coverage was popular in the newspapers of the early 1900s. In November 1901 A. L. Riker timed a 1:08 run in his electric carriage on a one-mile straightaway at the Long Island Automobile Club races. The cars in this race were stripped down to the frame and seat. Auto racing also saw its share of casualties. One incident occurred in 1902 when a Baker Electric racer attempted a new land speed record at Staten Island, New York. W. C. Baker designed the vehicle along the lines of an earlier Riker racing car. The machine's aerodynamics was ahead of its time, with a torpedo-shaped body tapered at both ends. Its iron frame was covered with wood and fabric. The wheels had three-inch pneumatic tires mounted on wooden rims covered with a canvas fabric. The auto weighed 3,000 pounds, a hefty machine for a racer. The weight was primarily due to the batteries and controlling apparatus, consisting of forty cells of "light-weight" Gould lead-zinc accumulators, assembled around the vehicle in a U shape on each side of the operator's seats.

Two people were required to operate the racer. The driver peered through a small isinglass window. The test became a disaster when the car reached about 60 mph, swerved to the right and struck some trolley tracks. The vehicle left the ground, and when it touched down, the hand brakes had been applied with an uneven distribution and the car

Baker Racing electric car, 1902[84]

smashed broadside into a crowd of spectators. The drivers were unhurt, but two onlookers were killed and a half dozen others were injured. This caused the sponsor, the Automobile Club of America, to cancel all further road speed tests and concentrate the energies of its members on the "development of the pleasure of commercial automobiles."[85] A 1917 run sponsored by the Electric Vehicle Association achieved a new record for an intercity run in an EV. The run from Atlantic City, New Jersey, to New York City was made in five hours and 48 minutes with an average speed of 20.5 mph over a 123-mile stretch.[86] These auto races showcased the EVs and reminded the public of their viability, but the ICE performance overshadowed the small strides made by EVs in distance and speed. The race coverage was more likely to point out the electric's inability to match performance with the ICEs.

The Solar Electric 500, sponsored by local Phoenix, Arizona, EV car clubs, made its debut in April 1991. The clubs wanted to revitalize racing as a testing ground for new products and innovations in a way similar to the innovations gained during competitions in the early years of the electrics. The first year 13 cars competed. The entries averaged speeds of 54 miles per hour. Traveling distance was 108 miles. The Arizona Public Service utility company sponsored the APS Solar & Electric 500 race at the Phoenix International Raceway in 1992. It included fifty cars and four events, featuring a Saturn SC electric powered by nickel/cadmium batteries. The Saturn ran about eighty-four miles per hour for 125 miles without a pit stop. The Formula Lightning Classic in 1999 brought university teams from across the United States to compete at Indianapolis Raceway Park. Speeds reached 150 mph. For electrics, pit crews' jobs are a bit different from those of their NASCAR and Formula 1 counterparts. Their main job is to swap out batteries while the clock ticks out the seconds. Today, science and engineering students at high schools, colleges and universities are the designers and competitors in electric car racing.

At the Challenge Bibendum race in November 2001, Carroll Shelby introduced a Cobra CSX powered by a V-8 fueled by hydrogen. It generated 180 hp and went 108 mph. The event showcased more than fifty entries powered by natural gas, diesel and hybrid engines and brought fuel cell powered vehicles onto the public radar with test runs and races on major raceways in the United States and Europe. The 2003 challenge at Crissy Field in San Francisco continued with its theme of "sustainable mobility" and provided autos that are friendly to the environment without hindering the personal freedom that an auto provides. Small advances in fuel cell development such as the Volvo Multi-Fuel and Mercedes-Benz A-Class were showcased along with more efficient diesel and gasoline engines and a wide variety of hybrids. Success of the Prius and Civic Hybrid proved that consumers are willing to buy hybrids if the price is within reach. The manufacturers reacted with more research and design put in that direction. The Tzero AC Propulsion electric took the honors, going 0 to 60 mph in 3.6 seconds with a top speed of 100 mph. Acceleration, efficiency and emissions were factored into the scoring. Each year the challenge continues to showcase new possibilities and advances in technology for improving our vehicles. The commercial marketplace shares the spotlight. Its goal is to have a variety of energy sources fueling the vehicles to ensure that the market has competition to keep fuel costs affordable.

Using the AC Propulsion system, Ian Wright, a former employee of Tesla Motors, follows in the racing tradition of showing what can happen. He has taken his Wrightspeed X1 proof-of-concept car to the drag races and put in admirable performances. As of this writing the Wrightspeed website (http://www.wrightspeed.com/x1.html) showed performance data as follows:

> 0–30 mph: 1.35 sec
> 0–60 mph: 3.07 sec in 117 feet
> 0–100 mph: 6.87 sec
> 0–100–0 mph 11.2 sec

The car is intended to be concept only and is not fitted with additional safety gear required for production autos. The intent is to show that electrics do have the capacity to go fast.

Most diehard racing fans enjoy the sounds of the cars on the track as a basic part of the sport. Twenty hybrid electric vehicles whispering around the track just doesn't make good entertainment. While there is a duty to help the environment, racing fans will always want to hear the sweet music, the thunder of engines.

Challenges for the EV market

EVs have always held the trophy in environmental points against their gasoline engine competitors. It has been their major competitive lead. With the advances being made in fuel efficiency, this lead is growing smaller. Which technology will have the competitive edge with tomorrow's consumers? Who is interested in buying an EV?

- People who are concerned about the environment and want to help keep it clean and quiet
- People who want leading-edge technology such as fuel cell and hybrid technology in their lives
- People who want fuel-efficient cars with good mileage
- Households with a combined income of over $120,000

Will consumers who want environmentally friendly autos support the EV in the marketplace? Will providing charging stations really be the key to boosting EV sales? Has the bloom of the hybrid faded as competitors find higher fuel mileage and lower pollution emissions in the more conventional engines? Are buyers still interested in making an environmental statement by keeping the air cleaner or do they view the electrics and hybrids as "Your eco-green tree-hugger-mobile is a half an eyedropper full of medicine for a big, sick planet, and owning one is like having the only deck chair on the Titanic made from renewable bamboo and organically grown hemp fibers."[87]

By 1993 the GM electric vehicle marketing department was exploring ways to attract buyers. The major problem in marketing EVs is that the product is not market-driven but mandated by law. *Ward's Auto World* conducted an Electric Vehicle Study in 1993 which showed that two-thirds of the respondents doubted that EVs would be sold in significant numbers in any state that does not require them by law.[88]

GM's marketing director John Dabels said, "Introducing electric vehicles is a lot like convincing consumers to try other technologically advanced products. The major difference is that no government body ever passed legislation requiring marketers of microwave ovens and compact discs to meet certain sales goals."[89] GM decided the best approach was to join in a consortium with Ford Motor Company and Chrysler to develop technology and manufacturing techniques. The companies began building prototypes to be used in fleets for utility companies and government entities. These could be used as tests to gather information about consumer reactions in real-world use. Dabels said, "We want to put people in the vehicles and ask them what they really think after they sit in it, drive it, go shopping and take the kids places."[90] During the same time, the Japanese formed the Japan Electric Vehicle Association to research, develop and popularize electric vehicles in Japan. GM's marketing department identified price, range and infrastructure as the major areas to address. A study showed that most people in Boston and Los Angeles were driving about seventy-five miles per day, well within the range of the electric vehicles available. The infrastructure needed would be charging stations at work, shopping centers and restaurants, as well as at homes. They proposed small charging stations, similar to parking meters, that would accept credit cards. GM has formed partnerships with companies like the Los Angeles Department of Water and Power, Southern California Edison, San Diego Gas & Electric, Pacific Gas & Electric, Sacramento Municipal Utility District, Arizona Public Service, and Tucson Electric Power Company to build an electric car charging infrastructure.

By 2003, more than 1,100 chargers had been installed and were in use by EV1 customers in California and Arizona. Nearly 500 public charging stations are located at shopping malls, restaurants, beaches, airports, Saturn retail facilities, and key workplaces. For the near future, most of them are free.[91]

Other major metropolitan areas along the West Coast of the United States followed, slowly building an infrastructure for the electric car owners. By 2008, King County, Washington had charging facilities in two community garages, with plans for sockets in three new facilities. Portland General Electric added five stations in Portland, Salem and Lake Oswego, Oregon. California had its Couloub Technology, Inc., and Project Better Place. But most plug-in owners carry long extension cords and rely on the generosity of others to allow them to plug in. Each project is moving forward. The difficulty in providing the service is, as always, a balance between the cost for installation and the demand for the service. As in the past, families could use an electric car for short shopping trips and still have a traditional ICE vehicle for longer tips. The prevailing thought of the day is to get the message out to the consumers and then find out what they want.

Honda began its experiments with a battery-only vehicle in the late 1990s with the EV Plus. Designed from the ground up, it was not a conversion based on an existing platform. Honda marketed the car heavily in southern California using newspaper advertising. This resulted in sales of only 300 vehicles in two and a half years. The problems again were lack of public demand due to the inconvenience of "plugging in" and the cost of the batteries. The battery pack weighed in at about a thousand pounds, cost forty thousand dollars and would last for only about five years. Cold weather climates reduced the range and hot weather climates resulted in battery failures. Steve Ellis, manager of American Honda's Alternative Fuel Vehicle Sales and Marketing division, noted in an interview that even if the cost of the battery pack was reduced by half, to twenty thousand dollars, that would equal the price of a new Honda Civic Hybrid or a Natural Gas Civic.[92] The Natural Gas Civic came on the market in 1998, had a range of two hundred miles and carried an SULEV rating. Honda sells approximately one thousand Natural Gas Civics a year, primarily for fleet use. They have not been marketed to the general retail consumer because of infrastructure challenges. Honda's all-electric EV Plus did not find a market.

In 1996 France was thought be a good market for electric vehicles partly because nuclear generating stations were producing most of the country's electricity. The French government was also subsidizing electric vehicles to keep costs in line with conventional ICEs. But sales were only about one-third of what was expected in 1996 and most of the units were going to fleet use. Gut Sarre, an engineer for SAFT SA, a French battery company, said, "I don't think we can develop a market by regulation and restraint. We develop a market by having a good product at a low cost."[93] Even with abundant power available, the French preferred the ICEs.

A *Business Week* analysis and commentary article in 1997 stated, "Motown [Detroit, Michigan] insists the public doesn't want them [EVs]. With gasoline cheaper than bottled water, American consumers seem unable — or unwilling — to curtail their addiction to gas-guzzlers. Chrysler Corporation claims fuel economy ranks 19th among buyers' criteria in picking cars — right after 'quality of air conditioning.'"[94] With Japan's Toyota Prius newly on the horizon, Stephen Girsky, an auto analyst for the Morgan Stanley Group, said, "Eventually the Big Three will be forced to field a car like this."

By 1998 the Big Three automakers were spending about 10 percent of their budgets on research and development on alternative fueled vehicles. Fuel cell technology was becoming less of a dream and looking more like a real solution for new cars, a solution that might be available within ten years. With no infrastructure for hydrogen filling stations to fuel the cells, researchers looked to gasoline for a hydrogen supply source. Extracting hydrogen from gasoline still produces carbon dioxide at levels not acceptable to those supporting zero emissions. David E. Cole, director of the University of Michigan's Office for the Study of Automotive Transportation, said, "The fuel cell has great potential, but it's certainly not the solution to global warming."[95] By 1999, polls indicated that the public was enamored, not so much with the ICE, but with the concept of a private automobile. Many would be willing to buy an electric vehicle if its performance and price were comparable to the ICE. Range is the performance issue most often mentioned. Consumers want to travel several hundred miles on a single charge at a comparable price. The electric is also at a disadvantage because the designers had not found an alternative to using the battery for powering the federally required heating. The energy must come from the battery, reducing power and range. Other factors include the fact that consumers want luxury extras, like air conditioning, power steering, power windows, and so forth. All of those add-ons deplete the batteries and shorten range considerably. The trade-off is not one the buying public is interested in making. Others polled named battery replacement and driving around in a vehicle filled with acid as factors that made them resistant to buying EVs. These perceptions make marketing an EV challenging, but still give promise that buyers will come if the product meets the buyers' expectations.

As stated by the *ACEEE's Green Book* car guide, "Perhaps the best green consumer news is that most of this year's [2001] Greenest Vehicles list is comprised of gasoline-powered cars."[96] The list is topped by the Honda Insight and Toyota Prius, hybrids that use standard gasoline and do not need to be plugged in. They are alternatives to ICEs yet can be treated "like a regular car," with no special plug, cords or charging stations. This remarkable recommendation by an environmentally friendly publication emphasizes that EVs are not in demand by the general public and that battery technology alone has not progressed as expected, but the technology for hybrid electrics keeps moving forward. The results are catching consumers' attention. When they first came on the market, new hybrid vehicles were priced at about $20,000 and in 2000 involved a waiting period of three to four months for delivery. There was also a growing market of used hybrids, primarily the Toyota Prius and the Honda Insight. A used 2001 Toyota Prius ranged in price from $17,000 to $21,000. The price for a used 2000 Honda Insight ranged from $14,000 to $15,000.

The Honda Insight was the first hybrid available in the United States (2000). It is still available, but the Toyota Prius and the Honda Civic Hybrid get all the attention of the press. However, the Insight gets better mileage, 50-plus versus 40 mpg for the competitors. The early Insight does not have the look of a conventional auto; it seats only two and has a swooping, aerodynamic body style, but those who have them own the first hybrid model to be marketed in the United States.

The 2008 Kelley Blue Book pricing indicated that each of these initial hybrid vehicles has kept a moderate price for the market and held value.

Consumers reacted positively to the limited variety of hybrid-gasoline vehicles available when they appeared on the market, and buyers adjusted to their little quirks. The original Honda Insight is a two-door hatchback with strong aerodynamic lines, and the Toyota Prius has four doors and a trunk. When either car stops at a light, the engine is shut off and the driver must fight the initial response to reach for the key and start the car. Owners report actual mileage well over 50 mpg and have a good feeling about driving an environmentally friendly car that gets good gas mileage. The Prius has a gasoline engine on one side of the engine bay and an electric motor on the other, connected by a planetary gear transmission. Five microprocessors determine which engine will drive the car. The NiMH batteries are behind the back seat and are charged by the gasoline engine. Hard acceleration engages both power sources. The Honda's electric motor/generator and gasoline engine are also balanced using computers. Their configuration provides the buyer the option of either a manual 5-speed or continuously variable automatic transmission. Each uses regenerative braking and has proven to be environmentally friendly, with the Insight having slightly higher efficiency in producing less carbon dioxide. Each vehicle also meets California's SULEV (super ultra low emission vehicle) standards, positioning at 75 percent cleaner than the ULEV (ultra low emission vehicle). Both the Toyota Prius and the Honda

Model	Year	Price Range
Toyota Prius (new)	2009	$22,000 – $24,270
Toyota Prius	2006	$22,000 - $24,800
Toyota Prius	2003	$22,000 - $24,270
Honda Insight	2010	Not available yet
Honda Insight	2006	$17,150 - $17,550
Honda Insight	2003	$12,950 - $13,650
Honda Civic Hybrid (new)	2009	$23,550 - $26, 270
Honda Civic Hybrid	2006	$19,600 - $21,100
Honda Civic Hybrid	2003	$14,250 – $15,000

Table 1. 2008 Kelley Blue Book Pricing.

Insight enjoyed higher-than-expected sales in 2000, the Prius with 5,562 sales in 2000 and the Insight with 4,099 sales through February 2001. In May 2007, the Honda Civic Hybrid replaced the Insight and its sales totaled 4,520. In May 2008 the total was 4,676. The Prius met with unexpected success. By 2008 its total sales worldwide topped 1 million. The Insight's success prompted Honda to advance plans for the Insight technology. It is currently implemented in its highly successful Civic Hybrid models and is being reintroduced in the Insight 2010. Both manufacturers have attracted consumer attention with the technical advances of combining electric motors with convenient gasoline engines. The success of these early models opened the gates to a wider selection of hybrids. The more the cars were bought, the more manufacturers moved to design and build that type of auto.

EV Testing

The Department of Energy (DOE) is in charge of testing EVs. Its Field Operations Program uses four testing methods to produce repeatable results. The first is called Baseline Performance and involves testing on closed tracks or with dynamometers. The test parameters include acceleration, range, handling, charging, maximum speed and braking. The second is called Accelerated Reliability Testing and includes accruing high mileage, up to 25,000 to 30,000 miles per year. The testing includes energy use, maintenance requirements and the effect of mileage on range. The third is EV Fleet Testing, wherein Qualified Vehicle Testers (QVTs) collect data on electric vehicles within commercial fleets. This includes energy use, maintenance requirements, mileage, range and reliability. The fourth is Urban and Neighborhood Electric Vehicle Testing. This involves small pure-electric vehicles about the size of golf carts, and consequently a slightly different set of performance goals from those for the full-size electric vehicle.

The DOE has also been involved with hybrid electric vehicles since 1993 in a partnership with the PNGV. The official name is National Renewable Energy Laboratory (NREL). The NREL uses the assistance of the Big Three automakers, Ford, General Motors and DaimlerChrysler, for technical work. They test vehicle performance, battery thermal management and auxiliary loads reduction.

The Fleets Market

Conventional EV manufacturers have struggled to find a technology breakthrough that will provide a product to meet the buyer's expectations. Since individual consumer acceptance has not materialized, retail markets will develop only when there is value for the customer. The auto dealers expanded sales efforts to public agencies and private industry in an attempt to put their product in the public eye and meet ZEV obligations. In 1998 over 90 percent of all EVs sold were for fleet use. This included the Ford Ranger Electric, GM EV1 and the Toyota RAV4 EV.

GM's EV1, an all-electric zero emission vehicle developed by its Saturn division, originally leased for $480 a month after government incentives, but in 1996, GM had to cut the payment by 25 percent due to disappointing sales. GM offered a nickel metal-hydride battery that doubles the 70–90 mile range of the lead acid battery. In 1997 GM spent $10 million for advertising in Los Angeles, San Diego and Sacramento, California; and Phoenix and Tucson, Arizona. By 1998, with little response to television ads, GM switched to print advertising and direct mail to increase public awareness of its product. GM discontinued the EV1 in 1999, but production facilities remain in place.

Honda began selling its ultra–low emission (ULEV) Accord in 1998, the SULEV in 1999, and the Civic GX (SLEV) in 2001. The ZLEV technology was introduced at the Tokyo show in 1997. Honda promised to have a ZLEV engine in production in a few years, but in 2006 no production models were on the market, suggesting that Honda's research and design monies were channeled toward other possibilities.

Ford introduced its Ford Ranger Electric Vehicle in 1998. It used NiMH batteries and advertised a range of ninety to one hundred miles between charges. It could take a full charge at six to eight hours, but had an 80 percent recovery after four hours. By 2003, the vehicle had been replaced by a hybrid model.

Hybrids have had a bit more success in the fleet market. In 2005, Chicago's city-vehicle fleet included 45 Prius cars and 18 Ford Escape Hybrids. At the time Chicago was the eighth largest market for hybrid vehicles in the country, and was the only city on the list that was not on the East or West Coast. Hybrid vehicle registrations in the Chicago area grew by 72 percent from 2003 to 2004, but still accounted for only one-half of one percent of the total new vehicle registrations. By 2007, Maryland had 30 hybrids in its fleet of 9,000 and projected that 100 more would be added by 2011. Maryland's Public Works Department made a commitment that forty percent of its vehicle purchases between 2009 and 2011 would be biofuel and hybrids. This would require additional commitment in the area for building a strong infrastructure to support those vehicles. When the state government made that commitment in 2007, there was only one ethanol station in the system.

The private sector showed some interest in a greener world as well. With the expansion of the hybrid options, government incentive programs, and the environmentally friendly image associated with cars like the Prius and Ford Escape Hybrid, companies like Google, Roche, and Bank of America moved to replace some company cars with hybrids and alternative fuel vehicles, and also gave cash incentives (in some cases up to $5,000) to encourage their employees to purchase hybrids. The CEO of ETM Electromatic, Tom Hayse, chose to support a grassroots organization called Plug-in Bay Area, and ordered 10 vehicles for his company's fleet in anticipation that General Motors, Toyota and Nissan would soon go beyond the prototype and put the concept into production. He also joined other companies in offering the $5,000 incentive to his employees to encourage purchase of a hybrid vehicle for their personal transportation. In 2006 the American Jewish Committee announced a program that would give its employees a bonus of up to $2,500 for buying a hybrid vehicle. Executive Director David A. Harris described the program as "integral to AJC's long-term commitment to developing a serious energy policy in the U.S."[97]

Rental agencies are also seeing the benefits of offering hybrids to their customers. Hertz, Enterprise Rent-A-Car and Avis promote their hybrid offerings in major metropolitan airports worldwide, and consumers are willingly paying the added daily charge to drive the gas-electrics.

Better batteries, convenient refueling/recharging, and competitive pricing continue to challenge the EV industry as it strains to be competitive against the advances made in the ICE's lower tailpipe emissions, increased fuel efficiency and the emergence of alternate fuel vehicles. In the early 1900s moguls in the electric vehicle industry believed that any substantial increased use of electric vehicles would naturally be followed by an increase in charging stations. Even with the ad campaigns sponsored by the associations and support from manufacturers and EV enthusiasts, sales were disappointing. Although a few major urban areas are experimenting with charging posts at shopping centers and by major downtown buildings, and batteries are improving with the lithium-ion and lithium-ploy, electrics still have not caught the interest of many fleet managers beyond the government's required mandate.

From the beginning of the motor age, the touring motorist needed both good roads and refueling or recharging stations. Roads improved through the efforts of pioneers like Colonel Albert A. Pope, the "father of good roads." In the mid–1890s he rose as a leader of the League of American Wheelmen (LAW), a national organization of bicycle enthusiasts, and promoted research and design centered on road construction. The United States Post Office started rural free delivery in 1896 and politicians followed the public demand for good roads by increasing the monies to be spent.[98] Better roads spurred more auto travel. Gas stations soon dotted the landscape at convenient locations. Gasoline suppliers saw an opportunity and quickly took advantage of the interest in ICEs. The oil and ICE auto industries were able to combine resources to build an infrastructure to support the needs of the touring motorist. Electricity suppliers did not give coverage in large enough numbers for the electrics to have the same convenient fuel stations. Electric grids existed mainly in towns, and most rural areas had cars before lightbulbs.[99]

A century later, electric vehicles and, more recently, hybrid fuel-cell electrics, have not seen an infrastructure develop. That picture may be changing. Today, electrics continue to operate in a Catch-22. Although the sale of gasoline hybrid electrics continues to expand, the volume of sales for other alternate fuel vehicles is too low to make recharging or alternate-fuel stations for hydrogen, natural gas or methanol attractive to suppliers. This is partly due to vehicle cost. However, in order to increase sales and lower costs, refueling stations must be in place. Utility deregulation for natural gas looked like it might have possibilities for AFVs. As an alternative to a natural gas refueling station, deregulation has allowed an individual who owns a home that is piped for natural gas to install a refueling station next to the driveway (it must be outside the residence). The installation cost to provide the overnight refueling is about $5,000. It is an expensive investment, which the buying public did not find appealing. To make the electric vehicles interesting to potential owners, both competitive cost and fuel availability have to be in place.

Private/public ventures like Elektromotive, Ecofactor, Coulomb and Project Better Place may spark more interest as they begin to build infrastructures for the electrics. If they find success in Israel, Denmark, Australia, England and California, the plans hold excellent possibilities for being adopted on a worldwide scale. With infrastructure in place and improvement seen in batteries for recharging times, size and weight, the electric may once again find a profitable market niche.

Elektromotive, based in Brighton, UK, had installed 68 recharging stations by summer 2008. The system uses its newly developed power line communication technology as a data exchange mechanism for billing, power requirement identification and transaction security.[100] Venture capitalist Shai Agassi is tackling the problem of lack of infrastructure for electric vehicles through his Project Better Place organization. Its market strategy is to alleviate consumers' fear of being stranded in their EVs with no place to recharge. The plan provides "islands," or geographic areas with available charging. As confidence builds and more customers begin to drive EVs, island areas will expand, creating more demand for the electrics. Agassi and his business partners see the future of automotives in a new all-electric paradigm supported by the grid. Islands will eventually blend to provide car owners with recharging stations at any point needed. His goal is to create a network and sign contracts with motorists for use of a specified number of kilowatts per month to power their electric cars. The project brings private enterprise, utility companies and government interests together to create the power network and find willing customers. Renault Nissan Alliance, partners in Project Better Place, teamed with Israel to introduce 500,000 charging stations to that country with plans to market all-electric vehicles there by 2012. The Israel project has the benefit of large urban areas within close proximity, weather that lends itself to solar technology and a political climate that encourages reduction in the need for foreign oil. Their project will use lithium-ion batteries in cars supplied by Renault and Nissan. Israel guarantees substantial tax breaks for the cars through 2015. Similar projects are cropping up worldwide, with alliances in Portugal and Denmark leading the Renault Nissan list. Denmark, through Project Better Place, is taking advantage of its wind power energy and is setting up battery recharging and swapping stations in its plan. DONG Energy and Renault Nissan are partners in the project. Again, this seems a rich possibility for the electrics. With strong environmental interests and a moderate population of about 5.4 million, Denmark, like Israel, has great potential for electrics to become mainstream transportation. Initial investments came from Investors Israel Corp., Ofer Shipping Holdings, Morgan Stanley, VantagePoint Venture Partners and private investors; the entire project is expected to cost at least $1 billion.

EcoFactor and Project Better Place, with financing from Macquarie Capital Group, moved into Australia's market. In 2008, it became the world's largest infrastructure recharging stations operation. The initiative carried a $1 billion (Australian) price tag to cover over 2 million charging stations powered by renewable energy. The promotion package carries the option that was popular with electric marketers in the early 1900s. At least 500 battery swapping facilities will be available for those who prefer not to wait for the recharging. Freeway travelers who need a break will find recharging stations at rest areas along the freeways. Australia was chosen as a third site, after Israel and Denmark, to show that the idea of the grid is feasible in a huge country whose urban areas are miles apart as well as in countries with smaller land area and more proximate cities. Australia is also a country with a host of car lovers. Australia has more cars per capita than countries in the United Kingdom or in the United States.

By 2011, Norway plans to have about 400 recharging stations available. As was common with the first electrics, EV manufacturers plan to promote use of the service in hope of creating a wider market for their vehicles. ElbilNorge is increasing assembly of the all-electric Buddy to about 300 per year; a similar strategy is being used for the Th!nk. Increased production is based on increased availability for fast fuel infrastructure for their EVs. Not to be outdone by their fellow Scandinavians, Sweden (via the Finnish-based company Fortum) and Toyota are moving ahead, installing recharging posts in business district parking lots in Stockholm. And in France, Électricité de France has a similar project with Toyota as its partner.

Coulomb Technologies, Inc., began a similar project in San Jose, California, just outside San Francisco, in 2008. Its market plan differs from that of Project Better Place. With so many different standards and configuration for EV and hybrids, Coulomb is not including the battery swap-out option. It is putting its efforts toward the charging stations' locations and subscription payment options available for EV owners.

Electrics are not the only models benefiting from the move to alternate fuels. Iceland, with its hydroelectric and geothermal resources, saw hydrogen fuel cell powered vehicles as a plausible market solution in its quest for energy independence. Iceland's New Energy was the first to have public hydrogen fueling stations. Its Shell stations worked very well and advertising created a demand, but automakers have not been able to supply enough cars to meet the interest. The 2008 Reykjavik Driving Sustainability Conference centered on all-electrics. With the vehicle supply shortage, critics of the hydrogen infrastructure are seeing a "window of opportunity" to promote their electrics.

Enthusiasts of the plug-in hybrids, like Hybrid Owners of America, backed by the Civil Society Institute, found support for plug-ins in a July 2007 report by the Electric Power Research Institute and the Natural Resources Defense Council. The report reinforced the idea that electric (plug-in) hybrids will provide cleaner emissions as the cars age, unlike ICEs which tend to degrade with age. Their position relies on standards and technologies that make modern power plants, and particularly coal plants, run cleaner with fewer harmful emissions. The studies also estimated that using off-hours for recharging and the addition of personal solar panels and wind power installations will provide enough auxiliary power to fill the needs of the electrics without requiring more power plants to be built. They are proposing the usual incentives—subsidies and rebates—to offset the 10 percent to 20 percent ($2,000 to $5,000) higher cost for purchasing the PHEVs because the batteries are an added expense. The offset for buyers is the reduced maintenance for the electric portion of the auto. The study does not take into account the possibility of an increase in electric costs as the "off hours" become more heavily used for recharging. They assume that power companies will decrease the cost per kilowatt to give incentive for recharging at night.

The plug-in hybrid caught the consumer's attention again when gas prices soared in 2007. The concept had been surfacing on the test grid in a number of labs. Some high profile testing occurred with General Motors prototypes of the Saturn VUE SUV and the Chevy Volt; Ford's Escape; Chrysler's Sprinter delivery vans; United States Department of Energy's "Future Truck" competition (University of California at Davis's Hybrid Research Center was a frequent winner); and DaimlerChrysler's partnering with California's Electric Power Research Institute and Southern California Edison to test NiMH and lithium-ion batteries with diesel and gasoline engines. The United States Marine Corps also did some testing with General Dynamics trying out the possibilities of a diesel-electric plug-in Humvee. Not to be outdone, Toyota tried this market as well, but with less than stellar results. Its nickel-metal-hydride battery gave only 7 miles on the charge before the gasoline engine kicked in. Toyota's competitors, using types of lithium-ion batteries, got up to forty miles on their overnight charging. Despite the rhetoric, which sounds much like that used at the turn of the 20th century for a new battery being "just around the corner," the plug-in continues to be in development. Programs like the Advanced Vehicle Initiative in Port of Chelan County, Washington, which provides conversion to plug-in services for Prius owners, continue to move the electric concept forward. Safe, usable standards, robust suppliers of electric motors, and development of a low cost, smaller, long range battery are its greatest challenges.

Marketing Obstacles and Strategies

In the second decade of the 21st century, manufacturers are still weighing the viability of the battery versus the fuel cell, or the ICE and hybrids. Which technology will become a standard and be attractive to the public? Where are the dollars for research and development best spent? In 1880 Edison demonstrated the use of electricity by stringing wires for a central electric grid. This marketing was used to create public demand. But Edison was adamant about retaining DC (short range) current over changing to AC (long range), which he said was dangerous. He locked into the wrong technology, was forced out of the scene, and lost his company. Ford won market share by knowing what the customer was able to understand and afford. What direction will this century take?

At the 1914 convention of the Electric Vehicle Association, members supported an advertising campaign for electrics. Conventioneers expressed concern about producing low-priced cars and whether electrics should be marketed as touring cars. A paper was presented by George H. Kelly titled "The Cost of Electric Vehicles." He pointed out that the demand for electric cars fluctuated widely from month to month and this made it impossible for the manufacturer to anticipate production. At the time, the use of high-grade materials and expert workmanship also increased the price of the electric passenger cars. Kelly proposed creating a demand for the electrics by implementing an extensive advertising campaign. Part of this campaign would be to educate the public in what the electric was, what it could do and show how it could do more to reduce the price over other choices. The suggested advertising plan included sending printed materials such as booklets and charts to potential customers to spark interest and a desire for the product. This, Kelly noted, should be followed by personal letters and other forms of communication. Trained salesmen should answer every inquiry that was received, and women demonstrators should be employed to demonstrate passenger cars to prospective buyers.[101] The convention was divided on two issues: production of large heavy vehicles versus the lighter models of earlier years, and touring cars versus city-use cars. Kelly presented arguments that the public would not accept an electric car for touring purposes until the speed could be increased and the batteries could be perfected to last an entire day or could be recharged or exchanged in less time than it would take to fill a gasoline tank. J. M. Skinner, of the Philadelphia Storage Battery Company, claimed it was possible for the electric cars to be used in touring throughout the entire eastern states, and claimed he frequently made the trip from Washington, D.C., to Boston without difficulty, averaging fifty miles per charge. The consensus of the convention, however, was to recommend that people not go touring in the country with the ordinary electric vehicle, "as trouble will surely be encountered."[102]

The HEV industry today is facing a marketing issue similar to the problems confronted by the EVs of the early 20th century. Internal combustion engines are entrenched in our culture. Comfort, convenience and cargo space are part of the life style. We are familiar with their maintenance, enjoy their power and speed, and rely on the freedom they provide. To be successful, the HEV industry will have to show its cars' strengths over ICEs (both traditional gasoline and the bio-fuel models) and conventional battery-powered EVs. The industry is making progress. Consumers are seeing a variety of models using many different hybrid technologies, from those that use electrics to boost power or run accessories, to those that run on either the electric or the alternate or gasoline fueled engine. Motors may run on all battery or use fuel cells to generate electricity to store in the batteries. Concept cars are moving to test markets, on to production floors, and to showrooms.

A quality of EVs that was considered a selling point in the early years is a drawback for fellow motorists and pedestrians, both sighted and visually impaired. Electric cars can cause problems by being too quiet. People are apt to dart out in front of moving EVs, because they cannot hear the cars approaching. Some drivers even complain about the silence as the motor stops at a traffic light. The silent running, while a welcome relief from noise pollution for some, is hazardous for others.

Fuel cell development is gaining a higher profile as hydrogen stations begin to appear. One key advantage of the fuel cell is its capacity to be refueled. Unlike batteries, which must be recharged or discarded, fuel cells can mimic ICEs in convenient "fill-ups." This aspect alone, if used in a customer-awareness campaign, presents the potential for taking market share from other automobiles, as the HEV has convenience, economy and technological advances in fuel cell development.

Convincing the public to buy the alternate fuel products is not easy. ICEs have become more fuel efficient, cost effective and less polluting. In fuel economy statistics from 2006, the Honda Fit got 34 mpg (cost, $15,200), the Nissan Versa 33 mpg (cost, $12,000) and the Toyota Yaris 36 mpg (cost, $12,430). The ICEs are familiar and trusted vehicles.

Although both EVs and HEVs have many positive environmental aspects, they each have image problems. Where EVs must overcome consumers' dislike of battery replacement and fear of the battery overheating and igniting, fuel cell technology must overcome the public perception that hydrogen is dangerous. Even though Honda's extensive crash testing with its FCX has proved it safer than conventional cars, many people still remember the *Hindenburg* airship disaster and connect it with the dangers of having hydrogen on board. This continues to haunt advocates of the fuel cell.

In 2007, AFS Trinity advanced its Extreme Hybrid (HX), a concept car consisting of a two-part energy storage system, a power converter and control software. The plug-in hybrid could achieve 250 mpg in the five-passenger sedan or 150 mpg in the SUV version. The exceptional mileage is achieved because the flex-fuel engine runs on the electrics for 40 miles per day before it turns on its gasoline or diesel engine. Most Americans drive less than 40 miles per day. The HX provides rapid acceleration, a top speed of over 90 mph and meets the PZEV and SULEV vehicle standards. To demonstrate the potential, AFS modified two Saturn VUEs and displayed them at the North American Automobile Show in Detroit in January 2008. Part of its marketing and investing strategy involved lobbying Congress and presidential candidates to ensure that small independent auto companies are included in the federal $25 billion auto stimulus package.[103] The nonprofit CalCars (California Cars) Initiative is also committed to promoting the plug-in alternative and to impelling the automotive industry into providing cars that are equipped to use local power outlets.

Malcolm Bricklin, an auto entrepreneur, was planning to build plug-in hybrid cars in China by 2009 and distribute them in the United States via a network called Visionary Vehicles. Using lithium-ion batteries, the car could be recharged using a conventional power outlet. The cars were meant to compete with the Chevrolet Volt. The arrangement didn't materialize. The Chinese government was slow to grant approval for the partnership, pushing the start date back from 2007 to 2008–2009. Visionary's partnership with Chevy in China ended. Visionary, GM and Chrysler each introduced lawsuits against Chevy over intellectual property rights.

China is also advancing dramatically, faster than the United States in fuel-cell technology. It is likely that China could soon out-produce California by 10 to 1 in the fuel-cell wars. China is well placed to enter the hydrogen power market. It has a diversity of energy resources ranging from nuclear to water power. The Three Gorges Dam, the largest in the world, has the potential of producing power equivalent to a dozen nuclear power plants. This could be used to produce hydrogen via electrolysis. China has another advantage in the area of new development. Unlike America or Europe, where roads are built and in place,

China has a very small network of roads. This allows China more opportunities to develop a new green infrastructure from the start. China has the added advantage of not suffering from a "stranded assets" problem, where fear of switching to something new could wipe out past investment spending.[104]

A wide variety of new concept cars were introduced at the 2008 Challenge Bibendum auto show in Shanghai. *AutoWeek* reporters were amazed at the diversity of selections, to the point of being confused as to whether the competitive entries rushing by were on a test drive or merely an event shuttle. Most entries were not aimed at the American market. The exhibitors showed varieties of bicycles, three-wheeled two-seaters, scooters and diesel-fueled buses for their target buyers—China, India and Europe. Concept cars give a window to the future, and that future shows clean, economically viable transportation for millions of new drivers. While people are currently living with existing technologies, concept cars inspire a cost-effective future and showcase innovation to spur the marketplace. The success of hybrid marketing has been a boon to the traditional market as well. Existing ICE technologies have improved. Spark plug technology is making strides in improving fuel efficiency for traditional engines. Incorporating the element iridium in the center electrode as an alloy with platinum, the spark plugs are less susceptible to corrosion and erosion. This makes for quicker starts, more efficient fuel combustion and a longer performance life. Some testing has indicated a fuel savings of nearly five percent using a four-electrode plug.[105] ICEs need less frequent oil changes than in the past, and most average more miles per gallon than the CAFE requirements.

Through advanced technology, diesel power has come back as a competitor in the AFV market. Peugeot introduced its concept diesel hybrid car at the Paris motor show in August 2008. It is called the Hymotion4 and has a very racy design. A production crossover is scheduled for 2010 and promises near 70 mpg fuel economy.

In 2008, Volkswagen introduced the Jetta TDI "Clean Diesel" engine, which runs on ultra-low-sulfur fuel. Diesel emissions are reduced dramatically by the ultra-low-sulfur fuel, which is 95 percent lower in sulfur content than other diesel fuels. The VW TDI engines also feature an "emission-capturing" technology to further reduce what comes out of the tailpipe. Diesel hybrid buses are already on the road in many United States cities, including New York and Washington, improving mileage by up to fifty percent.[106] Alternate fuel development and advances in automotive technology are booming in the concept car world and rapidly moving into production models.

Paralleling the environmental interest, many people consider buying an EV or hybrid as a patriotic issue. The price of patriotism comes high. When non–ICE cars first appeared in the marketplace, it took up to ten years before the owner saw cost savings over the fuel, maintenance and purchase costs of an ICE; by 2007 that recovery was reduced to 5 years through more efficient technology and the rising cost of gasoline. This brings greater incentive to reduce dependence on foreign oil. For those looking at the United States job market, another consideration is that successful hybrids today are manufactured primarily in Japan and therefore contribute to the United States trade deficit.[107] Defining the issue in this manner, a patriotic buyer weighs which area is more important to him, foreign oil dependence or local economic strength.

The fuel cell industry and HEV manufacturers are aware of the obstacles in moving their product to the marketplace. Firoz Rasul, chairman and CEO of Ballard Systems Fuel Cell Company, said in 2000 that his company was taking on some major market forces: the automotive industry, oil industry, utilities and the government. Ballard is concentrating on obtaining patents and intellectual property now, while investing in research and product development with the help of consumers, then will focus on mass production 3–5 years down the road.[108]

"People have to want to buy fuel efficient vehicles," says Chrysler vice president Robert Libaeratore. "We will go wherever customers go." The price remains high in part because the volume of sales is just not there, and the volume remains low because the initial price is too high.

Advertising must hit the right chord to bring in the buyers. Honesty, not hype, may be expected, but *caveat emptor*—let the buyer beware. Actual gas mileage versus the mileage advertised runs high on the "questionable" meter.

There is some hype about hybrid cars concerning the efficiency of the hybrid over an ICE. Some experts claim the fuel effiency is overestimated by as much as 25 percent. This could be attributed to driving habits by consumers that are not taken into consideration in testing. The battery-powered electric engine works only at low speeds, but many people don't drive at those speeds, even in the city. Hybrids use a combination of gas and electric when accelerating. With more traffic congestion, drivers tend to jackrabbit through the city and traffic jams on the freeways, braking more and accelerating faster, thus losing the advantage of slow speeds for the electric motor.[109]

The hybrid's environmental friendliness is a strong selling point, and consumers expect truth in advertising. In 2007, Toyota came under scrutiny by the United Kingdom's Advertising Standards Authority (ASA) when an ad touting the Prius' green credentials was questioned. In the ad, Toyota claimed that its car emitted "One tonne of CO_2 less than the equivalent family vehicle with a diesel engine."[110] ASA found Toyota's methodology to be flawed because the mileage per year reflected United States and not United Kingdom mileage and because Toyota had used both petrol and diesel engines in the calculations.[111] Although the Prius was still strong in the marketplace, the overestimated mileage did cause consumers to question the true value of the hybrid and especially of the Prius.

Toyota has spent millions of dollars each year to keep the Prius in the public eye. Despite a few suspicious advertisements, the campaigns have been extremely successful, raising consumers' awareness of the environmental benefits for driving a Prius. Many drivers buy hybrid cars like the Toyota Prius in order to help reduce oil dependence and provide a cleaner environment. Some think it is about saving the world, a little bit every day. They cite reports that estimate that transportation accounts for about one quarter of the greenhouse gases released into the atmosphere, and put carbon dioxide in the category of pollutant. The "hybrid phenomenon" allows drivers to feel that they are changing the world.[112] People feel that they are part of a global community that is promoting environmental sustainability, an effective marketing approach for a specific audience.

Profiles of hybrid car owners are an excellent example of showing that data can show any viewpoint you would like to promote. A 2006 report listed on Hybridcars.com touts studies that show the drivers are affluent (42 percent have incomes above $100,000), live on the West Coast of the United States, have higher than average education levels, are technically savvy and like skiing and organic food. Politically they are 38 percent Democrat, 34 percent Independent and 14 percent Republican.[113] Statistics gathered by the *Chicago Tribune* in that same year counter that report. The *Tribune*'s data showed that only 16 percent of hybrid owners live on the West Coast, with 21 percent in the Midwest and 31 percent in the Northeast. Also, 43 percent of hybrid owners are under the age of 45, but that means 57 percent are older than 45. So much for "young." As for education, 24.5 percent of hybrid owners have a college degree. The majority of hybrid owners have an annual household income of less than $60,000, with 35 percent making less than $40,000. Politically, 40 percent are Republicans and 36 percent are Democrats. The demographics also show that hybrid ownership is split equally between males and females.[114] Statistics provide as varied a report as miles per gallon for the hybrids.

Statistics also give us a picture of increased demand for hybrids as more models come on the market. The *Detroit Free Press* reported in September 2007 that the number of hybrid electric vehicles on the United States roads had grown by 49 percent over the previous year, with the Midwest seeing the sharpest uptick. Oklahoma led all states, with a growth of more than 143 percent, while Hawaii was the only state to show a decline in new vehicle registrations, by about 5 percent. Once again, the Toyota Prius led the pack, with an increase of 88 percent in the Midwest, followed by the Toyota Camry Hybrid. As of April 2007, Portland, Oregon, had become the hybrid car capital of the nation, outdoing San Francisco with numbers of 11.19 per 1,000 households versus 8.76 in the Bay Area. Prospective buyers of hybrid vehicles nationwide increased by five percent to 71 percent from the year before. Los Angeles, with a much larger population than Portland, has a higher number of hybrids overall, but Portland has about twice as many per household. Two other Oregon cities made the top ten — Bend, Oregon, in sixth place and Eugene in 10th place. California had five cities in the top ten list. Oregon's showing may be due in part to the car's availability and the state giving a tax credit of $1,500 toward the purchase of a hybrid car. Dealerships have cars in stock. Buyers no longer have to be on a waiting list or pay higher than sticker price to get a Prius. Sales of the Prius in 2007 doubled over those of a year earlier.[115] Increased percentages in sales show the increased popularity of hybrids, but hybrids still make up less than three percent of the vehicles on the road.

What does a hybrid vehicle "think about" while it's being driven? Dave Hermance of Toyota says that the onboard computers take into consideration the driver's every move of the throttle and brake pedal and then calculate the most fuel efficient outcome: "The processor is looking at three inputs. They include current vehicle speed, throttle position, and auxiliary loads such as air conditioning.... It sums up the total demand and says, 'When I get to a power level where I know the gas engine is efficient, I'll start it. When I'm below that level, I'll keep the engine off and run on batteries.' It's a sophisticated algorithm."[116]

Hybrid cars have the advantage of being more flexible in design; they can have a variety of combinations. There are two basic types of hybrid vehicles, series and parallel. In the series, a gasoline engine generates power to drive the electric motor. In parallel, the two systems are separate, being able to propel the vehicle independently or together. To gain higher fuel economy on the highway, engine designs have been developed that shut down one or more cylinders to adjust to various power needs for the vehicle. A hybrid can be gasoline-electric, fuel cell-electric, diesel-electric, CNG/LNG-electric, methanol/ethanol-electric, and more.

The year 2006 brought a flicker of interest among hybrid enthusiasts who believe the power grid is the best source for the electric energy needed to run the hybrid in urban traffic. The plug-in conversion kit, primarily for the Prius, became a popular item for a niche market in urban areas along the West Coast. Hybrids are competitive, even while being sold at a loss. In the first decade of the 21st century, government subsidies continued to bolster hybrid production. In 2008, Toyota took advantage of Australia's $6.2 billon available for participation in the thirteen-year green car innovation program. Had the monies not been available, the company's business would have gone to Japan or Thailand. Even with increased demand and production, automakers are still taking advantage of government funding to supplement their production costs for hybrids.[117] CARB is reevaluating whether plug-in conversion shops should have to meet the same requirements as automakers to get a PLEV emissions rating. Plug-in enthusiasts see this as a positive. Automakers must sell 66,000 PEVs between the years 2012 and 2014, according to current CARB regulations. The cost of complying with the current automaker standards would prohibit most small businesses from converting the vehicles. This lessening of the requirements for the converted hybrids will allow small businesses to continue the conversions and may give incentive for moving more plug-ins to the road. More cars on the road will show automakers they are a viable product that should be manufactured — and, in the Henry Ford tradition, it may encourage consumers to buy one because they see so many on the road. This may lead to a competitive advantage in the marketplace. Buyers have shown that there is a market for this technology; it is an option to consider seriously, if the price is right.

Fleet Testing

Fleets are a main market niche for electric vehicles. Although there have been some difficulties with cost and supply, from the onset their reliability and usefulness as commercial and government transport was touted. Between 1905 and 1917 EVs were used as ambulances, patrol wagons and delivery vehicles. By 1917 some units had been in service for close to eighteen years. The New York Edison Company had a fleet of 105 electric vehicles in 1912. The general inspector of the company conducted a study of its fleet and determined the vehicles could be run practically twenty-four hours a day with a number of shifts in drivers. In comparison, no one could get more than eight hours of work out of a horse. Two-thirds of the orders for electric vehicles for commercial use were reorders. Once again, however, their usefulness decreased with better roads and wider territories to cover. Limited range became the downfall of the electric vehicle in all but a limited fleet market.

Both small and large manufacturing companies supplied EVs for fleet service, some with more satisfactory results than others. In 1975 American Motors Corporation supplied the United States Postal Service with a fleet of 352 jeep-size electric vans. The initial cost was twice as much as an ICE and the expected life of the EV was only eight years.[118] But two years of fleet testing revealed the EVs were about 30 percent less expensive to operate than comparable internal combustion vans. This type of vehicle is perfectly suited for postal service needs, as they travel only eight to fifteen miles a day making 100 to 300 stops. When stopped to deliver mail, the motor is turned off and expends no energy. The Batronic Truck Corporation of England provided 107 trucks to over fifty United States utility companies in 1975. The trucks cost about $10,000 and carried loads weighing about 500 pounds. Unfortunately Batronic, a small manufacturer, could not supply replacement parts readily and many of the trucks sat idle for months at a time.[119] Generally, companies wanting electric vehicle fleets find suppliers who stock the models the company needs within the price range they can afford.

Today, government agencies, utilities and corporations are dabbling in the more environmentally accepted alternate fuel vehicles for their fleets, while keeping an eye on the bottom line. By 1992, electric vehicles were seen as playing a major part in the reduction of air quality problems, such as those addressed by CARB in 1990. Marketing strategists thought that if utilities and government agencies participated in fleet ownership and testing, their satisfaction could be used to promote the general acceptance of electric vehicles. By using electrics, government agencies could show support for air quality programs. In 1992 the Electric Vehicle Coalition predicted an EV fleet market of 5,000 vehicles by 1997, with about half being ordered by utilities and the other half by government agencies. The actual figure was about five hundred vehicles due to competition and cost-cutting by state governments and the high price of the EVs. The realities of using all electrics did not match expectations, and fleet managers looked at other options. In 1999 DaimlerChrysler and Ford announced a test fleet of fuel-cell-powered vehicles to be used in Los Angeles. Honda joined the group, putting 20 FCX cars into the California testing arena. In 2007 GM announced Project Driveway to put 100 vehicles built with the Chevrolet Equinox Fuel Cell into testing in New York, California and Washington, D.C. In 2000, of the 17,000 EVs sold in the United States, approximately 10 percent went into fleet use. This was an acceptable showing, but the same problems continue to hamper these vehicles even in this specialized market. The lack of infrastructure (too few fueling stations and no funds to build those stations) is still the most commonly reported problem. This is followed by high initial purchase cost, maintenance costs, range, availability and performance.[120] Most fleet operators show a dichotomy in their approach to the economics of hybrid electric vehicles, citing economics both as a reason to use HEVs and also as an obstacle to obtaining them. Fleet use surveys show a strong interest in performance and costs with little regard for emissions information. Products were selected based on information gathered from a variety of sources by the fleet operators. The sources included the Internet, government publications, trade publications and direct mail.[121] Trade publications were the preferred source of information. Hybrid and flex-fuel vehicles are gaining the interest of fleet operators. The advancing technology meets the public's environmental concerns and decreases dependence on foreign oil without having to immediately adopt a completely electric vehicle.

Natural gas, a major competitor of EVs and HEVs in the fleet market, is another fuel option. The mixture is primarily methane with propane and ethane and is environmentally friendly. It produces 85 percent less nitrogen oxide and 74 percent less carbon monoxide. Natural gas must be compressed (CNG) or liquefied (LNG) to be convenient and useful. Most heavy-duty vehicle fleets comprising trucks and buses use LNG, while fleet cars use CNG. Natural-gas-powered vehicles have the same drawbacks as EVs. The conversion of a vehicle to natural gas adds about $5,000 to the cost. Public access to natural gas infrastructure is a problem. In 2001 there were about 1,300 high-pressure–refueling natural gas sta-

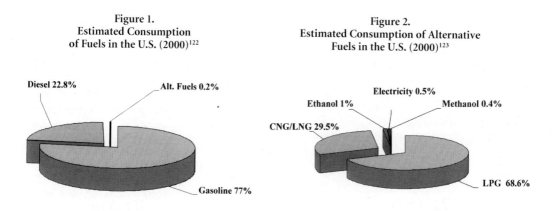

Figure 1.
Estimated Consumption
of Fuels in the U.S. (2000)[122]

Diesel 22.8%   Alt. Fuels 0.2%

Gasoline 77%

Figure 2.
Estimated Consumption of Alternative
Fuels in the U.S. (2000)[123]

Electricity 0.5%

Ethanol 1%   Methanol 0.4%

CNG/LNG 29.5%

LPG 68.6%

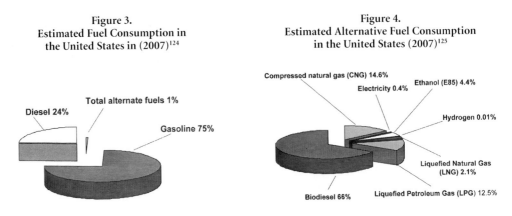

Figure 3.
Estimated Fuel Consumption in
the United States in (2007)[124]

Figure 4.
Estimated Alternative Fuel Consumption
in the United States (2007)[125]

tions in the United States. However, more than 40 percent of these are privately owned, or owned by local governments for their fleet cars, and are not open to the public. Many stations require use of a special key card to use the pump. Each utility company provides its own unique charge card, greatly decreasing the accessibility of the CNG infrastructure. Deregulation laws passed in 2000, stipulating that the industry cannot pass on the cost of infrastructure building to consumers, also hampered infrastructure development and made the natural gas alternative less competitive. Some manufacturers claim a range for their vehicles of over 300 miles, but actual road tests show a range of about 120 miles. Some of the vehicles equipped for natural gas are the Volvo V70 (dual fuel), Honda Civic GX, Toyota Camry CNG and a variety of Ford models, including the Contour and Crown Victoria. In 2001, there were 28 natural gas stations in the Phoenix, Arizona, area, 44 stations in British Columbia, Canada, 191 stations in California and 89 in Texas.

By 2004, the Natural Gas Coalition found approximately 1,500 stations, half of them open to the public, in the United States. Fleets in both public and private sectors account for the majority of the expansion.

Although these fleet alternate fuel vehicles and EVs are in competition, they have similar issues. It is easy to buy a natural gas vehicle, but the infrastructure is not in place, and it is easy to use the electric grid infrastructure, but the vehicles are too expensive. This cycle might be shifting slightly in urban areas, and thanks to the increased availability of alternate fuels and alternate, flex-fuel and dual-fuel vehicles. A 2007 study based on data from 2000 was done by Marc Melaina and Joel Bremson at the Institute of Transportation Studies (University of California, Davis). It indicates that a viable infrastructure is closer than had been thought. Their data found that spatial coverage for gasoline service station availability in densely populated areas across the United States was more than sufficient to provide refueling stations for alternate-fuel vehicles in normal city driving. They concluded that "some 51,000 stations could pro-

Region	LPG	CNG	Methanol	Ethanol	EVs	Total
Northeast	376	162	0	0	19	577
South	1,222	407	0	3	129	1,761
Midwest	760	204	0	103	10	1,077
West	924	468	3	5	399	1,799
Total	3,282	1,261	3	111	557	5,214

Table 2. Number of fueling stations by census region and fuel type, February 8, 2001.[126]

vide a sufficient level of refueling availability for the general public in urban areas, while still allowing for some degree of retail competition. This sufficient coverage estimate for urban areas offers an improved representation of refueling availability needs for AFVs." The coverage for rural areas varied and still presents a challenge for refueling alternate fuel vehicles.[127] Even with these challenges, by 2007 there were over 695,000 alternative and electric vehicles on the road.

For over a century, the auto industry has used many methods for providing convenience to their customers and finding ways to attract the buyer's attention. In 1896 Morris and Salom began an electric cab company instead of selling the autos to individuals because they believed the EV needed to be under a regular maintenance schedule and the electric vehicle was too complicated and unreliable for lay operators. Electric cabs caught on and a market opened. Electric-cab drivers in the Boston area in 1900 earned about $14 a week for twelve hours of work and claimed that "the people they served were more agreeable than the ordinary street car passenger."[128]

In today's market, automakers are looking for that competitive edge as marketing strategies evolve. In 1993, Nissan created its first advertising slogan for its FEV concept car: "Gentle to People, Gentle to Society, Gentle to Earth."[129] GM's strategy mirrored the Morris and Salom philosophy. The EV1 was leased exclusively to customers and not sold. The Saturn division offered to send a representative to help consumers make the right EV1 selection. Ford and DaimlerChrysler are working in conjunction with the Ballard Fuel Cell Company to develop a vehicle that is better than conventional vehicles. It would offer enough electricity to power air conditioning, electric brakes, electric steering, Internet-capable dashboard, drive-by-wire capability, and a video screen in the back for the kids. Even with the new approaches, attracting buyers continues to be a problem for updated century-old concepts, but attitudes may be changing in favor of the EVs and HEVs.

A report in *Business Economics* in October 2000 projected global sales of more than one million electric vehicles by the year 2007. This would represent 1.5 percent of the total global motor vehicle production and 0.5 percent of the motor vehicles on the road. The authors wrote, "Clearly, we are looking at a narrow, albeit fast-growing market."[130] They also predicted that most of the electric vehicles would be battery-powered, and that hybrids and fuel-cell-powered cars would increase faster in the second half of the decade.

Business reports agree that between 2000 and 2007 sales of hybrids increased each year. Although exact percentages vary from report to report, they come to similar conclusions. Car buyers, especially in the United States, are becoming hybrid-auto owners. From 2000 to 2004, sales of hybrid cars increased 88.6 percent. Sales of hybrids in 2000 were about 9,000 vehicles. In 2003, registrations for hybrids counted 43,435. United States sales for all cars in 2003 were 16.7 million. Sales of hybrid cars doubled from 2004 to 2005, accounting for 1.3 percent of total car sales. The United States accounted for nearly 70 percent of those hybrid purchases. Sales of hybrid vehicles rose 28 percent in 2006, but growth in the segment began to slow. The *Seattle Post-Intelligencer* wrote, "R.L. Polk & Co., which collects and analyzes auto-registration data, said the Toyota Prius accounted for almost 43 percent of new hybrid sales in 2006. Overall, United States consumers bought 254,545 hybrids in 2006, up from 199,148 a year earlier."[131] One effective marketing strategy Toyota used to boost sales of backlog inventory in Michigan, Ohio, and Kentucky was to offer financing through Toyota for 3.9 percent for 36 months. (Toyota spends almost twice as much advertising its hybrids as its other models.)[132] More than 16,000 Toyota Prius cars were sold in July 2007; 4,329 units of the Toyota Camry Hybrid made it the second-best-selling hybrid model; and 2,493 units of the Honda Civic Hybrid gave it third place. Toyota Prius sales were surging, but the Chevy Cobalt, Ford Focus and Ford Fusion hybrids outsold them in 2007.[133] Honda announced in 2006 that it would build a new plant in Decatur County, Indiana, to produce its new version of the fuel-efficient four-cylinder Honda Fit. At the same time, Ford announced it would give up on its promise made in 2005 to build 250,000 hybrid gasoline-electric vehicles as part of its financial turnaround effort, due to low consumer demand.

Sales strategies differ in the global hybrid market. Toyota and Honda represent two marketing theories. Toyota has hybrids throughout its lineup, and sells its technology to others in the industry, expanding its impact in the market. Honda has found that hybrids are most profitable and efficient in its smaller-vehicle lines, like the Civic, and is concentrating hybrid development in that area.

Hybrids have become part of our vocabulary. Their popularity has the potential for becoming our future standard. Sales of electric-gas hybrids (with 11 models available) numbered approximately 212,000 in 2005, and are forecasted to be 780,000 in 2012, or about 4.2 percent of total sales. J. D. Power and Associates Automotive Forecasting Services predicts this boom will result from an increased number of models available, with as many as 52 hybrid models available in 2012.[134] Anthony Pratt, senior manager of global powertrain forecasting at J. D. Power, said in 2006, "By 2012, consumers will have the opportunity to purchase a hybrid vehicle in nearly all segments, including full-sized pickups, minivans and luxury cars."[135]

Consumers and investors do need to be cautious in this emerging electric car market. A 2007 article in *Forbes* magazine by Jonathan Fahey describes the questionable business practices of the Santa Rosa, California, based company ZAP. It has excellent marketing promotions with a history of telling potential buyers and stockholders about the technology that is just around the corner. Its Zap-X "is a marvel. It solves every problem that has foiled attempts to build electric vehicles.... The company even asks for deposits of $5,000 on the cars—without saying how much they will eventually cost or when they will arrive."[136] ZAP has a history of promises for its prospective investors and customers and a trail, according to Fahey's research, of questionable business practices in its wake.

China America Cooperative Automotive, Inc. (Chamco Auto) and the Miles Automotive Group came to the 2007 National Automakers Convention in Las Vegas, hoping to

Left: ZAP Sedan, 2009. *Right:* ZAP XBRA Truck, 2009.

find dealers for two product lines of all-electrics built in China by Tianjin Qingyaun Vehicle Electric and by Zhongxing Automobile Co. The appeal was a low startup investment, and a few dealers were willing to sign on. As of late 2007, these deals were still in the planning stages and moving to have the cars certified in the United States. Investors and buyers need to move cautiously in the niche markets.

The industry is seeing rising competition among the traditional manufacturers in their ICE and HEV lines. IntelliChoice, a company providing cost analysis of the automotive industry, looks at the depreciation, fuel, financing, insurance, repairs, and maintenance and state fees in its survey results. Its results for the 2007 model year showed that although, over the previous five years, Toyota Prius (-$10,288) and Honda Civic Hybrid (-$6,250) still hold the highest savings versus their non-hybrid counterparts, Ford Escape Hybrid 2WD (-$5,975) and Mercury Mariner Hybrid (-$5,768) are decreasing the gap in cost value.[137]

Battery technology, a major drawback to EVs for over a century, is finally seeing some innovations. In 2008 the preferred battery was the NiMH cell, but it was being challenged by the new Li-Ion and li-poly cell batteries. The NiMH battery is more responsive to discharging and recharging rapidly. The new lithium-ion and lithium-polymer batteries, although more expensive, are more suited to the deep draw-down and recharge cycles expected of plug-in vehicles. New developments in these batteries show promise for making the EVs and HEVs more cost effective and convenient for buyers.

SYNC technology, which allows customers to integrate Bluetooth-enabled cell phones and MP3 players into their autos, proved to be an effective marketing move for Ford Motor Company in its hybrid lines. Sales of both their hybrid and conventional ICEs— ICEs that boasted gas mileage similar to the hybrids— rose between 2006 and 2007 from 19 percent to over 63 percent depending on the model.

Large numbers of electric vehicles will appear first in the densely populated cities of the world. The consensus remains that air pollution is easier to control at central power generating plants than from individual vehicles. This leads to the promotion of greater use of electric vehicles while controlling emissions from plants generating electricity. Disposal and recycling of lead-acid batteries has been partially resolved. New types of batteries are being developed, with thought to environmental concerns. Fleet sales continue to be a major portion of overall EV sales.[138] The recharging and alternative fuel infrastructures continue to grow with major contributions from such nations as Iceland and Denmark, from private entrepreneurs like Project Better Place, and from more modest efforts by local governments and private industry. General acceptance of the EV is here, but consumers are still slow to open their wallets. Consumers are willing to consider alternatives to the ICEs if the new auto power plants and design fit the image and reflect the owner's lifestyle. Markets open when products meet buyers' expectations and catch their fancy.

6

CONCLUSION

Publications of the day chronicle the electric vehicle's roller-coaster existence. Their prose captures the early optimism of EV dominance in the 1890s and today's more practical approach to the market's attitude about electrics. The following pages highlight the EV's story from optimism to realism. It is obvious, based on the limited progress over one hundred years, that a new battery technology that would increase range and decrease costs dramatically will not take place overnight or in the near future, if ever. This may leave the battery-only vehicles in a niche market. There is, however, a great deal of genuine optimism concerning the hybrid vehicles already on the road and the nascent fuel cell technology. These developments, combined with the more–fuel-efficient ICE engines being developed, appear to be the obvious next steps in reducing our dependence on foreign oil and eventually replacing the traditional internal combustion engine with one that is more environmentally friendly. EVs continue to provide an incentive to improve our means of transportation. Writers throughout the past century have captured the acceptance, flaws and development cycles of the electric vehicle. As each generation rediscovers the EV, we see the same points recur.

As early as 1897, comments about electric vehicles were showing up in print. One of the earliest reports on the new electric taxicabs in New York City strikes a slightly negative note. The *New York Journal* printed a column titled "A Chappie and a Horseman Try the New Horseless Carriage." In it, pseudonymous columnist "Cholly Knickerbocker" chronicles an outing in an electric cab taken by him and his new bride as a diversion on their honeymoon. He noted,

> There is a sense of incompleteness about it. You seemed to be sitting on the end of a huge pushcart, propelled by an invisible force and guided by a hidden hand. Gradually, I felt I did not need the protection of a horse in front of me. I congratulate myself that I survived the ordeal. The horseless carriage will have to be improved before it becomes popular in chappiedom.[1]

On another ride with a portly friend, the two of them weighing approximately 425 pounds in total, Morris and Salom's cab was put out of balance. Knickerbocker's friend Francis Trevelyan said:

> I do not think the [electric] motor cab will be anything more than a fad. The horses, especially when they are well-bred trotters, regard it rather curiously, but on the whole contemptuously; but in the bosom of the average cyclist it seems to arouse derision, scorn and contempt. It gives the occupant a hopeless sensation of being perpetually shot through a chute, with the pleasing possibility of being utilized as a battering ram in a collision with a cable car or a runaway team.[2]

Fortunately for the future of EVs, not everyone considered them just a passing fad. Some periodicals predicted a rosy future for the electrics. *Scientific American* proclaimed in its May 13, 1899, issue:

Electricity, too, has made its "debut" in locomotion. An almost perfect electric motor has been found. Backward and forward motion, and excellent brake arrangement, absence of noise, smell or vibration, are only a few of the qualities of this wonderful motor. It has only one fault, an immense quantity of electricity is wanted. Then they have to be refilled at the works [recharging station]. Accordingly, electric carriages can only be employed within a small radius of these works, from which the supply of energy is obtained. Still, they seem to be destined for a great future in town locomotion by reason of the ease with which accumulators [batteries] may be obtained.[3]

The optimism of the enthusiasts showed dreams of a new era of companionship and travel. An article in *McClure's Magazine* in 1899 declared,

It is not hard to imagine what a country touring station will be like on a summer afternoon some five or ten years hence. Long rows of vehicles will stand backed up comfortably to the charging bars each with its electric plug filling the battery with power. The owners will be lolling at the tables on the verandas of the nearby road house. Men with repair kits will bustle about tightening up a nut here, oiling this bearing and regulating that gear. The new electric cabs are unquestionably immensely popular as fashionable conveyances.[4]

Fashion was not the only vision the EV supporters saw. They realized the problems that were already plaguing cities: the use of horses had long caused one environmental problem, and the early ICEs had brought another. The electric automobile was considered the perfect solution for city use at the turn of the 20th century. That new era would mean quieter streets and cleaner air. In 1899 *Scientific American* said,

There seems to be a general impression that for passenger transportation in and around our cities the electric automobile is the best. It has the great advantage of being silent, free from odor, simple in construction and gearing, capable of ready control, and having a considerable range of speed.[5]

Some manufacturers saw the electric's potential and were eager to get into the business of designing a product that would grab the customer's attention. Colonel Albert A. Pope in 1900 was one of these entrepreneurs. An auto historian wrote:

Fifteen thousand of his bicycle agents throughout the country were "fairly howling" for automobiles to meet an enormous demand. Pope knew the need was for a reliable automobile that would sell for less than $1,000. Although he recognized that the current automobiles fell far short of this standard, he confidently hoped that "next year we will currently have a machine near perfection."[6]

Marketing on fuel economy alone did not seem to interest the early adopters. In the 1900 Paris-Dijon road race, one electric car traveled 164 miles at an average speed of ten miles per hour on a single charge:

In energy equivalence, this electric car traveled 183 miles per gallon. At the time, steam vehicles were achieving six miles per gallon, over atrocious roads, and gasoline powered cars 12 miles per gallon. Fuel costs have had little impact on the choice of the motive power of cars, indicating there have been other subjective and objective reasons.[7]

Around the same time, the motoring magazine *Horseless Age* noted that during the period from July 1 to December 31, 1902, it published "five articles listing new electric cars,

67 announcing gasoline-powered cars and 19 introducing steam cars."[8] By 1905 there had been several experiments with hybrid gasoline-electric vehicles. *The Automobile* devoted an entire chapter to these gasoline-electric vehicles and observed that the combination of the two motors could have the advantage of balancing the disadvantages of each. It noted,

> The greatest inconvenience of the petrol motor, as has been shown, is its want of elasticity [efficiency], as it must have an excess of power which there is no use for in ordinary circumstances where the petrol spirit yields only a part of its theoretical heat energy. To obtain variable speeds with a petrol motor there has to be a complicated system of spur gears or of pulleys and belts, which, of course, wastes much power. On the other hand, a large amount of energy can be carried on a petrol car, and further supplies can be easily obtained on the road. Opposite in every way to this is the electric motor; this has remarkable elasticity being able to bring the requisite amount of energy into play at each moment and to dispense with [a] mechanical speed changing gear, but its great disadvantage is that frequent new supplies are essential. This balancing of advantages and disadvantages naturally has led to the idea of associating two motors, one of each type, in the same car. The weight of the petrol-electric car is a consideration ... as the whole mechanism is essentially heavier.... [This] type of vehicle is proving itself highly successful for lurries [trucks] and omnibuses, where actual weight is comparatively unimportant. How far it can be adapted for passenger vehicles and pleasure cars of the lighter kind remains to be seen.[9]

By 1907 "the electric vehicle [had] taken its logical position as a means of freight and passenger traffic in cities and for short tours out of town; while the gasoline machine [was] rapidly gaining recognition as the automobile *par excellence*."[10]

In 1910, the *Cyclopedia of Automobile Engineering* pronounced great promise in using electrics for touring. The article proclaimed:

> [T]hese have not been trips around a circle or through a certain territory but have been right across the country. They show it is perfectly feasible to tour in an electric where the driver is sufficiently familiar with his machine and the methods by which it may be charged to take advantage of the current supply where the ordinary facilities for charging are lacking. North of the Ohio and east of the Mississippi, cities and towns where electric current may be obtained are so numerous and so close together that there is practically no part of this large territory in which a car would have to be driven much beyond its ordinary mileage in order to reach a charging current. In view of the number of garages that are equipped with the necessary facilities for taking care of electric cars to be found in every town and city, it is possible to lay out extended touring routes anywhere in the territory in question. Runs of 50 to 80 miles per day may be averaged and while touring is not recommended by its builders, these performances have shown in a very striking manner of what it is capable.[11]

In that same year, while he sold an electric car battery of his own, Thomas Edison predicted widespread popularity for electric cars. He told Walter Baker of the Baker Electric Company, "If you continue to make your present caliber of automobile, and I my present quality of battery, the gasoline buggies will be out of existence in no time."[12] To promote their transportation concept, the Electric Vehicle Association of America partnered with electric utility companies in 1912 for a joint EV advertising campaign:

> An advertising fund of large proportions we are about to solicit and secure. Our idea is, by means of this fund [for a publicity campaign], to advertise all over the land that the electric vehicle is a perfect device, and that it can and does perform certain services better and cheaper than any other agency. We are to *sing the praises* [italics added] of the electric vehicle as such, and to get the public to adopt and use the electric vehicle.[13]

In 1911, *Scientific American* noted,

> The electric pleasure car is coming into its own. For certain kinds of service it is ideal. Its simple and responsive control will always be its most remarkable feature. The gasoline car has perhaps obscured the development which the electric has been undergoing in recent years. [In the following article] will be found a summary of those mechanical and electrical perfections which have been introduced in recent cars, and which have elevated the pleasure vehicle to a remarkable pitch of perfection. Popular misconceptions are corrected, so far as the function and energy of the storage battery are concerned, and the remarkable luxurious furnishing of the electric carriage is illustrated. The many mechanical expedients devised to make the electric carriage a comfortable and easily operated vehicle, are set forth.[14]

A 1911 *Electrical World* article reiterated a theme seen from the EV's earliest days that would persist through the century: "If charging stations could readily be found in every town where there is electric service, the use of electric pleasure cars on fairly long runs would become much more common than it is now."[15]

The October 1912 report to the Electric Vehicle Association of America was presented by the publicity committee complete with illustrations. The presentation included lantern slides of the images. The report covered the progress of the previous two years of its national cooperative advertising campaign. The campaign was fairly well supported by the members and subscribers, and various editorial comments reflected this consensus of opinion. Remarks included:

> We are very well satisfied with the results of our campaign last year, and the writer has been so well pleased with the efforts and beauty of the E.V.A. matter that we are very desirous of again going on into our local campaign and of co-operating with the E.V.A. so as to use their copy concurrently in our newspapers.
> ...There can be no question whatever that such extensive and excellent promotion must have the effect of popularizing the electric vehicle. We are, of course, conducting local campaigns with this same object in view.[16]

There is a sense, however, reading between the lines, that the electrics were losing the battle. The president stated:

> The aim of the Electrical Association of America is to promote the use of the electric vehicle for business and pleasure purposes. One of our first duties, we believe, is to educate the public as to the advantages of electric propulsion. It is *hoped* [italics added] that the national advertising will be supplemented by consistent and continuous local advertising, both on the part of vehicle manufacturers and the central stations.[17]

A 1912 article in the *Horseless Age* claimed charging stations had been established to the limited extent that an electric car owner could travel between New York and Buffalo, and from Philadelphia to New York, this representing "touring." Auto historian Ernest Wakefield wrote, "This development was an infrastructure that enhanced the value of an electric car, an omission which today limits the value of the modern electric automobile. The gasoline station, in contrast, is everywhere present."[18] A 1912 *Scientific American* article observed optimistically,

> It is remarkable to note the extraordinary favor with which the electric vehicle is being accepted in the commercial world to-day. But, popular as the electric vehicle is at present it is bound to find far greater favor as its advantages become more appreciated. In fact the mechanism of an electric car is so simple that there are only two things upon which there can be any extensive improvement, i.e. the battery and the motor.[19]

The year 1915 saw electrics promoted as perfect, yet manufacturers kept improving them. *The Automobile* carried especially glowing comments about the beautiful electrics:

> Although many people are apparently settled in the belief that the electric passenger car has reached perfection and no further improvement is possible without some radical departure from accepted construction, the car makers themselves are far from sharing this view of the matter, each year surpassing themselves in the improved appearance and in luxurious fittings, finish and equipment. These features, developed to the extent that they might be referred to as boudoirs on wheels, render the electric passenger car, as built today, especially attractive to women, and at the same time not too ornate for the every-day use of even the most conservative business man....
>
> Chassis have been simplified, lightened and made more accessible wherever possible without impairing the solidity of construction. The increased use of worm, spiral-bevel and herringbone gears in the final drive has done much to promote efficiency. Weight reductions due to chassis simplification and the use of aluminum for bodies, together with the elimination of resistance from the presence of dirt and grit in the working parts by the provision of improved protection, and the more thorough utilization of battery equipment have done much towards increasing mileage per charge, and at the same time towards cutting down operating expense for the owner.[20]

A 1921 article in *Electrical World* indicated that the electrics had not had the success expected in 1915, but supporters remained optimistic. It stated, "A new day has dawned for the electric vehicle after a period of sub-normal appreciation of its economic capabilities.... The line of new installations is rapidly lengthening and many of the foremost men in the industry are standing up to be counted as believers in the electric vehicle opportunity."[21] Thomas A. Edison noted, "I am pleased to hear that the electric vehicle for city traffic is receiving more attention lately from the electric lighting companies. Any merchant who keeps accurate costs will buy electrics."[22] *Electrical World* continued: "Those who have cast their lot with the transportation side of the great electrical industry will realize they have not labored in vain."[23]

In 1922, in response to an assertion that the price of electric vehicles was too high and might be inordinately profitable, a *London Electrical Review* article noted, "As an answer to this totally erroneous view, it may be stated, as an incontrovertible fact, that, in this postwar period, no British firm building electric vehicles has made any profit worth speaking of—indeed, it would be safe to say that most, if not all of them, have made losses on the business done."[24] The article went on to list three justifications for the high initial cost of the electric: It cited a lack of demand, but pointed out that the initial high cost could be offset by the electric's long useful life — twice that of a comparable gasoline vehicle. Finally, the magazine declared it the best long-term investment for short-distance haulage. Businessmen generally accepted electrics as delivery vehicles after a trial period; not so the public. The lack of convenient charging stations, even in a country like England where the distances between towns were relatively short, continued to be problematic for the average consumer. The *London Electrical Review* was still optimistic, stating,

> There are good reasons for predicting the employment of electric vehicles upon a considerable scale in the near future. It will, no doubt, be mainly in urban areas, but any improvement upon the present type of battery in the direction of increased capacity per unit of weight will widen the field of utility, and if, concomitantly with such improvement, we come to the establishment of the battery exchange system and sufficiently numerous exchange stations, it will undoubtedly lead to electrics being employed in rural or long-distance transport. With the improvement, which is continuously in progress in road construction, we

may very likely see the electric entering this wider field of employment at no very distant date.[25]

Little was written about electric vehicles again until World War II. By 1940, gasoline was needed for war. Electrics came back into service to keep people and products moving without sapping precious fuel from the military effort. The electrics' use was encouraged, while their limitations were acknowledged:

From the national and patriotic standpoint, too, every gallon of petrol saved improves our position for waging the war and it is estimated that if electric vehicles were given their rightful place in the transport services of this country no fewer than 70,000,000 gallons of petrol would be saved every year.... The long life of the electric vehicle is a further point that would appeal to those responsible for conserving our national resources. In this connection it must be remembered that practically all the lead in an old battery is recoverable and can be used again.[26]

As in the early years, the dream of improved technology was also a consideration in 1940.

When a lighter or standard battery appears on the scene, a new vista will be opened for electric vehicles for private purposes. Even now they have a limited market as town runabouts for doctors, lady shoppers, business men, etc., and, as in the case of a vehicle just purchased by Ferguson, Pailin, Ltd., for running between a factory and a station, etc. With a maximum range of about 50 miles and a maximum speed of 30 MPH, the vehicle for private use will necessarily be favoured only by people who possess another car.[27]

The *Saturday Evening Post* in 1960 saw renewed interest in electrics creeping into society.

Production of "the old square jobs" ceased thirty years ago, and no one expects their return. Like the Stanley Steamer, they lost out to the gasoline engine. The steamers are gone for good, but electrics are coming back, in a variety of forms. With stream lined bodies and updated innards, new electric trucks and passenger cars are rolling now in Atlantic City, Lansing, Detroit, Cleveland and Spokane, and in several towns in France and England.

Most of the experimental electrics are good-looking on the outside, pretty crude inside. I have driven two experimental models. They were silent, of course, and they handled well. My wife tried them too—and got an I'd-like-one look in her eye. If we lived in a city or suburb, instead of far out in the country, she'd have a case. Trouble is, these cars run only eighty miles or so on a fresh battery charge, so they won't do for long trips. But for in-town use by a two-car family they are unbeatable on several counts.[28]

Environmental concerns became prevalent in the 1960s, with optimism for solutions running high. A *Scientific American* article in 1966 proclaimed:

Some engineers have never lost faith in the electric car, and the basic arguments for its revival are cogent and becoming stronger year by year. Chief among these is the increasingly dangerous pollution of our air by the millions of gasoline burning vehicles invading our cities and countryside. We also face the inescapable fact that the supply of cheap gasoline will not last many decades longer at the present rate of consumption of fossil fuels. And while the cost of gasoline is rising, electricity is becoming more plentiful and cheaper. Only technical problems have stood in the way of producing an electric car that could replace the internal combustion one. Solutions for these problems are now definitely in sight.[29]

Distance and battery technology continued to be discussed as a drawback of the EVs. In 1967, *Science News* predicted:

An automobile, even a small car, cannot have a range of 150 miles with any presently available storage battery systems. It may be five to ten years before more advanced systems now being studied are ready for road testing.[30]

More recently, in 2002 Steve Thompson of *Car and Driver* had a different take on the environmentalist concerns:

> The real social force behind what B. Bruce-Briggs aptly called *The War Against the Automobile* in his '70s book with that title was not environmentalism, safety consciousness or the national-security concerns of dependence on foreign oil. Instead, Williams concluded that a new Puritanism was abroad in the land, in the form of what he called "The Alliance Against Fun."
> It has taken the ensuing decades to show how right I think Williams was in his judgment that it wasn't really what the cars of the era actually did (or didn't do) that made so many in his theoretical Alliance hate them. It was what cars are: expressions of individual choice and freedom of action.
> If Williams' hypothesis about car haters is correct, it means that moving from an oil economy to a hydrogen economy via hybrids, NGVs and other interim solutions will have no effect on these New Puritans, who will continue not only to be haunted by the fear that someone, somewhere is happy in an automobile, but is actually using it.[31]

The 1970 Clean Air Car Race, run cross-country from Pasadena, California, to Cambridge, Massachusetts, was covered by the *New York Times*. It reported that the race was not "a stunt, is neither a campus caper, nor a far-out demonstration. The more such activity and awareness [of alternative fuel vehicles] spreads, the less automakers can expect to put-off that change at their pleasure."[32] General Motors had two internal factions concerning the concept of electric vehicle production: "Yes, an electric vehicle can really perform.... At what cost?"[33]

The 1973–74 energy crisis provided a long-awaited reawakening in the interest in electric vehicles. The "just around the corner" theme surfaced again, as in this suggestion from *Industry Week*:

> Today's fuel shortage and tomorrow's projected per-gallon costs for gasoline appear to create the correct timing for the fledgling electric car industry."[34]

Later in 1974, *Industry Week* approached the continual problem of limited range of electric cars by stating,

> ...high-density batteries are surely just around the corner, which would swing all logic to electrics. We look to the battery industry for a technology breakthrough.[35]

In a 1989 article, A. F. Burke found lacking the advancement of battery technology for electrics. He stated,

> Methods for accurately including the effects of changes in battery temperature and age must be developed and demonstrated before any battery state-of-charge unit can be used with confidence in a vehicle. None of the battery management systems tested established sufficiently accurate and reliable operation in both the charge and discharge modes that they could be used in the test programs to control the cycling of the batteries.... [While] considerable progress has been made in battery management systems for electric vehicles in recent years the available systems are insufficiently dependable for unattended use.[36]

Ernest Wakefield expressed a historical perspective in comparing early discoveries to today's product:

It is interesting to note that after a century of effort, the most commercially suitable battery in 1990 for electric vehicle propulsion is a derivation of Plante's lead-acid battery of 1859. Also, the modern version is less than twice the delivered energy per unit weight of Julien's 1888 lead-acid battery.[37]

The Department of Energy, with the Idaho National Engineering and Environmental Laboratory (INEEL) and other partners, worked on developing advanced batteries, such as nickel/iron, lithium-ion, and nickel/zinc, as noted in 1986:

> Although these advanced batteries show exciting promise, the problems of solving the associated research problems and of producing a practical battery at low cost is a great challenge. These advanced batteries may hold out the best hope for a substantial replacement of gasoline cars with electric cars.[38]

In 1996 increased pollution caused by generating the additional power needed for electric vehicles was examined.

> The debate about electric vehicles often revolves around whether increased smokestack emissions—from power plants generating the electricity needed to recharge all those EV batteries—will offset the reduction in pollution from tailpipes.[39]

The adverse effects of increasing lead-acid batteries needed to power zero-emission electrics were also an environmental concern. An abstract from *Environmental Science and Technology* predicted that the CARB mandate requiring that 10 percent of motor vehicles must be zero emission vehicles by 2003 would add 500,000 batteries for disposal:

> In contrast to the small ozone-related benefits from BPVs, the potential environmental problems are considerable. Mining, smelting, and recycling more than 500kg of lead batteries per vehicle would result in environmental lead releases 80 times greater per vehicle mile than those of a gasoline-powered vehicle with a current starter battery. Half a million lead-acid BPVs would increase national lead discharges to the environment by about 20 percent.[40]

In 1997, *Scientific American* again took a look at hybrids.

> There are actually hundreds of engineers around the world who are working on hybrid electric vehicles. But almost a century after the hybrid was first conceived, more than 25 years after development work began on them in earnest, and after more than $1 billion has been spent worldwide in recent years on development, not a single hybrid vehicle is being offered to the public by a large automaker. In fact, not a single design is anywhere near volume production. In the U.S., where the government has spent about $750 million since 1994 on almost frenzied efforts to advance the technology of hybrid electric vehicles [HEVs], the concept is still a political football rather than a commercial reality.[41]

Revisiting hybrids included reviewing the fuel cell as a possible energy source. In 1998, reviews on fuel cells were mixed. *Business Week*'s Science and Technology section stated:

> Other pieces of the fuel-cell puzzle are falling into place. Impressive progress has been made in developing transmissions, for instance. While consumers haven't flocked to battery-powered cars, the research and design that went into them helped Detroit cut the cost and improve the reliability of the motors and generators. Insiders say that GM, thanks to its EV1 electric car, has an edge in electronic controllers, which coordinates all high-voltage operations of the drive system. By 2000, these sources expect GM to have an electric transmission equal in cost to a traditional automatic transmission.
>
> Still. Researchers may have trouble keeping up with the public-relations machine. Already, engineers are looking for wiggle room in the pronouncements by senior managers. Even Ford's Bates has a hard time accepting the newfound optimism. "We really have no

confidence these things will completely deliver on their promise," he admits. "But the promise is so great, you just have to give it a go." Or risk seeing more German and Japanese cars in the driveways.[42]

The fuel-cell-powered vehicle had its skeptics at the turn of the 21st century. In response to the NECAR 4 and P2000, *Car and Driver* featured these comments.

In Sacramento, California, DaimlerChrysler and Ford scored first in the headline wars with a press intro of their NECAR 4 and P2000 fuel-cell-powered machines as part of the widely ignored Earth Day festivities. These vehicles were the opening salvo in a test fleet of 45 cars and buses to be powered by the magic cells in Los Angeles basin over the next four years.

Yes, fuel-cell cars powered by hydrogen are zero-emission units, but several issues have been conveniently ignored by the press during its euphoric announcements, including the "total energy" process required to produce, deliver and consume fuel in any vehicle. In this context, a gasoline-powered engine is radically more efficient than any fuel-celled alternative.[43]

Environmentalists of the 1990s stressed the impact ICEs had on an international issue of the day, global warming. Discussions on global warming included the need to find ways of coping with the problem ICEs cause with their exhaust. The Sierra Club in 1999 and *Time* in 2002 earmarked the problem and a possible solution in the not-too-distant future. The Sierra Club magazine stated:

Motor vehicles consume half the world's oil and account for a quarter of its greenhouse gas emissions. The biggest source of air pollution in a majority of the world's cities is auto exhaust.[44]

And *Time* said:

Hybrids are the first viable alternative to the gasoline engine. Cars that run on fuel cells— widely expected to be the next technological advance in automotive power — are at least ten years off.[45]

In the early 21st century, carmakers maintain that EVs cost about $20,000 more to manufacture than a gasoline vehicle. Manufacturers met government mandates for zero emission vehicles with varying degrees of enthusiasm, but the demand was not there.

[The] oil industry acted aggressively against both the CARB mandate and the electric car. General Motors worked against the mandate only, and has been fairly enthusiastic about having an advanced electric car for sale. Ford and Chrysler have not to the same degree been enthusiastic about electric cars, and certainly not about the mandate. Toyota is taking a more active role in Japan.[46]

The Honda Insight Hybrid and Toyota Prius began to get consumers' attention soon after their U.S. arrival. Well-known talk-radio hosts Tom and Ray Magliozzi of *Car Talk* test-drove the cars in 2001 and concluded:

The Honda Insight is currently the second best hybrid vehicle on sale in the United States. We should also mention that there are only two hybrids in that category. The other is the Toyota Prius. We can sum up the differences between the Insight and Prius this way: The Insight is a vehicle for people whose first and foremost goal in life is to get the best possible gasoline mileage, everything else be damned. And the Prius is a great little car that happens to get outstanding gas mileage.[47]

In 2003 General Motors' vice president for research and development, Larry Burns, had a novel approach to the AFV concept:

"The Stone Age didn't end because we ran out of stones." This Larry Burns aphorism is one you hear from his acolytes at General Motors' facilities around the world. He means it to suggest that a superior technology can replace a proven one by offering advantages, rather than by waiting for a resource to run out. We didn't stop heating our homes with logs because the trees were all gone, and we didn't put ourselves on wheels because there was a global shortage of horses.

Burns doesn't aim to replace stones or trees or even wheels, but internal combustion engines. He is passionate about this, and he has GM chairman and CEO Richard Wagoner backing him up. They're driven, you might say, to push the transition away from internal combustion of petroleum derivatives and into fuel cells running on hydrogen. And by repeating his "Stone Age" line, what his minions mean to convey is they share Burns' conviction that fuel cells can be made into a superior alternative, one that can attract consumers on its own merits rather than being foisted on them by force of government decree or onerous taxation.[48]

Acceptance of electric, hybrid and alternative fuel vehicles has vacillated over the last one hundred years. Optimism prevailed in the early years when many predicted the dominance of the electrics, but their battery cost and performance could not compete with the distance and speed of ICEs. After a century of research and development and commercial availability, battery technology, lack of infrastructure, and sluggish consumer support continue to be stumbling blocks for electric vehicles. The logic that if there were more cars, charging stations would be more prevalent has been repeated time and again, through five wars, energy crises and whenever concerns about environmental issues arise.

The year 2009 found the world in an economic recession. There was concern about climate change, and President Barack Obama pledged to create 5 million green jobs in the next two decades. Green jobs include such things as installing solar panels, engineering algae for biofuels or building windmills to generate clean power. But a dollar spent on green sources may displace the dollar spent in conventional power generation, and persuading consumers to practice energy conservation may decrease demand, again resulting in job loss. Finding a reasonable balance is not easy.

How does this relate to the auto industry? Electric and hybrid cars fit the green energy profile. Their emissions are cleaner and their engines efficient. Their customer base during periods of energy awareness grows and the market responds. Small businesses are emerging around tuning and repairing electric and hybrid vehicles. Auto racing interests are involved in promoting green technology. The large car companies are competing in a very-high-stakes game to become the first to create a "new" battery, a "new" fuel cell or a flex-fuel vehicle at a competitive price. Competition runs high to be the first to create something new, not only for the "naming rights" but also for the billions of dollars possible to make on the open market. This is a huge opportunity for everyone, and the competition is fierce.

Looking at a microeconomic opportunity, in 2009, economic developers in Portland, Oregon, invited makers of the Th!nk electric vehicle (the Ford-affiliated Norwegian corporation) to consider opening a plant in Portland that would employ 300 people. It would be capable of producing 16,000 cars per year and could grow to 60,000 cars per year employing 900 people. The Th!nk is an all-electric vehicle that is capable of running 60 mph and will go 112 miles on one charge. This is the type of growth in green jobs that could make the economic future look brighter.

As of this writing China is poised to become the number-one car producer in the world very soon. Some 5.2 million cars were sold last year, and the numbers are expected to expand greatly. How many of these vehicles will be electric and hybrid? The only hybrids currently available in China are from Japan — the Toyota Prius and Honda Civic Hybrid. They are assembled in China, but with China's heavy import taxes on parts, they cost double what they do in the United States. The Chinese are attempting to design and build their own hybrid, but, at the moment, the future of green cars in this emerging market looks dim.

The major auto industry manufacturers readily finance research and development in the 21st century to develop new technologies. Since gasoline is still the most widely available fuel, the current infrastructure still relies on gasoline. Consumer acceptance varies widely. Small pockets of enthusiasts are scattered throughout the continents and many more are poised to revisit EVs. The consumers' view of electric vehicles has not varied much over the past one hundred years. The concept of an environmentally friendly machine continues to grab their attention, and if the electric meets their expectation of convenience, performance and cost, many will buy it by choice. The most promising development to replace the ICE and dependence on foreign oil supplies seems to be the hybrid engine, with fuel cell vehicles possibly emerging as a viable alternative in about ten years.

Will this prediction come any closer to fulfillment than so many other predictions of the last hundred years? We will all just have to wait and see.

APPENDIX
HYBRIDS DEFINED

Full Hybrids: can run on electricity alone, and use the gas engine to recharge the battery

Hollow hybrids: have idle-off and regenerative braking and use the electrics to power accessories and air conditioning.

Light hybrids: use the electrics and computer to control fuel mileage by temporarily shutting down the engine automatically whenever the vehicle stops, and restarting it when needed.

Mild Hybrids: are internal combustion engines that use the electric motor to increase fuel efficiency by assisting the engine. They are cheaper to build than full hybrids and cannot be converted to plug-ins or run on electricity alone.

Muscle hybrids: are internal combustion engines that use electric motors to improve acceleration and power and fuel mileage. They also have regenerative braking.

Plug-in hybrids: use large battery packs and recharge from external power supplies. They may have small auxiliary gas engines to provide additional recharging. They are the closest to all-electric cars.

CHAPTER NOTES

Preface

1. Wakefield, Ernest H., *History of the Electric Vehicle*, Warrendale, Pa.: Society of Automotive Engineers, 1994.

Introduction

1. Emmanouilides, Nick. "The Rambler and 'I Spy.'" *AutoWeek* 57:52 (December 24, 2007), p. 18.

2. Thompson, Steve. "SUV: Appropriate Technology." *AutoWeek* 57:34 (August 20, 2007), p. 14.

3. Ibid.

4. *Scientific American* LXXXVII:16 (October 18, 1902), p. 266.

5. *The Horseless Carriage* 1:11 (September 1896), p. 18.

6. Kirsch, David A. "The Electric Car and the Burden of History: Studies in Automotive Systems Rivalry in America 1890–1996." *Business & Economic History* 26:2 (Winter 1997), pp. 304–310.

7. *The Horseless Age* 2:5 (March 1897), p. 5.

8. *Cyclopedia of Automobile Engineering, Vol. 3*, Chicago: American Technical Society, 1910, p. 11.

9. Schiffer, Michael B., Butts, Tamara C., and Grimm, Kimberly K., *Taking Charge*, Washington, D.C.: Smithsonian Institution Press, 1994, p. 70.

10. Ibid.

11. Kirsch, David A., *The Electric Vehicle and the Burden of History*, New Brunswick, N.J.: Rutgers University Press, 1964, p. 93.

12. *The New York Times*, December 21, 1906, 10:1.

13. *Scientific American* LXXX:19 (May 13, 1899), p. 304.

14. Villano, Matt, "Plug in a Car and Give It Juice," http://future.newsday.com/4/fbak0430.htm (accessed April 5, 2001).

15. *The Horseless Age* 7:11 (December 12, 1902), p. 22.

16. *Cyclopedia of Automobile Engineering, Vol. 3*, Chicago: American Technical Society, 1910, p. 12.

17. *Electrical World* 57:25 (June 22, 1911), p. 1590.

18. Ibid.

19. *Electrical World* 57:22 (June 11, 1911), p. 1437.

20. *Electrical World* 57:25 (June 22, 1911), p. 1590.

21. *The Automobile* 31 (October 22, 1914), pp. 753–754.

22. *Country Life in America* 23 (January 1913), pp. 23–26.

23. Ibid.

24. *The Automobile* 35 (January 20, 1916), pp. 122–129.

25. Fogelberg, Hans, *The Electric Car Controversy*, Gothenburg, Sweden: Department of History and Technology and Industry, Chalmers University of Technology, 1998, p. i.

26. De Luchi, Mark, Michael Quanlu Wang, and Daniel Sperling, "Electric Vehicles: Performance, Life-Cycle Costs, Emissions, and Recharging Requirements," *Transportation, 1989, Research Part A*, Vol. 23A, No. 3.

27. Rowland, Karen. "Fuel-cell Vehicles Stalled by Price Tag." *Washington Times*, February 20, 2008. http://www.washingtontimes.com (accessed February 28, 2008).

28. *Scientific American* LXXXVII:16 (October 18, 1902), p. 266.

29. *Life* XLV:1159 (January 12, 1906), p. 59.

30. Vance, Bill, "Stanley and the Steam-Powered Automobiles," http://www.canadiandriver.com/articles/bv/stanley.htm (accessed May 21, 2001).

31. Gallivan, Leo G., "Steam Vehicles Assure a Cleaner Environment," *Utility & Telephone Fleets* (December/January 1997–1998), p. 40.

32. Ibid. p. 41.

33. Ibid. p. 42.

34. Pool, Robert, *Beyond Engineering: How Society Shapes Technology*, New York: Oxford University Press, 1997, pp. 152–154.

35. Gallivan, Leo G., "Steam Vehicles Assure a Cleaner Environment," *Utility & Telephone Fleets* (December/January 1997–1998), p. 43.

36. *Scientific American* LXXX:19 (May 13, 1899), p. 300.

37. "Electric Cars: The Drive Toward Fresh Air," *Humanist*, 54:3 (May/June 1994), p. 43.

38. Morrison, Mac, "Solid Option." *AutoWeek* 57:17 (April 23, 2007), p. 23.

39. Grunwald, Michael. "The New Action Heroes," *Time* (June 14, 2007) http://www.time.com/time/nation/article/0,8599.1632736-3.00.html (accessed July 19, 2008).

Chapter 1

1. "Research and Markets: Understand the Technological Basis of a Hybrid Vehicle and the Basic Differentiation Between Electric and Hybrid Vehicles." *M2 Presswire*. Retrieved from Lexis-Nexis (accessed September 14, 2007).

2. Anonymous.

3. Tomaine, Bob. "Top Brass." *AutoWeek* 57:11 (March 12, 2007), p. 25.

4. Fogelberg, Hans, *The Electric Car Controversy*,

Gothenburg, Sweden: Department of History and Technology and Industry, Chalmers University of Technology, 1998, p. 31.

5. "Automobile Motors," *Scientific American* 81:82 (August 5, 1899), cited in Flink, James J., *America Adopts the Automobile, 1895–1910*, Cambridge, Mass.: MIT Press, 1970, p. 238.

6. *The Automobile, Vol. 1*, New York: Cassell, 1905, p. 347.

7. Ibid.

8. *Scientific American* LXXXI:9 (September 2, 1899), p. 153

9. *Scientific American* LXVI:1 (January 9, 1892), p. 18.

10. Schiffer, Michael B., Butts, Tamara C., and Grimm, Kimberly K., *Taking Charge*, Washington, D.C.: Smithsonian Institution Press, 1994, p. 36.

11. *Scientific American* LXVI:1 (January 9, 1892), p. 18.

12. *Scientific American* LXXII:12 (March 23, 1895), p. 177.

13. Ibid.

14. *Scientific American* LXXXI:81 (November 18, 1899), p. 324.

15. Ward, Ian, *The World of Automobiles, Vol. 5*, Milwaukee: Purnell Reference Books, 1977, p. 693.

16. Ibid.

17. Wakefield, Ernest H., *History of the Electric Automobile: Hybrid Electric Vehicles*, Warrendale, Pa.: Society of Automotive Engineers, Inc., 1998. p. v.

18. Olama, Mark, "Ferdinand Porsche." http://www.foi.hr/~molama/History.htm (accessed July 15, 2002).

19. *Scientific American Supplement* 1451, October 24, 1903, p. 23,253.

20. *Scientific American* LXXX:18 (May 13, 1899), p. 294.

21. *Scientific American Supplement* 49:1253 (January 6, 1900), p. 20,088.

22. *The Horseless Age* 2:9 (August 1897), p. 12.

23. *Scientific American* LXXVI:21 (May 22, 1897), p. 331.

24. Schiffer, Michael B., Butts, Tamara C., and Grimm, Kimberly K., *Taking Charge*, Washington, D.C.: Smithsonian Institution Press, 1994, p. 58.

25. *Scientific American* LXXVI:21 (May 22, 1897), p. 331.

26. *Scientific American* LXXXVII:24 (December 13, 1902), p. 427.

27. Lavergne, Gérard, *The Automobile, Vol. II*, New York: Cassell, 1905, p. 697.

28. Ibid., p. 700.

29. Ibid., p. 749.

30. Ibid., p. 750.

31. Georgano, Nick, *The Beaulieu Encyclopedia of the Automobile, Vol. 1, Chicago:* Fitzroy Dearborn Publishers, 2000, p. 160.

32. Dorrington, Leigh. "The Makings of a Muscle Car." *AutoWeek*, February 27, 2006, p. 23.

33. Gallivan, Leo G., "Steam Vehicles Assure a Cleaner Environment," *Utility & Telephone Fleets* (December/January 1997–1998), p. 42.

34. *Scientific American* LXXXI:78 (October 14, 1899), p. 244.

35. Ibid.

36. McShane, Clay, *The Automobile*, Westport, Conn.: Greenwood Press, 1997, p. 24.

37. Georgano, Nick, *The Beaulieu Encyclopedia of the Automobile, Vol. 1, Chicago:* Fitzroy Dearborn Publishers, 2000, p. 1334.

38. *Scientific American* LXXX:18 (May 13, 1899), p. 294.

39. *Scientific American* LXXXIII (December 22, 1900), p. 389.

40. Ward, Ian, *The World of Automobiles, Vol. 10*, Milwaukee: Purnell Reference Books, 1977, p. 1237.

41. *The Automobile* 31 (September 24, 1914), p. 567.

42. Ibid.

43. Georgano, Nick, *The Beaulieu Encyclopedia of the Automobile, Vol. 1, Chicago:* Fitzroy Dearborn Publishers, 2000, p. 489.

44. *The Motor World* LX:4 (August 7, 1902), p. 540.

45. *Electrical World* 57:11 (March 16, 1911), p. 679.

46. Ibid.

47. *Life* LIII: 1381 (April 15, 1909).

48. Ward, Ian, *The World of Automobiles, Vol. 5*, Milwaukee: Purnell Reference Books, 1977, p. 93.

49. *Electrical World* 57:22 (June 1, 1911), p. 1436.

50. Handy, Galen, "Rauch & Lang," (2008) personal research papers.

51. 1923 Rausch & Lang electric car, http://www.econogics.com/ev/raulangl.jpg (accessed March 10, 2001).

52. Georgano, Nick, *The Beaulieu Encyclopedia of the Automobile, Vol. 1, Chicago:* Fitzroy Dearborn Publishers, 2000, p. 326.

53. *Electrical World* 64 (September 19, 1914), p. 573.

54. *Illustrated World* XXVI:2 (October 1916), p. 229.

55. Georgano, Nick, *The Beaulieu Encyclopedia of the Automobile, Vol. 1, Chicago:* Fitzroy Dearborn Publishers, 2000, p. 1037.

56. *Electrical World* 57:11 (March 6, 1911), p. 678.

57. Baker Electric Vehicles advertisement, http://www.econogics.com/ev/bkr1908.jpg (accessed March 10, 2001).

58. Ward, Ian, *The World of Automobiles, Vol. 5*, Milwaukee: Purnell Reference Books, 1977, p. 154.

59. Ibid.

60. *The Automobile* 32 (January 21, 1915), p. 138.

61. Georgano, Nick, *The Beaulieu Encyclopedia of the Automobile, Vol. 1, Chicago:* Fitzroy Dearborn Publishers, 2000, p. 258.

62. Century electric car, http://www.econogics.com/ev/century.jpg (accessed March 10, 2001).

63. Ward, Ian, *The World of Automobiles, Vol. 5*, Milwaukee: Purnell Reference Books, 1977, p. 96.

64. *Electrical Review* 67 (October 2, 1915), pp. 641–643.

65. Tomaine, Bob. "Age: Just a Number." *AutoWeek* 57:50 (December 10, 2007), p. 29.

66. Georgano, Nick, *The Beaulieu Encyclopedia of the Automobile, Vol. 1, Chicago:* Fitzroy Dearborn Publishers, 2000, p. 430.

67. 1914 Detroit Roadster Model 46, http://www.econogics.com/ev/model46.jpg (accessed March 10, 2001).

68. Georgano, Nick, *The Beaulieu Encyclopedia of the Automobile, Vol. 1, Chicago:* Fitzroy Dearborn Publishers, p. 430.

69. 1915 Milburn, http://www.econogics.com/ev/rlmilbu2.jpg (accessed April 2, 2001).

70. *Literary Digest* LII:13 (March 25, 1916), p. 857.

71. *The New York Times*, January 7, 1917, III, 15:1.

72. *Electrical World* 71 (June 15, 1918), p. 1264.

73. Facts on File World News Service, March 29, 2007. "Today's Science@Facts.com: Garrett Augustus Morgan: Innovation in the Face of Adversity."

74. Georgano, Nick, *The Beaulieu Encyclopedia of the*

Automobile, Vol. 1, Chicago: Fitzroy Dearborn Publishers, 2000, p. 1557.

75. Ibid., p. 490.

76. Illustration of Enfield 8000, http://www.econogics.com/ev/enfield.jpg (accessed February 20, 2000).

77. Georgano, Nick, *The Beaulieu Encyclopedia of the Automobile, Vol. 1,* Chicago: Fitzroy Dearborn Publishers, 2000, p. 488.

78. Gritzinger, Bob, "1966 GMC Electrovan," *Auto Week* 51:1 (January 1, 2001), p. 27.

79. *Automotive News* 69:5581 (December 5, 1994), p. 2i (supp).

80. Schroeder, Don, "General Motors EV1," *Car & Driver* 42 (October 1996), p. 77+.

81. Ibid.

82. Supplied by Corbin Motors, 2001.

83. *Facts on File World News Digest* March 19, 2007. http://www.2facts.com (accessed April 1, 2007).

84. "This Week: Extra Fighting for Green." *AutoWeek* 57:26 (June 25, 2007), p. 10.

85. Vaughn, Mark. "ECO-Smooth." *AutoWeek* 57:36 (September 3, 2007), p. 9.

86. Neff, Natalie. "GM Plugs into Hybrid Pickups." *AutoWeek* 58:36 (September 8, 2008), p. 9.

87. *PR Newswire US,* May 22, 2007, Dearborn, Mich.

88. Kudirka, Scott. "Hold Your Breath," *AutoWeek* 17:18 (April 23, 2007), p. 18.

89. Tesla EV, http://stadium.weblogsinc.com/auto blog/videos/hirezpics/IMG_6847.jpg (accessed February 16, 2008).

90. "Fisker Karma." http://www.fiskerautomotive.com (accessed January 3, 2009).

91. Kurczewski, Nick. "Taking a Flyer." *AutoWeek* 57:49 (December 3, 2007), p. 9.

92. Wilson, Kevin A. "The Idea of a Germ." *Auto Week* 58:17 (April 21, 2008), p. 52.

93. Segan, Sascha. "Go Green with Hybrid Cabs and Rental Cars." *Frommer's.* http://www.frommers.com/deals/north_america/article.cfm?dealID=NORTH_AMERICA&articleid=3857&t=Go%20Green%20with%20Hybrid%20Cabs%20and%20Rental%20Cars (accessed August 2, 2008).

94. Ibid.

95. Nielsen, Susan. "Opinion." *Oregonian,* January 27, 2008, Section E5.

96. Ibid.

Chapter 2

1. Vaughn, Mark. "Who Killed the Electric Car?" *AutoWeek* 56:25 (June 19, 2006), p. 36.

2. Coradato, Roy E., "Markt-based Environmentalism and the Free Market," *Independent Review,* 1:3 (Winter 1997), p. 371.

3. Sperling, Daniel, *Future Drive,* Washington, D.C.: Island Press, 1995, pp. 10–11.

4. Moore, Bill, "Shell's H2 Future." http://www.ev world.com/article.cfm?storyid=396 (accessed November 1, 2009).

5. "Fuel Cell Works," *Europa,* February 25, 2008. http://www.fuelcellsworks.com/Supppage8460.html (accessed February 28, 2008).

6. Moore, Bill, "California's Line in the Sand." http://evworld.com/article.cfm?storyid=388 (accessed November 1, 2009).

7. Boschert, Sherry. *Plug-in Hybrids: The Cars That Will Recharge America.* Gabriola Island, B.C.: New Society Publishers, 2006, pp. 162–165.

8. Gleisner, B. B., and S. A. Weaver. "Cars, Carbon, and Kyoto: Evaluating an Emission Charge and Other Policy Instruments as Incentives for a Transition to Hybrid Cars in New Zealand." *Kotuitui: New Zealand Journal of Social Sciences* 1:1 (May 2006), pp. 81–89.

9. *Scientific American Supplement* LV:1431 (June 6, 1902), p. 22,929.

10. Flink, James J., *America Adopts the Automobile, 1895–1910,* Cambridge, Mass.: MIT Press, 1970, p. 327.

11. *North American Review,* August 1904, pp. 168–177.

12. Ibid.

13. Ibid.

14. *Scientific American* 85:407 (December 21, 1901), p. 407.

15. *The New York Times,* November 11, 1899, 6:2.

16. Ibid.

17. *The Horseless Age* V:17 (January 24, 1900), p. 17.

18. *Scientific American* LXXX:18 (May 6, 1899), p. 278.

19. *North American Review,* August 1904, pp. 168–177.

20. *The New York Times,* March 11, 1906, 10:5.

21. *The New York Times,* March 11, 1906, 11:2.

22. *The New York Times,* July 8, 1906, 18:4.

23. *Outlook* 47 (January 1906), pp. 502–504.

24. Ibid.

25. Ibid.

26. Rollins, Mongomery, *Outlook* 92 (August 7, 1909), pp. 859–860.

27. *Outlook* 84 (December 15, 1906), pp. 903–904.

28. *Harper's Weekly* 51 (March 30, 1907), p. 470.

29. Ibid.

30. *The Nation* 87:2283 (September 3, 1908), pp. 199–200.

31. *Outlook* 92 (June 12, 1909), pp. 342–343.

32. Wurzer, Cathy, *Tales of the Road: Highway 61.* St. Paul: Minnesota Historical Society Press, 2008, p. 3.

33. *The New York Times,* June 24, 1917, 2, 4.1.

34. *Literary Digest* 67 (November 6, 1920), pp. 80–88.

35. *Scientific American Supplement* 130 (April 1924), p. 252.

36. *The Literary Digest* 76 (March 24, 1923), p. 25.

37. Facts on File World News Service, March 29, 2007. "Today's Science@Facts.com: Garrett Augustus Morgan: Innovation in the Face of Adversity."

38. "The Civil Shaping of Technology: California's Electric Vehicle Program," *Science, Technology & Human Values* 26:1 (Winter 2001), pp. 56–82.

39. *The Wall Street Journal,* January 18, 1974, 30:1.

40. Ibid.

41. *The Wall Street Journal,* February 21, 1974, 32:1.

42. Ibid.

43. Schoenbrod, David, *Saving Our Environment from Washington: How Congress Grabs Power, Shirks Responsibility, and Shortchanges the People.* New Haven, Conn.: Yale University Press, 2005, p. 35.

44. Ibid., p. 44

45. "Energy Policy," *Facts on File Issues & Controversies,* January 9, 2006. Facts on File News Service. http://www.2facts.com (accessed March 29, 2007).

46. Ibid.

47. U.S. Department of Transportation, U.S. Department of Energy, U.S. Environmental Protection Agency, *Report to Congress: Effects of the Alternative Motor Fuels Act CAFE Incentives Policy,* March 2002, pp. iv–v.

48. Wakefield, Ernest H., *History of the Electric Automobile: Battery-Only Powered Cars,* Warrendale, Pa.: Society of Automotive Engineers, 1994, p. 284.

49. U.S. Department of Energy. *Clean Cities: Participating Countries*. U.S. Department of Energy. Energy Efficiency and Renewable Energy Clean Cities. http://www1.eere.energy.gov/cleancities/participating_countries.html (accessed March 5, 2008).

50. Bergeron, P., and V. Putsche. "Clean Cities Annual Metrics Report 2006, Prepared under Task No. FC07.2200. NREL/TP-540-41753, July 2007." National Renewable Energy Laboratory, Department of Energy, Office of Energy Efficiency and Renewable Energy. http://www.nrel.gov/docs/fy07osti/41753.pdf (accessed March 30, 2008).

51. Baumgartner, William, and Gross, Andrew, "Global Market for Electric Vehicles," *Business Economics* 35:4 (October 2000), p. 51.

52. *The New York Times*, February 23, 2008, p. A01.

53. *WARD'S Auto World* 28 (June 1992), p. 32.

54. Ibid.

55. Ibid.

56. McCool, Bob, "Are Oil Companies Trying to Kill the Electric Auto?" *Oil & Gas Journal* 93:37 (September 11, 1995), p. 21.

57. "Canada's Hydrogen and Fuel Cell Sector." Randall Anthony Communications. http://www.randallanthony.com/canadas-hydrogen-and-fuel-cell-sector (accessed March 13, 2008).

58. Industry Canada. *Canadian Hydrogen and Fuel Cell Sector Profile 2007*. http://www.hydrogeneconomy.gc.ca (accessed April 5, 2008).

59. "Ford Delivers First Fuel Cell Cars in Canada to Vancouver Fuel Cell Vehicle Program." *Hydrogen Forecast*. http://www.hydrogenforecast.com/wireitems/hfc_nb0043.html (accessed March 3, 2008).

60. "Alternate Fuels and Advanced Data Center." *State and Federal Incentive Laws*. http://www.eere.energy.gov/afdc/incentives_laws.html (accessed June 17, 2008).

61. *The Oregonian*, December 9, 1996, p. B02.

62. Boschert, Sherry, *Plug-in Hybrids: The Cars That Will Recharge America*. Gabriola Island, B.C.: New Society Publishers, 2006, p. 122.

63. Kempton, Willett, Tomic, Jasna, Letendre, Steven, Brooks, Alec N., and Lipman, Timothy E. *Vehicle-to-Grid Power: Battery, Hybrid, and Fuel Cell Vehicles as Resources for Distributed Electric Power in California*. Institute of Transportation Studies, University of California, Davis. Research Report UCD-ITS-RR001-03. http://pubs.its.ucdavis.edu/publication_detail.php?id=360 (accessed February 21, 2009).

64. Gage, Thomas B. *Final Report: Development and Evaluation of a Plug-in HEV with Vehicle-to-Grid Power Flow*. CARB Grant Number ICAT 01-02. Prepared by AC Propulsion, Inc. December 17, 2003. http://www.udel.edu/V2G/docs/ICAT%2001-2-V2G-Plug-Hybrid.pdf (accessed February 10, 2007).

65. Brown, M. H., and Breckenridge, Leah, *State Alternative Fuel Vehicle Incentives: A Decade and More of Lessons Learned*. Washington, D.C: National Conference of State Legislatures, 2001, pp. 42–50, 54–64.

66. Ibid., p. 20.

67. "Campaigns Against Electric Cars Gaining Strength," *National Petroleum News* 87 (July 1995), p. 18+.

68. Ibid.

69. "Basement Mandarins," *Newsweek* 133:12 (March 22, 1999), p. 50.

70. Welch, David, "The Eco-Cars," *Business Week*, August 14, 2000, pp. 62–68.

71. Hanssen, Greg, "Is CARB Getting Real or Caving In?," November 30, 2002. http://evworld.com/article.cfm?storyid=458 (accessed October 10, 2009).

72. Surber, F. T., et. al., "Hybrid Vehicle Potential Assessment," #5030-345, California Institute of Technology, Pasadena, CA: Jet Propulsion Laboratory, 1980.

73. "Hybrid Electric Vehicles," *Scientific American* 277:4 (October 1997), p. 71.

74. "Why Detroit's Going Green," *Sierra* 84:4 (July/August 1999), p. 38.

75. "Energy Storage Technologies." *CQ Congressional Testimony*, October 3, 2007, p. 12.

76. "Why Detroit's Going Green," *Sierra* 84:4 (July/August 1999), p. 38.

77. Sperling, Daniel, *Future Drive*, Washington, D.C.: Island Press, 1995, p. 144.

78. United States Department of Energy, *Alternative Fueling Stations*. U.S. Department of Energy. Energy Efficiency and Renewable Energy. http://www.eere.energy.gov/afde/fuels/stations.html (accessed March 5, 2008).

79. "State of the Union: The Advanced Energy Initiative." January 31, 2006. http://www.whitehouse.gov/news/releases/2006/01/print/20060131-6.html (accessed April 5, 2007).

80. Chess, Dave, "Hybrid Hustle." *AutoWeek* 56:35 (August 28, 2006), p. 4.

81. Block, Sandra, "For 2006 Taxes, Hybrid Vehicle Tax Credits Have Gotten a Bit Complicated." *USA Today*, February 20, 2007. http://search.ebscohost.com/login.aspx?direct=aph&AN=JOE320038947807&site=ehost-live (accessed March 1, 2007).

82. Eudy, Leslie, *Field Operations Program: Overview of Advanced Technology Transportation, Update for CY2001*. Golden, Colo.: National Renewable Energy Laboratory, April 2001, p. 7.

83. Arizona Department of Administration, "Use of Alternative Fuels and Clean Burning Fuels in the State Motor Vehicle Fleet." November 2008.

84. Francfort, J., and Carroll, M., *Field Operations Program Incremental Funding Activities Status Report*, March 2001.

85. Ibid.

86. "Ethanol Fuel." *Issues & Controversies on File*, July 21, 2006. Facts on File News Service http://www.2facts.com (accessed March 29, 2007).

87. Ibid.

88. Ibid.

89. Kable, Greg. "How Low Can You Go." *AutoWeek* 57:39 (September 24, 2007), pp. 7–9.

90. Ibid., p. 8

Chapter 3

1. Wakefield, Ernest H., *The Consumer's Electric Car*, Ann Arbor, Mich.: Ann Arbor Science Publishers, 1977, p. vi.

2. Brown, Jordana, "Fuel for Thought." *Vegetarian Times*, March 2006, pp. 55–59.

3. Nathanson, Scott, "Not All Hybrids Are Created Equal," *Futurist* 41:4 (July/August 2007), p. 24.

4. Crockett, Jim, "Is Muddier Shade of Green OK? I Think So," *Consulting-Specifying Engineer* 40:5 (November 2006), p. 7.

5. EV1 Club. "Who Killed the Electric Car? The Facts — Footnotes." http://www.sonyclassics.com/whokilledtheelectriccar/pages/footnotes_facts.html (accessed May 26, 2007).

6. McCluggage, Denise, "Now and Then." *Auto Week* 57:11 (March 12, 2007), p. 10.

7. Carson, Iain. "A Hundred Years on the Clock." *The Economist* 339:7971 (June 22, 1996), p. 3.

8. "Hybrids in the Third World?" *Business Week Online* (July 31, 2006): 2–2. Business Source Complete, EBSCOHost (accessed February 6, 2007).

9. *Globe and Mail*, September 16, 1999, p. 17.

10. Transportation Research Board, National Research Council, *Toward a Sustainable Future: Addressing the Long-Term Effects of Motor Vehicle Transportation on Climate and Ecology*, Washington D.C.: National Academy Press, 1997.

11. Bachram, Heidi, "Climate Fraud and Carbon Colonialism: The New Trade in Greenhouse Gases," *Capitalism, Nature, Socialism* 15:4 (December 2004), p. 6.

12. Harper, Jennifer. "'Carbon neutral' Called Hottest New Word of '06." *The Washington Times*, November 14, 2006. Retrieved from Regional Business News, EbscoHost (accessed March 20, 2007).

13. Transportation Research Board, National Research Council, *Toward a Sustainable Future: Addressing the Long-Term Effects of Motor Vehicle Transportation on Climate and Ecology*, Washington D.C.: National Academy Press, 1997.

14. Moore, Bill, "Can Wind Compete with Coal?" http://evworld.com/databases/storybuilder.cfm?storyid=250&first=3052&end=3051 (accessed June 2, 2002).

15. Pedersen, Sigurd Lauge, "The Danish CO_2 Emissions Trading System." *Reciel* 3 (2000), pp. 223–225.

16. Dyer, Gwynne, *The Spectator*, November 17, 1998, A10.

17. McElroy, Joe. "Green Is the New Granite." *Planning* 73:7 (July 2007), pp. 20–25.

18. Fernandez, Maria Luisa, and Blass, Soto, "Green House Gas Emissions Trading Scheme and Their Fiscal Implications," *Journal of American Academy of Business* 9:1 (March 2006), p. 33.

19. *The New York Times*, July 4, 1899, 6:4.

20. Wakefield, Ernest H., *History of the Electric Automobile*, Warrendale, Pa.: Society of Automotive Engineers, 1994, p. 127.

21. *Scientific American* LXXX (February 18, 1899), p. 98.

22. *Scientific American* LXXXV:407 (December 21, 1901), p. 407.

23. *Scientific American* LXXX:1 (October 18, 1904), p. 5.

24. Ibid., p. 4.

25. Wilson, Kevin A., "Opposite Lock." *AutoWeek* 52:36 (September 2, 2002), p. 9.

26. *Outing* 47 (January 1906), pp. 502–504.

27. *Scientific American* 100 (March 27, 1909), p. 238.

28. "Danger in Gas Exhaust Fumes," *The New York Times*, December 16, 1917, 2, 11:4.

29. Bedard, Patrick, "Filling Up with Clean, Free Wind, and Other EV Fantasies," *Car & Driver* 44:7 (January 1999), p. 19.

30. Camerota, Alisyn, "Wind Farms Fan Flames of Controversy," Fox News, August 21, 2003. http://www.foxnews.com/story/0,2933,95273,00.html (accessed August 22, 2003).

31. Krauss, Clifford, "Move Over, Oil, There's Money in Texas Wind." *The New York Times*, February 23, 2008. http://www.nytimes.com/2006/02/23/business/23wind.html (accessed February 25, 2008).

32. Ibid.

33. Carlson, Scott. "Wind Turbines: Not Always a Breeze for Colleges." *The Chronicle of Higher Education* 54:16 (December 14, 2007). http://chronicle.com/article/Wind-Turbines-Not-Always-a/18233. (accessed November 1, 2009).

34. Lave, L. B, et al., "Battery Powered Vehicles: Ozone Reduction Versus Lead Discharges." *Environmental Science and Technology* 30:9 (1996), pp. 402A–407A.

35. DeCicco, John and Kliesch, James, *ACEEE's Green Book: The Environmental Guide to Cars and Trucks, Model Year 2001*, Washington, D.C. : American Council for an Energy Efficient Economy, 2001, p. 26.

36. "How Green Is Your Hydrogen?" *The Economist* 355:8164 (April 1, 2000), p. 74.

37. Leung, D. "How the Ballard Fuel Cell Works." *The Ottawa Citizen*, May 24, 2001. http://www.tcp.com/~ether/articles/fuel-cells.html (accessed September 2, 2001).

38. Motavalli, Jim, "Your Next Car?," *Sierra* 84:4 (July/August 1999), p. 41.

39. International Energy Agency, "Honda Solar Hydrogen Refueling Station," International Energy Agency Hydrogen Implementing Agreement. http://www.ieahia.org/pdfs/honda.pdf (accessed January 9, 2008).

40. Fuel Cells 2000, "Frequently Asked Questions." http://www.fuelcells.org/basics/faqs.html (accessed October 15, 2009).

41. *Mass Transit* 24:4 (July 1998), p. 32.

42. Weissmann, Jordan, "On the Road Again." *The Washington Post*, August 26, 2008, p. D01.

43. Kamalick, Joe, "Bush Plan Pointless—but Passable." *ICIS Chemical Business Americas* 271:4 (January 29, 2007), p. 19.

44. Tilman, David, and Hill, Jason, "Not All Alternative Biofuels Are Created Equal." *The Sunday Oregonian*, April 1, 2007, Section E2, p. 2.

45. Kudirka, Scott, "Hold Your Breath," *AutoWeek* 57:17 (April 23, 2007), p. 59.

46. Vettraino, J.P., "Racing Green," *AutoWeek* 57:17 (April 23, 2007), p. 59.

47. Tilman, David, and Hill, Jason, "Not All Alternative Biofuels Are Created Equal." *The Sunday Oregonian*, April 1, 2007, Section E2, p. 2.

48. Richtel, Matt, "Green Energy Enthusiasts Are Also Betting on Fossil Fuels." *The New York Times*, March 16, 2007. http://www.nytimes.com (accessed March 16, 2007).

49. Lofton, Lynn, "New Technology Brings Increased Oil and Gas Activity to Mississippi." *Mississippi Business Journal* 29:30 (July 23, 2007), pp. 1, 28.

50. Pope, Carl, March 6, 2002. http://newyork.sierraclub.org/rochester/hybrid.htm (accessed December 14, 2002).

51. Moore, Bill, "Can Wind Compete with Coal?" October 20, 2001. http://evworld.com/databases/storybuilder.cfm?storyid=250 (accessed June 2, 2002).

52. Ryan, Don, Associated Press, image number 6207733 (3P1X1). March 26, 2002.

53. "The Wind Powered Automobile." *Scientific American* 129 (September 1923), p. 171.

54. Ball, Jeffrey, "Wind Power May Gain Footing Off Coast of U.S." *The Wall Street Journal Online*. September 3, 2008. http://online.wsj.com/ (accessed September 9, 2008).

55. Thwaites, Tim, "A Bank for the Wind." *New Scientist* 193:2586 (January 13, 2007), pp. 39–41.

56. Ibid. p. 41.

57. O'Mara, Kathleen, with assistance from Phillip

Jennings, "Wave Energy," The Australian Renewable Energy Website. http://www.acre.murdoch.edu.au/ago/ocean/wave.html (accessed June 6, 2002).

58. "Fuel Research: Data on Fuel Research Described by Researchers at University of Queensland, 2009." *Energy Weekly News*, April 3, 2009, p. 352.

59. Fischer, Perry A., "Editorial Comment." *World Oil* 227:11 (November 2006), p. 1.

60. Woodward, Colin, "Iceland Strides Toward a Hydrogen Economy." *Christian Science Monitor,* February 12, 2009. http://feature.csmonitor.com/environment/2009/02/12/iceland-strides-toward-a-hydrogen-economy (accessed March 20, 2009).

61. U.S. Car Council for Automotive Research. http://www.uscar.org/techno/vrp1.htm (accessed April 20, 2000).

62. Arp, Fredrik, "Ford to Establish Hybrid Development Center in Sweden; Volvo Cars to Invest $1.4 Billion in Environmental R&D." *Green Car Congress,* June 30, 2006. November 1, 2009).

63. "Toyota's Fuel Cell Vehicles." http://www.toyota.com/html/about/environment/partner_tech/fuelcell_hybrid.html#fchv-5 (accessed January 22, 2001).

64. "RechargeIT Driving Experiment." RechargeIT.org: A Google.org Project. http://www.google.org/recharge/experiment (accessed September 6, 2008).

65. Becker, Daniel, September 19, 2002. http://newyork.sierraclub.org/rochester/hybrid.htm (accessed December 14, 2002).

66. Willett, David, "Sierra Club Welcomes Honda's New Civic Hybrid." December 20, 2001. http://lists.sierraclub.org/SCRIPTS/WA.EXE?A2=ind0112&L=ce-sc news-releases&D=1&T=0&H=1&O=D&F=&S=&P=825 (accessed February 15, 2002).

67. "Environment: EPA Proposes New Fuel-Economy Ratings." *Facts on File World News Digest* (accessed March 29, 2007).

68. "Hybrid Cars Try Merging into the Mainstream." http://www.thenewenvironmentalist.com/articles_0702/transport1.html#2008 (accessed February 15, 2002).

69. Wouk, Victor, "Hybrid Electric Vehicles." *Scientific American* 277:4 (October 1997), p. 71.

Chapter 4

1. Helmut Weule, head of Daimler-Benz research and technology, at the company's fuel cell vehicle unveiling in April 1994.

2. "Recent Improvements in Electric Vehicles," *Scientific American* CVII:10 (September 7, 1912), p. 194.

3. Gritzinger, Bob, "Beta vs. VHS?" *AutoWeek* 52:21 (May 20, 2002), p. 6.

4. Terrell, Kenneth, "Running on Fumes." *U.S. News and World Report,* 132:14 (April 29, 2002), p. 58.

5. Ibid.

6. Interview with Hugh Holman by authors, Technology Analyst, CIBC, March 29, 2000.

7. Kirsch, David A., *The Electric Vehicle and the Burden of History,* New Brunswick, N.J.: Rutgers University Press, 1964, p. 89.

8. Ibid., p. 88.

9. Adler, Cy A., and Reibsamen, Gary G., *Electric Vehicles at a Glance,* New York: McGraw-Hill, 1978, p. 12.

10. Kirsch, David A., *The Electric Vehicle and the Burden of History,* New Brunswick, N.J.: Rutgers University Press, 1964, p. 93.

11. *Scientific American* LXXXIII:25 (December 22, 1900), p. 389.

12. Ibid.

13. *Scientific American* 107 (September 7, 1912), p. 194.

14. *Scientific American* CIV:2 (January 14, 1911), p. 31.

15. Ibid.

16. *Country Life in America* 23 (January 1913), pp. 23–26.

17. Hawker Energy Products, Inc., "An Introduction to Batteries." http://www.hepi.com/basics/history.htm (accessed April 10, 2000).

18. *Scientific American* CIV:2 (January 14, 1911), p. 30.

19. *Scientific American* 80 (May 13, 1899), p. 295.

20. *Scientific American* LXXXIV:23 (June 8, 1901), p. 357.

21. Ibid., p. 356.

22. *Scientific American* LXXXIII:25 (December 22, 1900), p. 389.

23. *Iron Age* 221 (September 24, 1978), p. 21.

24. "EV Batteries," http://www.radix.net/~futurev/battery.html (accessed October 11, 2000).

25. McCormick, J. Byron, and Huff, James R., "The Case for Fuel-Cell-Powered Vehicles," *Technology Review* 82 (August/September 1980), p. 56.

26. Ibid.

27. "The Fuel Cell's Bumpy Ride," *The Economist* 358:8214 (March 24, 2001), p. 39.

28. Woodward, Colin, "Iceland Strides toward a Hydrogen Economy." *The Christian Science Monitor* 101:54 (February 12, 2009) http://features.csmonitor.com/2009/02/12/environment/iceland-strides-toward-a-hydrogen-economy (accessed March 23, 2009).

29. "Ballard Systems." http://www.ballard.com (accessed February 12, 2000).

30. McGowan, Elizabeth, "EPA Takes Hydrogen Fuel Cell Car for a Spin," *Waste News* 14:11 (September 29, 2008), p. 15.

31. Interview with Hugh Holman, Technology Analyst, CIBC, March 29, 2000.

32. Sperling, Daniel, *Future Drive,* Washington, D.C.: Island Press, 1995, p. 144.

33. "Volkswagen Jetta ZEM" http://dealer.vw.com/vwpress/fullStoryA.html?release_id=4904 (accessed April 12, 2000).

34. *Scientific American Supplement* LVI: 1451 (October 24, 1903), p. 23,253.

35. Ibid.

36. *Scientific American* LXXXVII:12 (September 20, 1902), p. 196.

37. http://prius.toyota.com/interior/index.html (accessed January 12, 2000).

38. http://Karma.Fiskerautomotive.com (accessed January 29, 2009).

39. Clynes, Tom, "The Energy Fix." *Popular Science* 269:1 (July 2006), p. 47.

40. http://prius.toyota.com (accessed March 15, 2000).

41. Demirdoven, Nurettin, and Deutch, John. "Hybrid Cars Now, Fuel Cell Cars Later." *Science* 305:5686 (August 13, 2004), pp. 974–976.

42. "Insight." http://www.honda2001.com/models/insight/customize.html (accessed March 12, 2000).

43. Pope, Bryon, "Honda Insight," *AutoWeek* 51:3 (January 15, 2001), p. 15.

44. "2120 Honda Insight: Overview." HybridCars.Com. http://www.hybridcars.com/compacts-sedans/honda-insight-overview.html (accessed February 9, 2009).

45. Brown, Jordana. "Fuel for Thought." *Vegetarian Times,* March 2006, pp. 55–59.

46. Edmunds.com. http://www.Edmunds.com. August 22, 2006. (accessed April 8, 2007).

47. Ibid.

48. "Tribrids." Her Electric Vehicle. http://www.her electricvehicle.com/tribrid.html (accessed July 16, 2008).

49. Corbin Motors. http://www.corbinmotors.com/about.htm (accessed March 15, 2000).

50. "NmG." Myers Motors. http://www.myersmotors.com/buynow.html (accessed January 5, 2009).

51. "GM Energy and Environment Strategy." http://www.gm.com/company/environment/products/chart/index.html (accessed February 12, 2000).

52. Ford Motor Company, Technical Information Division, Dearborn, Mich.

53. "Think Global Gets Investment from GE, Launches Th!nk City, Introduces New Crossover EV Concept and Signs Li-Ion Supply Deal with A123Systems." *Green Car Congress*, March 5, 2008. http://www.greencarcongress.com/2008/03/think-global-ge.html (accessed April 30, 2008).

54. Bedard, P., "Why EVs Are No-Shows," *Car & Driver* (March 2000), p. 137.

55. EVRental.com. http://www.evrental.com/cars.shtml (accessed March 15, 2000).

56. "Ethanol Fuel." *Issues & Controversies on File,* July 21, 2006. Facts on File News Service. http://www.2facts.com (accessed March 29, 2007).

57. Wilson, Kevin A., "The Idea of a Germ: Ethanol from Cellulose? Coskata Doesn't Stop There." *AutoWeek* 58:17 (April 21, 2008), p. 42.

58. Carr-Ruffino, Norma, and Acheson, John, "Efficiency: Well-to-Wheel Analysis." *Futurist* 41:4 (July/August 2007), p. 19.

59. "Aerovironment Electric Vehicle Travels 777 Miles in 24 Hours." http://www.aerovironment.com/news/news-archive/news-fastchrgrecord.html (accessed March 12, 2000).

Chapter 5

1. Appleton, Victor, *Tom Swift and His Electric Runabout, Or the Speediest Car on the Road,* New York: Grosset & Dunlap, 1910.

2. Edsall, Larry, "The Michelin Guide." *AutoWeek* 53:43 (October 27, 2003), pp. 22–30.

3. Fernandez, Tommy, "Hybrid Car Sales Not Up to Speed." *Crain's New York Business* 22:15 (April 10, 2006), p. 1.

4. *Kiplinger's Personal Finance* 60:5 (May 2006), pp. 102–104.

5. Murray, Charles J., "I Killed the Electric Car." *Design News* 62:1 (January 8, 2007), p. 14.

6. Design News Staff, "Poor Marketing Killed the EV." *Design News* 62:3 (February 26, 2007), p. 12.

7. Ibid., p. 8.

8. Lynch, Charles J., "Emerging Power Sources." *Science and Technology,* October 1967, pp. 36–48.

9. Ibid.

10. Fogelberg, Hans, *The Electric Car Controversy,* Gothenburg, Sweden: Department of History and Technology and Industry, Chalmers University of Technology, 1998, p. 3.

11. Kirsch 2000, Schiffen 1994, Volti 1990.

12. Schrage, Michael, "Toys for Big Boys." *Across the Board* 32:4 (April 1995), p. 47.

13. Ibid.

14. *The New York Times,* March 9, 1971, 42:1.

15. *House Beautiful* 35 (January 1914), pp. 56–57.

16. Ibid.

17. *Life* LIII:1376 (March 11, 1909), p. 330.

18. *The Literary Digest* XLV:1 (July 20, 1912), p. 115.

19. Babcock Electrics advertisement, www.econogics.com/ev/babcock.jpg (accessed March 12, 2001).

20. *Life* LII: 1376 (March 11, 1909), p. 331.

21. *Outing* 44 (May 1904), pp. 154–159.

22. Ibid.

23. *The New York Times,* March 4, 1906, 12:1.

24. *Scientific American* 97 (November 9, 1907), p. 330.

25. *The New York Times,* January 24, 1909, 4, 4:1.

26. Ibid.

27. *The Literary Digest* 46 (February 8, 1913), p. 299.

28. Ibid., p. 1068.

29. *The Literary Digest* 46 (May 10, 1913), p. 1068.

30. *Electrical World* 63 (June 6, 1914), p. 1318.

31. Ibid., p. 1319.

32. *The Automobile* 32 (January 21, 1915), p. 127.

33. *Electrical World* 70 (August 4, 1917), pp. 212–213.

34. *The New York Times,* June 24, 1917, II, 4:4.

35. *The New York Times,* January 7, 1917, III, 18:1.

36. Wurzer, Cathy, *Tales of the Road: Highway 61.* St. Paul: Minnesota Historical Society Press, 2008.

37. Ibid., pp. 10–11.

38. Sloan, John French, Letter to Walter Pach, from the Archives of American Art Digital Collections. http://www.aaa.si.edu/collections/digitalcollections (accessed November 14, 2007).

39. *Electrical World* 69 (January 6, 1917), p. 29.

40. Ibid.

41. *The Literary Digest* 76 (February 3, 1923), pp. 60–64.

42. *Life* LIII:1387 (May 27, 1909), p. 744.

43. *Life* LVII:1747 (April 20, 1916), p. 777.

44. Ibid.

45. *Life* LIII (May 27, 1909), p. 744.

46. *Ladies' Home Journal* 29:11 (June 1912), p. 79.

47. *The New York Times,* February 23, 1913, VIII, 6:1.

48. *The New York Times,* January 7, 1917, 3, 11:1.

49. *Life* LIII:1387 (May 27, 1909), p. 542.

50. *Ladies' Home Journal* 29:3 (March 1912), p. 69.

51. *Life* LVII:1741 (March 9, 1916), p. 744.

52. *Walt Disney's Donald Duck Beach Party,* New York: Dell Publishing, No. 5, 1958.

53. Dye, Brandon, "Girls on the Road." *AutoWeek* 56:35 (September 4, 2006), p. 34.

54. Crane, Laura Dent, *The Automobile Girls Along the Hudson, or Fighting Fire in Sleepy Hollow.* Philadelphia: Henry Altemus, 1910.

55. Ibid., p. 19.

56. Ibid., p. 33.

57. *The New York Times,* January 7, 1917, 3, 11:1.

58. Ibid.

59. *Scientific American* LXXXVII: 24 (December 13, 1900), p. 422.

60. *Scientific American* LXXXVII: 24 (December 13, 1900), p. 422.

61. *The Cosmopolitan* XXIX:4 (August 1900), p. 5.

62. *The Motor World* 89:4 (August 7, 1902), p. 540.

63. *The Horseless Age* 5:17 (January 24, 1900), p. 12.

64. *The New York Times,* December 21, 1906, 10:1.

65. *The New York Times,* January 24, 1909, 4:1.

66. *The Literary Digest* LII:16 (April 15, 1916), p. 1121.

67. *Life* LII:1367 (January 7, 1909), p. 37.

68. Ibid.

69. *Life* LIII:1388 (June 3, 1909), p. 783.

70. *Life* LIII:1381 (April 15, 1909), p. 533.

71. *Life* LIII:1377 (March 18, 1909), p. 375.

72. *Life* LII:1381 (February 4, 1909), p. 148.

73. Electric Vehicle Association of America, *Report of*

the Publicity Committee on the National Co-operative Advertising Campaign of the Electric Vehicle Association of America, New York: J. Kempster Print, 1912, p. 6.

74. Ibid., p. 9.

75. Ibid., p. 19.

76. *The Literary Digest* 63:12 (December 20, 1919), p. 107.

77. *Harper's Weekly* LV:2850 (August 5, 1911), p. 29.

78. *Life* LVII:1741 (March 9, 1911), p. 744.

79. *Harper's Weekly* LV:2845 (July 1, 1911), p. 24.

80. *Electrical World* 57:22 (June 1, 1911), p. 1374.

81. Handy, Galen. Personal research, 2008.

82. *The New York Times*, September 20, 1953, II, 11:3.

83. "Doubts Cast on Hybrid Efficiency." *The Daily Auto Insider*, April 3, 2006. http://www.caranddriver.com/dailyautoinsider/1087/doubts-cast-on-hybrid-efficiency.htm (accessed February 13, 2007).

84. *Scientific American* LXXXVI: 24 (June 14, 1902), p. 419.

85. Ibid.

86. *The New York Times*, June 24, 1917, II, 4:4.

87. Vaughn, Mark, "Buying Green," *Crain's Detroit Business*, 23:44 (October 29, 2007), p. 25.

88. Ferris, Deebe, "Big Three Team Up on Electric Vehicles," *WARD'S Auto World*, 29 (January 1993), p. 51.

89. Sarafin, Raymond, "How to Plug Electric Cars," *Advertising Age*, 64:2 (January 11, 1993), p. 12.

90. Ibid.

91. General Motors Corporation, "Charging Toward the Future," http://www.gmev.com/charging/charging.htm (accessed October 22, 2002).

92. Landis, Josh, "Honda Insight — Part 3," *EV World*, August 09, 2003. http://evworld.com/databases/storybuilder.cfm?storyid=453&first=5687&end=5686 (accessed October 23, 2002)

93. Diem, William. "EVs Prove a Tough Sell in France," *Automotive News*, 71:5683 (October 21, 1996), p. 34i.

94. Naughton, Keith. "Can You Have Green Cars Without the Red Ink?; The Big Three Scramble to Match Toyota's Clean Affordable Prius." *Business Week*, No. 3559 (December 29, 1997) p. 50.

95. Naughton, Keith. "Detroit's Impossible Dream." *Business Week*, No. 3567 (March 2, 1998), p. 66.

96. DeCicco, John and Kliesch, James, *ACEEE's Green Book, The Environmental Guide to Cars and Trucks, Model Year 2001*, Washington, D.C.: American Council for an Energy Efficient Economy, 2001, p. 25.

97. "The Jewish Agency Offers Bonus to Staffers Buying Hybrid Cars," *Christian Century*, 123:14 (July 25, 2006), p. 14.

98. Kirsch, David A., *The Electric Vehicle and the Burden of History*, New Brunswick, N.J.: Rutgers University Press, 1964, p. 170.

99. Ibid., p. 174.

100. The Institution of Engineering and Technology. "Recharging Stations 'Talk' to Electric Cars." *Transport News*, September 22, 2008 http://kn.theiet.org/news/sep08/elektrobay.cfm (accessed October 30, 2008).

101. *Electrical Review and Western Electrician*, October 31, 1914, Vol. 65, pp. 868–74.

102. *The Automobile*, October 22, 1914, Vol. 31, pp. 753–4.

103. AFS Trinity Power Corporation, "A Revolution in Fast Energy Storage, Featuring the Extreme Hybrid." http://www.afstrinity.com (accessed April 12, 2008).

104. Carson, Iain, and VijayVaitheeswaran. *ZOOM*. New York: Hachette Book Group USA, 2007.

105. "A Heated Discussion." *AutoWeek* 58:37 (September 15, 2008), p. 6.

106. Voelcker, John. "Diesel Hybrids: Clean and Mean." *Popular Science* 269:2 (August 2006), p. 26.

107. Moore, Bill, "California Cruising by Civic Hybrid — Part 3," *EV World*, August 09, 2003, http://evworld.com/databases/storybuilder.cfm?storyid=419&first=3960&end=3959&subcookie=1 (accessed July 5, 2008).

108. Interview with Hugh Holman, Technology Analyst, CIBC 3/29/00.

109. MacDonald, Nancy "Hybrids Suck Gas." *Maclean's* 118:49 (December 5, 2005), p. 44.

110. "Toyota Forced to Scrap TV Advert for 'Green' Prius Car, *Professional Engineering*, 20:11 (June 13, 2007), p. 13.

111. Ibid.

112. "The Hybrid Phenomenon." *The Futurist* 40:4 (July-August 2007), p. 17.

113. "Profile of Hybrid Drivers." *Hybridcars*, March 31, 2006, http://www.hybridcars.com/hybrid-drivers/profile-of-hybrid-drivers.html (accessed December 15, 2008).

114. Mateja, Jim. "Jim Mateja Column," *Chicago Tribune*, November 21, 2006, p. 22.

115. Tilman, David, and Jason Hill." Not All Alternative Biofuels Are Created Equal." *The Sunday Oregonian*, April 1, 2007, p. E2.

116. *AutoWeek* 56:51 (December 11, 2006), p. 5 (advertisement).

117. Hopkins, Philip, "Subsidy Key to Hybrid Production: Toyota," *The Age*, http://www.theage.com.au/action/printArticle?id=289460 (accessed November 29, 2008).

118. *Barron's* 57 (June 13, 1977), p. 11+.

119. Ibid.

120. Whalen, M.V., *HEV Information Needs Study — Summary of Results*, Golden, CO: NREL, U.S. Dept. of Energy, July 2000.

121. Ibid.

122. Eudy, Leslie, Field Operations Program-Overview of Advanced Technology Transportation, Update for CY 2001, Golden, CO: NREL (National Renewable Energy Laboratory), April 2001, p. 5.

123. Ibid.

124. Energy Information Administration. *Alternative to Traditional Transportation Fuels 2007*. April 2009, http://www.eia.doe.gov/cneaf/alternate/page/atftables/afv-atf2007.pdf (accessed May 15, 2009). [The diesel fuel consumption number was taken from the U.S. General Services Administration 2007 Fuel Consumption Report because it was not available in the EIA table.]

125. Ibid.

126. Eudy, Leslie, Field Operations Program-Overview of Advanced Technology Transportation, Update for CY 2001, Golden, CO: NREL (National Renewable Energy Laboratory), April 2001, p. 7.

127. Melaina, Marc, and Joel Bremson. "Refueling Availability for Alternative Fuel Vehicle Markets: Sufficient Urban Station Coverage." *Energy Policy* 36 (2008), pp. 3233–3241.

128. *The Horseless Age* 5:37 (January 24, 1900), p. 13.

129. McWhirter, William, "Off and Humming," *Time*, 141:17 (April 26, 1993), p. 53.

130. Baumgartner, William, and Gross, Andrew, "The Global Market for Electric Vehicles," *Business Economics* 35:4 (October 2000), p. 51.

131. "Hybrid Sales Rise, but Growth Is Slowing"

March 2, 2007, http://seattlepi.nwsource.com/wheels/305485_twl02.html (accessed April 8, 2007).

132. Halliday, Jean, "Hybrid Strategy Forces Foes' Hands," *Advertising Age* 77:46 (November 13, 2006), p. M-5.

133. Wilson, Kevin A. "Spinning Wheels." *AutoWeek* 57:16 (April 16, 2007), p. 16.

134. "Sale of Hybrid Vehicles in the US May Triple in 7 Years," *The Washington Times*, January 5, 2006, http://www.washtimes.com/autoweekend/20060105-114917-2019r.htm (accessed April 8, 2007).

135. Ibid.

136. Fahey, Jonathan, "Shock Jocks," *Forbes* 179:13 (June 18, 2007), p. 50.

137. "IntelliChoice.com Survey: Hybrids Continue to Reward of the Long Term," *IntelligChoice.com*, http://www.intellichoice.com/press/Hybrid-Survey-2007 (accessed July 12, 2008).

138. Baumgartner, William, and Gross, Andrew, "The Global Market for Electric Vehicles," *Business Economics* 35:4 (October 2000), p. 51.

Chapter 6

1. *The Horseless Age* 2:5 (March 1897), pp. 15–16.

2. Wakefield, Ernest H., *History of the Electric Automobile*, Warrendale, Pa.: Society of Automotive Engineers, 1994, p. 50.

3. *Scientific American* LXXX:19 (May 13, 1899), p. 293.

4. Wakefield, Ernest H., *History of the Automobile: Battery-only Powered Cars*, Warrendale, Pa.: Society of Automotive Engineers, 1994, p. 127.

5. *Scientific American* LXXXI (September 2, 1899), p. 153.

6. "Fairly Howling," *Motor World* 1:17 (October 11, 1900), quoted in Flink, James J., *America Adopts the Automobile, 1895–1910*, Cambridge, Mass.: MIT Press, 1970, pp. 35, 238.

7. Wakefield, Ernest H., *History of the Automobile: Battery-only Powered Cars*, Warrendale, Pa.: Society of Automotive Engineers, 1994, p. 213.

8. Ibid.

9. *The Automobile, Vol. II*, New York: Cassell, 1905, pp. 730–733.

10. Fogelberg, Hans, *The Electric Car Controversy*, Gothenburg, Sweden: Department of History and Technology and Industry, Chalmers University of Technology, 1998, p. 71.

11. *Cyclopedia of Automobile Engineering, Vol. 3*, Chicago: American Technical Society, 1910, pp. 101–103.

12. Wakefield, Ernest H., *History of the Automobile: Battery-only Powered Cars*, Warrendale, Pa.: Society of Automotive Engineers, 1994, p. 219.

13. Electric Vehicle Association of America, *Report of the Publicity Committee on the National Co-operative Advertising Campaign of the Electric Vehicle Association of America*, New York: J. Kempster Print, 1912, p. 1.

14. *Scientific American* CIV:2 (January 14, 1911), p. 31.

15. *Electrical World* 57:25 (June 22, 1911), p. 1590.

16. Electric Vehicle Association of America, *Report of the Publicity Committee on the National Co-operative Advertising Campaign of the Electric Vehicle Association of America*, New York: J. Kempster Print, 1912, p. 15.

17. Ibid.

18. Wakefield, Ernest H., *History of the Automobile*

Battery-only Powered Car, Warrendale, Pa.: Society of Automotive Engineers, 1994, p. 247.

19. *Scientific American* CVII:10 (September 7, 1912), p. 194.

20. "Electric Cars," *The Automobile* 32 (January 21, 1915), p. 132.

21. *Electrical World* 77 (June 11, 1921), p. 1357.

22. Ibid.

23. *Electrical World* 77 (June 11, 1921), p. 1358.

24. *London Electrical Review* 91 (November 17, 1922), pp. 740–741.

25. Ibid.

26. *Electric Review*, February 16, 1940, pp. 177–180.

27. Ibid.

28. Furnas, J. C. "Are Electric Cars Coming Back?" *Saturday Evening Post* 323:7 (March 12, 1960), pp. 20, 56–63.

29. *Scientific American* 215:4 (October 1966), pp. 34–40.

30. "Electric Cars: They're Cleaner, but..." *Science News* 91:10 (March 11, 1967), p. 232.

31. Thompson, Steve, "At Large." *AutoWeek* 52:46 (November 11, 2002), p. 15.

32. Wilford, John Noble, "Clean Air Cars Line Up for Cross-Country Race," *The New York Times*, August 30, 1970, IV, 10:1.

33. Wakefield, Ernest H., *History of the Automobile: Battery-only Powered Cars*, Warrendale, Pa.: Society of Automotive Engineers, 1994, p. 278.

34. *Industry Week* 180 (January 28, 1974), p. 24+.

35. *Industry Week* 181 (June 3, 1974), p. 42.

36. Burke, A. F., *Evaluation of State-of-Charge Indicator Approaches for EVs*, SAE 8990816, Warrendale, Pa.: Society of Automotive Engineers, 1989.

37. Wakefield, Ernest H., *History of the Automobile: Battery-only Powered Cars*, Warrendale, Pa.: Society of Automotive Engineers, 1994, p. 155.

38. Zodronik, Jeff, *Eighth International Electric Vehicle Symposium*, Washington, D.C., 1986.

39. Kodjak, Drew, "EVs: Clean Today, Cleaner Tomorrow." *Technology Review* 99:6 (August/September 1996), p. 66.

40. Lave, Lester B., Russell, A. G., Hendrickson, Chris T., McMichael, Francis C., "Battery-powered Vehicles: Ozone Reductions versus Discharges," *Environmental Science and Technology* 30:9 (1996), p. 402A.

41. Wouk, Victor, "Hybrid Electric Vehicles." *Scientific American* 277:4 (October 1997), p. 70.

42. Naughton, Keith, "Detroit's Impossible Dream." *Business Week* 3567 (March 2, 1998), p. 68.

43. "Fuel-cell Miracles and Urban Sprawl," *Car and Driver* 45:2 (August 1999), p. 30.

44. Motavalli, Jim, "Your Next Car?" *Sierra* 84:4 (July 1999), p. 34.

45. Hamilton, Anita, Goldstein, Andrew, Ressner, Jeffery, Szczesny, Joseph R., and White, Roy B. "Why Hybrids Are Hot." *Time* 159:17 (April 29, 2002), p. 52.

46. Fogelberg, Hans, *The Electric Car Controversy*, Gothenburg, Sweden: Department of History and Technology and Industry, Chalmers University of Technology, 1998, p. 95.

47. "Honda Insight 2001," http://cartalk.cars.com/Info/Testdrive/Reviews/honda-insight-2001.html (accessed August 3, 2003).

48. Wilson, Kevin A., "Green Machines and Politics," *AutoWeek* 53:2 (January 13, 2003), p. 16.

Selected Bibliography

Bedard, Patrick. "Filling Up with Clean, Free Wind, and Other EV Fantasies." *Car & Driver*, January 1999, p. 19.
  The author objects to what he perceives as environmentalists' denial of all forms of power plants, whether fossil fuel-based or alternative, and asserts that "EVs, in the real world, don't pass the laugh test."

_____. "GEM E825: Why EVs Are No-Shows." *Car & Driver*, March 2000, p. 137.
  The author makes a five-point argument that ZEV technology is not important in 2000. It includes an interesting observation from Daniel Sperling, director of the Institute of Transportation Studies at the University of California–Davis, that the "new" gasoline cars with RFG are "for all practical purposes, zero emitting." Bedard claims that EV advocates are "giving up" and CARB is "backpedaling." He notes that the U.S. Advanced Battery Consortium (USABC), an industry/government partnership formed in1991 to produce a practical EV battery, has not been successful, finding itself in a double bind: The battery technology cannot deliver the performance and range expected by consumers and the vehicles must be sold at a loss. Consumers are not willing to spend more money for less-than-average performance.

Boschert, Sherry. *Plug-in Hybrids: The Cars That Will Recharge America.* Gabriola Island, B.C.: New Society, 2006.
  A good history of why plug-in hybrids have caught the public's attention and why the author sees it as a better alternative solution than electric, fuel cell or biofuel vehicles for moving to a cleaner, less-oil-dependent environment. It includes interesting stories that illustrate technology development and the politics that surround the plug-in hybrid. An engaging read.

Brown, Mark B. "The Civil Shaping of Technology: California's Electric Vehicle Program." *Science, Technology and Human Values* 26:1 (Winter 2001), p. 56.
  Lengthy technical and political discussion of how government shapes technology policy for people and how people shape civic policies. Points out that while government has a role to play in shaping new technologies, its policies are also shaped by citizens. CARB is an example in its setting regulations and later revising them. Initial CARB policy in 1990 was designed to promote a "participatory conception of citizenship." When CARB realized in 1996 that the public was not particularly interested in buying EVs, it began changing factors involving technical criteria and postponed initial sales mandates. This shift in policy recognized a "consumer conception of citizenship." The "person as citizen" and "the person as consumer" play different roles. While a citizen may favor a regulation promoting EVs, the consumer does not act on it by purchasing an EV.

Brown, Stuart F. "It's the Battery, Stupid." *Popular Science*, February 1995, p. 62.
  Considers the situation of the government's issuing policies when the technology is not yet ready. The author questions CARB's mandate that 2 percent of all vehicles sold in California by 1998 must be ZEVs. The price of an electric vehicle was too high, requiring subsidies and tax credits. Even with that stimulus, EVs were not a marketable alternative. He also notes that the mandate required manufacturers to build electric cars, but not necessarily to sell them.

Carson, Iain, and Vijay V. Vaitheeswaran. *Zoom: The Global Race to Fuel the Car of the Future.* New York: Grand Central, 2007.
  The authors explore the economic and geopolitical forces affecting the oil industry and its links

to the auto industry. They cover green innovators and new energy systems for autos (flex-fuels, biofuels, electricity, hydrogen) and share a view that a world without cars would be joyless and lack freedom and prosperity. Technology and clean vehicles, they say, are the solution. They promote new energy policies while showing that oil companies are not inherently evil and give a balance to the benefits brought to the economy and quality of life in most of the work.

Crane, Laura Dent. *The Automobile Girls Along the Hudson, or Fighting Fire in Sleepy Hollow.* Philadelphia: Henry Altemus, 1910.
  The Automobile Girls series was advertised, with a number of other young adult series, as "The Best and Least Expensive Books for Real Boys and Girls. These fascinating volumes will interest boys and girls of every age under sixty." The price was 50 cents per volume. This series followed the adventures of four young women and their aunt as they motored (in an automobile they had to start by cranking) outside New York City. The descriptions of clothing and sentiments about driving reflect those of both electric and gasoline motorist enthusiasts of the era.

"An Interesting Automobile Damage Case." *Scientific American* 85 (December 21, 1901), p. 407.
  Describes a case in Bridgeport, Connecticut, in 1901 that involved a silent electric vehicle approaching a horse-drawn carriage from behind. The horse was spooked and the carriage driver was thrown down and dragged. Part of the complaint argued that the electric vehicle was so noiseless that it was dangerous. The carriage driver lost his case, but the important part historically was not the case itself but the judge's instructions to the jury. The growing realization was that motoring interest was expanding and that all must recognize a personal responsibility and show a respect for the right-of-way of fellow motorists, and that carriage riders must accommodate the faster motorized transports.

"Maryland Favors Auto Reciprocity." *New York Times*, March 3, 1912, sec. 4, 10:1.
  Examines early state laws concerning the use of roadways by automobiles licensed in various states. New Jersey had passed a bill allowing nonresident tourists to use the highways for a period of fifteen days. The new Maryland law would repeal the current law requiring nonresidents to affix a tag to the rear of their vehicle before using the Maryland roads. It also included a provision that would require motorists to display at least one bright light during the period from one hour after sunset to one hour before sunrise.

McConnell, Curt. "*A Reliable Car and a Woman Who Knows It*": The First Coast-to-Coast Auto Trips by Women, 1899–1916. Jefferson, N.C.: McFarland, 2000.
  This is an account of the first coast-to-coast road trips made by women, beginning with the courageous trail breakers, Alice Ramsey and three female companions, in 1909. It is hard to imagine making this drive with no highways available, but this book brings the trip to life. Alice Ramsey and her friends left New York City and arrived in San Francisco just 59 days and some harrowing adventures later. The information about the five excursions by the adventurous women is taken from the women's personal journals and from newspaper accounts.

McCormick, J. Byron, and James R. Huff. "The Case for Fuel-Cell-Powered Vehicles." *Technology Review* 82:54 (1980).
  Good brief history of fuel-cell development from 1839 through the 1970s. Mentions that Wilhelm Ostwald in 1894 foresaw the pollution problems caused by the internal combustion engine, but his electrochemical strategy was not understood and so not implemented. Touches on research by Allis-Chalmers Manufacturing Company into the hydrogen/propane oxygen fuel cell, the predecessor of the cells used in the spacecraft *Apollo*'s backup system; cells using phosphoric acid electrolyte; potassium hydroxide electrolyte; the six-kilowatt alkaline fuel cell built by Karl Kordesch of Union Carbide; and briefly on the feasibility studies in 1978 for economic potential of fuel cells. Result of the study: the technology was there, but the economics were still out of reach.

Michaels, Patrick J., and Robert C. Balling, Jr. *Climate of Extremes: Global Warming Science They Don't Want You to Know.* Washington, D.C.: Cato Institute, 2009.
  Discusses the impact of politics on the information the public hears about climate change/global warming. Provides examples of the way in which scientific discourse is suppressed through ridicule, intimidation, blacklisting and loss of the employment for those who show facts that oppose the mainstream discussion on global climate change. The authors bring information about how data is collected, selected and presented. They supply explanations of how different the analysis and conclusions look if the entire range of data is included in the product. They give examples of what

is not being presented in an effort to quell p the fear and show how the data, as with any statistics, has been ignored or misused to promote a political agenda. Gives many clear examples of how the earth's climate works. Has extensive references and selected readings.

Neil, Dan. "Pump This!" *Car & Driver*, April 1999, p. 110.
Amusing tale of an attempted journey across country in 1999 by two reporters using a natural-gas-fired car. They run into a few problems. Although they had been told the car would have a range of about 300 miles, it actually was more like 120 miles. Their bible was the *Directory of U.S. Natural Gas Vehicle Fueling Stations*, which they found was loaded with "out-of-date and erroneous information that has been painstakingly tabulated by chimps." Many of the stations required a unique charge card. They discover that due to recent industry deregulation, natural gas companies cannot pass on the price of infrastructure-building to consumers, resulting in more CNG outlets closing instead of opening. They gave up the trip in Colorado after eighty hours of travel averaging 26 miles per hour.

Perrin, Noel. *Solo: Life with an Electric Car*. New York: W.W. Norton, 1992.
Noel Perrin drove his new electric car in 1991 from California to Vermont and this book describes his journey. The car was a converted solar-electric Ford Escort with a cruising speed of 65 mph and a range of 45–60 miles. Hills, mountains and finding a place to recharge make for an entertaining adventure. He arrived in Vermont after three weeks and put the car to use as a daily commuter.

Raynal, Wes. "Honda Insight — The Smart Car." *AutoWeek*, 50:32 (July 31, 2000), p. 13.
Positive report about the beginning of a year-long test drive of the Honda Insight. The *AutoWeek* test driver planned to use the car under normal driving conditions for one year; initially the car got 55 mpg. The only negatives were a lousy stereo system and noise at freeway speeds.

Schiffer, Michael Brian. *Taking Charge: The Electric Automobile in America*. Washington, D.C.: Smithsonian Institution Press, 1994.
A very good history. Emphasizes Ford and Edison working together. Places demise of electric cars on social factors. Women wanted them, but didn't have the financial influence to affect the market.

Schrage, Michael. "Toys for Big Boys." *Across the Board*, 32:4 (April 1995), p. 22.
Points out perceived differences between men and women in their preferences in vehicles: men want cars as "toys" for power, touring, racing and adventure; women want reliability, comfort, safety and cleanliness. "The patriarchal family structure [of the early 1900s] and the economic nature of the middle class is what doomed the electric car." Points out that EVs are a good idea, but that doesn't necessarily make them a viable innovation.

Scott, Robert F. "Does Mourning Become the Electric?" *Automobile Quarterly* 5 (1966), pp. 194–207.
The article touches on the battery development, beginning with early inventions, to be refined by Gaston Plante in 1860, and traces the decline of electric vehicles through World War I, the depression years, and World War II. There is a brief mention of fuel cells as a possible replacement for batteries, but Scott focuses on auto racing and land speed records set by electrics. His tone is optimistic about the future of electric cars.

Sperling, Daniel. *Future Drive*. Washington, D.C.: Island Press, 1995.
Takes an assertive stance promoting environmental and economic transportation as soon as possible. Looks at the history of electric vehicles and briefly considers the politics of CARB. Explains a variety of unconventional solutions. Feels the government is best equipped to guide consumers and encourage experimentation with vehicles and fuels in a benign way.

Wakefield, Ernest H. *History of the Electric Automobile: Battery-Only Powered Cars*. Warrendale, Pa.: Society of Automotive Engineers, 1994.
Definitive and thorough history of battery-powered vehicles. Includes many photographs and technical charts concerning batteries.

_____. *History of the Electric Automobile: Hybrid Electric Vehicles*. Warrendale, Pa.: Society of Automotive Engineers, 1998.
Comprehensive coverage and historical account of hybrid automobiles involving electricity, flywheels, gasoline and solar power. Includes many photographs and technical drawings. Briefly mentions the Toyota Prius, introduced in Japan in 1997. About half the book is dedicated to solar

power. Some discrepancies with other sources in historical accounts of the early auto companies, but excellent for the descriptions of the technology. It is extensively documented, with about 30–40 references per chapter.

Zittel, John D. "Electric Vehicles from Letters to the Editor." *Issues in Science and Technology* 11:14 (Spring 1995).
In response to Sperling's article "Gearing Up for Electric Cars," Zittel argues that consumers will respond to EVs only if they are competitive with conventional vehicles. Zittel challenges Sperling's suggestion that EV government mandates are the only way, and suggests that the USABC shows promise in delivering a suitable battery. It may be that flexibility for manufacturers is a better means for meeting the environmental problems as EV mandates may indicate that electric is better than internal combustion, but the environmental costs of exotic materials for the auto and auto battery components is less clear.

INDEX

Numbers in *bold italics* indicate pages with photographs.